BIRDS
OF
QUEENSLAND'S WET TROPICS
AND
GREAT BARRIER REEF

COOKTOWN TO TOWNSVILLE
NORTH-EASTERN QUEENSLAND
AUSTRALIA

First published 1996 by
GERARD INDUSTRIES PROPRIETARY LIMITED
12 Park Terrace
Bowden
SOUTH AUSTRALIA 5007

Text © 1996 by Lloyd Nielsen
Illustrations © 1996 by Lloyd Nielsen
Maps © 1996 by Lloyd Nielsen

National Library of Australia
Cataloguing-in-Publication data:

Nielsen, Lloyd.
    Birds of Queensland's Wet Tropics and Great Barrier Reef.

    Includes indexes.
    ISBN 0 646 27200 4.

    1. Birds — Queensland — Identification.
    2. Birds — Tropics — Identification.
    3. Birdwatching — Queensland — Guidebooks.
    I. Gerard Industries.
    II. Title.

598.29943

This field guide is dedicated to my mother, Isabelle Nielsen

CONTENTS

I wish to thank the many people who gave valuable assistance and advice during the compilation of this field guide. Francis Crome, John Crowhurst PSM, Keith and Lindsay Fisher, Charles and Joan Freestun, Cliff and Dawn Frith, Andrée Griffin, David James, Dawn and Arnold Magarry, Nick Marshall, John McLean, Elinor Scambler, John Squire, David Stewart and Klaus Uhlenhut either gave freely of their notes, read earlier drafts of the manuscript, provided constructive comments, or performed all three.

Special thanks to John Young whose immense field knowledge of the birds of north-eastern Queensland I was able to tap at any time.

Many thanks to Glenn Holmes for reading the final draft of the manuscript and providing professional advice.

For friendship, support and faith in the project whilst getting it off the ground, thanks go to Chris Dahlberg and Denise Collins. To Del Richards for his assistance and the part he played in our discovery of the Pacific Swallow, and to both Del and his wife Pat for their friendship. Ian and Pauline Clayton provided valuable information concerning their home territory, the Townsville region. Thanks to several people in the Department of Environment, especially Rupert Russell, Mossman and Jenny Smith, Innisfail for providing information about plants and birds from their own districts.

Rainfall and temperature graphs were kindly supplied by the Bureau of Meteorology, Brisbane.

Garry and Nada Sankowsky were always available to offer expert advice and guidance whenever computer problems arose. Grateful thanks to Geoff and Sandra Nicholson for their support over several years.

Dorothy Window transformed my much-edited and jumbled draft into a readable manuscript.

I am most grateful to Robert Gerard, Chairman of Gerard Industries Pty Ltd, the makers of Clipsal electrical wiring accessory products, who agreed to underwrite this publication. We hope this will be the first of a series of Clipsal Guides.

Finally, my deepest gratitude goes to Mervyn and Anne Chappel. Their faith in my project brought it to reality.

On two occasions over a time span of 20 years, namely in 1975 and 1995, I have had the pleasure of visiting North Queensland and doing some birding in the Wet Tropics. For me, these were highly memorable and exciting trips to a region that has one of the most fascinating avifaunas and diversity of habitats of anywhere I have been. Where else will you find two of the greatest World Heritage Areas, the forests of the Wet Tropics and the Great Barrier Reef, side by side?

Visitors to the Wet Tropics, even if they have only a cursory interest in nature, must notice quickly that the forests along the northern east coast of Australia are very special indeed. Tropical forests in general are not only the most threatened ecosystems of the world, but also the richest in terms of diversity and uniqueness of the plants and animals that live there. The forests of North Queensland are of particular global importance, being so limited in their extent compared to the larger tracts we still find in New Guinea or Amazonia, for example.

We are in the fortunate situation that, because of the popularity of ornithology and birdwatching, we now know much about the distribution and status of the world's birds; many species are proving to be good indicators for the condition and health of an ecosystem, and of our environment in general. The Wet Tropics also contains indicator bird species — foremost probably being the Cassowary, a major attraction for birdwatchers from far afield. This giant and secretive bird needs a lot of quiet forest habitat and does not adapt well to the slow encroachment of human activities into this habitat. This species appears to be in a slow but steady decline, which is greatly worrying since its numbers have never been very high.

North Queensland is currently undergoing enormous economic development, with tourism growing particularly quickly. As has sadly happened in many other fragile places around the world, this could pose a serious threat to the unique habitats of the region. People will make increasing demands for infrastructures, reaching deeper and deeper into the forests, the wetlands and the islands of the Barrier Reef. But it could also be an opportunity for ecologically sound development, where conservation objectives, such as the survival of the Cassowary, are an integral part of regional planning, and economic development is balanced against maintaining the very resource that provides the region's livelihood. The opportunity for such *sustainable* development still exists in North Queensland.

To appreciate the beauty and biological uniqueness of the Wet Tropics people must be able to go and see, and experience it. They must have guidance as to what they may encounter and where, how to get there, how to identify the various species — in short they need a good field guide. This new beautifully illustrated book by Lloyd Nielsen is an extremely welcome tool for any amateur and professional ornithologist who would like to explore the secrets and riches of the Wet Tropics.

Dr Christoph Imboden
Director-General
BirdLife International
Cambridge

February 1996

Welcome to the Wet Tropics!

Probably the first thing you will notice when you thumb through this guide is a departure from the standard format widely used for field guides throughout the world. During several years as a wildlife guide in Lamington National Park, southern Queensland, I was frequently asked questions such as 'What is the small bird with a yellow breast that clings sideways to tree trunks?' or 'What is the large brown rainforest bird with the long tail?' or 'Which bird has a white head and black wings?' It soon became very obvious to me that birdwatchers possess varying degrees of competency in their bird identification skills. A regional field guide, arranged in clear and simple format, seemed the answer. Thus *Birds of Lamington National Park and Environs* was self-published in 1991.

A similar distinctive identification system has been devised for this field guide. I have incorporated much previously unpublished material drawn from my field notes collated over 25 years of visiting and residing in the Wet Tropics region and also from the generous assistance of my birdwatching colleagues. Thus a clearer picture of the status and range of most species has emerged. With this as a base, our knowledge of the birds of the Wet Tropics can only be enhanced.

My aim has been to create a field guide not only for dedicated birdwatchers, but for anyone with an interest in natural history, the environment and its birds, whether this interest be on a casual or professional level. This guide describes the most important sites for birds in the Wet Tropics, the birds that frequent them, and how and when to see them at their best.

Good birding!

THE WET TROPICS

The Wet Tropics is an important biogeographic region in north-eastern Queensland. It is essentially a narrow, mountainous rainforested region, up to 80 kilometres wide, embracing coastal plain, mountain ridges and tablelands, running from the vicinity of Cooktown to the vicinity of Townsville approximately 450 kilometres to the south. Not only has it the highest rainfall in Australia but it contains the greatest diversity of plants and animals on the Australian continent.

In 1988 these rainforests were placed on the World Heritage List. Officially, the area was given the name 'The Wet Tropics of Queensland'. Eighty-five per cent of remaining tropical rainforest in the region is now protected within World Heritage borders covering almost 9000 square kilometres. Today, the use of the title 'Wet Tropics' has been generalised, mostly by the tourism industry, to embrace the entire region from Cooktown to Townsville.

THE GREAT BARRIER REEF

Inscribed on the World Heritage List in 1981, the Great Barrier Reef is the longest and most extensive complex of coral reefs and islands in the world. Covering 2000 kilometres in length, it extends from Cape York, through the western Coral Sea to just south of Gladstone, and ranges from 180 kilometres to a mere few kilometres from the coastline. Indeed, lowland rainforest and fringing reefs meet at Cape Tribulation, a phenomenon unique in Australia and rare worldwide.

As well as providing specialised habitat for countless forms of marine and bird life, this living museum contains nesting grounds of global significance for species such as the endangered green and loggerhead turtles. Humpback whales migrate from the Antarctic to give birth, and dugong rely upon the seagrass beds for sustenance.

THE BIRDS

The Wet Tropics and the Great Barrier Reef contain a larger number of bird species than any other region of similar size in Australia. Over 430 species have so far been recorded, being more than half the total number of bird species for the entire Australian continent. Importantly, 13 species are endemic, while a number of others are represented by distinct subspecies. To convey some idea of the richness of the region, all 24 species of Australia's birds of prey; 14 of 18 species of terns; 7 of the 9 species of owls; 9 of the 10 species of kingfishers; all species of ducks and geese, as well as 38 of the 76 species of honeyeaters have been recorded.

Some of Australia's most spectacular birds occur here, perhaps none more so than the Buff-breasted Paradise-Kingfisher. But the beautiful fruit-doves, tiny fig-parrots, Yellow-bellied Sunbird, the brilliant Crimson Finch and the delicately-coloured Black-throated Finch also vie for attention. Metallic Starlings, black at a distance but displaying a brilliant luminescence when viewed at close range in full sunshine; the glowing Golden Bowerbird, and metallic green and black of Victoria's Riflebird are but a few examples of what lies in store in the Wet Tropics.

Still others are rare or elusive, a challenge to locate and view. Of these, the giant Southern Cassowary proves to be one of the most elusive. The owls, some of which fall into this category, or the rare or accidental shorebirds which suddenly appear on Cairns Esplanade all combine to make this one of the best birdwatching destinations Australia has to offer.

THE ENDEMICS

LESSER SOOTY OWL *Tyto multipunctata*
FERNWREN *Oreoscopus gutturalis*
ATHERTON SCRUBWREN *Sericornis keri*
MOUNTAIN THORNBILL *Acanthiza katherina*
MACLEAY'S HONEYEATER *Xanthotis macleayana*
BRIDLED HONEYEATER *Lichenostomus frenatus*
GREY-HEADED ROBIN* *Heteromyias albispecularis*
CHOWCHILLA *Orthonyx spaldingii*
BOWER'S SHRIKE-THRUSH *Colluricincla boweri*
PIED MONARCH *Arses kaupi*
VICTORIA'S RIFLEBIRD *Ptiloris victoriae*
TOOTH-BILLED BOWERBIRD *Scenopoeetes dentirostris*
GOLDEN BOWERBIRD *Prionodura newtoniana*
* Extends to New Guinea where several subspecies occur in montane forest.

INTRODUCED BIRDS

Unfortunately, for various reasons, a number of species were introduced into Australia from other continents many years ago. Some such as Common Myna and House Sparrow have become well-established in the Wet Tropics, often to the detriment of native species. Nutmeg Mannikin, Spotted Turtle-dove and Rock-dove have also become established, but in smaller numbers.

THE SEASONS

Rather than distinctive seasonal changes, the seasons in tropical Australia are measured by rainfall or the absence of it. Much of the rain falls during 'the Wet', between December and March. The remainder of the year is referred to as 'the Dry'. Thunderstorms during November and December herald the onset of the Wet. Annual rainfall varies enormously in the region, from an average of 8600 millimetres (340 inches) on the high peaks of Bellenden Ker and Bartle Frere, to 880 millimetres (35 inches) and less along the dry western fringe.

Many birds breed through the late Dry when rainforest and other trees are fruiting. The few aquatic species which breed in the region delay their breeding until the Wet, while some seed-eating species, e.g. Squatter Pigeon and finches breed through the early Dry when their food is most plentiful.

In the ornithological world, birds are described as 'summer' or 'winter' visitors, and in most instances these terms have been retained. Usually, summer breeding migrants arrive about September (early spring) and depart about March (autumn). Winter visitors arrive about April (autumn) and depart about August (late winter).

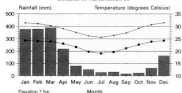

MEAN MONTHLY RAINFALL AND TEMPERATURE FOR TOWNSVILLE AMO
BUREAU OF METEOROLOGY

Elevation 7.5m

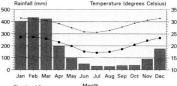

MEAN MONTHLY RAINFALL AND TEMPERATURE FOR INNISFAIL
BUREAU OF METEOROLOGY

Elevation 4.2m

MEAN MONTHLY RAINFALL AND TEMPERATURE FOR MAREEBA (QWRC)
BUREAU OF METEOROLOGY

Elevation 405.7m

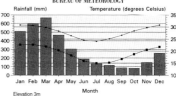

MEAN MONTHLY RAINFALL AND TEMPERATURE FOR CAIRNS
BUREAU OF METEOROLOGY

Elevation 3m

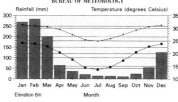

MEAN MONTHLY RAINFALL AND TEMPERATURE FOR COOKTOWN
BUREAU OF METEOROLOGY

Elevation 6m

■ Mean Mthly Rainfall ← Mean Maximum Temp ◆ Mean Minimum Temp

MIGRATION

Migration into and through the region is strong and obvious. Some of the most notable migrants are the shorebirds which arrive from their Asian and Arctic breeding grounds during September and October. Many continue southward on their journey, but large numbers remain in the Wet Tropics during our summer months. March and April sees most of the population departing for their northern breeding grounds. However, individuals of some species (probably immature birds) remain through the entire winter without returning to their Northern Hemisphere breeding grounds.

The swifts, Oriental Cuckoo, Barn Swallow and others which breed in the Northern Hemisphere, 'winter' in Australia during our summer. Some Australian species which breed as far south as the south-eastern parts of the continent (and sometimes Tasmania) pass through the Wet Tropics to and from their wintering grounds (usually in the islands to the north); often there is a local breeding population. These include Channel-billed Cuckoo, Koel, Dollarbird and Leaden Flycatcher. Much of the breeding populations of the migratory Metallic Starling and Buff-breasted Paradise-Kingfisher are to be found within the Wet Tropics. Only a small number travel farther south to the rainforests of central Queensland. Still others winter in the Wet Tropics, moving out of colder southern Australia during autumn. Thus birds such as Rainbow Bee-eater, Leaden Flycatcher and Welcome Swallow arrive to augment, and probably replace, local populations for a few short months.

THE HABITATS

LOWLAND RAINFOREST
Before the impact of early European settlement, lowland rainforest covered vast areas of the coastal plain. Over the ensuing years most was cleared to make way for agriculture, principally the growing of sugar-cane. While small pockets or remnants exist here and there, the only large tract remaining lies north of the Daintree River. Lowland rainforest is the most luxuriant of all Australian rainforests and contains the most plant species. However, the forest floor is usually sparse. In summer the atmosphere is often hot and steamy. Lowland rainforest is usually rich in birdlife, though strangely the tract north of the Daintree River, so rich in plant species, proves rather poor for birdlife.

UPLAND RAINFOREST
The upland rainforest of the Great Dividing Range and various mountainous offshoots form the greater part of the rainforest in the Wet Tropics. Upland rainforest is characterised by a distinct coolness in the air and often shrouded in cloud, resulting in an abundance of mosses, lichens and epiphytes. The floor has a denser layer of ferns, small palms, herbs and other plants than

lowland rainforest. Upland rainforest too is rich in birdlife. Some of the endemics like Fernwren, Atherton Scrubwren, Tooth-billed and Golden Bowerbirds are confined to these higher altitudes. Others such as Lesser Sooty Owl, Macleay's Honeyeater and Victoria's Riflebird extend to lowland areas.

GALLERY FOREST

A feature of the tropics are the ribbons of rainforest which follow streams flowing through the drier tropical woodland. Known as gallery forest, this habitat contains only a small variety of plants but is usually rich in birds, especially at the edges where the two habitats meet. The White-browed Robin exploits gallery forest exclusively.

WET SCLEROPHYLL FOREST

Along the main range and behind the coastal ranges, forests of tall eucalypts stand adjacent the rainforest. This forest is dominated by Flooded Gum *Eucalyptus grandis*, Mountain Stringybark *Eucalyptus resinifera* and Pink Bloodwood *Eucalyptus intermedia*. Often the understorey is dense and shrubby. One can find such species as Little Lorikeet, White-browed Scrubwren and White-naped Honeyeater — birds that exploit other habitats in more southern parts of the continent.

DRY SCLEROPHYLL FOREST

Fringing the Wet Tropics to the west of the rainforest, and sometimes adjacent to the wet sclerophyll, lies a dry sclerophyll forest consisting mostly of eucalypt species. Much of this habitat remains. Its poor worth for intensive agricultural use, and sometimes hilly terrain, have so far ensured its survival. With a low rainfall, and grassy understorey, this open forest allows some of the inland species to extend into the Wet Tropics. Here, Crested Pigeon, Diamond Dove, Apostlebird and others can be found, often only a short distance from tropical rainforest.

MIXED TROPICAL WOODLAND

On the coastal plain and parts of the tablelands lies a belt of woodland consisting of various *Melaleuca* spp. (paperbarks), eucalypts and acacias. Much has been cleared to make way for agriculture, but some areas remain, especially in the south-east and about the northern tablelands. Regrettably this habitat too is quickly disappearing in order to accommodate the ever-expanding sugar-cane industry. Mixed tropical woodland provides important habitat for a wide variety of birds, especially parrots, cuckoos, kingfishers, nomadic honeyeaters, flycatchers, fantails and cuckoo-shrikes.

THE WETLANDS

The bulk of the wetlands lie on the coastal plain, though some are to be found on the Atherton Tableland. Much of the wetland areas are seasonal, filling during the Wet and generally drying out through the Dry, but others which are more permanent, act as refuges through the late Dry.

Though much of the coastal wetlands were drained for agricultural purposes many years ago, those remaining are augmented by large permanent water storages such as Ross River and Tinaroo Falls dams. Though these support extensive populations of aquatic birds, all are utilised mostly as dry season refuges. Only limited breeding takes place. At the onset of the Wet, many species vacate the region.

PAPERBARK *(Melaleuca)* SWAMPS

Throughout the wetter lowlands, paperbark swamps have formed. This unique habitat not only supports some of the more specialised aquatic birds such as the elusive Black Bittern and pygmy-geese, but forms important habitat for the Brown-backed Honeyeater. Paperbark swamps are favoured roosting and nesting sites of the Barking Owl. Unfortunately many paperbark swamps have been drained and cleared to make way for agriculture. This practice continues.

THE MANGROVES

Fortunately mangrove forests have not suffered the same fate as other habitats through human exploitation. These tropical mangrove forests contain the richest variety of mangroves along the eastern Australian coastline.

A surprisingly large number of forest birds exploit the mangroves and often utilise them for breeding purposes. More importantly, mangroves have their own often elusive species, such as the Great-billed Heron, Collared Kingfisher, Mangrove Robin and Mangrove Golden Whistler.

BEACHES, MUDFLATS & ESTUARIES

Along nearly 500 kilometres of coastline are many sandy beaches, but interspersed with these, various estuaries and mudflats form extensive feeding grounds for the migratory shorebirds. Of these mudflats, the most noted is the Cairns Esplanade, which is constantly under threat from development. The future of the Cairns Esplanade remains uncertain. Here, such rarities as Asiatic Dowitcher, Common Redshank, Long-toed Stint, Dunlin and Laughing and Franklin's Gulls have been recorded.

THE GREAT BARRIER REEF, ISLANDS & CAYS

The Great Barrier Reef supports both continental islands close to the coast as well as coral islets or cays farther out in the Coral Sea. The continental islands, usually with a covering of adjacent mainland flora, share many forest birds with the mainland, but some seabirds often breed on them and feed out from them. The coral cays and islets, such as Michaelmas Cay, have a covering of vegetation and provide nesting sites for terns and noddies. Others, devoid of vegetation, are mostly utilised as roosting sites.

Some tropical petrels, storm-petrels and others such as shearwaters, boobies and jaegers sometimes reach the outer edge of the Reef.

FARMLAND

The arrival of European settlers saw the creation of a new habitat — farmland. Where rainforests and tropical woodland once flourished, large areas of open farmland, pasture and sugar-cane now stand. The most significant farmland for birdlife is pasture and cropland much of which lies across the Atherton Tableland. Quail, kites, harriers, cranes, rails, button-quail, lapwings and others exploit this habitat.

On the other hand, land used for sugar-cane farming is generally devoid of birdlife. As an example, the area about Pickford Road near Mareeba, which was used for rice farming, soon became widely known for its prolific birdlife. Then, for economic reasons, rice crops were replaced with fields of sugar-cane. Today, little can be seen about Pickford Road apart from a few Black Kites.

OTHER SMALLER SPECIALISED HABITATS

Some small areas of specialised habitats occur throughout the Wet Tropics. Though insignificant in stature, they considerably augment the richness of the local bird scene.

Short-grassed aerodromes and turf farms provide habitat for Little Curlew, Oriental and Australian Pratincoles and Yellow Wagtail. **Heathland** about Cooktown provides habitat for the White-streaked Honeyeater. The Zitting Cisticola inhabits **couch grass flats or saline grassland** at the inland edge of mangroves in the southern part of the region. Behind the beaches where urban development has not yet encroached grows a low, dense vegetation known locally as **dune scrub**. This habitat supports populations of birds such as Lovely Fairy-wren, Fairy Gerygone and Varied Triller.

THE SIZE OF BIRDS

Each bird has been designated as either tiny, small, medium-sized, large, very large or huge. This categorisation is based entirely on visual appearances. Measurements, which have been included, can often prove misleading, since they encompass tail and bill lengths. Thus a small bird with a long bill or tail (or both) will give a greater measurement than a larger bird with a short bill or tail or both.

Briefly, very small birds such as Weebill are designated as tiny, while birds up to the size of Eastern Yellow Robin are designated as small. Those from shrike-thrush to Australian King-Parrot and Brown Cuckoo-Dove are medium-sized, while birds from Topknot Pigeon and Galah and larger are designated as large. Birds such as Wedge-tailed Eagle are designated very large or huge.

Be aware that designated size should be taken only as a general guide. Sizes quoted in centimetres are given as an average size to aid identification and comparison with other species.

ENGLISH OR COMMON NAMES

English names for Australian birds have been 'revised' several times in recent years, sometimes for valid reasons, but unfortunately often for little reason other than change or at the whim of academia. Names were again revised in 1995 following a popular vote. This was a necessary move in order to eliminate some unsuitable names foisted upon the birdwatching community some years ago by a committee.

This field guide incorporates the current English names; *see* Christidis, L. and Boles, W. E. 1994, 'The Taxonomy and Species of Birds of Australia and Its Territories', *Royal Australasian Ornithologists Union Monograph 2*, RAOU, Melbourne. Previous names used in other publications are included, with an appropriate referral, in the index. I would strongly suggest that current names be used for all birds in order to lessen the widespread confusion which presently exists.

BINOCULARS & TELESCOPES

For those about to embark upon an interest in the birds about them, binoculars are a necessity. The best binoculars for birdwatching are the wide angle 7x35s or 8x40s, although the lighter 8x30s are adequate. Some of the smaller pocket binoculars such as 7x20s are surprisingly good, but the heavier 10x50s, 12x50s, or 16x50s especially, are not entirely suitable.

One of the most important things to bear in mind when buying binoculars is to perhaps pay a little extra and purchase one of the better brands. The old adage that one only gets what one pays for has never been more true than when purchasing binoculars. A pair of Leica binoculars or similar will last a lifetime, while very cheap brands perhaps one or two years at best.

A telescope is a wonderful aid for those more serious birdwatchers who want to see finer detail or identify difficult shorebirds. The use of a tripod, which is necessary with a telescope, provides a view free of the 'shakes' commonly associated with the use of binoculars. As with binoculars, the more one pays, the better the performance. An eyepiece is an important key to a useful telescope. Standard 20x or 30x eyepieces are available. My favourite is a 20–60x zoom which allows me to view details such as the diagnostic markings on the gape of an egret one kilometre away!

WHEN TO VISIT

While birding throughout the year proves fruitful in the Wet Tropics, the optimum time is October to January. Migrants, having wintered in the islands to the north of Australia, return to breed. Migratory shorebirds have returned to their Australian 'wintering' quarters, and aquatic birds congregate in large numbers throughout the drying wetlands. Fruit-eating pigeons usually become more obvious as they feast upon an abundance of rainforest fruits. The weather, pleasantly warm though dry, proves ideal for birdwatching!

HANDY HINTS

You may be fortunate enough to see a cassowary in the wild. If so, remain still or very slowly move away. Never approach a cassowary, particularly if the male has chicks in tow. Cassowaries can be inquisitive animals, but any sudden movement may cause them to react unfavourably. If driving, observe road signs where cassowaries are known to cross. Do not offer food to the birds.

Be aware that crocodiles may lurk about coastal rivers and billabongs any time of year. They pose no threat if common sense is observed. Heed warning signs where posted and do not stand close to the water's edge. Automobiles pose a far greater danger!

Always carry insect repellent, and avoid becoming a target for the scrub itch mite by not sitting on the ground or logs in rainforest.

During the Wet, check road conditions before setting out. Waterways can rise with alarming speed.

SIGHTINGS OF RARE BIRDS

From time to time, species new or rare to the Australian continent appear in this region. Our proximity to New Guinea and south-east Asia, coupled with the frequency of cyclones during the summer, guarantees the ongoing likelihood of such occurrences.

In order to have such sightings officially accepted, a carefully prepared proposal must be submitted to a records appraisal committee: either Queensland Ornithological Society Inc., Post Office Box 97, St Lucia Qld. 4067 or Royal Australasian Ornithologists Union, 415 Riversdale Road, Hawthorn East, Vic. 3123.

If a sighted bird is suspected as being rare or not recorded for Australia previously, one should record as much detail as possible such as colours, patterns, shape, other species which it resembles; bill, leg and eye colour; call (if any), as well as locality, date, weather, light conditions and the like. If possible, confirmation by another observer should be obtained. Better still, if practicable, photographs should be taken. A useful trick is to use your binoculars as a telephoto lens, with a standard camera. If the binoculars can be steadied on a rock or something similar, press the camera lens against the rubber eyepiece of the binoculars. You now have a 400 mm plus lens. The results will not be masterpieces, but will often provide an adequate picture for identification purposes.

Take time to submit a well-presented proposal. State what species you suspect the bird to be, and your reasons why you think it is so. Consider all other species it might be and eliminate each of these with an explanation why your bird is not one of them.

The onus is on the observer to prove to the committee that the bird in question is the rare or new one he or she thinks it to be. If proven, and the record accepted, then there is no dispute. The record becomes official and the observer given the credit.

Records appraisal committees were formed to combat a trend when a growing number of misidentifications (some very blatant) found their way into print. A few rather lax journal and newsletter editors accepted sightings without question. Consequently the literature remains littered with many of these worthless records.

AERIAL
  Swifts, Swallows & Martins 154–6
  others 156–7
AQUATIC
  freshwater swimming 163–5
  freshwater waders 165–70
  Geese, Ducks & Swans 170–3
  of reedbeds & stream margins 173–5
BACK
  olive-green 108
BILL
  long, excluding shorebirds 81–2
  red or orange
    small/medium 83–5
    large/very large 86
  short straight, shorebirds 182–4
  medium-length straight, shorebirds 184–6
  long straight, shorebirds 186
  upcurved, shorebirds 187
  downcurved, shorebirds 187–9
BIRDS OF PREY
  diurnal 175–81
BREAST
  yellow 71–4
  chestnut, rufous, orange or buff
    small 63–5
    medium/large 65–6
BREASTBAND
  black or dark 78–9
CREST 87–8
DIFFICULT GROUPS
  Birds of Prey: diurnal 175–81
  Bronze-Cuckoos 198–9
  Cisticolas: Zitting & Golden-headed 204
  Corvids: Australian Raven & Torresian Crow 203
  Cuckoos: plain underparts, excluding juvenile Bronze-Cuckoos 197
  Cuckoos: barred underparts 198
  Egrets 196–7
  Flycatchers: Broad-billed, Leaden, Satin 202
  Friarbirds: Helmeted, Silver-crowned, Noisy 201
  Gerygones: Brown, Mangrove, Western, Large-billed 200
  Honeyeaters: Lewin's, Yellow-spotted, Graceful 201–2
  Owls: Masked, Barn, Grass 199
  Reed-Warblers: Clamorous & Oriental 203

POSSIBILITIES

WHITE-RUMPED SWIFTLET
Collocalia spodiopygius   11 cm
Aerial; dark grey; **small greyish-white patch on
rump; stiff-winged flight**; usually in flocks.
Appears over most habitats at all altitudes.
May be confused with: NONE. Distinctive flight
separates it from other aerial birds.

WHITE-THROATED NEEDLETAIL
Hirundapus caudacutus   20 cm
Migrant, present Oct.–Apr.; aerial; small to medium-
sized dark bird; **long slender swept-back wings**;
white throat; short square tail **white underneath**.
Swift flight. Appears over most areas at all altitudes.
May be confused with: FORK-TAILED and HOUSE
SWIFTS, but look for large swift with short square tail
white underneath.

FORK-TAILED SWIFT
Apus pacificus   17 cm
Migrant, present Oct.–Apr.; small to medium-sized
dark aerial bird; **long swept-back wings**; pale throat;
white rump; long deeply forked tail. Flight is slower
than that of the WHITE-THROATED NEEDLETAIL.
Appears over most areas at all altitudes. *May be
confused with:* WHITE-THROATED NEEDLETAIL
and HOUSE SWIFT. Look for long thin tail and white
rump. Fork in tail often indiscernible.

HOUSE SWIFT   *Apus affinis*   15 cm
Rare summer visitor; aerial; mostly blackish; underside
of wings two-toned; **small and stocky; pale throat
and white rump; slightly forked tail becomes
square when fanned.** *May be confused with:* Other
swifts, swiftlets, swallows and martins, but look for
slight fork in tail, pale throat and white rump.

PAINTED HONEYEATER
Grantiella picta   16 cm
Rare; blackish upperparts; white underparts;
**broad yellow margin to flight and tail feathers;
pinkish-red bill.** Drier open forest and woodland
mostly in western areas.

BANDED HONEYEATER
Certhionyx pectoralis   13 cm
Black upperparts; white underparts; white rump; **thin
black band across breast.** Dry open forest and
woodland especially where eucalypts and paperbarks
are blossoming.

WHITE-EARED MONARCH
Monarcha leucotis 13 cm
Greyish-white underparts; black tail tipped
white; **three white patches about eye in black head**.
Coastal rainforest, sometimes upland rainforest.
May be confused with: Perhaps VARIED TRILLER
which has buff lower belly and under tail-coverts.

PIED MONARCH *Arses kaupi* 14 cm
White collar; **erectile frill on nape; wide black
breastband on white underparts; blue eye-ring**.
Female: broader breastband, incomplete collar and
greyish nape. Rainforest, moreso at lower altitudes.

LEADEN FLYCATCHER
Myiagra rubecula (Male) 15 cm
Constantly quivers tail; blue-grey upperparts which
sometimes appear black; glossy leaden head and upper
breast **distinctly demarcated by white upperparts**.
Eucalypt forest, woodland, mangroves, parks and
gardens. *May be confused with:* Male SATIN
FLYCATCHER. See p. 202.

SATIN FLYCATCHER
Myiagra cyanoleuca (Male) 16 cm
A rare migrant seen on passage Aug.–Sept. and Mar.–Apr.;
similar to LEADEN FLYCATCHER. *May be confused
with:* Male LEADEN FLYCATCHER. See p. 202.

RESTLESS FLYCATCHER
Myiagra inquieta 20 cm
Black upperparts; white underparts from throat to
under tail; **faint buff on breast**; longish straight tail
which it **sweeps from side to side; frequently
hovers**. Open forest and woodland, often near water
and sometimes about farmhouses. *May be confused
with:* WILLIE WAGTAIL, but look for white throat.

WILLIE WAGTAIL
Rhipidura leucophrys 20 cm
Active, common bird; black upperparts; **black throat**;
white eyebrow; white underparts; tail partly spread
and **twitched frequently**. Lightly timbered country,
farmland and urban areas. *May be confused with:*
RESTLESS FLYCATCHER, but look for black throat.

WHITE-WINGED TRILLER
Lalage sueurii (Breeding Male) 18 cm
Black crown, back and tail; all-white underparts;
white shoulder; grey rump; no eyebrow. Develops
brown non-breeding plumage Feb.–Aug. Open
woodland and eucalypt forest. *May be confused with:*
NONE within its habitat. Male VARIED TRILLER has
buff lower belly and under tail-coverts and prefers
denser habitat.

VARIED TRILLER

Lalage leucomela (Male) 19 cm
Blackish crown and nape, back and tail; white to off-white underparts from chin to belly; prominent white eyebrow; grey rump; **buff lower belly and under tail-coverts**. Gallery forest, rainforest, denser eucalypt forest and paperbark woodland, sometimes mangroves. *May be confused with:* NONE. Buff lower belly and under tail-coverts separate it from all other species.

WHITE-BACKED SWALLOW

Cheramoeca leucosternus 14 cm
Rare; distinct black and white aerial bird; **white throat**, **breast**, **crown and back**; plain deeply forked tail. Open woodland.

TREE MARTIN *Hirundo nigricans* 12 cm
Aerial; dark back and wings; whitish underparts; **white rump which appears dirty**; **square tail**; **dark crown**. Open areas and farmland; often perches with other aerial birds on powerlines. *May be confused with:* FAIRY MARTIN which has rusty crown.

FURTHER POSSIBILITIES
Male HOODED ROBIN — rare.
WHITE-BREASTED WOODSWALLOW
Juvenile BARN SWALLOW

MEDIUM-SIZED BLACK & WHITE BIRDS

POSSIBILITIES

BLACK-WINGED STILT

Himantopus himantopus 37 cm
Distinctive boldly marked wading bird; white head and body; black nape and wings; longish needle-like bill; **extremely long pink legs**; often 'yaps' like a small dog. Shallow freshwater lakes, swamps and riverbeds, sometimes estuaries and mudflats.

WHITE-HEADED PIGEON

Columba leucomela 40 cm
White head and underparts; **black back**, **wings and tail**; **red bill**; **red about eye**. Rainforest at all altitudes, but moreso in higher areas.

PIED IMPERIAL-PIGEON

Ducula bicolor 42 cm
Migrant, present Aug.–Apr.; predominantly white pigeon; **black flight feathers and lower half of tail**; head may be soiled brownish from fruit stains. Rainforest and mangroves in coastal lowlands and offshore islands.

CHOWCHILLA
Orthonyx spaldingii (Male) 27 cm
A darkish bird of the rainforest floor; all-white underparts; **conspicuous white eye-ring**. Rainforest, moreso in upland areas.

MAGPIE-LARK *Grallina cyanoleuca* 27 cm
Common, distinctive black and white bird; short white bill; white eye. Juvenile: dark bill; brown eye. **Walks on ground with head-nodding movement**. Usually in vicinity of water in open areas, creeks, swamps, farmland, parks and gardens.

PIED BUTCHERBIRD
Cracticus nigrogularis 34 cm
Black head and 'bib'; thick blue-grey finely hooked bill tipped black. In flight, shows prominent **white rump and black triangle on back**. **Hops** while on ground. Open lightly timbered areas and farmland. *May be confused with:* Perhaps AUSTRALIAN MAGPIE, but look for black 'bib'.

FURTHER POSSIBILITIES
GREY BUTCHERBIRD sometimes appears black and white but has a grey back.

LARGE BLACK & WHITE BIRDS
POSSIBILITIES

LITTLE PIED CORMORANT
Phalacrocorax melanoleucos 52 cm
Aquatic; black upperparts; white underparts; white face; **shortish yellow hooked bill**. Mostly freshwater lakes, swamps, rivers, creeks, also estuaries and mangroves. *May be confused with:* PIED CORMORANT, but look for white face and shorter yellow bill.

PIED CORMORANT *Phalacrocorax varius* 72 cm
Aquatic; black upperparts; white underparts; **horn-coloured hooked bill**; **orange-yellow facial and throat skin**; **black flank**. Estuaries and bays, larger lagoons and lakes. *May be confused with:* LITTLE PIED CORMORANT, but look for orange-yellow facial skin and black flank.

GREAT FRIGATEBIRD
Fregata minor (Female) 92 cm
Mostly black aerial seabird with **long slender wings and deeply forked tail**; **white throat and breast**. Soars high on motionless wings. Usually with all-black males. Offshore waters and islands of Great Barrier Reef, sometimes over coastal shorelines. *May be confused with:* Female LESSER FRIGATEBIRD which has all-black head and throat.

Male *Female*

23

LESSER FRIGATEBIRD

Fregata ariel (Female) 75 cm
Very similar to GREAT FRIGATEBIRD and inhabits
similar oceanic areas. **All-black head and throat;**
white 'armpits' in flight. *May be confused with:*
GREAT FRIGATEBIRD, but look for all-black head
and white 'armpits'.

PIED HERON   *Ardea picata*   46 cm

Rare wading bird; blue-black body; long thin
neck; white cheeks, throat and neck; **black crown**
and crest; long thin sharp **yellow bill; yellow legs.**
Juvenile: lacks black crown and crest. Freshwater
swamps and lagoons, pasture, mudflats, mangroves
and tidal rivers. *May be confused with:* Adult: NONE.
Juvenile: the larger WHITE-NECKED HERON, but
look for yellow bill and legs.

AUSTRALIAN WHITE IBIS

Threskiornis molucca   70 cm
Mostly white wading bird; **bare black head; black**
tail; long curved black bill; plumage often soiled.
Shallow fresh water, grassland, tidal flats, mangroves
and city parks.

STRAW-NECKED IBIS

Threskiornis spinicollis   70 cm
Wading bird; black back; white neck and
underparts; **bare black head; long curved black**
bill. Adult has yellow straw-like plumes on neck. Wet
or dry grassland, pasture, swamps and city parks.

PIED OYSTERCATCHER

Haematopus longirostris   50 cm
Distinctive shorebird; black head, back, wings
and tail; white breast, belly and under tail-coverts;
conspicuous **red bill, eye-ring, legs and feet.** Mostly
sandy beaches, also mudflats and estuaries.

AUSTRALIAN MAGPIE

Gymnorhina tibicen   43 cm
Mostly black; **rounded white patch on back of neck;**
white patch on wing; white under tail; thick robust
whitish bill tipped black. Feeds mostly on ground;
walks. Open lightly timbered areas and farmland.
May be confused with: Perhaps PIED BUTCHERBIRD,
but look for all-black underparts and white patch on
back of neck. BUTCHERBIRD hops when on ground.

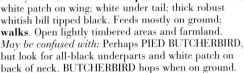

PIED CURRAWONG   *Strepera graculina*   46 cm

Predominantly black when perched; black and white in
flight; some white in wing; white tail tip, under tail-
coverts and rump; **prominent yellow eyes;** heavy
black bill. Hillside eucalypt forest, rainforest canopy
and open woodland; lowlands in winter.

WHITE-WINGED CHOUGH

Corcorax melanorhamphos   45 cm

Large nearly all-black bird; **white patch in each wing conspicuous in flight**; small curved bill; red eye. **Feeds on ground in family groups**. Noisy when alarmed. Note range. Open dry forest. *May be confused with:* PIED CURRAWONG which has yellow eye and stout bill. AUSTRALIAN RAVEN and TORRESIAN CROW are all-black with stout bill.

FURTHER POSSIBILITIES

With little doubt the PAPUAN HARRIER occurs in the region as a vagrant. See Diurnal Birds of Prey, pp. 175–81

MEDIUM-SIZED BLACK, WHITE & GREY BIRDS
POSSIBILITIES

GREY BUTCHERBIRD

Cracticus torquatus   30 cm

Black head, wings and tail; **grey back**; white underparts from chin to tail; **thick, longish hooked blue-grey bill tipped black**. Drier open forest and woodland.

SMALL & MEDIUM-SIZED BLACK OR DARK-COLOURED BIRDS
POSSIBILITIES

DUSKY MOORHEN

Gallinula tenebrosa   39 cm

Medium-sized, short-tailed aquatic bird; dark olive-brown; **small red head shield, red bill tipped yellow and two white markings under tail** distinguish it from all other aquatic birds. Freshwater swamps, lakes, creeks, dams, especially those with open aquatic vegetation. *May be confused with:* PURPLE SWAMPHEN has heavier all-red bill and all-white under tail-coverts.

BLACK-TAILED NATIVE-HEN

Gallinula ventralis   34 cm

Rare, medium-sized short-tailed **bantam-like** aquatic bird; plain dark olive-brown above; slate-grey below; **bright red legs, several white spots on flanks and green and red bill** distinguish it from all other aquatic birds.

EURASIAN COOT   *Fulica atra*   37 cm

Medium-sized, almost tailless aquatic bird; overall dark slate-grey with **white bill; white head shield**. Open sheets of deep fresh water.

COMMON KOEL

Eudynamys scolopacea (Male) 43 cm
Migrant, present Sept.–Apr.; medium-sized black
bird with **long straight tail**; **red eye**; **pale bill**.
Usually timid and skulking. Denser open forest and
woodland, gallery forest, dense trees in farmland,
parks and gardens. *May be confused with:* SPANGLED
DRONGO which has fish tail and dark bill. Male
SATIN BOWERBIRD has short tail, longish pale legs
and violet eye. Look for long tail and pale bill.

DOLLARBIRD *Eurystomus orientalis* 29 cm

Migrant, present late Sept.–Apr./May; medium-sized;
plump; short tail; overall dark greyish to greenish-blue;
thin blue stripe along edge of wing; **broad red bill**;
red feet; **shows large white spot in each wing in
flight**. Sparsely timbered areas, especially along
watercourses, open woodland and farmland.

CHOWCHILLA

Orthonyx spaldingii 27 cm
Medium-sized darkish bird of the rainforest floor;
conspicuous white eye-ring. Male: all-white
underparts. Female: rufous throat and breast; white
belly. Rainforest, moreso in upland areas.

EASTERN WHIPBIRD

Psophodes olivaceus 27 cm
Dark olive-green body; black head **white cheek
patches**; **small black crest** sometimes carried flat on
back of head; **long tail.** Juvenile lacks white cheek
patches. Lower strata of rainforest at higher altitudes,
occasionally adjacent eucalypt forest. Sometimes coastal.

SHINING FLYCATCHER

Myiagra alecto (Male) 17 cm
Small; **entirely glossy blue-black**; raises crown
feathers in a small crest; usually with bright rufous,
black and white female. Mangroves, sometimes
adjacent paperbark forest and riverside vegetation.
Occasionally well upstream in some larger rivers.

SPANGLED DRONGO *Dicrurus bracteatus* 30 cm

Noisy medium-sized black bird; **fish tail**; **red eye**;
shrugs shoulders and flicks tail somewhat 'crazily'
while calling. Mostly edges of rainforest and adjacent
woodland throughout, but moreso at lower altitudes,
sometimes in mangroves. *May be confused with:* Male
COMMON KOEL, BLACK BUTCHERBIRD and male
SATIN BOWERBIRD, but look for fish tail. Only the
DRONGO flicks its tail. Occasionally the DRONGO
with outer tail feathers moulted or abraded has been
mistaken for the TRUMPET MANUCODE, a rainforest
bird of northern Cape York Peninsula.

CICADABIRD *Coracina tenuirostris* (Male) 25 cm
Migrant, present Oct.–Apr.; medium-sized; overall dark
grey, appearing **almost black with darker face**; fast
flight; usually wary. Eucalypt forest, vine thickets,
paperbark woodland, mangroves, canopy of lowland
rainforest.

DUSKY WOODSWALLOW
Artamus cyanopterus 18 cm
Small; overall dark smoky-brown; bluish-black wings;
bluish bill; black tail tipped white frequently wagged;
thin white wing-stripe. Open woodland and open
areas with dead timber. *May be confused with:* LITTLE
WOODSWALLOW which lacks white wing-stripe.

LITTLE WOODSWALLOW
Artamus minor 14 cm
Rare; dark chocolate-brown; deep blue-grey wings;
blackish-grey tail tipped white; **bluish bill**; **no wing-
stripe**; tail frequently wagged. Open and grassy
woodland. *May be confused with:* DUSKY
WOODSWALLOW which has white wing-stripe.

BLACK BUTCHERBIRD *Cracticus quoyi* 36 cm
Medium-sized; totally black; **thick, longish, finely
hooked blue-grey bill tipped black**. All denser
habitats, e.g. rainforest moreso at lower altitudes,
mangroves. *May be confused with:* Perhaps male
COMMON KOEL, and male SATIN BOWERBIRD in
upland rainforest, but look for distinctive bill.

VICTORIA'S RIFLEBIRD
Ptiloris victoriae (Male) 24 cm
Medium-sized; velvety-black; iridescent metallic-green
crown and triangular patch on throat; **long curved
black bill**; short tail. Rainforest at all altitudes. *May
be confused with:* Perhaps male SATIN BOWERBIRD,
but long curved bill readily distinguishes it.

APOSTLEBIRD
Struthidea cinerea 31 cm
Unspectacular dark grey bird; robust black bill; **black
tail; brownish flight feathers**; usually in family
groups; noisy when approached. Drier open forest and
woodland.

SATIN BOWERBIRD
Ptilonorhynchus violaceus (Male) 24 cm
Medium-sized; **glossy blue-black; shortish tail;
pale bill; violet eye**. Upland rainforest, rainforest
margins and adjacent open forest.
May be confused with: Male COMMON KOEL,
SPANGLED DRONGO, BLACK BUTCHERBIRD and
male VICTORIA'S RIFLEBIRD, but look for shortish
tail, short pale bill and violet eye.

METALLIC STARLING *Aplonis metallica* 24 cm
Medium-sized gregarious bird; plumage appears
glossy-black but with purple and green iridescence.
Prominent, **bulging red eye**; **long**, **sharply pointed**
tail. Rainforest and remnants of rainforest mostly at
lower altitudes; sometimes mangroves.

FURTHER POSSIBILITIES
WHITE-WINGED CHOUGH appears all-black but has white
patches in wings in flight.

LARGE BLACK OR DARK-COLOURED BIRDS
POSSIBILITIES

DARTER *Anhinga melanogaster* (Male) 90 cm
Blackish aquatic bird; **long thin neck**; **sharp**
yellowish bill. Swims with body submerged with only
slender head and neck visible above surface. Deeper
fresh water, sometimes river estuaries.

LITTLE BLACK CORMORANT
Phalacrocorax sulcirostris 62 cm
Black aquatic bird which dives for fish; **dark face**;
dark hooked bill. Lakes, rivers, swamps, sometimes
estuaries and bays. *May be confused with:* GREAT
CORMORANT, but look for dark face.

GREAT CORMORANT *Phalacrocorax carbo* 82 cm
Black aquatic bird which dives for fish; **yellowish**
face; white chin and white patch on flank in breeding
plumage; hooked, dark horn-coloured bill. Larger areas
of deeper water, rivers, lakes, bays, estuaries.
May be confused with: LITTLE BLACK CORMORANT
which is smaller. Look for yellowish face.

EASTERN REEF EGRET
Egretta sacra (Grey phase) 62 cm
Marine wading bird; **slate-grey**; **thin white streak**
down throat. Exclusively coastal – rocky shores, coral
reefs, mudflats, offshore islands and beaches.
May be confused with: WHITE-FACED HERON which
has white face and throat, all-black bill, yellow legs
and is paler grey. STRIATED HERON which has black
cap and yellow to orange legs.

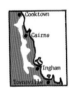

BLACK BITTERN *Ixobrychus flavicollis* 60 cm
Secretive, dark sooty-coloured wading bird; breast and
sides of neck streaked yellowish **with yellowish plume**
on side of neck; **dark bill**; **olive-brown legs**. Female:
duller. Juvenile: sooty-brown with paler edging to
feathers, pale neck plume; yellow-brown legs. Feeds at
dusk and dawn. Freshwater swamps, especially paperbark swamps, well-vegetated streamsides, sometimes
mangroves. *May be confused with:* Perhaps STRIATED
HERON, which has black cap and yellow to orange legs,
but look for neck plume and olive-brown legs.

GLOSSY IBIS *Plegadis falcinellus* 55 cm
Wading bird; appears black at a distance but
is dull reddish-brown. Purple-green sheen on wings;
long black curved bill. Shallow freshwater swamps,
sometimes mangroves and mudflats. *May be confused
with:* Generally NONE. However, in flight, can be
confused with LITTLE BLACK CORMORANT. Look for
drooping, extended neck and more downcurved wings.

BLACK FALCON
Falco subniger Male 49 cm Female 55 cm
Rare; dark sooty-brown; **faint pale chin and face**; older
birds have white-speckled throat developing into an
extensive white 'bib'; **plain tail**. Open grassland and open
woodland. *May be confused with:* BROWN FALCON
(dark form). See Diurnal Birds of Prey, pp. 175–81.
Sometimes can be mistaken for AUSTRALIAN RAVEN or
TORRESIAN CROW at a distance.

PURPLE SWAMPHEN *Porphyrio porphyrio* 49 cm
Aquatic; dark **purplish-blue**; **thick red bill**; **large
red head shield**; **all-white under tail-coverts**.
Margins of lakes, swamps and nearby grassland.
May be confused with: Possibly DUSKY MOORHEN,
but look for all-white under tail-coverts. DUSKY
MOORHEN has two white markings under tail.

SOOTY OYSTERCATCHER
Haematopus fuliginosus 50 cm
Sooty-black marine shorebird; conspicuous **red bill**,
eye-ring, **legs and feet**. Rocky coastlines, exposed reef
flats, mostly on offshore islands.

RED-TAILED BLACK-COCKATOO
Calyptorhynchus banksii 56 cm
Black; **broad red panels in tail** visible only when tail
is spread. Male: dark grey bill and rounded crest.
Female: whitish bill; fine yellow spots and barring in
plumage; tail panels more yellow-orange, finely barred
black. Open forest, woodland, sometimes over
rainforest and about cities and towns.

PHEASANT COUCAL
Centropus phasianinus (Breeding plumage) 70 cm
Clumsy-looking; **outsized tail**; skulking; black head
and body from about Sept.–Mar./Apr.; brown wings;
dark tail has paler barring. Lives mostly on the ground
in tall grassy areas in open forest and farmland.

AUSTRALIAN RAVEN
Corvus coronoides 52 cm
Totally black; heavy black bill; black legs. Adult:
white eyes. Juvenile: brown eyes. Open, lightly
timbered areas and farmland.
May be confused with: TORRESIAN CROW.
See p. 203.

TORRESIAN CROW
Corvus orru 50 cm
Similar to AUSTRALIAN RAVEN. *May be confused*
with: AUSTRALIAN RAVEN. See p. 203.

FURTHER POSSIBILITIES
FRIGATEBIRDS which sometimes appear over the coastline.
See also Diurnal Birds of Prey, pp. 175–81.
Medium-sized and Large Brown Birds of the Rainforest Floor, pp. 142–3.
Aquatic Birds, pp. 163–75.

VERY LARGE & HUGE BLACK OR DARK-COLOURED BIRDS
POSSIBILITIES

SOUTHERN CASSOWARY
Casuarius casuarius 200 cm
Huge flightless black bird; bare blue skin on head
and neck; two red wattles; large grey 'helmet'.
Juvenile: quite brown. Rainforest at all altitudes.

EMU *Dromaius novaehollandiae* 200 cm
Huge well-known bird; flightless; dark brown;
shaggy feathers; blue skin on sides of head and
throat. Drier open woodland and grassland.

BLACK SWAN *Cygnus atratus* 125 cm
Well-known, very large, distinctive and graceful
waterbird; black; **long neck**, **bright red bill**; shows
white wing feathers in flight. Nearly always on water.
Larger expanses of open water, mostly fresh water.

GREAT-BILLED HERON *Ardea sumatrana* 105 cm
Very large grey-brown aquatic bird; **large dark sharp
bill**, dull yellow at base of lower mandible; **pale throat**;
long thin neck; **yellow eye**. Mostly mangroves and
associated tidal channels, mudbanks, freshwater creeks
and rivers. *May be confused with:* Juvenile BLACK-
NECKED STORK which is sometimes misidentified as a
GREAT-BILLED HERON, but look for pale throat and
yellow eye, long thin neck, folded in flight.

BLACK-NECKED STORK
Ephippiorhynchus asiaticus (Juvenile) 120 cm
Huge, long-legged, grey-brown wading bird; **heavy
long bill**; **grey face**; **black eye**; flies with neck
extended. Usually freshwater swamps, sometimes
estuaries and mangroves. *May be confused with:*
GREAT-BILLED HERON, but look for heavy bill, long
legs and black eye, extended neck in flight.

WHITE-BELLIED SEA-EAGLE
Haliaeetus leucogaster (Juvenile and Immature) Male
76 cm Female 83 cm. A huge dark brown eagle; short
buffy-white rather rounded tail. In flight, shows
**upswept wings with a pale half-moon near the tip
on underside of each wing**. Estuaries, bays, larger
lakes and rivers and offshore islands. *May be confused
with:* Other large birds of prey. See pp. 175–81.

WEDGE-TAILED EAGLE

Aquila audax   Male 91 cm Female 100 cm
Huge dark eagle ranging from brown to near black;
thickly-feathered legs; heavy, hooked pale bill; **longish
wedge-shaped tail**. In flight, look for upswept wings
and wedge-shaped tail which distinguishes it from all
other birds of prey. Mountainous forest to lowland
tropical woodland. Generally avoids rainforest.
May be confused with: Other large birds of prey.
See Diurnal Birds of Prey, pp. 175–81.

SMALL BIRDS WITH SOME BLUE PLUMAGE
POSSIBILITIES

AZURE KINGFISHER *Alcedo azurea*   18 cm
Deep blue head, back and wings;
disproportionately-long, thin black bill; short tail;
completely orange underparts. Freshwater streams,
often in rainforest. Sometimes in mangroves.

LITTLE KINGFISHER *Alcedo pusilla*   13 cm
Tiny; **deep blue head, back, wings, tail and sides of
breast**; white underparts; two white spots on forehead;
white tuft on side of neck; disproportionately-long,
thin black bill; short tail. Somewhat elusive.
Mangroves, freshwater creeks in rainforest. *May be
confused with:* Larger conspicuous FOREST
KINGFISHER which is often mistaken for LITTLE.
Look for white neck tuft and noticeably tiny size.

FOREST KINGFISHER
Todiramphus macleayii   21 cm
Usually looks immaculate; two-toned blue upperparts;
white underparts; **white collar** (not entire in female);
large black bill; two prominent white spots on
forehead; **white 'window' in each wing in flight**.
Perches openly on powerlines, posts, open limbs. The
most common kingfisher in the Wet Tropics. Open
forest, woodlands, open areas, farmland and gardens.
May be confused with: LITTLE KINGFISHER, but
look for white collar, white 'windows' in wing in flight
and open perching habit. COLLARED and SACRED
KINGFISHERS lack white spots on forehead and white
'windows' in wings in flight. RED-BACKED
KINGFISHER has red rump and streaked crown.

RED-BACKED KINGFISHER
Todiramphus pyrrhopygia   22 cm
Rather dull kingfisher; upper back, wings and tail pale
blue and whitish-blue; **streaked crown; reddish-
orange rump**. Open woodland and sparsely timbered
areas. *May be confused with:* Perhaps other
kingfishers, but look for rump colour and streaked
crown.

SACRED KINGFISHER *Todiramphus sanctus* 21 cm
Blue wings, tail and rump; blue-green back and crown;
white to buff underparts; **buffy-white** collar; **buff**
spot in front of eye. Open forest, paperbark woodland,
farmland, edges of mangroves, sometimes about
beaches. *May be confused with:* FOREST and
COLLARED KINGFISHERS. The SACRED in the Wet
Tropics is mainly a winter visitor when underparts
become pale buff to buff, making it distinct. The
spring/summer breeding population about Kaban and
the western edge of the Wet Tropics has white
underparts but lacks the white spots on the forehead
and white wing patches (in flight) of the FOREST.
RED-BACKED KINGFISHER has a reddish-orange
rump and streaked crown.

RAINBOW BEE-EATER
Merops ornatus 23 cm
Blue-green; light blue rump and belly; **orange-yellow**
throat underlined blackish; two long feathers
protrude from blackish tail; triangular pointed
wings show **bright rufous** underneath in flight.
Juvenile: lacks black in throat. Open, lightly timbered
areas and farmland.

LOVELY FAIRY-WREN
Malurus amabilis 15 cm
Long cocked bluish tail. Male: blue head and ear-
coverts; black throat and breast; chestnut rump.
Female: **dull blue head, back and tail; pale blue**
ear-coverts; white throat and underparts. Denser
tropical woodland, coastal paperbark swamps and
mangroves. *May be confused with:* NONE. Sometimes
misidentified as VARIEGATED FAIRY-WREN which
does not occur in the Wet Tropics.

BLUE-FACED PARROT-FINCH
Erythrura trichroa 12 cm
Rare; **rich grass-green; blue face; dark reddish-**
brown rump. Face mid-blue in male, duller in female
and green in juvenile. Mostly rainforest at higher
altitudes.

FURTHER POSSIBILITIES
Male KING QUAIL has slate-blue sides of face, chest and
flanks — an elusive ground-dweller.
BLUE-TAILED BEE-EATER *Merops philippinus* 28 cm
A species of New Guinea. A chance that it may eventually
occur in the Wet Tropics. Similar to RAINBOW BEE-EATER
but with **blue tail and plain chestnut throat.**

POSSIBILITIES

RAINBOW LORIKEET

Trichoglossus haematodus 28 cm
The most common parrot; medium-sized; green back,
wings and tail; **deep blue head**; orange breast and
bill; noisy. Eucalypt forest, rainforest edges, open
areas, parks and gardens.

CRIMSON ROSELLA

Platycercus elegans 33 cm
Medium-sized; striking blood-red head and
underparts; **blue cheeks; broad blue edges to wings**;
long dark-blue tail. Upland rainforest and nearby
eucalypt forest.

PALE-HEADED ROSELLA

Platycercus adscitus 30 cm
Medium-sized; **pale yellow to white head and
throat; red under tail-coverts**; greenish-blue belly;
blue edges to wings; yellow and black back; long tail.
Eucalypt forest, tropical woodland, lightly timbered
grassland.

LAUGHING KOOKABURRA

Dacelo novaeguineae 46 cm
Large; overall brown and white; heavy stout bill;
whitish head; brown crown; **dark mark through eye**;
dark eye; underparts faintly barred, sometimes stained;
sky-blue on shoulders. Open forest and woodland,
farmland, cities and towns. *May be confused with:*
Perhaps BLUE-WINGED KOOKABURRA, but look for
brown crown, dark mark through eye and dark eye.

BLUE-WINGED KOOKABURRA

Dacelo leachii 43 cm
Large; whitish streaked head; faintly barred whitish
underparts; heavy stout bill; **large blue patch on
wings; blue rump**; white eye (dark in juvenile). Male:
blue tail. Female: tail reddish-brown barred darker.
Eucalypt forest and paperbark woodland. *May be
confused with:* Perhaps LAUGHING KOOKABURRA,
but look for blue rump, pale head and crown and
white eye.

BUFF-BREASTED PARADISE-KINGFISHER

Tanysiptera sylvia 34 cm
Migrant, present Nov.–early Apr.; medium-sized;
distinctively spectacular; thick red bill; brilliant blue
and black above; rufous-orange below; centre of back
and rump white; **two very long, stiff, white tail
feathers** sometimes broken-off during or after
breeding. Mostly lowland rainforest.

COLLARED KINGFISHER
Todiramphus chloris 26 cm
Mangrove-dwelling kingfisher; **blue and green above** (mostly blue in the Wet Tropics); white below; white collar. Mangroves, sometimes adjacent paperbark swamps. Frequently inhabits the zone between the two. *May be confused with:* FOREST KINGFISHER is more blue with prominent white spots on forehead and white 'window' in wing in flight. Wintering SACRED KINGFISHER inhabits mangrove and adjacent habitats and is distinctive, with pale buff to buff underparts.

DOLLARBIRD *Eurystomus orientalis* 29 cm
Migrant, present late Sept.–Apr./May; medium-sized; plump; short tail; overall dark-greyish to greenish-blue; thin blue stripe along edge of wing; **broad red bill; red feet; shows large white spot in each wing in flight.** Sparsely timbered areas, especially along watercourses, open woodland and farmland.

NOISY PITTA *Pitta versicolor* 18 cm
Medium-sized, short-tailed bird of the rainforest floor; **blue shoulders; black throat and mask extending to back of head;** buff breast; green back and wings; black patch on belly; red lower belly. Rainforest at all altitudes.

SMALL BRIGHTLY-COLOURED BIRDS
POSSIBILITIES

AZURE KINGFISHER *Alcedo azurea* 18 cm
Deep blue head, back and wings; completely orange underparts; disproportionately-long, thin black bill; short tail. Freshwater streams, often in rainforest. Sometimes in mangroves.

LITTLE KINGFISHER *Alcedo pusilla* 13 cm
Tiny; **deep blue head, back, wings, tail and sides of breast;** white underparts; two white spots on forehead; **white tuft on side of neck;** disproportionately-long, thin black bill; **short tail.** Somewhat elusive and secretive. Mangroves and freshwater creeks in rainforest. *May be confused with:* Larger conspicuous FOREST KINGFISHER which is often mistaken for LITTLE KINGFISHER. Look for white neck tuft and noticeably tiny size.

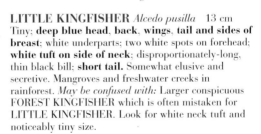

FOREST KINGFISHER
Todiramphus macleayii 21 cm
Usually looks immaculate; two-toned blue upperparts; white underparts; **white collar** (not entire in female); large black bill; two prominent white spots on forehead; **white 'window' in each wing in flight.** Perches openly on powerlines, posts, open limbs. The common kingfisher in the Wet Tropics. Open forest,

woodland, open areas, farmland and gardens.
May be confused with: LITTLE KINGFISHER, but
look for white collar, white 'windows' in wing in flight
and open perching habit. SACRED and COLLARED
KINGFISHERS lack white spots on forehead and white
'windows' in wings in flight. RED-BACKED
KINGFISHER has red rump and streaked crown.

RAINBOW BEE-EATER *Merops ornatus* 23 cm
Blue-green; light blue rump and belly; **orange-yellow
throat underlined blackish; two long feathers protrude
from blackish tail;** triangular pointed wings show **bright
rufous** underneath in flight. Juvenile: lacks black on
throat. Open lightly timbered areas and farmland.

LOVELY FAIRY-WREN
Malurus amabilis (Male) 15 cm
**Long cocked bluish tail; blue head and ear-
coverts;** black throat and breast; chestnut rump.
Denser tropical woodland, coastal paperbark swamps
and mangroves. *May be confused with:* NONE.
Sometimes misidentified as the VARIEGATED FAIRY-
WREN which does not occur in the Wet Tropics.

RED-BACKED FAIRY-WREN
Malurus melanocephalus (Male) 12 cm
Black body; black head; **brilliant red back and
rump; long cocked tail.** Long grass in and adjacent
to woodland, grassy areas in farmland.

SPOTTED PARDALOTE
Pardalotus punctatus (Male) 9 cm
Tiny short-tailed, well-spotted bird; black crown well-
spotted white; yellow throat; red rump; **lines of white
spots on black wings.** Open forest and wet
sclerophyll mostly at higher altitudes.
May be confused with: RED-BROWED and
STRIATED PARDALOTES which have wing stripes
and yellow and buff rumps respectively. Look for
much spotting and red rump.

SCARLET HONEYEATER
Myzomela sanguinolenta (Male) 11 cm
Brilliant red head, centre-back and rump; red
often continues down front to belly (immature male
shows varying amount of red); greyish-white belly;
black wings and tail. Flowering trees and shrubs —
eucalypts, paperbarks, bottlebrush, sometimes
rainforest trees, sometimes mangroves.
May be confused with: NONE, however the RED-
HEADED HONEYEATER may occur in some more
extensive mangrove habitats. The male is similar to the
male SCARLET HONEYEATER, but with a dark
breast and belly, sharply demarcated from red head;
lacks the beautiful song of the SCARLET.

Scarlet

Red-headed

CRESTED SHRIKE-TIT
Falcunculus frontatus (Male) 18 cm
Olive-green back; yellow breast; **black head with white markings; black crest and throat.** Female has olive-green throat. Usually high in foliage. Drier eucalypt forest and woodland. *May be confused with:* Males of GOLDEN and MANGROVE GOLDEN WHISTLERS, but look for black crest and black or olive-green throat.

GOLDEN WHISTLER
Pachycephala pectoralis (Male) 17 cm
Olive-green back; yellow underparts; **black head; prominent white throat bordered with a black band across breast.** Rainforest at higher altitudes, sometimes coastal in winter. *May be confused with:* CRESTED SHRIKE-TIT, but look for white throat. Male MANGROVE GOLDEN WHISTLER. See p. 202.

MANGROVE GOLDEN WHISTLER
Pachycephala melanura (Male) 16 cm
Only known population is in Hinchinbrook Channel. Similar to male GOLDEN WHISTLER. Mangroves. *May be confused with:* CRESTED SHRIKE-TIT, but look for white throat. Male GOLDEN WHISTLER. See p. 202.

CRIMSON FINCH
Neochmia phaeton (Male) 13 cm
Striking; **deep crimson face, bill, rump and underparts;** black belly; long brown tail washed crimson; flanks spotted white. Coastal paperbark swamps and rank grass, edges of sugar-cane fields.

YELLOW-BELLIED SUNBIRD
Nectarinia jugularis (Male) 11 cm
Olive-green upperparts; yellow underparts; **iridescent blue-black patch on throat and breast;** long fine curved bill; short tail. Rainforest margins, woodland, gallery forest, parks and gardens and about dwellings. Mostly at lower altitudes.

MISTLETOEBIRD
Dicaeum hirundinaceum (Male) 10 cm
Black head, back and wings; **red throat and breast; red under tail-coverts;** short tail; **black stripe down white belly;** active. All forested habitats wherever mistletoe grows.

FURTHER POSSIBILITIES
BUDGERIGAR — rare.
BLUE-TAILED BEE-EATER. See p. 32.
Male RED-CAPPED ROBIN — rare.
GOULDIAN FINCH — probably extinct in the Wet Tropics region. See p. 74.

POSSIBILITIES

WOMPOO FRUIT-DOVE
Ptilinopus magnificus 37 cm
Large pigeon of mid and upper strata of
rainforest; green upperparts; **greyish-white
head**; **purple breast**; **yellow belly**. Rainforest
at all altitudes, occasionally in tropical woodland.

SUPERB FRUIT-DOVE
Ptilinopus superbus (Male) 23 cm
Beautiful multi-coloured small pigeon; mid-green
above; vivid **purple crown**; **orange hind neck**; **blue-
black band across lower breast**; **white belly**; red
feet. Rainforest at all altitudes. *May be confused with:*
ROSE-CROWNED FRUIT-DOVE, but look for blue-
black breastband and white belly.

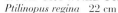

ROSE-CROWNED FRUIT-DOVE
Ptilinopus regina 22 cm
Small pigeon; **rose-pink crown**; pink across lower
breast; **yellow belly and broad yellow tail tip**; grey
feet. Rainforest but moreso on coast, especially
offshore islands, mangroves. *May be confused with:*
SUPERB FRUIT-DOVE, but look for yellow belly and
tail tip.

GALAH
Cacatua roseicapilla 36 cm
Large bird with **pink head and body**; **grey back,
wings and tail**; white crown and bill. Open woodland
and open grassland.

RAINBOW LORIKEET
Trichoglossus haematodus 28 cm
The most common parrot; medium-sized; green back,
wings and tail; **deep blue head**; **orange breast and
bill**; noisy. Eucalypt forest, rainforest edges, open
areas and parks and gardens.

AUSTRALIAN KING-PARROT
Alisterus scapularis (Male) 42 cm
Striking; **brilliant red head and underparts**; long
dark bluish tail; **dark green back and wings**. Mostly
upland rainforest and nearby eucalypt forest.

RED-WINGED PARROT
Aprosmictus erythropterus (Male) 32 cm
Medium-sized; **overall green**; **spectacular red patch
on wing**; black back; blue rump; orange bill. Open
drier woodland and lightly timbered country.

CRIMSON ROSELLA
Platycercus elegans 33 cm
Medium-sized; striking **blood-red head and underparts**; long dark-blue tail; **blue cheeks and broad blue edges to wings**. Upland rainforest and nearby eucalypt forest.

PALE-HEADED ROSELLA
Platycercus adscitus 30 cm
Medium-sized; **pale yellow to white head and throat; red under tail-coverts**; greenish-blue belly; blue edges to wings; yellow and black back; long tail. Eucalypt forest, tropical woodland, lightly timbered grassland.

BUFF-BREASTED PARADISE-KINGFISHER
Tanysiptera sylvia 34 cm
Migrant, present Nov.–early Apr.; medium-sized; **distinctively spectacular**; thick red bill; brilliant blue and black above; rufous-orange below; centre of back and rump white; **two very long, stiff, white tail feathers** sometimes broken-off during or after breeding. Mostly lowland rainforest.

NOISY PITTA
Pitta versicolor 18 cm
Medium-sized, short-tailed bird of rainforest floor; **blue shoulders; black throat and mask extending to back of head;** buff breast; green back and wings; black patch on belly; red lower belly. Rainforest at all altitudes.

FIGBIRD
Sphecotheres viridis race *flaviventris*
(Male — yellow-bellied race) 28 cm
Medium-sized; deep olive-green back and wings; bright yellow underparts; black head and black tail with white edges; large area of **red skin about eye**. Rainforest edges and remnants, gallery forest and nearby open forest, parks and gardens.

GOLDEN BOWERBIRD
Prionodura newtoniana (Male) 24 cm
Striking; **golden-olive above; golden-yellow below**. Upland rainforest above 900 m, sometimes lower.

POSSIBILITIES

SUPERB FRUIT-DOVE

Ptilinopus superbus (Female and Juvenile) 23 cm
Female: medium-sized plump short-tailed bird; overall greenish; **bluish patch on rear of crown; extensive area of white on belly**; greyish feet. Juvenile: overall greenish; underparts flecked or mottled with yellow. Rainforest at all altitudes. *May be confused with:* Female: ROSE-CROWNED FRUIT-DOVE, but note colour of belly which is white in SUPERB and yellow in ROSE-CROWNED. Juveniles of SUPERB and ROSE-CROWNED are almost impossible to separate.

Female

ROSE-CROWNED FRUIT-DOVE

Ptilinopus regina (Juvenile) 22 cm
Similar to juvenile SUPERB FRUIT-DOVE. Rainforest at all altitudes but moreso on the coast, especially offshore islands, mangroves. *May be confused with:* Female SUPERB FRUIT-DOVE which has white belly. Juveniles of SUPERB and ROSE-CROWNED are almost impossible to separate.

SCALY-BREASTED LORIKEET

Trichoglossus chlorolepidotus 23 cm
Medium-sized overall green bird; **yellowish 'scaly' pattern on breast; red bill; orange under wings in flight**. Strong direct flight. Eucalypt forest, parks and gardens wherever there is blossom.

LITTLE LORIKEET *Glossopsitta pusilla* 15 cm
Small overall green parrot; **red forehead and throat; small black bill;** short tail. Taller eucalypt forest, mainly at higher altitudes. *May be confused with:* DOUBLE-EYED FIG-PARROT which has thick dark bill; more colourful facial pattern with some blue. Look for red forehead and throat in a green face.

DOUBLE-EYED FIG-PARROT

Cyclopsitta diophthalma 14 cm
Small mostly all-green parrot; very short tail; **thick dark bill;** colourful facial pattern. Male: **red cheek; red forehead; blue about eye.** Female: similar, but face mainly blue with buffy cheek patch. Rainforest at most altitudes but mainly in the lowlands, often breeding in nearby paperbark swamps.
May be confused with: LITTLE LORIKEET, but look for thick dark bill; some blue on face; very short tail.

LEWIN'S HONEYEATER *Meliphaga lewinii* 20 cm
Small overall olive-green bird; **pale yellow earpatch;** pale yellow line from bill to under eye. Rainforest and adjacent tall eucalypt forest, usually above 450 m.
May be confused with: YELLOW-SPOTTED and GRACEFUL HONEYEATERS. See pp. 201–2.

YELLOW-SPOTTED HONEYEATER
Meliphaga notata 18 cm
Similar to LEWIN'S HONEYEATER and difficult to
separate. Rainforest, adjacent eucalypt forest,
woodland and gardens, usually below 600 m.
May be confused with: LEWIN'S and GRACEFUL
HONEYEATERS. See pp. 201–2.

GRACEFUL HONEYEATER
Meliphaga gracilis 15 cm
Similar to LEWIN'S HONEYEATER and difficult to
separate. Rainforest, gallery forest, adjacent eucalypt
forest and woodland, mostly below 400 m.
May be confused with: LEWIN'S and YELLOW-
SPOTTED HONEYEATERS. See pp. 201–2.

YELLOW ORIOLE *Oriolus flavocinctus* 28 cm
Medium-sized **yellow-green** bird with some striations;
**red bill and eye; edges of wing feathers and tail tip
yellow.** Juvenile: well-striated; bill and eye brownish.
Rainforest, gallery forest at low altitudes, and
mangroves. *May be confused with:* OLIVE-BACKED
ORIOLE, but look for overall yellow-green colouration
and yellow tips and edges of wing feathers.

FIGBIRD *Sphecotheres viridis* race *vieilloti*
(Male — green-bellied race) 28 cm
Medium-sized; deep olive-green back, wings and breast;
white lower belly; black head; black tail with white
sides; **red skin about eye.** Feeds in fruiting trees. A
southern race extending northward to the vicinity of
Townsville. Rainforest edges and remnants, gallery
forest, nearby open forest, parks and gardens.

SPOTTED CATBIRD *Ailuroedus melanotis* 28 cm
Medium-sized bird with deep green back and wings;
paler underparts spotted buffy-white; **brownish
crown and throat, heavily spotted white; dark ear-
coverts; red eye.** Rainforest at all altitudes.

SATIN BOWERBIRD
Ptilonorhynchus violaceus (Female) 24 cm
Medium-sized olive-green bird; paler underparts with
darker 'scaly' pattern from throat to belly; blue
eyes; longish, pale legs. Rainforest margins and
adjacent open forest at higher altitudes.

BLUE-FACED PARROT-FINCH
Erythrura trichroa 12 cm
Rare; **rich grass-green; blue face; dark reddish-
brown rump.** Face mid-blue in male, duller in female
and green in juvenile. Mostly rainforest at higher
altitudes.

FURTHER POSSIBILITIES
BUDGERIGAR — rare.

POSSIBILITIES

DIAMOND DOVE *Geopelia cuneata* 20 cm
Rare, rather plain long-tailed bird; **white spotting on wings; red eye-ring.** Juvenile: white bars in place of spots. Mostly dry open forest.
May be confused with: PEACEFUL DOVE, but look for red eye-ring and absence of barring.

PEACEFUL DOVE
Geopelia striata 20 cm
Fine black barring on breast, nape, hind neck and wings; blue eye-ring; long tail. Often sitting on powerlines. Eucalypt woodland, lightly timbered grassland, open forest, parks and gardens.
May be confused with: DIAMOND DOVE, but look for blue eye-ring and extensive barring.

BLACK-EARED CUCKOO
Chrysococcyx osculans 19 cm
Rare; rather inconspicuous brownish-grey bird; paler below; **curved black mark through eye; thick white eyebrow; pale rump; white tail tip.** Drier woodland and open forest. *May be confused with:* Juvenile HORSFIELD'S BRONZE-CUCKOO which is smaller; browner; has dark rump; eyebrow almost absent; rufous margins to upper tail feathers. Look for thick eyebrow and pale rump and tail tip.

BROWN GERYGONE
Gerygone mouki 10 cm
Small, active, plain-greyish bird; paler below; white eyebrow. Mostly upland rainforest above 250 m. *May be confused with:* Other grey gerygones. See p. 200.

MANGROVE GERYGONE
Gerygone levigaster 10 cm
Small, plain, active, greyish bird similar to BROWN GERYGONE. Mangroves and adjacent forest. *May be confused with:* Other grey gerygones. See p. 200.

WESTERN GERYGONE
Gerygone fusca 10 cm
Rare; small active greyish bird similar to BROWN GERYGONE. Dry open forest and woodland. *May be confused with:* Other grey gerygones. See p. 200.

LARGE-BILLED GERYGONE
Gerygone magnirostris 11 cm
Small, active, greyish bird similar to BROWN GERYGONE. Along streams, about paperbark swamps and mangroves, mostly in lowlands. *May be confused with:* Other grey gerygones. See p. 200.

WHITE-GAPED HONEYEATER

Lichenostomus unicolor 19 cm

Plain grey-brown nondescript bird; **small white mark between eye and bill** (pale yellow in juvenile). Gallery forest and adjacent woodland, suburban gardens and about farmhouses. *May be confused with:* Perhaps the smaller BROWN HONEYEATER which is sometimes misidentified as the WHITE-GAPED. BROWN has a yellow mark between eye and bill and yellowish wash on flight and tail feathers.

MANGROVE ROBIN

Eopsaltria pulverulenta 16 cm

Rather **plain unobtrusive bird of denser mangroves.** Can initially appear greyish but has brownish wings; white underparts; **blackish tail with white sides at base.**

GOLDEN WHISTLER

Pachycephala pectoralis (Female) 17 cm

Overall grey-brown; **yellow under tail-coverts; black eye.** Immature similar, with rufous margins to wings. Rainforest at higher altitudes, sometimes coastal in winter. *May be confused with:* GREY WHISTLER at lower altitudes, but look for yellow under tail-coverts.

GREY WHISTLER

Pachycephala simplex 17 cm

Plain; paler underparts; **very pale yellow lower breast and belly** barely noticeable. Mostly lowland rainforest. *May be confused with:* Female GOLDEN WHISTLER which has yellow under tail-coverts. The larger GREY SHRIKE-THRUSH has faint white spots on forehead.

RUFOUS WHISTLER

Pachycephala rufiventris (Female) 17 cm

Initially appears grey but has **lightly streaked pale buff underparts** from chin to tail. Open eucalypt forest and woodland.

MISTLETOEBIRD

Dicaeum hirundinaceum (Female) 10 cm

Rather plain; short tail; faint eyebrow; **pale red under tail-coverts;** active. All forested habitats wherever mistletoe grows.

FURTHER POSSIBILITIES

Female RED-CAPPED ROBIN — rare.
Female HOODED ROBIN — rare.
Both recorded only from extreme south-west of region.

POSSIBILITIES

CRESTED PIGEON
Ocyphaps lophotes 33 cm
Overall grey; **erect dark crest; red about eye; red legs;** iridescent bronze and green patch on wings. Feeds on ground. Open, sparsely timbered areas and about farmhouses.

COCKATIEL *Nymphicus hollandicus* 32 cm
Long-tailed parrot; **upright yellow crest; large white shoulder patch.** Male: large yellow cheek patch and orange ear patch. Female: much duller. Open drier woodland and lightly timbered country.

PALLID CUCKOO *Cuculus pallidus* 31 cm
Overall greyish cuckoo; long tail 'notched' white; **small white spot on nape; faint darker curved line through eye and down to shoulder;** yellow eye-ring; grey feet. Open woodland.

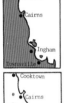

AUSTRALIAN OWLET-NIGHTJAR
Aegotheles cristatus 22 cm
Nocturnal, moth-like greyish bird; **double collar on hind neck;** large black eyes; bristles about bill. Sometimes flushed from hollows by day. Open forest and woodland, occasionally rainforest.

NOISY MINER *Manorina melanocephala* 27 cm
Pesky; **black mask about eye and over crown;** white forehead and throat; yellow spot behind eye; yellow bill; **grey rump.** Open, drier eucalypt forest. *May be confused with:* YELLOW-THROATED MINER, but look for grey rump, black crown and white throat.

YELLOW-THROATED MINER
Manorina flavigula 27 cm
Similar to NOISY MINER, but with **white rump; yellow forehead and crown.** Open, drier eucalypt forest. *May be confused with:* NOISY MINER, but look for white rump which is conspicuous and diagnostic.

GREY SHRIKE-THRUSH
Colluricincla harmonica 22 cm
Plain grey; black bill and eye; **white mark between bill and eye.** Female: slightly striated throat and upper breast. Immature: buff in front of eye. Eucalypt and casuarina forest and dry woodland, mostly at higher altitudes. *May be confused with:* Female GOLDEN WHISTLER which has yellow under tail-coverts. GREY WHISTLER lacks white mark between bill and eye and has lemon wash on underparts. Both are smaller.

BLACK-FACED CUCKOO-SHRIKE
Coracina novaehollandiae 33 cm
Immaculate; **refolds wings on alighting.** Adult: **large prominent black face.** Immature: **broad black line through and behind eye only.** Eucalypt forest and woodland, open areas, and about cities and towns. *May be confused with:* Adult: NONE. Immature: WHITE-BELLIED CUCKOO-SHRIKE, but look for black mark extending well behind eye. WHITE-BELLIED has fine white part eye-ring behind eye.

BARRED CUCKOO-SHRIKE
Coracina lineata 27 cm. Immaculate; **refolds wings on alighting; fine barring** from lower breast to under tail; yellow eye; black wing and tail tips. Rainforest at all altitudes. *May be confused with:* Perhaps adult ORIENTAL CUCKOO which has similar barring, but dark eye, yellow eye-ring and feet and long 'notched' tail.

WHITE-BELLIED CUCKOO-SHRIKE
Coracina papuensis 28 cm
Plain grey; **refolds wings on alighting; black mark between bill and eye;** white part eye-ring behind eye. Open forest, woodland, open areas, mangroves, sometimes about urban areas. *May be confused with:* Immature BLACK-FACED CUCKOO-SHRIKE, but look for black mark extending only to eye, and white part eye-ring.

MASKED WOODSWALLOW
Artamus personatus 19 cm
Rare; mid-grey; paler below; bluish bill; tail grey, tipped white, frequently wagged. Male: **large black face edged white.** Female: **subdued dusky-grey face.** Drier, open, lightly timbered country. *May be confused with:* Male: NONE. Female and juvenile: BLACK-FACED WOODSWALLOW, but look for large dusky-grey face and grey tail.

BLACK-FACED WOODSWALLOW
Artamus cinereus 18 cm
Smoky-grey; **bluish bill; small black face; black tail tipped white;** white under tail-coverts; tail frequently wagged. Open, lightly timbered areas and almost treeless grassland. *May be confused with:* Female and juvenile: MASKED WOODSWALLOW, but look for small black face and black tail.

APOSTLEBIRD *Struthidea cinerea* 31 cm
Unspectacular dark grey; robust black bill; **black tail; brownish flight feathers.** Usually in family groups, noisy when approached. Drier open forest and woodland.

FURTHER POSSIBILITIES
BRUSH CUCKOO
Immature WHITE-HEADED PIGEON
LITTLE FRIARBIRD

GREAT BOWERBIRD
See also Aquatic Birds,
pp. 163–75.

POSSIBILITIES

AUSTRALIAN WOOD DUCK
Chenonetta jubata   48 cm
Brown head; black along middle of back; female
duller than male with **white line above and below
eye.** On and about freshwater lagoons, swamps and
farm dams.

WHITE-FACED HERON
Egretta novaehollandiae   67 cm
Overall medium-grey wading bird; long thin neck;
white face and throat; long sharp black bill; **yellow
legs.** Shallow fresh water, short wet grassland,
mudflats, parks and gardens. *May be confused with:*
Grey phase of EASTERN REEF EGRET, but look for
white face and throat and black bill.

EASTERN REEF EGRET
Egretta sacra   (Grey phase) 62 cm
Slate-grey marine wading bird; **a thin white streak
down throat;** yellowish bill. Exclusively coastal, rocky
shores, coral reefs, mudflats, offshore islands.
May be confused with: WHITE-FACED HERON which
has white face and throat, all black bill, yellow legs
and is paler grey. STRIATED HERON which has
black cap and yellow to orange legs.

STRIATED HERON
Butorides striatus   (Adult) 47 cm
Blue-grey wading bird; **black cap;** long pointed black
and yellow bill; **yellow or orange legs and feet;**
usually feeds with a distinctive **crouched posture.**
Juvenile: well-striated. Mangroves, lower reaches of
rivers, tidal flats. *May be confused with:* Generally
NONE. Look for bright yellow or orange legs and
crouched stance. Female BLACK BITTERN is dark
grey but distinguished by yellow neck plumes. Juvenile
NANKEEN NIGHT HERON and juvenile LITTLE
BITTERN are well-striated.

GREY GOSHAWK
Accipiter novaehollandiae
(Grey phase) Male 38 cm Female 52 cm
Rather long powerful **yellow legs and feet; yellow
cere;** red eyes; grey above; white below; **fine grey
barring on breast.** Rainforest and adjacent tall
eucalypt forest of higher areas, sometimes in coastal
woodland, and on rainforested offshore islands.
May be confused with: In flight, can be overlooked for
SULPHUR-CRESTED COCKATOO. GOSHAWK
usually circles. COCKATOO has direct flight.

BUSH STONE-CURLEW
Burhinus grallarius 55 cm
Nocturnal; ground-dwelling; streaked greyish plumage;
long legs; buffy underparts; **whitish forehead and
eyebrow; large yellow eyes;** moves slowly and
deliberately when disturbed by day. Open forest, open
lightly timbered areas. Often in urban localities.

TOPKNOT PIGEON
Lopholaimus antarcticus 43 cm
Overall grey pigeon: **prominent chestnut 'bun' on
back of head; black tail with whitish band.** Often
flies above canopy, sometimes high. Rainforest, moreso
at higher altitudes. *May be confused with:* NONE.
Look for whitish tail band in flight.

CHANNEL-BILLED CUCKOO
Scythrops novaehollandiae 64 cm
Migrant, present Sept.–Apr.; overall grey; **large heavy
pale curved bill; red about eye.** In flight, the **long
wings and tail** give it a distinctive hawk-like
appearance. Eucalypt forest, rainforest edges, gallery
forest and farmland, wherever figs abound.

BARKING OWL *Ninox connivens* 40 cm
Nocturnal, greyish-brown owl: **streaked grey
underparts; large staring yellow eyes** focused
forward. Open forest with some dense cover, rainforest
margins, paperbark swamps and woodland. *May be
confused with:* The smaller, browner SOUTHERN
BOOBOOK which has distinct 'goggles' about eyes.

TAWNY FROGMOUTH
Podargus strigoides 39 cm
Nocturnal, grey or brownish bird; **short broad heavy
bill; tuft of plumes over bill;** sparse black streaking
on underparts; long tail; **yellow eyes;** adopts a stick-
like attitude when approached by day. Eucalypt forest
and woodland. *May be confused with:* PAPUAN
FROGMOUTH which is much larger. Eye colour is the
most reliable feature to separate the two frogmouths.
Each inhabits distinct habitat.

PAPUAN FROGMOUTH
Podargus papuensis 49 cm
Nocturnal. Male: greyish. Female: more reddish.
Similar to TAWNY FROGMOUTH but underparts
more speckled or mottled with some streaking; **red
eyes.** Gallery forest and similar dense vegetation,
paperbark swamps, mangroves, and sometimes upland
rainforest. *May be confused with:* TAWNY
FROGMOUTH, but look for red eyes.

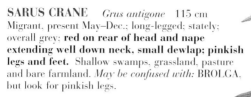

POSSIBILITIES

SARUS CRANE *Grus antigone* 115 cm
Migrant, present May–Dec.; long-legged; stately;
overall grey; **red on rear of head and nape
extending well down neck, small dewlap; pinkish
legs and feet.** Shallow swamps, grassland, pasture
and bare farmland. *May be confused with:* BROLGA,
but look for pinkish legs.

BROLGA *Grus rubicunda* 115 cm
Almost identical to SARUS CRANE, but red does not
extend as far down neck; **dark grey legs; heavy
dewlap.** Similar habitat. *May be confused with:*
SARUS CRANE, but look for grey legs.

AUSTRALIAN BUSTARD
Ardeotis australis Male 110 cm Female 80 cm
A heavy-bodied **stately ground bird;** brown
upperparts; white underparts; black band across breast;
yellowish legs. Walks slowly with **head held high.**
Open grassland, sparse open forest and pastures.

VERY LARGE GREY & WHITE OR BLACK & WHITE BIRDS
POSSIBILITIES

MAGPIE GOOSE
Anseranas semipalmata 80 cm
Very large black and white aquatic bird; black head,
neck, rump and tail; fleshy-grey bill and part of face;
yellow legs; **black knob on top of head.** Most
wetlands, especially those with dense reeds.

AUSTRALIAN PELICAN
Pelecanus conspicillatus 165 cm
Well-known, huge black and white waterbird;
enormous flesh-coloured bill; black flight feathers,
shoulders, rump and tail; white head and underparts.
Larger areas of deeper fresh water, also along
foreshore.

WHITE-NECKED HERON
Ardea pacifica 87 cm
Very large wading bird; blackish body; white head and
long thin white neck; **black bill and legs;
conspicuous white patch on leading edge of wing
in flight;** looks very large in flight, and sometimes
resembles a bird of prey at a height. Shallow
freshwater swamps, dams, streams and lake edges,
sometimes open grassland. *May be confused with:* The
smaller juvenile PIED HERON which has yellow bill
and legs; rare.

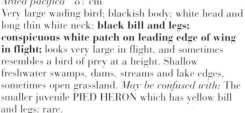

BLACK-NECKED STORK
Ephippiorhynchus asiaticus 120 cm
Huge black and white wading bird with long red legs; black head and neck; large heavy black bill. In flight, appears mostly white with black wingbar and flies with neck outstretched. Usually freshwater swamps, sometimes estuaries and mangroves.

WHITE-BELLIED SEA-EAGLE
Haliaeetus leucogaster
(Adult) Male 76 cm Female 59 cm
Huge grey and white fishing eagle; grey back, wings and base of tail; graceful flight with **upswept wings; white, broad, short, rather rounded tail.** Estuaries, bays, larger lakes and rivers, and offshore islands.

NONDESCRIPT – WITHOUT OBVIOUS MARKINGS
POSSIBILITIES

FERNWREN
Oreoscopus gutturalis (Juvenile) 13 cm
Rich olive-brown upperparts; slightly paler below; **long, thin, buff eyebrow; longish bill.** Upland rainforest, usually above 600 m, sometimes lower. *May be confused with:* ATHERTON and LARGE-BILLED SCRUBWRENS, but look for thin eyebrow and longish bill.

EASTERN WHIPBIRD
Psophodes olivaceus (Juvenile) 27 cm
Overall olive-brown; **small crest** sometimes carried flat on back of head; **long tail.** Lower stratum of rainforest at higher altitudes, occasionally adjacent eucalypt forest. Sometimes coastal.

ATHERTON SCRUBWREN
Sericornis keri 13 cm
Small brown bird of lower stratum of upland rainforest above 750 m; dark eye in a plain face.
May be confused with: Juvenile FERNWREN which is rich olive-brown above with long thin buff eyebrow, darker face and eye and longish bill. LARGE-BILLED SCRUBWREN. See p. 200.

LARGE-BILLED SCRUBWREN
Sericornis magnirostris 13 cm
Small brown bird of mid-stratum of rainforest, almost identical to ATHERTON SCRUBWREN. Rainforest at all altitudes, but mostly below 1000 m. *May be confused with:* Juvenile FERNWREN which is rich olive-brown above with long thin buff eyebrow and darker face and eye. ATHERTON SCRUBWREN. See p. 200.

BROWN GERYGONE

Gerygone mouki   10 cm
Small, active, greyish bird; paler below; white eyebrow.
Mostly upland rainforest above 250 m. *May be
confused with:* Other grey gerygones. See p. 200.

MANGROVE GERYGONE

Gerygone levigaster   10 cm
Small, active, greyish bird similar to BROWN
GERYGONE but inhabiting mangroves and adjacent
forest. *May be confused with:* Other grey gerygones.
See p. 200.

WESTERN GERYGONE

Gerygone fusca   10 cm
Rare; small active greyish bird similar to BROWN
GERYGONE. Dry open forest and woodland. *May be
confused with:* Other grey gerygones. See p. 200.

LARGE-BILLED GERYGONE

Gerygone magnirostris   11 cm
Small, active, greyish bird similar to BROWN
GERYGONE. Along streams, about paperbark swamps
and mangroves, mostly in lowlands. *May be confused
with:* Other grey gerygones. See p. 200.

LITTLE FRIARBIRD

Philemon citreogularis   26 cm
A medium-sized bird; mid-brown above; paler below;
patch of blue-grey facial skin from bill to under eye.
Lacks knob on bill of other friarbirds. Eucalypt forest
and tropical woodland. *May be confused with:* NONE.
Look for blue-grey facial skin.

WHITE-GAPED HONEYEATER

Lichenostomus unicolor   19 cm
Small grey-brown bird; **small white mark between
bill and eye** — pale yellow in juvenile. Gallery forest,
adjacent woodland, suburban gardens and about
farmhouses. *May be confused with:* Perhaps the
smaller BROWN HONEYEATER which is sometimes
misidentified as the WHITE-GAPED. Note position
and colour of small mark. BROWN has yellowish wash
on flight and tail feathers.

YELLOW HONEYEATER

Lichenostomus flavus   17 cm
Small; **entirely bright olive-yellow;** faint dusky mark
through eye; faint whisker below chin; loud cheerful
call. Tropical woodland, margins of rainforest, about
farmhouses, parks and gardens.

BROWN HONEYEATER
Lichmera indistincta 12 cm
Small, dull-brown bird. Adult: **triangular yellowish spot behind eye;** longish curved black bill; yellowish wash on flight and tail feathers. Juvenile: lacks spot behind eye. Open forest, parks and gardens, mangroves and paperbark swamps. *May be confused with:* WHITE-GAPED, DUSKY and female SCARLET HONEYEATERS, but look for triangular spot behind eye and yellowish wash on flight feathers. Juvenile can be difficult to separate from juvenile RUFOUS-THROATED HONEYEATER, but BROWN has a darker face and is usually loudly vocal.

RUFOUS-THROATED HONEYEATER
Conopophila rufogularis (Juvenile) 12 cm
Overall brown, nondescript bird; **yellow edges to wing and tail feathers.** Open forest, parks and gardens, paperbark swamps. *May be confused with:* Adult BROWN HONEYEATER which has triangular yellowish spot behind eye. Difficult to separate from juvenile BROWN HONEYEATER, but BROWN is usually loudly vocal. DUSKY HONEYEATER is very dark brown, and female SCARLET HONEYEATER has reddish wash on chin.

DUSKY HONEYEATER
Myzomela obscura 13 cm
Small, **very dark brown** bird; longish curved bill. Very active. Rainforest at all altitudes, gallery forest, mangroves and open forest. *May be confused with:* The paler BROWN and female SCARLET HONEYEATERS with which it sometimes associates.

SCARLET HONEYEATER
Myzomela sanguinolenta (Female) 11 cm
Small, active brown bird; paler below; longish curved bill; **reddish wash on chin.** Flowering trees and shrubs, eucalypts, bottlebrush, paperbarks, sometimes rainforest trees, sometimes mangroves.
May be confused with: BROWN and DUSKY HONEYEATERS, but look for reddish chin. In more extensive areas of mangroves, it is possible that the RED-HEADED HONEYEATER may occur. The female is similar to the female SCARLET but has reddish wash on **both chin and forehead.** Usually with distinct males.

GOLDEN WHISTLER
Pachycephala pectoralis (Female) 17 cm
Small grey-brown bird; **yellow under tail-coverts;** black eye. Immature similar with rufous margins to wings. Rainforest at higher altitudes, sometimes coastal in winter. *May be confused with:* GREY WHISTLER at lower altitudes, but look for yellow under tail-coverts.

GREY WHISTLER *Pachycephala simplex* 17 cm
Small greyish bird; paler underparts: **very pale yellow lower breast and belly** barely noticeable. Mostly lowland rainforest. *May be confused with:* Female GOLDEN WHISTLER which has yellow under tail-coverts. GREY SHRIKE-THRUSH has faint white spots on forehead, is larger and usually inhabits drier habitats.

LITTLE SHRIKE-THRUSH
Colluricincla megarhyncha 18 cm
Medium-sized **plain brown** bird; slightly striated on throat and upper breast; longish **pink-brown** bill; shortish tail. Rainforest moreso at lower altitudes, gallery forest and mangroves. *May be confused with:* BOWER'S SHRIKE-THRUSH which has dark grey back and head and black bill.

GREY SHRIKE-THRUSH
Colluricincla harmonica 22 cm
Medium-sized **plain grey** bird; black bill and eye; **white mark between bill and eye.** Female: lightly striated throat and upper breast. Immature: buff in front of eye. Eucalypt and casuarina forest and dry woodland, mostly at higher altitudes. *May be confused with:* Female GOLDEN WHISTLER which has yellow under tail-coverts. GREY WHISTLER lacks white between bill and eye and has lemon wash on underparts. Both are smaller.

APOSTLEBIRD *Struthidea cinerea* 31 cm
Medium-sized, unspectacular dark grey bird; robust black bill; **black tail; brownish flight feathers.** Usually in family groups, noisy when approached. Drier open forest and woodland.

GOLDEN BOWERBIRD
Prionodura newtoniana (Female) 24 cm
Medium-sized; **olive back with ash-grey underparts;** short bill; yellow eye. Upland rainforest usually above 900 m, sometimes lower.

MISTLETOEBIRD
Dicaeum hirundinaceum (Female) 10 cm
Small grey bird; short tail; faint eyebrow; **pale red under tail-coverts.** Active. All forested habitats wherever mistletoe grows.

CLAMOROUS REED-WARBLER
Acrocephalus stentoreus 17 cm
Small brownish bird of reedbeds; paler underparts; **pale eyebrow.** Rather elusive. Reedbeds in freshwater swamps and streams. *May be confused with:* ORIENTAL REED-WARBLER. Extremely difficult to distinguish from CLAMOROUS. See p. 203.

FURTHER POSSIBILITIES
Female RED-CAPPED ROBIN — rare.
Female HOODED ROBIN — rare.
Both recorded only from extreme south-west of region.

POSSIBILITIES

RED-BACKED FAIRY-WREN
Malurus melanocephalus (Male) 12 cm
Long cocked tail; brilliant red back and rump;
black head and body. Long grass in and adjacent to
woodland, grassy areas in farmland.

SCARLET HONEYEATER
Myzomela sanguinolenta (Male) 11 cm
Brilliant red head, centre back and rump; red often
continues down front to belly (immature males show
varying amounts of red); greyish-white belly; black wings
and tail. Flowering trees and shrubs — eucalypts, paperbarks, bottlebrush; sometimes rainforest trees, sometimes
mangroves. *May be confused with:* NONE, however the
RED-HEADED HONEYEATER may occur in some more
extensive mangrove habitats. The male is similar to the
male SCARLET, but with a dark breast and belly,
sharply demarcated from red head; lacks the beautiful
song of the SCARLET. See p. 35.

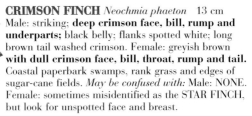

CRIMSON FINCH *Neochmia phaeton* 13 cm
Male: striking: **deep crimson face, bill, rump and
underparts;** black belly; flanks spotted white; long
brown tail washed crimson. Female: greyish brown
with dull crimson face, bill, throat, rump and tail.
Coastal paperbark swamps, rank grass and edges of
sugar-cane fields. *May be confused with:* Male: NONE.
Female: sometimes misidentified as the STAR FINCH,
but look for unspotted face and breast.

STAR FINCH *Neochmia ruficauda* 11 cm
Probably extinct in the Wet Tropics region.
Conspicuous red face and bill; olive back and breast;
whitish belly; dull reddish-brown tail; **white spotting
on lower face, breast, sides of body and rump.**
Immature: grey head and face. Rank watercourse
vegetation and wet areas, e.g. reeds in eucalypt forest
and woodland. *May be confused with:* Female
CRIMSON FINCH is sometimes misidentified as STAR
FINCH but look for well-spotted face and breast.

RED-BROWED FINCH
Neochmia temporalis (Adult) 11 cm
Olive-green and grey; **red rump, bill and
eyebrow;** black tail. Margins of rainforest,
regrowth and adjacent shrubby and grassy areas.

MISTLETOEBIRD
Dicaeum hirundinaceum (Male) 10 cm
Black head, back and wings; **red throat and breast;
red under tail-coverts; short tail;** black stripe down
white belly. Active. All forested habitats wherever
mistletoe grows.

FURTHER POSSIBILITIES
Male RED-CAPPED ROBIN — rare. Recorded only from
extreme south-west of region.

POSSIBILITIES

RED-NECKED CRAKE
Rallina tricolor   30 cm
Medium-sized bird initially appearing dark brown;
rich chestnut head, neck and breast; dark brown
body; short tail often flicked. Floor of rainforest,
especially close to water.

RED-TAILED BLACK-COCKATOO
Calyptorhynchus banksii   56 cm
Large black bird; **broad red panels in tail** visible
only when tail is spread. Male: dark grey bill and
rounded crest. Female: whitish bill; fine yellow spots
and barring in plumage; tail panels more orange-
yellow, finely barred black. Open forest, woodland,
sometimes over rainforest and about cities and towns.

AUSTRALIAN KING-PARROT
Alisterus scapularis   42 cm
Male: striking; **brilliant red head and underparts;**
dark green back and wings; long dark bluish tail.
Female and immature: **dark green head,** back and
wings; red lower breast and belly. Mostly upland
rainforest and nearby eucalypt forest.

RED-WINGED PARROT
Aprosmictus erythropterus   32 cm
Medium-sized; overall pale green; orange bill; red
wing patch. Male: **large spectacular red wing patch;**
black back; blue rump. Female and immature: small
duller wing patch. Open drier woodland and lightly
timbered country.

CRIMSON ROSELLA
Platycercus elegans   33 cm
Striking **blood red head and underparts;** long dark-
blue tail; **blue cheeks and broad blue edges to
wings.** Upland rainforest and nearby eucalypt forest.

PALE-HEADED ROSELLA
Platycercus adscitus   30 cm
Medium-sized; **pale yellow to white head and
throat; red under tail-coverts;** greenish-blue belly;
blue edges to wings; yellow and black back; long tail.
Eucalypt forest, tropical woodland, lightly timbered
grassland.

POSSIBILITIES

SPOTTED HARRIER
Circus assimilis   Male 53 cm Female 59 cm
Large, graceful, slow-flying bird of prey with long
upswept wings; smoky-grey above; distinct **chestnut
owl-like facial disc; underparts rich chestnut,
finely spotted white;** grey, heavily barred tail; long
yellow legs. Open grassland and farmland.

SPOTTED TURTLE-DOVE
Streptopelia chinensis   27 cm
Introduced, medium-sized, long-tailed bird or large
dove; brown; **back of neck black, spotted white.**
Well-established in most cities and towns.
May be confused with: BAR-SHOULDERED DOVE,
but look for white spotting on black, on back of neck.

DIAMOND DOVE
Geopelia cuneata   20 cm
Rare, small, rather plain long-tailed grey bird; **white
spotting on wings; red eye-ring.** Mostly dry open
forest. *May be confused with:* PEACEFUL DOVE, but
look for red eye-ring and spotting on wings.

RED-TAILED BLACK-COCKATOO
Calyptorhynchus banksii   (Female) 56 cm
Black; **broad red panels in tail, finely barred black**
visible only when tail is spread; fine yellow spots and
barring in plumage; lower belly and under tail-coverts
barred orange-red; whitish bill. Open forest, woodland,
sometimes over rainforest and about cities and towns.

COMMON KOEL
Eudynamys scolopacea   (Female) 43 cm
Migrant, present Sept.–Apr.; rather shy long-tailed
bird; brown back and wings **heavily spotted white;
black head; red eye;** brown tail barred white;
underparts whitish barred brown. Juvenile: similar;
more chestnut; no black crown. Denser open forest,
woodland, gallery forest, dense trees in farmland,
parks and gardens.

SPOTTED PARDALOTE
Pardalotus punctatus   9 cm
Tiny, short-tailed, well-spotted bird; black crown
spotted white; yellow throat; red rump; **lines of white
spots on black wings.** Open forest and wet
sclerophyll mostly at higher altitudes.
May be confused with: Other pardalotes (which have
wing-stripe and yellow or buff rump). Look for much
spotting and red rump.

RED-BROWED PARDALOTE
Pardalotus rubricatus   11 cm
Rare; tiny short-tailed bird predominantly fawn-grey;
yellowish breast; yellow rump; **black crown spotted
white; yellow edges to wing feathers; small orange
to red eyebrow.** Dry open forest. *May be confused
with:* Other pardalotes, but look for spotted crown and
orange-red eyebrow; yellow stripe in wings.

SPOTTED CATBIRD
Ailuroedus melanotis   28 cm
Medium-sized bird with deep green back and wings;
paler underparts spotted buffy-white; **brownish
crown and throat heavily spotted white; dark ear-
coverts; red eye.** Rainforest at all altitudes.

STAR FINCH *Neochmia ruficauda*   11 cm
Probably extinct in the Wet Tropics region. Small;
conspicuous red face and bill; olive back and
breast; whitish belly; dull reddish-brown tail; **white
spotting on lower face, breast, sides of body and
rump.** Immature: grey head and face. Rank
watercourse vegetation and wet areas, e.g. reeds in
eucalypt forest and woodland. *May be confused with:*
Female CRIMSON FINCH which is sometimes
misidentified as STAR FINCH, but look for well-
spotted face and breast. CRIMSON has spotting only
on the flanks and is usually with the more spectacular
males.

FURTHER POSSIBILITIES
PAINTED BUTTON-QUAIL
SOUTHERN BOOBOOK
LESSER SOOTY, MASKED, BARN and GRASS OWLS
ZEBRA, DOUBLE-BARRED, CRIMSON
and PLUM-HEADED FINCHES

MEDIUM-SIZED & LARGE WHITE BIRDS
POSSIBILITIES

LITTLE EGRET *Egretta garzetta*   56 cm
Large all-white wading bird or small egret; **long thin
neck;** long legs; long sharp black bill; stalks prey in
shallow water. Freshwater swamps, sometimes about
mangroves and foreshores.
May be confused with: Other egrets. See pp. 196–7.

EASTERN REEF EGRET
Egretta sacra   (White phase) 62 cm
Large all-white marine wading bird similar to LITTLE
EGRET but larger. Exclusively coastal — rocky shores,
coral reefs, mudflats, offshore islands and beaches.
May be confused with: Other egrets. See pp. 196–7.

GREAT EGRET

Ardea alba   83 cm
Similar to LITTLE EGRET but larger with longer neck. Usually utters a gutteral croak when it takes flight. Inhabits similar habitat.
May be confused with: Other egrets. See pp. 196–7.

INTERMEDIATE EGRET

Ardea intermedia   65 cm
Similar to LITTLE EGRET but larger. Inhabits similar habitat.
May be confused with: Other egrets. See pp. 196–7.

CATTLE EGRET   *Ardea ibis*   51 cm

Large bird usually about cattle; similar to LITTLE EGRET; develops **orange head and neck and orange-red bill** during breeding season Sept.–Feb. Open grassy paddocks, occasionally swamps.
May be confused with: In breeding plumage: NONE. In non-breeding plumage: other egrets. See pp. 196–7.

AUSTRALIAN WHITE IBIS

Threskiornis molucca   70 cm
Large wading bird appearing all-white at a distance; **bare black head; black tail; long curved black bill;** plumage often soiled. Shallow fresh water, grasslands, tidal flats, mangroves and city parks.

ROYAL SPOONBILL *Platalea regia*   77 cm

Large wading bird; long **black bill spoon-shaped at tip; black legs;** black face. Breeding birds develop a long tuft on back of head — usually Sept.–Mar. Fresh, brackish or saltwater swamps, mudflats and mangroves.

YELLOW-BILLED SPOONBILL

Platalea flavipes   83 cm
Similar to ROYAL SPOONBILL but with **pale yellow bill; yellowish legs.** Does not develop breeding tuft. Habitat similar to ROYAL SPOONBILL'S.

BLACK-SHOULDERED KITE

Elanus axillaris   36 cm
Medium-sized immaculate-looking bird, appearing white at a distance but with grey back, wings and tail; **black shoulder patches; red eyes. Frequently hovers.** Open grassland and farmland.
May be confused with: Usually NONE, but LETTER-WINGED KITE sometimes appears as a vagrant. The GREY GOSHAWK lacks black shoulder patch and inhabits denser forest.

GREY GOSHAWK   *Accipiter novaehollandiae*
(White phase) Male 49 cm Female 59 cm
Large bird with long powerful **yellow legs and feet;
yellow cere;** red eyes. White phase is scarce. Grey
phase can also appear whitish at a distance, especially
in flight. Rainforest and adjacent tall eucalypt forest of
higher areas, sometimes in coastal woodland.
Rainforested offshore islands. *May be confused with:* In
flight, can be overlooked for SULPHUR-CRESTED
COCKATOO. GOSHAWK usually circles. COCKATOO
has direct flight.

PIED IMPERIAL-PIGEON *Ducula bicolor* 42 cm
Migrant, present Aug.–Apr.; predominantly white
pigeon; **black flight feathers and lower half of tail;**
head may be soiled brownish from fruit stains.
Rainforest and mangroves on coastal lowlands and
offshore islands.

LITTLE CORELLA *Cacatua sanguinea*   38 cm
Medium-sized cockatoo; **white bill; bare bluish eye
patch;** short crest; usually in flocks. Open forest, open
grassy areas, sometimes outskirts of urban areas.

SULPHUR-CRESTED COCKATOO
Cacatua galerita   49 cm
Large; **obvious yellow crest on back of head**
spectacular when erect; small black eye in white face.
Often extremely noisy. Most habitats at all altitudes.

FURTHER POSSIBILITIES
GULLS
TERNS
SEABIRDS

SMALL & MEDIUM-SIZED PREDOMINANTLY YELLOW BIRDS
POSSIBILITIES

WEEBILL   *Smicrornis brevirostris*   8 cm
Tiny plain bird of eucalypt foliage; olive-yellow above;
yellow below; **short horn-coloured bill; whitish eye;**
faint creamy eyebrow. Drier eucalypt forest and open
woodland. *May be confused with:* Female and juvenile
FAIRY GERYGONE; juvenile WHITE-THROATED
GERYGONE; BUFF-RUMPED and YELLOW
THORNBILLS. WEEBILL is overall more yellowish.
Look for pale bill and whitish eye.

YELLOW THORNBILL *Acanthiza nana*   10 cm
Small, active bird; olive-green above; yellowish below;
streaked patch behind eye; sharp black bill; dark
eye. Drier woodland, especially where there are denser
stands of casuarina, sometimes nearby eucalypt forest.
May be confused with: WEEBILL, female and juvenile
FAIRY GERYGONE, BUFF-RUMPED THORNBILL.
Look for streaked patch behind dark eye.

YELLOW HONEYEATER
Lichenostomus flavus   17 cm
Small; **entirely bright olive-yellow;** faint dusky mark through eye; faint whisker below chin. Tropical woodland, margins of rainforest, about farmhouses, parks and gardens.

GOLDEN BOWERBIRD
Prionodura newtoniana   (Male) 24 cm
Striking; **golden-olive above; golden-yellow below.** Upland rainforest, usually above about 900 m, sometimes lower.

FURTHER POSSIBILITIES
BUDGERIGAR — rare.
WHITE-PLUMED HONEYEATER *Lichenostomus pencillatus* 16 cm Rare; yellowish; white plume with black edge on side of neck. Recorded only from extreme south-west of region.
YELLOW WHITE-EYE *Zosterops luteus* 11 cm A small resident population to the south of the Wet Tropics. Yellow-olive above; bright yellow below; white eye-ring.

Yellow White-eye

BIRDS WITH BARRED UPPERPARTS
POSSIBILITIES

PEACEFUL DOVE *Geopelia striata*   20 cm
Small grey long-tailed bird; **fine black barring on breast, nape, hind neck and wings; blue eye-ring.** Often sitting on powerlines. Eucalypt woodland, lightly timbered grassland, open forest, parks and gardens. *May be confused with:* DIAMOND DOVE, but look for blue eye-ring and extensive barring.

BAR-SHOULDERED DOVE
Geopelia humeralis   28 cm
Medium-sized, appearing brownish; **dark 'scaly' pattern on a chestnut patch on back of neck;** back, wings and rump brown barred blackish in a 'scaly' pattern; long tail. Rainforest edges, eucalypt forest with denser understorey, farmland and mangroves. *May be confused with:* SPOTTED TURTLE-DOVE in urban areas, which has black patch spotted white on back of neck.

BRUSH CUCKOO
Cacomantis variolosus   (Juvenile) 24 cm
Medium-sized overall brownish bird heavily mottled; **barred brown and buff on back and wings;** barred underparts from throat to **long 'notched' tail;** grey feet. Rainforest at most altitudes and most other forested habitats. *May be confused with:* Juvenile and immature ORIENTAL and PALLID CUCKOOS and juvenile FAN-TAILED CUCKOO. See p. 198.

GROUND CUCKOO-SHRIKE

Coracina maxima (Juvenile) 36 cm
Rare; greyish; **dark wings which it refolds on
alighting; long dark forked tail;** throat, breast, belly
and rump finely barred; scallops on back of head and
neck; **pale rump and back conspicuous in flight.**
Drier open forest and woodland.

FURTHER POSSIBILITIES

A rare, reddish-brown well-barred phase of ORIENTAL
CUCKOO. See p. 198.
Each of the following, with some barring on upperparts, has
more prominent features:
CRESTED PIGEON
BUDGERIGAR
AUSTRALIAN OWLET-NIGHTJAR
BASSIAN and RUSSET-TAILED THRUSHES

SMALL BIRDS WITH CHESTNUT BACK, WINGS & TAIL
POSSIBILITIES

SHINING FLYCATCHER

Myiagra alecto (Female) 17 cm
A striking bird with **glossy blue-black head,
chestnut back, wings and tail** and white underparts;
usually with the all-glossy blue-black male.
Mangroves, sometimes adjacent paperbark forest and
riverside vegetation. Occasionally well upstream in
some larger rivers.

SMALL BIRDS WITH WELL-BARRED UNDERPARTS
POSSIBILITIES

PEACEFUL DOVE *Geopelia striata* 20 cm
**Fine black barring on breast, nape, hind neck and
wings; blue eye-ring;** long tail. Often sitting on
powerlines. Eucalypt woodland, lightly timbered
grassland, open forest, parks and gardens.
May be confused with: DIAMOND DOVE, but look for
blue eye-ring and extensive barring.

HORSFIELD'S BRONZE-CUCKOO

Chrysococcyx basalis 17 cm
Small cuckoo; brownish above with iridescent sheen;
white underparts boldly barred brownish; **barring
does not meet in centre.** Open forest, woodland,
lightly timbered areas, swampy areas, sometimes parks
and gardens. *May be confused with:* Other bronze-
cuckoos. See pp. 198-9.

SHINING BRONZE-CUCKOO

Chrysococcyx lucidus 17 cm
Small cuckoo with iridescent **golden-green back,
wings and tail;** boldly barred underparts from chin to
tail; **bars complete.** Upland rainforest, especially
about clearings. *May be confused with:* Other bronze-
cuckoos. See pp. 198-9.

LITTLE BRONZE-CUCKOO
Chrysococcyx minutillus   16 cm
Small cuckoo; dull bronze-green above; white below with
bold barring from chin to tail. Male: **red eye-ring.** Female:
tan eye-ring. Open forest, paperbark forest, tropical
woodland, moreso to the west of the Wet Tropics. *May be
confused with:* Other bronze-cuckoos. See pp. 198–9.

GOULD'S BRONZE-CUCKOO
Chrysococcyx russatus   17 cm
Almost identical to LITTLE BRONZE-CUCKOO.
Mostly coastal. Rainforest, open forest, paperbark
woodland, gallery forest, also mangroves. *May be
confused with:* Other bronze-cuckoos. See p. 198–9.

BAR-BREASTED HONEYEATER
Ramsayornis fasciatus   14 cm
Rare; distinctive; paler underparts; **bold black
broken bars across breast and flanks;** crown
scalloped black and white. Paperbark swamps,
mangroves and gardens.

VARIED TRILLER
Lalage leucomela   (Female) 19 cm
Blackish crown and nape, back and tail; lightly barred
white to off-white underparts from chin to belly; **buff
lower belly and under tail-coverts;** prominent white
eyebrow; grey rump. Gallery forest, rainforest, denser
eucalypt forest and paperbark woodland, sometimes
mangroves. *May be confused with:* NONE. Buff lower
belly and under tail-coverts separate it from all other
species.

ZEBRA FINCH   *Taeniopygia guttata*   (Male) 10 cm
Distinctive, beautifully-marked bird; greyish; **finely
barred throat and breast; chestnut sides spotted
white;** short thick red bill; chestnut ear patch.
Grassland studded with shrubs and small trees.

DOUBLE-BARRED FINCH
Taeniopygia bichenovii   10 cm
White face and underparts; **two thin black bars
across breast;** black wings heavily spotted white.
Grassy woodland, open forest, parks and gardens.

PLUM-HEADED FINCH   *Neochmia modesta* 11 cm
Rare; brownish; short thick black bill; black tail;
**prominent brown barred underparts; shoulders
spotted white; barred white rump.** Gregarious.
Taller grassland and lightly timbered grassy areas,
often close to streams.

FURTHER POSSIBILITIES
The elusive BAILLON'S and AUSTRALIAN SPOTTED CRAKES
have barred bellies which are not very obvious in the field. Some
juvenile BRONZE-CUCKOOS have faint barring on underparts.
BROWN-BACKED HONEYEATER has faint barring on sides of
breast.

POSSIBILITIES

COLLARED SPARROWHAWK

Accipiter cirrhocephalus Male 31 cm Female 37 cm
A small hawk appearing quite brown. Adult: greyish-brown upperparts; **finely barred pale rufous underparts;** rufous collar; longish yellow legs; **square tail.** Juvenile: overall brown; streaked throat and upper breast; heavily barred lower breast and belly. Open eucalypt forest and woodland. *May be confused with:* BROWN GOSHAWK which is almost identical in all stages but is larger with a rounded tail.

BUFF-BANDED RAIL *Gallirallus philippensis* 31 cm

Shy, brownish ground bird; chestnut crown and stripe through eye; **grey eyebrow; chestnut patch on breast; extensive fine barring** on underparts. Juvenile: duller. Dense damp grassland, vegetation about swamps and streams. *May be confused with:* The rare LEWIN'S RAIL, but look for grey eyebrow and chestnut on breast.

LEWIN'S RAIL *Rallus pectoralis* 22 cm

Rare, shy ground bird; dark upperparts; **rich chestnut head and nape** with black streaks; **slate-grey throat and breast;** barred wings, belly and under tail-coverts; **long black-tipped pink bill.** Damp grassland and reedy swamps. *May be confused with:* BUFF-BANDED RAIL, but look for long bill, absence of eyebrow and slate-grey extending from throat to upper belly.

ORIENTAL CUCKOO *Cuculus saturatus* 31 cm

Long-tailed greyish bird; long wings and long tail give it a hawk-like appearance in flight; **boldly barred lower breast and belly;** yellow eye-ring and feet. Juvenile: dark brown barring from throat to tail. Eucalypt forest and woodland, paperbark swamps, sometimes about rainforest clearings, moreso at lower altitudes. *May be confused with:* Adult: BARRED CUCKOO-SHRIKE has similar barring, yellow eye, black legs and feet and refolds wings on alighting. Juvenile and immature: juvenile and immature PALLID, BRUSH and FAN-TAILED CUCKOOS. See p. 198.

PALLID CUCKOO

Cuculus pallidus (Immature) 31 cm
Long-tailed brown bird; **mottled brown and buff** on back and wings; lightly barred underparts heavier on breast; **streaked crown; 'notched' tail;** grey feet. Open woodland. *May be confused with:* Juvenile ORIENTAL, BRUSH and FAN-TAILED CUCKOOS. See p. 198.

BRUSH CUCKOO

Cacomantis variolosus (Juvenile) 24 cm
Overall brownish; heavily mottled; **barred brown and buff on back and wings;** barred underparts from throat to tail; **long 'notched' tail;** grey feet. Rainforest at most altitudes and most other forested habitats. *May be confused with:* Immature ORIENTAL and PALLID CUCKOOS and juvenile FAN-TAILED CUCKOO. See p. 198.

FAN-TAILED CUCKOO

Cacomantis flabelliformis (Juvenile) 26 cm
Slender; brown upperparts; paler underparts **faintly barred; long 'notched' tail;** grey feet. Rainforest and denser eucalypt forest. *May be confused with:* Juvenile and immature ORIENTAL, PALLID and BRUSH CUCKOOS. See p. 198.

COMMON KOEL

Eudynamys scolopacea (Female) 43 cm
Migrant, present Sept.–Apr.; rather shy long-tailed bird; skulking; brown back and wings **heavily spotted white; black head; red eye;** brown tail barred white; underparts whitish barred brown. Juvenile: similar, more chestnut, no black crown. Denser open forest, woodland, gallery forest, dense trees in farmland, parks and gardens.

BARRED CUCKOO-SHRIKE

Coracina lineata 27 cm
Immaculate; **refolds wings on alighting;** grey with fine barring from **lower breast to under tail; yellow eye;** black wing and tail tips. Rainforest at all altitudes. *May be confused with:* Perhaps adult ORIENTAL CUCKOO which has similar barring but dark eye, yellow eye-ring and feet and long 'notched' tail.

CICADABIRD *Coracina tenuirostris* (Female) 25 cm

Migrant, present Oct.–Mar./Apr.; mid-brown with paler **creamy-buff underparts barred dark brown.** Does not refold wings. Fast flight. Usually wary. Eucalypt forest, vine thickets, paperbark woodland, mangroves, canopy of lowland rainforest. *May be confused with:* Perhaps juvenile FAN-TAILED and BRUSH CUCKOOS which have long 'notched' tails.

GROUND CUCKOO-SHRIKE

Coracina maxima 36 cm
Rare; greyish with **black wings which it refolds on alighting; long black forked tail;** paler underparts barred on lower breast and belly; **white faintly barred back and rump conspicuous in flight;** white eye. Drier open forest and open woodland.

FURTHER POSSIBILITIES
PINK-EARED DUCK
GREEN PYGMY-GOOSE
Some SHOREBIRDS

POSSIBILITIES

PACIFIC BAZA
Aviceda subcristata Male 37 cm Female 44 cm
Grey; reddish-brown barring on belly; **small upright crest on back of head; large yellow eye.** Open forest, rainforest (especially the edges), gallery forest, forested farmland.

BROWN GOSHAWK
Accipiter fasciatus Male 42 cm Female 50 cm
Adult: greyish-brown upperparts; finely barred **pale rufous** underparts; rufous collar; longish yellow legs; **long rounded tail.** Juvenile: overall brown with heavily streaked throat and upper breast, barred lower breast and belly. Open eucalypt forest and woodland. *May be confused with:* Almost identical to the smaller COLLARED SPARROWHAWK in all plumages, but look for rounded tail.

RED-TAILED BLACK-COCKATOO
Calyptorhynchus banksii (Female) 56 cm
Black; **broad red panels in tail, finely barred black;** fine yellow spots and barring in plumage; lower belly and under tail-coverts barred orange-red; whitish bill. Open forest, woodland, sometimes over rainforest and about cities and towns.

RUFOUS OWL *Ninox rufa* 51 cm
Nocturnal, **rufous-brown owl** with large yellow eyes focused forward; **narrow dense rufous barring on underparts; darker barring on upperparts;** tail barred below; perches by day in dense foliage, e.g. rainforest, gallery forest; hunting out over woodland by night. Moreso at lower altitudes.

FURTHER POSSIBILITIES
GREY GOSHAWK

SMALL BIRDS WITH CHESTNUT, RUFOUS, ORANGE OR BUFF BREAST OR UNDERPARTS
POSSIBILITIES

AZURE KINGFISHER *Alcedo azurea* 18 cm
Deep blue head, back and wings; disproportionately-long, thin, black bill; short tail; **completely orange underparts.** Freshwater streams, often in rainforest. Sometimes in mangroves.

EASTERN SPINEBILL
Acanthorhynchus tenuirostris 15 cm
Active; blackish head; **rufous patch in white throat; long, fine, curved bill;** rufous belly; shows much white in tail in flight. Frequently hovers at blossom. Rainforest and nearby eucalypt forest at higher altitudes.

63

RUFOUS WHISTLER
Pachycephala rufiventris   (Male) 17 cm
Rufous breast extending to under tail; white throat margined black; greyish back. Open eucalypt forest and woodland.

BLACK-FACED MONARCH
Monarcha melanopsis   18 cm
Migrant, usually present Sept.–Mar./Apr.; mostly grey flycatcher; **rufous belly and under tail-coverts; grey breast sharply demarcated from belly; grey tail;** black forehead and throat. Juvenile: lacks black facial markings. Rainforest, moreso at higher altitudes. Often in more open country on migration. *May be confused with:* BLACK-WINGED and SPECTACLED MONARCHS, but look for grey wings and grey tail.

BLACK-WINGED MONARCH
Monarcha frater   18 cm
Rare in the Wet Tropics region. Present on northern Cape York Peninsula Oct.–Apr.; similar to BLACK-FACED MONARCH but with **black wings and tail and silver-grey upperparts.** *May be confused with:* BLACK-FACED and SPECTACLED MONARCHS, but look for black wings and tail.

SPECTACLED MONARCH
Monarcha trivirgatus   16 cm
Grey back; **rufous breast; white belly;** black forehead and throat; black mask about eyes; **black tail with broad white corners.** Juvenile: lacks black about face. Rainforest at all altitudes. *May be confused with:* BLACK-FACED MONARCH and the rare BLACK-WINGED MONARCH, but look for rufous breast and white belly and tail corners.

LEADEN FLYCATCHER
Myiagra rubecula   (Female) 15 cm
Constantly quivers tail; dull leaden-grey above; rusty-buff throat and upper breast; white underparts. Eucalypt forest, woodland, parks and gardens. *May be confused with:* BROAD-BILLED FLYCATCHER and female SATIN FLYCATCHER. See p. 202.

SATIN FLYCATCHER
Myiagra cyanoleuca   (Female) 16 cm
Rare passage migrant usually seen Aug.–Sept. and Mar.–Apr. Almost identical to LEADEN FLYCATCHER. *May be confused with:* BROAD-BILLED and female LEADEN FLYCATCHERS. See p. 202.

BROAD-BILLED FLYCATCHER
Myiagra ruficollis   16 cm
Rare; almost identical to female LEADEN and female SATIN FLYCATCHERS. Mangroves. *May be confused with:* Female LEADEN and female SATIN FLYCATCHERS. See p. 202.

VARIED TRILLER *Lalage leucomela*   19 cm
Blackish crown and nape, back and tail; white to off-white underparts from chin to belly; prominent white eyebrow; grey rump; **buff lower belly and under tail-coverts.** Female has lightly barred underparts from chin to belly. Gallery forest, rainforest, denser eucalypt forest and paperbark woodland, sometimes mangroves. *May be confused with:* NONE. Buff lower belly and under tail-coverts separate it from all other species.

BLACK-THROATED FINCH
Poephila cincta   10 cm
Brownish; grey head; **black throat and upper breast;** pale apricot-chestnut lower breast and belly; white under tail-coverts; short tail; short thick **black bill.** Two races occur in the Wet Tropics — black-rumped north from about Townsville; white-rumped from Townsville southward.

CHESTNUT-BREASTED MANNIKIN
Lonchura castaneothorax   10 cm
Appears brownish; **large black mask extending to throat; chestnut breast with a black band below;** creamy belly; yellowish-brown rump and tail. Grasslands, reedy areas, grassy roadsides, sugar-cane fields, farmland.

FURTHER POSSIBILITIES
RED-BACKED and RED-CHESTED BUTTON-QUAILS

MEDIUM-SIZED & LARGE BIRDS WITH CHESTNUT, RUFOUS, ORANGE OR BUFF BREAST OR UNDERPARTS
POSSIBILITIES

BRUSH CUCKOO *Cacomantis variolosus*   24 cm
Medium-sized grey-brown bird often appearing brownish; **grey eye-ring; near plain tail tipped white;** grey head, buffy-grey breast; buff belly. Rainforest at most altitudes and most other forested habitats. *May be confused with:* Perhaps FAN-TAILED and CHESTNUT-BREASTED CUCKOOS. See p. 197.

CHESTNUT-BREASTED CUCKOO
Cacomantis castaneiventris   24 cm
Rare; medium-sized; blue-grey above; **rich chestnut underparts;** yellow eye-ring and feet; **lower tail 'notched' white at sides.** Rainforest at all altitudes. *May be confused with:* FAN-TAILED CUCKOO. See p. 197.

FAN-TAILED CUCKOO
Cacomantis flabelliformis   26 cm
Medium-sized slender bird; slate-grey above with **pale rufous underparts; yellow eye-ring** and yellowish feet; fairly long tail markedly 'notched' white down each side. Rainforest and denser eucalypt forest. *May be confused with:* BRUSH and CHESTNUT-BREASTED CUCKOOS. See p. 197.

BUFF-BREASTED PARADISE-KINGFISHER

Tanysiptera sylvia 34 cm

Migrant, present Nov.–early Apr.; **distinctively spectacular;** thick red bill; brilliant blue and black above; rufous-orange below; centre of back and rump white; **two very long, stiff, white tail feathers** which are sometimes broken-off during or after breeding season. Mostly lowland rainforest.

NOISY PITTA

Pitta versicolor 18 cm

Medium-sized bird of the rainforest floor; **blue shoulders; black throat and mask extending to back of head;** buff breast; green back and wings; black patch on belly; red lower belly. Rainforest at all altitudes.

CHOWCHILLA

Orthonyx spaldingii (Female) 27 cm

Medium-sized darkish bird of the rainforest floor; **conspicuous white eye-ring;** rich rufous throat and breast; white belly. Rainforest, moreso in upland areas.

BOWER'S SHRIKE-THRUSH

Colluricincla boweri 20 cm

Medium-sized short-tailed bird initially appearing dark brown; **dark grey back and head; black bill;** rufous underparts; striated grey on throat and upper breast. Rainforest at higher altitudes, usually above 400 m.
May be confused with: LITTLE SHRIKE-THRUSH which has pinkish-brown bill and is overall brown.

WHITE-BROWED WOODSWALLOW

Artamus superciliosus 19 cm

Rare; medium-sized; deep blue-grey above; **chestnut lower breast and underparts;** dark grey face; **bluish bill; prominent white eyebrow;** grey tail tipped white. Wags tail. Female and juvenile: duller. Usually in noisy flocks. Drier, open, lightly timbered habitat.

VICTORIA'S RIFLEBIRD

Ptiloris victoriae (Female) 24 cm

Medium-sized short-tailed bird; **long curved black bill;** greyish-brown above; rufous-buff below with darker flecking. Rainforest at all altitudes.

FURTHER POSSIBILITIES
WANDERING and PLUMED WHISTLING-DUCKS
Introduced COMMON MYNA

POSSIBILITIES

SCALY-BREASTED LORIKEET

Trichoglossus chlorolepidotus   23 cm
Medium-sized mostly green bird or small parrot;
**yellowish 'scaly' pattern on breast; red bill; orange
underwings in flight.** Strong direct flight. Eucalypt
forest, parks and gardens wherever there is blossom.

SATIN BOWERBIRD

Ptilonorhynchus violaceus   (Female) 24 cm
Medium-sized olive-green bird; paler underparts with
darker 'scaly' pattern from throat to belly; blue
eyes; longish pale legs. Rainforest margins and
adjacent open forest at higher altitudes.

NUTMEG MANNIKIN *Lonchura punctulata* 11 cm
Introduced small brown bird; dark bill; darker brown
face; yellow rump; **finely-patterned 'scaly'
underparts.** Gregarious. Flicks tail from side to side.
Grassland, farmland, roadsides and fringes of towns.

BASSIAN THRUSH *Zoothera lunulata*   28 cm
Medium-sized brown bird with paler underparts;
prominent 'scaly' pattern from throat to belly. Feeds
on the ground. Rainforest at higher altitudes.
May be confused with: RUSSET-TAILED THRUSH
which is almost identical. See p. 204.

RUSSET-TAILED THRUSH

Zoothera heinei   27 cm
Similar to BASSIAN THRUSH and difficult to separate
in the field. Rainforest at higher altitudes. *May be
confused with:* BASSIAN THRUSH. See p. 204.

FURTHER POSSIBILITIES
BROWN QUAIL and female KING QUAIL
LESSER SOOTY OWL
Juvenile SACRED and juvenile FOREST KINGFISHERS —
faint 'scaly' pattern.

SMALL BIRDS WITH PROMINENTLY STRIATED UNDERPARTS
POSSIBILITIES

WHITE-THROATED TREECREEPER

Cormobates leucophaeus   14 cm
Brownish above; paler below; **small white throat
patch; heavily streaked underparts from lower
breast to tail.** Hops up tree trunks. Upland rainforest
and adjacent wet sclerophyll. *May be confused with:*
BROWN TREECREEPER which has prominent
whitish eyebrow and inhabits dry open forest.

MACLEAY'S HONEYEATER
Xanthotis macleayana   20 cm
Stocky bird initially appearing brownish; **boldly streaked; black cap; patch of orange skin about eye.** Rainforest, gallery forest, sometimes nearby eucalypt forest and gardens at all altitudes.

WHITE-STREAKED HONEYEATER
Trichodere cockerelli   17 cm
Olive-brown above; whitish below; **well-streaked white on light grey throat and breast;** dark grey head and sides of face; yellow edges to wing and tail feathers; **yellow ear-coverts.** Eucalypt forest, heathland, paperbark swamps.
May be confused with: NONE. WHITE-CHEEKED HONEYEATER has large white cheek patch.

WHITE-CHEEKED HONEYEATER
Phylidonyris nigra   18 cm
Black and white bird with boldly streaked underparts; **large white cheek patch; broad yellow panel in wing; yellow outer tail feathers.** Edges and clearings in upland rainforest, sometimes open forest with dense understorey, especially banksias, gardens.

JACKY WINTER *Microeca fascinans* (Juvenile) 13 cm
Grey-brown; paler below; dark brown striations on head, back and breast; **conspicuous white sides to tail feathers. Restlessly wags tail from side to side.** Usually with plain adults. Drier, open, sparsely timbered habitats. *May be confused with:* NONE. Tail wagging is distinctive. LEMON-BELLIED FLY-CATCHER has quite lemon underparts and plain tail.

VARIED SITTELLA *Daphoenositta chrysoptera* 11 cm
Short-tailed dark **heavily striated bird living on tree trunks and limbs; small white wingbar;** slightly upturned bill; yellow eye-ring, legs and feet. Male: dark crown. Female: dark head, throat and upper breast. Dry woodland and eucalypt forest, especially where Ironbark *Eucalyptus* spp. grow.

RUFOUS WHISTLER
Pachycephala rufiventris   (Female) 17 cm
Mostly grey upperparts; **lightly streaked pale buff underparts** from chin to tail. Open forest and woodland.

SINGING BUSHLARK *Mirafra javanica*   13 cm
Well-striated; brownish; paler below; **reddish patches on shoulders distinct in flight. Peculiar, jerky, fluttering and hovering flight** low over grass or high in the air in courtship display. Drier grassland, farmland and crops. *May be confused with:* RICHARD'S PIPIT, TAWNY GRASSBIRD, RUFOUS SONGLARK and female BROWN SONGLARK, but the jerky flight and reddish shoulders of SINGING BUSHLARK distinguish it from all other species.

RICHARD'S PIPIT *Anthus novaeseelandiae* 16 cm
Brown; well-striated; **teeters longish tail up and
down.** Open grassland and farmland. *May be confused
with:* SINGING BUSHLARK, TAWNY GRASSBIRD,
RUFOUS SONGLARK and female BROWN
SONGLARK, but the tail teetering habit of
RICHARD'S PIPIT distinguishes it.

RED-RUMPED SWALLOW *Hirundo daurica* 18 cm
Scarce summer visitor Dec.–Mar.; black upperparts;
**striated pale buffy underparts; long deeply forked
tail; conspicuous rufous rump.** Immature: duller.
Rests on powerlines with other swallows and martins.
Open areas and farmland.

FURTHER POSSIBILITIES
VARIED, PAINTED and juvenile BAR-BREASTED
HONEYEATERS
Juvenile EASTERN YELLOW ROBIN
Juvenile VARIED TRILLER

MEDIUM-SIZED BIRDS WITH PROMINENTLY STRIATED UNDERPARTS
POSSIBILITIES

SOUTHERN BOOBOOK
Ninox novaeseelandiae 32 cm
Nocturnal, small brown owl; **dark 'goggles' around
yellow eyes,** focused forward; white spots on wings;
underparts whitish with thick, blotchy brown streaks.
All open wooded habitats. The dark race *lurida* which
inhabits upland rainforest has spotted underparts. *May
be confused with:* Perhaps the larger BARKING OWL,
but look for 'goggles' about eyes.

YELLOW ORIOLE
Oriolus flavocinctus (Juvenile) 28 cm
**Well-striated yellow-green bird; bright yellow
margins** to brownish wing feathers; yellow-olive
underparts well-striated from throat to under tail;
brownish bill and eye. Rainforest, gallery forest at
lower altitudes and mangroves. *May be confused with:*
OLIVE-BACKED ORIOLE and perhaps female
FIGBIRD, but look for overall yellow-green colouration
and yellow tips and edges to wing feathers.

OLIVE-BACKED ORIOLE *Oriolus sagittatus* 27 cm
Olive-green back; dusky-grey or brownish wings; white
underparts with **'tear-drop' shaped striations; red
eye and bill.** Juvenile and immature: black eye and
bill; more heavily striated. Eucalypt forest and tropical
woodland. *May be confused with:* YELLOW ORIOLE,
female FIGBIRD and TOOTH-BILLED BOWERBIRD,
but look for white underparts with 'teardrop'
striations. Female FIGBIRD has bare grey skin about
eye and short thickish black bill.

FIGBIRD *Sphecotheres viridis* (Female) 28 cm
Brown upperparts; whitish underparts heavily streaked
brown; **bare grey skin about eye;** thickish black bill;
brown tail. Rainforest edges and remnants, gallery
forest, nearby open forest, parks and gardens. Feeds in
fruiting trees. *May be confused with:* Juvenile YELLOW
ORIOLE, OLIVE-BACKED ORIOLE (especially juvenile
and immature) and TOOTH-BILLED BOWERBIRD, but
look for bare grey skin about eye and thickish black bill.

TOOTH-BILLED BOWERBIRD
Scenopoeetes dentirostris 26 cm
Olive-brown; paler below; **coarse streaking on breast
and belly; robust dark bill.** Fast direct flight, quick
movements. Upland rainforest above 600 m,
sometimes lower. *May be confused with:* Juvenile and
immature OLIVE-BACKED ORIOLE. Female
FIGBIRD has bare grey skin about eye. Note habitat.

METALLIC STARLING
Aplonis metallica (Juvenile and Immature) 24 cm
Gregarious. Juvenile: dull black upperparts; dark eye.
Immature: glossy black upperparts; red eye. Both have
well-striated white underparts and **long sharply
pointed tail.** Usually in the company of glossy all-
black adults. Rainforest and remnant rainforest,
sometimes mangroves. Mostly at low altitudes.

FURTHER POSSIBILITIES
STUBBLE QUAIL
Juvenile LITTLE BITTERN
PAINTED BUTTON-QUAIL
SPINY-CHEEKED and STRIPED HONEYEATERS —
vagrants to extreme south of region.
SHOREBIRDS, see pp. 182–9.

LARGE BIRDS WITH PROMINENTLY STRIATED UNDERPARTS
POSSIBILITIES

STRIATED HERON *Butorides striatus* (Juvenile) 47 cm
Rather dumpy **blue-grey** small heron; well-striated
underparts continuing up onto sides of neck; **black
cap; yellow legs;** black and yellow bill. Usually feeds
with a distinctive **crouched stance.** Mangroves, lower
reaches of rivers and tidal flats. *May be confused with:*
Juvenile NANKEEN NIGHT HERON, juvenile
LITTLE BITTERN and BLACK BITTERN, but look
for plain black cap and bright yellow legs.

NANKEEN NIGHT HERON
Nycticorax caledonicus (Juvenile) 60 cm
Heavily striated brownish wading bird; greenish legs;
paler underparts well-striated; has a bittern-like
appearance and sometimes mistaken for one. Nocturnal;
rests by day in thick foliage. Freshwater swamps, lakes
and creeks. *May be confused with:* STRIATED HERON,
but look for well-striated head and body and greenish
legs. Often misidentified as a bittern.

BLACK BITTERN *Ixobrychus flavicollis* 60 cm
Secretive, **dark sooty** wading bird; yellowish streaked
breast and sides of neck; **yellowish plume on neck;
olive-brown legs; dark bill.** Female: duller. Juvenile:
sooty-brown with paler edging to feathers; pale neck
plume; yellow-brown legs. Feeds at dusk and dawn.
Freshwater swamps, especially paperbark swamps,
well-vegetated streamsides, sometimes mangroves.
May be confused with: Perhaps STRIATED HERON
which has black cap and yellow to orange legs, but
look for neck plume and olive-brown legs.

BUSH STONE-CURLEW *Burhinus grallarius* 55 cm
Nocturnal; streaked greyish plumage; long legs; buffy
underparts; **whitish forehead and eyebrow; large
yellow eyes.** Ground-dwelling. Moves slowly and
deliberately when disturbed by day. Open forest, open
lightly timbered areas, often in urban localities.

PHEASANT COUCAL
Centropus phasianinus (Non-breeding plumage) 70 cm
Clumsy-looking; outsized tail; skulking; brownish
Apr.–Aug.; head and body **heavily streaked;** long
broad dark tail with paler barring. Lives mostly on the
ground in tall grassy areas in open forest and farmland.

BARKING OWL *Ninox connivens* 40 cm
Nocturnal, greyish-brown owl; **streaked grey
underparts; large yellow staring eyes** focused
forward. Open forest with some dense cover, rainforest
margins, paperbark swamps and woodland. *May be
confused with:* The smaller, browner SOUTHERN
BOOBOOK which has distinct 'goggles' about eyes.

FURTHER POSSIBILITIES
Some SHOREBIRDS. See pp. 182–9.
Diurnal Birds of Prey. See pp. 175–81.
TAWNY and PAPUAN FROGMOUTHS

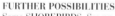

SMALL & MEDIUM-SIZED BIRDS WITH YELLOW BREAST OR UNDERPARTS
POSSIBILITIES

WEEBILL *Smicrornis brevirostris* 8 cm
Tiny plain bird of eucalypt foliage; olive-yellow above;
yellowish below; **short horn-coloured bill; whitish
eye;** faint creamy eyebrow. Drier eucalypt forest and
open woodland. *May be confused with:* Female and
juvenile FAIRY GERYGONE, juvenile WHITE-
THROATED GERYGONE, BUFF-RUMPED and
YELLOW THORNBILLS, but look for short pale bill
and whitish eye.

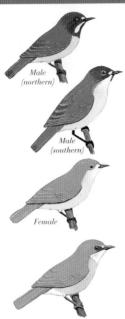

Male
(northern)

Male
(southern)

Female

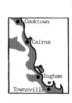

FAIRY GERYGONE *Gerygone palpebrosa* 11 cm
Small; greenish above; lemon underparts. Male: **white
'whisker' down each side of face from bill.** North of
about Innisfail, male has blackish-brown throat. South of
Innisfail, male resembles female with only a trace of white
'whisker' and small black chin. Female: **whitish throat
merging into pale lemon breast.** Lowland rainforest,
gallery forest, coastal vine scrubs and mangroves. Usually
below 500 m. *May be confused with:* WEEBILL: short
pale bill and white eye. WHITE-THROATED
GERYGONE: white throat, well-demarcated. (Female
FAIRY difficult to separate from juvenile WHITE-
THROATED which lacks well-demarcated white throat.)
BUFF-RUMPED THORNBILL: buff yellow rump.
YELLOW THORNBILL: striations behind eye. None
occurs in the denser habitats preferred by the FAIRY.

WHITE-THROATED GERYGONE

Gerygone olivacea 11 cm
Small; brown back; **yellow breast and belly; well-
demarcated white throat.** Juvenile: lacks white
throat. Eucalypt forest and open woodland. *May be
confused with:* WEEBILL, FAIRY GERYGONE, BUFF-
RUMPED and YELLOW THORNBILLS. In adults,
look for demarcated white throat. Juvenile is difficult
to separate from juvenile and female FAIRY, but
habitat should give some indication.

BUFF-RUMPED THORNBILL

Acanthiza reguloides 11 cm
Small; greenish-olive upperparts; yellow underparts;
buff-yellow rump; forehead and face scalloped
yellowish-cream; tail tipped pale yellow with broad black
band; dark bill; white eye. Dry open eucalypt forest and
casuarina thickets. *May be confused with:* WEEBILL,
FAIRY GERYGONE, juvenile WHITE-THROATED
GERYGONE and YELLOW THORNBILL, but look for
buff-yellow rump.

YELLOW THORNBILL *Acanthiza nana* 10 cm

Small active bird; olive-green above, yellowish below;
streaked patch behind eye; sharp black bill; dark
eye. Drier woodland, especially where there are denser
stands of casuarina, sometimes nearby eucalypt forest.
May be confused with: WEEBILL, female and juvenile
FAIRY GERYGONE, juvenile WHITE-THROATED
GERYGONE and BUFF-RUMPED THORNBILL, but
look for streaked patch behind dark eye.

VARIED HONEYEATER

Lichenostomus versicolor 19 cm. Small bird of
mangroves; olive-brown above; yellow underparts faintly
streaked brown; **thick black line through eye and down
side of neck, with yellow below black line, ending in
a white patch below ear.** Mangroves, sometimes adjacent
forest and gardens from about Cardwell north. *May be
confused with:* Perhaps the rather plain YELLOW
HONEYEATER, but VARIED is more brightly marked
about face and breast.

LEMON-BELLIED FLYCATCHER
Microeca flavigaster 12 cm
Small, active bird; brownish with **lemon underparts;
black legs and feet.** Tropical woodland and eucalypt
forest. *May be confused with:* JACKY WINTER which
has white underparts; white edges to dark tail. GREY
WHISTLER which has faint yellow wash on
underparts, grey legs and feet, is less active and
inhabits rainforest.

PALE-YELLOW ROBIN *Tregellasia capito* 13 cm
Small unobtrusive rainforest bird; greenish-grey
upperparts; **greenish-yellow** underparts; **buff from
bill to eye; white throat.** Clings sideways to tree
trunks. Rainforest at all altitudes.

EASTERN YELLOW ROBIN
Eopsaltria australis 15 cm
Small; medium-grey upperparts; **bright yellow
underparts and rump; grey face.** Tropical woodland
with some understorey and wet sclerophyll.

CRESTED SHRIKE-TIT *Falcunculus frontatus* 18 cm
Small; olive-green back; yellow breast; **black head
with white markings; black crest.** Male: black
throat. Female: olive-green throat. Drier eucalypt
forest and woodland. *May be confused with:* Males of
both GOLDEN and MANGROVE GOLDEN
WHISTLERS, but look for black crest and black or
olive-green throat.

GOLDEN WHISTLER
Pachycephala pectoralis (Male) 17 cm
Small; olive-green upperparts, yellow underparts; **black
head; prominent white throat bordered with a black
band across breast.** Rainforest at higher altitudes,
sometimes coastal in winter. *May be confused with:*
CRESTED SHRIKE-TIT, but look for white throat. Male
MANGROVE GOLDEN WHISTLER. See p. 202.

MANGROVE GOLDEN WHISTLER
Pachycephala melanura 16 cm
Only known population is about Hinchinbrook Channel.
Male: similar to male GOLDEN WHISTLER. Female:
grey-brown above with **yellow from breast to under
tail-coverts.** Mangroves. *May be confused with:* Male:
CRESTED SHRIKE-TIT, but look for white throat. Male
GOLDEN WHISTLER. See p. 202. Female: NONE.

YELLOW-BREASTED BOATBILL
Machaerirhynchus flaviventer 12 cm
Small black and yellow flycatcher; short
disproportionately-wide bill. Cocks tail. Male:
prominent **yellow eyebrow; white throat; yellow
underparts;** yellow rump. Female duller. Rainforest at
all altitudes.

FIGBIRD
Sphecotheres viridis race *flaviventris*
(Male — yellow-bellied race) 28 cm
Medium-sized; deep olive-green back and wings; yellow
throat, breast and upper belly; black head; black tail
with white edges; large area of **red skin about eye.**
Feeds in fruiting trees. Rainforest edges and remnants,
gallery forest, nearby open forest, parks and gardens.

GOLDEN BOWERBIRD
Prionodura newtoniana   (Male) 24 cm
A medium-sized striking bird; **golden-olive above;
golden-yellow below.** Upland rainforest above
900 m, sometimes lower.

YELLOW-BELLIED SUNBIRD
Nectarinia jugularis   11 cm
Short-tailed small bird; olive-green upperparts; **yellow
underparts;** long fine curved bill. Male: **iridescent
blue-black ' bib'.** Rainforest margins, gallery forest,
woodland, often about gardens and houses, mostly at
lower altitudes.

GREY WAGTAIL
Motacilla cinerea   20 cm
Rare summer visitor Nov.–Mar.; small; greyish;
yellowish underparts, brighter under tail; white
eyebrow; **yellowish-green rump; pale legs.
Constantly teeters long tail.** Mostly terrestrial. Open
areas in rainforest at high altitudes.
May be confused with: YELLOW WAGTAIL which has
greenish-grey rump; black legs; brownish-grey above;
paler below; visitor to lowland areas. Look for
yellowish-green rump, pale legs. Note habitat.

FURTHER POSSIBILITIES
GOULDIAN FINCH — probably extinct in the Wet Tropics
region.

BIRDS WITH RUFOUS, CHESTNUT OR BUFF THROAT
POSSIBILITIES

STUBBLE QUAIL
Coturnix pectoralis (Male) 18cm
Medium-sized brownish ground bird appearing tailless;
whitish streaks down back; **well-streaked
underparts heavier on breast forming black patch;
whitish eyebrow;** chestnut throat patch. Rank and
dry grassland, farmland and crops. *May be confused
with:* Other quail and button-quail, but fairly distinct.
Look for streaking, eyebrow and throat patch.

ORIENTAL PRATINCOLE
Glareola maldivarum   24 cm
Rare summer visitor; medium-sized long-winged olive-brown bird; buffish to white below; **buff throat edged with broken black line; long forked tail** with white sides and wide black margin at base; upper tail-coverts white; **chestnut underwing.** In flight, graceful and tern-like. Hawks flying insects over open short-grassed plains, claypans and mudflats. *May be confused with:* AUSTRALIAN PRATINCOLE which lacks throat patch. Look for broken edging to buff throat when sitting; chestnut underwing and long forked tail in flight. AUSTRALIAN teeters, ORIENTAL does not.

EASTERN SPINEBILL
Acanthorhynchus tenuirostris   15 cm
Small active bird; blackish head; dark back and wings; **rufous patch in white throat; long fine curved bill;** rufous belly. Shows much white in tail in flight. Frequently hovers at blossom. Rainforest and nearby eucalypt forest at higher altitudes.

BARN SWALLOW *Hirundo rustica*   16 cm
Summer visitor, present Nov.–Mar.; small mostly blue-black and white bird; blue-black upperparts; **whitish underparts; black breastband; rusty-red throat and forehead;** long, deeply forked tail. The BARN SWALLOW is in moult when it first arrives in Australia, and has a scruffy appearance and often no tail streamers. Attains full plumage before departing. Often associates with WELCOME SWALLOW. Rests on powerlines in open areas and open farmland. *May be confused with:* NONE. Even in moult has distinct whitish underparts.

WELCOME SWALLOW
Hirundo neoxena   15 cm
Small; blue-black upperparts; grey below; **rusty crown, throat and face;** deeply forked tail. Juvenile: almost no rust colour about head; short tail. Open areas, farmland, urban areas, often resting on powerlines. *May be confused with:* PACIFIC SWALLOW which has a shorter tail and different tail pattern. See p. 203.

PACIFIC SWALLOW *Hirundo pacifica*   13 cm
Almost identical to WELCOME SWALLOW with which it sometimes associates. Similar habitat. *May be confused with:* WELCOME SWALLOW which has longer tail and different tail pattern. See p. 203.

FURTHER POSSIBILITIES
SPINY-CHEEKED HONEYEATER — vagrant to extreme south of region.

POSSIBILITIES

KING QUAIL   *Coturnix chinensis*   (Male) 13 cm
Dark-coloured shy ground bird, appearing tailless;
brown back; **blue-grey breast and flanks; chestnut
belly; black and white throat pattern.** Farmland
and open grassy areas, also grassy casuarina forest and
sometimes wetter grassland about swamps.

BLACK-FRONTED DOTTEREL
Elseyornis melanops   17 cm
Freshwater wader; greyish-brown above; white below;
**black forehead; black band through eye connecting
with black breastband** which when viewed from the
front forms a **bold 'Y'** on breast; large white throat
patch; **red eye-ring.** Riverbeds, muddy margins of
freshwater swamps, lakes, dams and sewage ponds. *May
be confused with:* Perhaps RED-KNEED DOTTEREL,
but look for red eye-ring and greyish crown.

RED-KNEED DOTTEREL *Erythrogonys cinctus* 18cm
Greyish wader; **prominent black head and
breastband separated by large white throat patch;**
chestnut flanks. Bobs head. Mainly muddy edges of
lakes and swamps — fresh and brackish.
May be confused with: Perhaps BLACK-FRONTED
DOTTEREL, but look for black head, broad black
breastband and absence of eye-ring.

FERNWREN *Oreoscopus gutturalis*   13 cm
Rich olive-brown upperparts; slightly paler below; **white
eyebrow and throat, margined below by small black
'bib';** longish bill. Upland rainforest, usually above
600 m, sometimes lower. *May be confused with:*
YELLOW-THROATED and WHITE-BROWED
SCRUBWRENS, but look for dark eye and black 'bib'.

WHITE-BROWED SCRUBWREN
Sericornis frontalis   13 cm
Brown above; paler below; **white eyebrow over a
pale yellow eye; two small white markings on
shoulder.** Female: duller than male. Denser eucalypt
forest and rainforest **edges** in upland areas.
May be confused with: FERNWREN and YELLOW-
THROATED SCRUBWREN, but look for pale eye and
white throat without a black 'bib'.

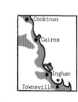

FAIRY GERYGONE
Gerygone palpebrosa   (Female) 11 cm
Greenish above; lemon underparts; **whitish throat
merging into pale lemon breast.** Lowland rainforest,
gallery forest, coastal vine scrubs and mangroves.
Usually below 500 m. *May be confused with:* WHITE-
THROATED GERYGONE which has well-demarcated
white throat. Juvenile WHITE-THROATED lacks white
throat. WHITE-THROATED usually does not occur in
denser habitats preferred by the FAIRY.

WHITE-THROATED GERYGONE
Gerygone olivacea   11 cm
Small; brown back; **yellow breast and belly; well-demarcated white throat** — only adult has white throat; **beautiful song.** Eucalypt forest and woodland. *May be confused with:* Female FAIRY GERYGONE. Look for demarcated white throat.

EASTERN SPINEBILL
Acanthorhynchus tenuirostris   15 cm
Active; blackish head; **rufous patch in white throat; long, fine curved bill;** rufous belly; shows much white in tail in flight. Frequently hovers at blossom. Rainforest and nearby eucalypt forest at higher altitudes.

PALE-YELLOW ROBIN
Tregellasia capito   13 cm
Small; unobtrusive; greenish-grey upperparts; **greenish-yellow** underparts; **buff from bill to eye; white throat.** Rainforest at all altitudes.

GOLDEN WHISTLER
Pachycephala pectoralis   (Male) 17 cm
Olive-green upperparts; yellow underparts; **black head; prominent white throat bordered with a black band across breast.** Rainforest at higher altitudes, sometimes coastal in winter. *May be confused with:* Male MANGROVE GOLDEN WHISTLER See p. 202.

MANGROVE GOLDEN WHISTLER
Pachycephala melanura   (Male) 16 cm
Only known population is about Hinchinbrook Channel. Similar to GOLDEN WHISTLER. Mangroves. *May be confused with:* Male GOLDEN WHISTLER. See p. 202.

RUFOUS WHISTLER
Pachycephala rufiventris   (Male) 17 cm
Rufous breast extending to under tail; white throat margined black; greyish back. Open eucalypt forest and woodland.

GREY FANTAIL   *Rhipidura fuliginosa*   16 cm
Small dark-grey active bird; pale buff belly; **large fanned tail;** white tip and shafts to each tail feather; white throat bordered by dark band; **short thick white eyebrow; white line behind eye.** Resident race *keasti* from upland rainforest is **darker** and slightly smaller than wintering southern race which inhabits open forest, woodland, mangroves and denser parks and gardens. *May be confused with:* NORTHERN FANTAIL, but look for thick white eyebrow and white mark behind eye. NORTHERN has a fine eyebrow only.

NORTHERN FANTAIL *Rhipidura rufiventris* 17 cm
Similar to GREY FANTAIL, but tail is less fanned;
more upright posture; broader duller breastband; **fine
white eyebrow only; no white line behind eye.**
Margins of rainforest, denser woodland, mangroves
and melaleuca woodland, moreso at lower altitudes.
May be confused with: GREY FANTAIL, but look for
fine white eyebrow and absence of white behind eye.

SMALL & MEDIUM-SIZED BIRDS WITH A BLACK OR DARK BREASTBAND
POSSIBILITIES

BLACK-FRONTED DOTTEREL
Elseyornis melanops 17 cm
Small freshwater wader; greyish-brown; white below;
**black forehead; black band through eye connecting
with black breastband** which when viewed from the
front forms a **bold 'Y'** on breast; large white throat
patch; **red eye-ring.** Riverbeds, muddy margins of
freshwater swamps, lakes, dams, sewage ponds. *May be
confused with:* Perhaps RED-KNEED DOTTEREL, but
look for red eye-ring and greyish crown.

RED-KNEED DOTTEREL
Erythrogonys cinctus 18 cm
Small greyish wader; **prominent black head and
breastband separated by large white throat patch;**
chestnut flanks. Bobs head. Mainly muddy edges of
lakes and swamps — fresh and brackish. *May be
confused with:* Perhaps BLACK-FRONTED
DOTTEREL, but look for black head, broad black
breastband and absence of eye-ring.

BANDED HONEYEATER
Certhionyx pectoralis 13 cm
Black upperparts; white underparts; white rump; **thin
black band across breast.** Dry open forest and
woodland, especially where eucalypts and paperbarks
are flowering.

GOLDEN WHISTLER
Pachycephala pectoralis (Male) 17 cm
Small; olive-green upperparts; yellow underparts;
**black head; prominent white throat bordered with
a black band across breast.** Rainforest at higher
altitudes, sometimes coastal in winter.
May be confused with: Male MANGROVE GOLDEN
WHISTLER. See p. 202.

MANGROVE GOLDEN WHISTLER
Pachycephala melanura (Male) 16 cm
Only known population is about Hinchinbrook
Channel. Similar to male GOLDEN WHISTLER.
Mangroves. *May be confused with:* Male GOLDEN
WHISTLER. See p. 202.

RUFOUS WHISTLER
Pachycephala rufiventris (Male) 17 cm
Small; greyish back; **rufous breast extending to under tail; white throat margined black across breast.** Open eucalypt forest and woodland.

PIED MONARCH *Arses kaupi* 14 cm
Small; white collar; erectile frill on nape; **wide black breastband on white underparts; blue eye-ring.** Female: broader breastband, incomplete collar and greyish nape. Rainforest, moreso at lower altitudes.

GREY FANTAIL *Rhipidura fuliginosa* 16 cm
Small dark-grey active bird; pale buff belly; **large fanned tail;** white tip and shafts to each tail feather, white throat bordered by dark band; **short thick white eyebrow; white line behind eye.** Resident race *keasti* from upland rainforest is **darker** and slightly smaller than wintering southern race which inhabits open forest, woodland, mangroves and denser parks and gardens. *May be confused with:* NORTHERN FANTAIL, but look for thick white eyebrow and white mark behind eye.

NORTHERN FANTAIL *Rhipidura rufiventris* 17cm
Similar to GREY FANTAIL, but tail is less fanned; more upright posture; broader duller breastband; **fine white eyebrow only; no white line behind eye.** Margins of rainforest, denser woodland, mangroves and melaleuca woodland, moreso at lower altitudes. *May be confused with:* GREY FANTAIL.

DOUBLE-BARRED FINCH
Taeniopygia bichenovii 10 cm
Small; brown back; white face and underparts; black wings heavily spotted white; **two thin black bars across breast.** Grassy woodland, open forest, parks and gardens.

CHESTNUT-BREASTED MANNIKIN
Lonchura castaneothorax 10 cm
Small; appears brownish initially; **large black mask extending to throat; chestnut breast with a black band below;** creamy belly; yellowish-brown rump and tail. Grassland, reedy areas, grassy roadsides, sugarcane fields and farmland.

BARN SWALLOW *Hirundo rustica* 16 cm
Summer visitor, present Nov.–Mar.; blue-black upperparts; **whitish underparts; black breastband; rusty-red throat and forehead;** long, deeply forked tail.The BARN SWALLOW is in moult when it first arrives in Australia, and has a scruffy appearance and often no tail streamers. Attains full plumage before departing. Often associates with WELCOME SWALLOW. Rests on powerlines in open areas and open farmland.

FURTHER POSSIBILITIES
BANDED LAPWING — rare.

POSSIBILITIES

RADJAH SHELDUCK
Tadorna radjah   54 cm
Rare; large bird; brown back; completely white head
and underparts; **thin chestnut breastband.** Lagoons,
swamps, river margins, tidal creeks, mudflats.

WHITE-NECKED HERON *Ardea pacifica* 87 cm
Very large wading bird with long thin neck; glossy-
black body; white head and neck; **black bill and legs;
conspicuous white patch on leading edge of wing
in flight.** Looks very large in flight and sometimes
resembles a bird of prey at a height. Shallow freshwater
swamps, dams, edges of streams and lakes, sometimes
open grassland. *May be confused with:* The smaller
juvenile PIED HERON, but look for black bill and legs.

PIED HERON *Ardea picata* (Juvenile) 46 cm
Rare; large wading bird with long thin neck; blue-
black body; dull-white head and neck; **yellow bill
and legs.** Freshwater swamps and lagoons, pastures,
mudflats, mangroves and tidal rivers.
May be confused with: the larger WHITE-NECKED
HERON, but look for yellow bill and legs.

OSPREY *Pandion haliaetus* Male 53cm Female 63 cm
Large fishing bird of prey; dark brown back, wings
and tail; white head and underparts; **heavy dark line
through eye and down neck; broken brownish
band across breast** generally heavier in female.
Coastal waters, estuaries, offshore islands, sometimes
larger rivers and lakes.

BRAHMINY KITE
Haliastur indus 48 cm
Large; deep-chestnut back, wings, lower body and tail;
conspicuous white head and breast. Mangroves,
estuaries, larger rivers, but sometimes open forest and
open areas some kilometres inland.

WHITE-HEADED PIGEON
Columba leucomela 40 cm
Medium-sized; white head and underparts; **black
back, wings and tail; red bill; red about eye.**
Rainforest at all altitudes, but moreso in higher areas.

WOMPOO FRUIT-DOVE
Ptilinopus magnificus 37 cm
Large colourful pigeon of mid and upper strata of
rainforest; green upperparts; **greyish-white head;
purple breast; yellow belly.** Rainforest at all
altitudes, occasionally in tropical woodland.

PALE-HEADED ROSELLA
Platycercus adscitus   30 cm
Medium-sized; **pale yellow to white head and throat; red under tail-coverts;** greenish-blue belly; blue edges to wings; yellow and black back; long tail. Eucalypt forest, tropical woodland, lightly timbered grassland.

BIRDS WITH A LONG BILL – EXCLUDING SHOREBIRDS
POSSIBILITIES

AUSTRALIAN PELICAN
Pelecanus conspicillatus   165 cm
Well-known huge black and white waterbird; **enormous flesh-coloured bill;** black flight feathers, shoulders, rump and tail; white head and underparts. Larger areas of deeper fresh water, also along foreshore.

GREAT-BILLED HERON
Ardea sumatrana   105 cm
Very large grey-brown aquatic bird; **large dark sharp bill,** dull yellow at base of lower mandible; **pale throat;** long thin neck; flies with neck folded; **yellow eye.** Mostly mangrove forests and associated tidal channels, mudbanks and freshwater rivers and creeks. *May be confused with:* Juvenile BLACK-NECKED STORK, but look for pale throat and yellow eye and long thin neck, folded in flight.

GLOSSY IBIS *Plegadis falcinellus*   55 cm
Large wading bird; appears black at a distance but is **dark reddish-brown;** purple-green sheen on wings; **long black curved bill.** Shallow freshwater swamps, sometimes mangroves and mudflats. *May be confused with:* Generally NONE, but can be confused with LITTLE BLACK CORMORANT in flight. Look for drooping, extended neck and more downcurved wings.

AUSTRALIAN WHITE IBIS
Threskiornis molucca   70 cm
Large mostly white wading bird; **bare black head; black tail; long curved black bill;** plumage often soiled. Shallow fresh water, grassland, tidal flats, mangroves and urban parks.

STRAW-NECKED IBIS
Threskiornis spinicollis   70 cm
Large wading bird; black back; white neck and underparts; **bare black head; long curved black bill.** Adult: yellow straw-like plumes on neck. Wet or dry grassland, pasture, swamps and urban parks.

ROYAL SPOONBILL *Platalea regia* 77 cm
Large white wading bird; **long black bill spoon-shaped at tip; black legs;** black face; breeding birds develop a long tuft on back of head — usually Sept.–Mar. Fresh, brackish or saltwater swamps, mudflats and mangroves.

YELLOW-BILLED SPOONBILL
Platalea flavipes 83 cm
Similar to ROYAL SPOONBILL, but with **pale yellow bill and legs.** Does not develop breeding tuft. Similar habitat.

BLACK-NECKED STORK
Ephippiorhynchus asiaticus (Adult) 120 cm
Huge black and white wading bird with long red legs; black head and neck; large heavy black bill. In flight, appears mostly white with black wingbar. Flies with neck outstretched. Usually freshwater swamps, sometimes estuaries and mangroves.

BLACK-NECKED STORK
Ephippiorhynchus asiaticus (Juvenile) 120 cm
Huge long-legged grey-brown wading bird; **heavy long bill; grey face; black eye.** Flies with neck outstretched. Usually freshwater swamps, sometimes estuaries and mangroves. *May be confused with:* GREAT-BILLED HERON, but look for heavy bill, long legs, black eye and extended neck in flight.

RED-NECKED AVOCET
Recurvirostra novaehollandiae 44 cm
Large distinctive black and white wading bird with **rufous head and upper neck; long, upcurved fine black bill.** Freshwater swamps, sometimes river beds, estuaries, mudflats and other saline areas.

AZURE KINGFISHER *Alcedo azurea* 18 cm
Small; **deep blue head, back and wings;** disproportionately-long thin black bill; short tail; **completely orange underparts.** Freshwater streams, especially in rainforest. Sometimes in mangroves.

LITTLE KINGFISHER *Alcedo pusilla* 13 cm
Tiny; **deep blue head, back, wings, tail and sides of breast;** disproportionately-long thin black bill; short tail; white underparts; **white tuft on side of neck.** Rather elusive. Mangroves, sometimes along freshwater creeks in rainforest. *May be confused with:* The larger FOREST KINGFISHER which is often mistaken for LITTLE KINGFISHER perches openly on powerlines, posts, open limbs. Look for white neck tuft and noticeably tiny size.

FURTHER POSSIBILITIES
EASTERN SPINEBILL
VICTORIA'S RIFLEBIRD

POSSIBILITIES

BUFF-BANDED RAIL *Gallirallus philippensis* 31cm
Medium-sized shy brownish ground bird; chestnut crown and stripe through eye; **grey eyebrow; chestnut patch on breast; extensive fine barring** on underparts. Dense damp grassland and vegetation about swamps and streams. *May be confused with:* The rare LEWIN'S RAIL, but look for grey eyebrow and chestnut on breast.

LEWIN'S RAIL *Rallus pectoralis* 22 cm
Rare medium-sized shy ground bird; dark upperparts; **rich chestnut head and nape** with black streaks; **slate-grey throat and breast;** barred wings, belly and under tail-coverts; **long black-tipped pink bill.** Damp grassland and reedy swamps.
May be confused with: BUFF-BANDED RAIL, but look for long bill, absence of eyebrow, and slate-grey extending from throat to upper belly.

DUSKY MOORHEN *Gallinula tenebrosa* 39 cm
Medium-sized, short-tailed aquatic bird; dark olive-brown; **red head shield, red bill tipped yellow; two white markings under tail** distinguish it from all other aquatic birds. Freshwater swamps, lakes, creeks, dams — especially those with open aquatic vegetation. *May be confused with:* PURPLE SWAMPHEN which has heavier all-red bill and all-white under tail.

BLACK-FRONTED DOTTEREL
Elseyornis melanops 17 cm
Freshwater wader; greyish-brown above; white below; **black forehead; black band through eye connecting with black breastband** which when viewed from the front forms a **bold 'Y'** on breast; large white throat patch; **red eye-ring.** Riverbeds, muddy margins of freshwater swamps, lakes, dams and sewage ponds. *May be confused with:* Perhaps RED-KNEED DOTTEREL, but look for red eye-ring and greyish crown.

RED-KNEED DOTTEREL
Erythrogonys cinctus 18 cm
Small greyish wader; **prominent black head and breastband separated by large white throat patch;** chestnut flanks. Bobs head. Mainly muddy edges of lakes and swamps — fresh and brackish.
May be confused with: Perhaps BLACK-FRONTED DOTTEREL, but look for black head, broad black breastband and absence of eye-ring.

WHITE-HEADED PIGEON
Columba leucomela 40 cm
Medium-sized; white head and underparts; **black back, wings and tail; red bill; red about eye.** Rainforest at all altitudes, but moreso in higher areas.

EMERALD DOVE *Chalcophaps indica* 26 cm
Medium-sized plump, ground-feeding bird or small pigeon; brown head and body; **deep green iridescent wings; red bill and legs;** white shoulder patch; **two white bars on lower back** obvious in flight. Rainforest at all altitudes.

RAINBOW LORIKEET
Trichoglossus haematodus 28 cm
The most common parrot; medium-sized; green back, wings and tail; **deep blue head; orange breast and bill.** Noisy. Eucalypt forest, rainforest edges, open areas, parks and gardens.

SCALY-BREASTED LORIKEET
Trichoglossus chlorolepidotus 23 cm
Medium-sized overall green bird; **yellowish 'scaly' pattern on breast; red bill; orange under wings in flight.** Strong direct flight. Eucalypt forest, parks and gardens, wherever there is blossom.

RED-WINGED PARROT
Aprosmictus erythropterus 32 cm
Medium-sized **pale green** bird. Male: **spectacular red wing patch;** black back; blue rump. Female: small duller red wing patch; blue rump. Open drier woodland and lightly timbered country.

BUFF-BREASTED PARADISE-KINGFISHER
Tanysiptera sylvia 34 cm
Migrant, present Nov.–early Apr.; **distinctively spectacular;** thick red bill; brilliant blue and black above; rufous-orange below; centre of back and rump white; **two very long, stiff, white tail feathers,** sometimes broken-off during or after breeding. Mostly lowland rainforest.

DOLLARBIRD *Eurystomus orientalis* 29 cm
Migrant, present late Sept.–Apr/May; medium-sized; plump; short tail; overall dark greyish to greenish-blue; thin blue stripe along edge of wing; **broad red bill; red feet; shows large white spot in each wing in flight.** Sparsely timbered areas — especially along watercourses, open woodland and farmland.

PAINTED HONEYEATER *Grantiella picta* 16 cm
Rare; blackish upperparts; white underparts; **broad yellow margins to flight and tail feathers; pinkish-red bill.** Drier open forest and woodland mostly in western areas.

YELLOW ORIOLE *Oriolus flavocinctus* (Adult) 28cm
Medium-sized **yellow-green bird with some striations; red bill and eye; edges of wing feathers and tail tip yellow.** Rainforest, gallery forest at low altitudes, and mangroves. *May be confused with:* OLIVE-BACKED ORIOLE, but look for overall yellow-green colouration and yellow tips and edges to wing feathers.

OLIVE-BACKED ORIOLE
Oriolus sagittatus (Adult) 27 cm
Medium-sized bird; olive-green back; dusky-grey or brownish wings; white underparts with **'tear-drop' shaped markings; red eye and bill.** Eucalypt forest and tropical woodland. *May be confused with:* YELLOW ORIOLE, but look for white underparts with 'tear-drop' striations.

ZEBRA FINCH
Taeniopygia guttata 10 cm
Small red-billed bird. Male: greyish; **finely barred throat and breast; chestnut sides of body spotted white;** chestnut ear patch. Female: plain greyish; white face. Grassland studded with shrubs and small trees.

CRIMSON FINCH
Neochmia phaeton 13 cm
Small; long-tailed. Male: striking **deep-crimson face, rump and underparts;** black belly; brown tail washed crimson. Female: greyish-brown, **dull crimson face, throat, rump and tail.** Coastal paperbark swamps, rank grass and edges of sugar-cane fields. *May be confused with:* Male: NONE. Female: sometimes misidentified as STAR FINCH, but look for unspotted face and breast.

STAR FINCH *Neochmia ruficauda* 11 cm
Probably extinct in the Wet Tropics region. **Conspicuous red face and bill;** olive back and breast; whitish belly; dull reddish-brown tail; **white spotting on lower face, breast, sides of body and rump.** Immature: grey head and face. Rank vegetation along watercourses and wet areas, e.g. reeds in eucalypt forest and woodland. *May be confused with:* Female CRIMSON FINCH which is sometimes misidentified as STAR FINCH, but look for well-spotted face and breast.

RED-BROWED FINCH
Neochmia temporalis 11 cm
Small olive-green and grey bird; **red rump, bill and eyebrow.** Usually gregarious. Margins of rainforest, regrowth, and adjacent shrubby and grassy areas.

FURTHER POSSIBILITIES
GULLS, see pp. 189–90.
TERNS, see pp. 190–3.
Male KING-PARROT has part-red bill which is overshadowed by its spectacular plumage.
SPINY-CHEEKED HONEYEATER — vagrant to extreme south of region.
BROWN-BACKED HONEYEATER has a pinkish-brown bill.

POSSIBILITIES

BLACK SWAN
Cygnus atratus   125 cm
Well-known very large, distinctive and graceful
waterbird; black; **long neck; bright red bill;** shows
white wing feathers in flight. Nearly always on water.
Larger expanses of open water — mostly fresh water.

PURPLE SWAMPHEN   *Porphyrio porphyrio* 49cm
Large aquatic bird; dark purplish-blue; **thick red bill;
large red head shield; all-white under tail-coverts.**
Margins of lakes, swamps and nearby grassland.
May be confused with: Possibly DUSKY MOORHEN
which has two white markings under tail, red bill
tipped yellow. Look for thick all-red bill and all-white
under tail.

PIED OYSTERCATCHER
Haematopus longirostris   50 cm
Distinctive large black and white shorebird; black
head, back, wings and tail; white breast, belly and
under tail-coverts; conspicuous **red bill, eye-ring,
legs and feet.** Mostly sandy beaches, also mudflats
and estuaries.

SOOTY OYSTERCATCHER
Haematopus fuliginosus   50 cm
Similar to PIED OYSTERCATCHER, but **overall
sooty-black.** Rocky coastlines, exposed reef flats —
mostly on offshore islands.

WOMPOO FRUIT-DOVE
Ptilinopus magnificus   37 cm
Large colourful pigeon of mid and upper strata of
rainforest; green upperparts; **greyish-white head;
purple breast; yellow belly.** Rainforest at all
altitudes, occasionally in tropical woodland.

TOPKNOT PIGEON
Lopholaimus antarcticus   43 cm
Large overall-grey pigeon: **prominent chestnut 'bun'
on back of head; black tail with whitish band.**
Often flies above canopy — sometimes high.
Rainforest, moreso at higher altitudes.

FURTHER POSSIBILITIES
RED-TAILED TROPICBIRD
CATTLE and INTERMEDIATE EGRETS develop red or orange
bills during the breeding season. See EGRETS, pp. 196–7.
GULLS, see pp. 189–90.
TERNS, see pp. 190–3.

POSSIBILITIES

ORANGE-FOOTED SCRUBFOWL
Megapodius reinwardt 40 cm
A large plain ground bird; dark slate-grey head, neck and upperparts; chestnut-brown above; prominent **crest on back of head;** powerful **orange legs and feet.** Rainforest, moreso at lower altitudes, coastal vine scrubs, also mangroves.

GREAT CRESTED GREBE
Podiceps cristatus 50 cm
Large brown and white aquatic bird appearing tailless; **rufous, black-tipped ruff or frill about neck, long crest-like ear tufts** in breeding plumage (Sept.–Mar.); ruff and ear tufts somewhat subdued in non-breeding plumage. Lakes and larger areas of fresh water.

PIED HERON   *Ardea picata*   (Adult) 46 cm
Rare wading bird; blue-black body; long thin white neck; white cheeks and throat; **black crown and crest;** long thin sharp **yellow bill and legs.** Freshwater swamps and lagoons, pasture, mudflats, mangroves and tidal rivers.

PACIFIC BAZA
Aviceda subcristata   Male 37 cm Female 44 cm
Large grey bird; **reddish-brown barring on belly; small upright crest on back of head; large yellow eye.** Open forest, rainforest (especially the edges), gallery forest and forested farmland.

LESSER CRESTED TERN
Sterna bengalensis 39 cm
Similar to CRESTED TERN, but smaller and paler, with **orange bill.** Islands, reefs, cays and ocean beaches. *May be confused with:* CRESTED TERN which has yellow bill.

CRESTED TERN *Sterna bergii* 47 cm
Large marine bird; grey wings, back and tail; white underparts; **yellow bill;** black legs. In breeding season **crown is black with shaggy black crest on nape.** Bays, inlets, tidal rivers, sandy beaches and offshore islands. *May be confused with:* LESSER CRESTED TERN which has orange bill.

CRESTED PIGEON *Ocyphaps lophotes* 33 cm
Medium-sized overall grey bird; **erect dark crest; red about eye; red legs;** iridescent-bronze and green patch on wings. Feeds on ground. Open, sparsely timbered areas and about farmhouses.

TOPKNOT PIGEON
Lopholaimus antarcticus   43 cm
Large, overall grey pigeon; **prominent chestnut 'bun' on back of head; black tail with whitish band.**
Often flies above canopy — sometimes high. Rainforest, moreso at higher altitudes. *May be confused with:* NONE. Look for white tail band in flight.

RED-TAILED BLACK-COCKATOO
Calyptorhynchus banksii   56 cm
Large black bird; **broad red panels in tail** visible only when tail is spread. Male: dark grey bill; rounded crest. Female: whitish bill; fine yellow spots and barring in plumage; tail panels more yellow-orange, finely barred black. Open forest, woodland, sometimes over rainforest, and about cities and towns.

SULPHUR-CRESTED COCKATOO
Cacatua galerita   49 cm
Large white bird; **obvious yellow crest on back of head** spectacular when erect; small black eye in white face. Often extremely noisy. Most habitats at all altitudes.

COCKATIEL
Nymphicus hollandicus   32 cm
Medium-sized; grey, long-tailed parrot; **upright yellow crest; large white shoulder patch.** Male: large yellow cheek patch; orange ear patch. Female: much duller. Open, drier woodland and lightly timbered country.

EASTERN WHIPBIRD
Psophodes olivaceus 27 cm
Medium-sized; dark olive-green body. Adult: black head; **white cheek patches; small black crest** sometimes carried flat on back of head; **long tail.** Juvenile: overall olive-brown; brown crest. Lower stratum of rainforest at higher altitudes, sometimes adjacent eucalypt forest. Sometimes coastal.

CRESTED SHRIKE-TIT
Falcunculus frontatus   18 cm
Small bird with olive-green back; yellow breast; **black head with white markings; black crest.** Male: black throat. Female: olive-green throat. Drier eucalypt forest and woodland. *May be confused with:* Males of GOLDEN and MANGROVE GOLDEN WHISTLERS, but look for crest and black or olive-green throat.

FURTHER POSSIBILITIES
ROYAL SPOONBILL develops a tuft of white feathers on the back of the head during the breeding season.
LITTLE EAGLE has a partial crest.
SHINING FLYCATCHER sometimes erects feathers on head to form a small crest.

POSSIBILITIES

BLACK-EARED CUCKOO
Chrysococcyx osculans 19 cm
Small rather inconspicuous brownish-grey bird; paler
below; **curved black mark through eye; thick white
eyebrow; pale rump;** white tail tip. Drier woodland
and open forest. *May be confused with:* Juvenile
HORSFIELD'S BRONZE-CUCKOO which is smaller;
browner; has dark rump; eyebrow almost absent;
rufous margin to upper tail feathers. Look for thick
eyebrow and pale rump and tail tip.

BLACK-FACED MONARCH
Monarcha melanopsis 18 cm
Migrant, usually present Sept.–Mar./Apr.; mostly grey
flycatcher; **rufous belly and under tail-coverts; grey
breast sharply demarcated from belly; grey tail;**
black forehead and throat. (Juvenile lacks black facial
markings.) Rainforest, moreso at higher altitudes.
Often in more open country on migration. *May be
confused with:* BLACK-WINGED and SPECTACLED
MONARCHS, but look for grey wings and grey tail.

BLACK-WINGED MONARCH *Monarcha frater* 18 cm
Rare in the Wet Tropics region; present on northern
Cape York Peninsula Oct.–Apr.; similar to BLACK-
FACED MONARCH, but with **black wings and tail
and silver-grey upperparts.** *May be confused with:*
BLACK-FACED and SPECTACLED MONARCHS, but
look for black wings and tail.

SPECTACLED MONARCH
Monarcha trivirgatus 16 cm
Grey back; **rufous breast; white belly;** black forehead
and throat; black mask about eyes; **black tail with
broad white corners.** (Juvenile lacks black about the
face.) Rainforest at all altitudes. *May be confused with:*
BLACK-FACED and BLACK-WINGED MONARCHS
but look for rufous breast, white belly and tail corners.

BLACK-FACED CUCKOO-SHRIKE
Coracina novaehollandiae 33 cm
An immaculate medium-sized grey bird; **refolds wings
on alighting.** Adult: **large prominent black face.**
Immature: **broad black line through and behind
eye only.** Eucalypt forest and woodland, open and
urban areas. *May be confused with:* Adult: NONE.
Immature: WHITE-BELLIED CUCKOO-SHRIKE.
Look for black mark extending well behind eye.

WHITE-BELLIED CUCKOO-SHRIKE
Coracina papuensis 28 cm
A medium-sized plain grey bird; **refolds wings on
alighting; black mark between bill and eye;** white
part eye-ring behind eye. Open forest, woodland, open
areas, mangroves, sometimes urban areas.
May be confused with: Immature BLACK-FACED
CUCKOO-SHRIKE, but look for black mark extending
only to eye, and white part eye-ring.

MASKED WOODSWALLOW

Artamus personatus 19 cm

Medium-sized mid-grey bird; paler below; **bluish bill;** grey tail tipped white, frequently wagged. Male: **large black face edged white.** Female: **subdued dusky-grey face.** Drier open lightly timbered country. *May be confused with:* Male: NONE. Female and juvenile: BLACK-FACED WOODSWALLOW, but look for large dusky-grey face and grey tail.

BLACK-FACED WOODSWALLOW

Artamus cinereus 18 cm

Smoky-grey; **bluish bill; small black face; black tail tipped white;** white under tail-coverts. Tail frequently wagged. Open, lightly timbered areas and almost treeless grassland. *May be confused with:* Female and juvenile MASKED WOODSWALLOW, but look for small black face and black tail.

CHESTNUT-BREASTED MANNIKIN

Lonchura castaneothorax 10 cm

Appears brownish initially; **large black mask extending to throat; chestnut breast with a black band below;** creamy belly; yellowish-brown rump and tail. Grassland, reedy areas, grassy roadsides, sugar-cane fields and farmland.

FURTHER POSSIBILITIES
AUSTRALIAN HOBBY
PEREGRINE FALCON
BLACK-FRONTED DOTTEREL
SINGING HONEYEATER — vagrant.
Male HOUSE SPARROW — mostly about urban areas.

BIRDS WITH BLACK & WHITE FACIAL MARKINGS
POSSIBILITIES

SQUATTER PIGEON *Geophaps scripta* 30 cm
Medium-sized; dull brown; broad white stripe bordering wings to flanks and belly; **prominent black and white facial pattern; tan eye-ring.** Drier open grassy woodland and open forest. *May be confused with:* Perhaps COMMON BRONZEWING which lacks the strong facial pattern and eye-ring.

NOISY MINER *Manorina melanocephala* 27 cm
Pesky, medium-sized grey bird; **black mask about eye and over crown;** white forehead and throat; yellow spot behind eye; yellow bill; **grey rump.** Open drier eucalypt forest. *May be confused with:* YELLOW-THROATED MINER which has yellow forehead and crown and a conspicuous and diagnostic white rump.

CRESTED SHRIKE-TIT
Falcunculus frontatus 18 cm
Small; olive-green back; yellow breast; **black head with white markings; black crest.** Male: black throat. Female: olive-green throat. Usually high in foliage. Drier eucalypt forest and woodland. *May be confused with:* Males of GOLDEN and MANGROVE GOLDEN WHISTLERS, but look for black crest and black or olive-green throat. All three prefer distinct habitats.

WHITE-EARED MONARCH
Monarcha leucotis 13 cm
Small, black white and greyish bird; **greyish-white underparts;** black tail tipped white; **three white patches about eye in black head.** Coastal rainforest, sometimes upland rainforest. *May be confused with:* Perhaps VARIED TRILLER which has buff lower belly and under tail-coverts.

FURTHER POSSIBILITIES
Male KING QUAIL
FLOCK BRONZEWING — vagrant.

BIRDS WITH BLUE FACIAL MARKINGS
POSSIBILITIES

PEACEFUL DOVE *Geopelia striata* 20 cm
Small grey long-tailed bird; **fine black barring on breast, hind neck and wings; blue eye-ring.** Often sitting on powerlines. Eucalypt woodland, lightly timbered grassland, open forest, parks and gardens. *May be confused with:* DIAMOND DOVE which has red eye-ring and no barring.

LITTLE CORELLA *Cacatua sanguinea* 38 cm
Medium-sized white cockatoo; **white bill; bare bluish eye patch;** short crest. Usually in flocks. Open forest, open grassy areas, sometimes outskirts of urban areas.

DOUBLE-EYED FIG-PARROT
Cyclopsitta diophthalma 14 cm
Small mostly all-green parrot; very short tail; **thick dark bill;** colourful facial pattern. Male: **red cheek and forehead, blue about eye.** Female: similar to male, but face mainly blue with buffy cheek patch. Rainforest at most altitudes, but mainly in the lowlands, often breeding in nearby paperbark swamps. *May be confused with:* LITTLE LORIKEET, but look for thick dark bill, some blue on face and very short tail.

PALE-HEADED ROSELLA
Platycercus adscitus 30 cm
Medium-sized; colourful long-tailed bird; **pale yellow to white head and throat; red under tail-coverts;** greenish-blue belly; blue edges to wings; yellow and black back. Eucalypt forest, tropical woodland and lightly timbered grassland.

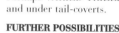
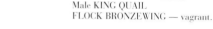

BLUE-FACED HONEYEATER
Entomyzon cyanotis 28 cm
Medium-sized; olive-green back and wings; white
underparts; **narrow dark smudgy mark on throat
and breast; large patch of blue skin about eye**
(green in juvenile). Shows pale patch in each wing in
flight. Dry woodland and eucalypt forest.

WHITE-THROATED HONEYEATER
Melithreptus albogularis 14 cm
Small; olive-green back, wings and tail; white
underparts; black head; white line across nape; **blue
crescent above eye.** Eucalypt forest and tropical
woodland, moreso in lowlands. *May be confused with:*
BLACK-CHINNED HONEYEATER, which has dark chin
and throat and pale blue crescent. WHITE-NAPED
HONEYEATER has red crescent above eye.

PIED MONARCH *Arses kaupi* 14 cm
Small; white collar; erectile frill on nape; **wide black
breastband on white underparts; blue eye-ring.**
Female: broader breastband; incomplete collar; greyish
nape. Rainforest, moreso at lower altitudes.

BLUE-FACED PARROT-FINCH
Erythrura trichroa 12 cm
Rare; **rich grass-green; blue face; dark reddish-
brown rump.** Face mid-blue in male, duller in female,
green in juvenile. Mostly rainforest at higher altitudes.

FURTHER POSSIBILITIES
LITTLE FRIARBIRD
The golden-backed race *laetior* of the BLACK-CHINNED
HONEYEATER has a blue eyebrow.

SMALL BIRDS WITH RED OR ORANGE FACIAL MARKINGS
POSSIBILITIES

LITTLE LORIKEET *Glossopsitta pusilla* 15 cm
Overall green parrot; **red forehead and throat; small
black bill;** short tail. Taller eucalypt forest, mainly at
higher altitudes. *May be confused with:* DOUBLE-
EYED FIG-PARROT, but look for red forehead and
throat in a green face.

DOUBLE-EYED FIG-PARROT
Cyclopsitta diophthalma 14 cm
Mostly all-green parrot; very short tail; **thick dark
bill;** colourful facial pattern. Male: **red cheeks and
forehead; blue about eye.** Female: similar to male,
but face mainly blue with buffy cheek patch; red
forehead. Rainforest at most altitudes, but mainly in
lowlands, often breeding in nearby paperbark swamps.
May be confused with: LITTLE LORIKEET, but look
for thick dark bill, some blue on face and very short
tail.

WHITE-NAPED HONEYEATER
Melithreptus lunatus 14 cm
Olive-green back, wings and tail; white underparts; black head; **white line across nape; red crescent above eye.** Eucalypt forest and edge of rainforest, e.g. at higher altitudes where stands of Flooded Gum *Eucalyptus grandis* are present. *May be confused with:* BLACK-CHINNED and WHITE-THROATED HONEYEATERS which have blue crescent above eye.

CRIMSON FINCH *Neochmia phaeton* (Female) 13 cm
Greyish-brown; **dull crimson face, throat, rump and tail.** Usually with the more spectacular males. Coastal paperbark swamps, rank grass and about the edges of sugar-cane fields. *May be confused with:* STAR FINCH but look for unspotted face and breast.

STAR FINCH *Neochmia ruficauda* 11 cm
Probably extinct in the Wet Tropics region.
Conspicuous red face and bill; olive back and breast; whitish belly; dull reddish-brown tail; **white spotting on lower face, breast, sides of body and rump.** Immature: grey head and face. Rank watercourse vegetation and wet areas, e.g. reeds in eucalypt forest and woodland. *May be confused with:* Female CRIMSON FINCH which is sometimes misidentified as STAR FINCH but look for well-spotted face and breast.

RED-BROWED FINCH
Neochmia temporalis 11 cm
Olive-green and grey; **red rump, bill and eyebrow.** Usually gregarious. Margins of rainforest, regrowth, and adjacent scrubby and grassy areas.

FURTHER POSSIBILITIES
BLACK-FRONTED DOTTEREL
DIAMOND DOVE
LITTLE and GOULD'S BRONZE-CUCKOOS
See also Birds with a Prominent Eye-ring, pp. 102–5.

MEDIUM-SIZED BIRDS WITH RED OR ORANGE FACIAL MARKINGS
POSSIBILITIES

BANDED LAPWING *Vanellus tricolor* 27 cm
Rare, medium-sized, ground-dwelling wading bird; brown back; black head; white underparts with **wide black breastband extending from sides of face;** white throat; yellow eye and bill; **small red wattle** on bill. Open bare areas, short grassland, farmland, aerodromes.

WHITE-HEADED PIGEON
Columba leucomela 40 cm
White head and underparts; **black back, wings and tail; red bill; red about eye.** Rainforest at all altitudes, but moreso in higher areas.

CRESTED PIGEON *Ocyphaps lophotes* 33 cm
Overall grey; **erect dark crest; red about eye; red legs;** iridescent-bronze and green patch on wings. Feeds on ground. Open sparsely timbered areas and about farmhouses.

COCKATIEL *Nymphicus hollandicus* 32 cm
Long-tailed grey parrot; **upright yellow crest; large white shoulder patch.** Male: large yellow cheek patch; orange ear patch. Female: much duller. Open, drier woodland and lightly timbered country.

FIGBIRD *Sphecotheres viridis* (Male) 28 cm
Deep olive-green back and wings; bright yellow underparts — greenish and variable in southern part of the Wet Tropics; black head; black tail with white edges; **large area of red skin about eye.** Feeds in fruiting trees. Rainforest edges and remnants, gallery forest, parks and gardens.

Northern race

Southern race

FURTHER POSSIBILITIES
DUSKY MOORHEN
COMB-CRESTED JACANA

SMALL BIRDS WITH WHITE FACIAL MARKINGS
POSSIBILITIES

WHITE-BROWED CRAKE *Porzana cinerea* 19cm
Aquatic bird; stubby tail; black and olive-brown upperparts; grey throat, neck and breast; white belly; **dark stripe through eye with white eyebrow and white stripe below eye.** Freshwater swamps, especially those with reedbeds and water-lilies, also rice fields and sometimes about sugar-cane fields. Moreso in the lowlands. *May be confused with:* The smaller BAILLON'S CRAKE which lacks white stripes about eye. WHITE-BROWED shows buffy flanks in flight.

FAIRY GERYGONE *Gerygone palpebrosa* (Male — northern race *personata* — north of Innisfail) 11 cm
Greenish above; lemon underparts; blackish-brown throat; prominent **white 'whisker' down side of face from bill.** Lowland rainforest, gallery forest, coastal vine scrub and mangroves.

WHITE-CHEEKED HONEYEATER
Phylidonyris nigra 18 cm
Black and white; boldly streaked underparts; **large white cheek patch; broad yellow panel in wing; yellow outer tail feathers.** Edges and clearings in upland rainforest, sometimes open forest with dense understorey, especially banksias, gardens.

SILVEREYE *Zosterops lateralis* 12 cm
Yellow-green, paler below; **prominent white ring around eye;** greyish breast and back. Rainforest margins, gallery forest, mangroves, parks and gardens.

FURTHER POSSIBILITIES
SPINY-CHEEKED HONEYEATER — vagrant to extreme south of region.
ZEBRA FINCH
GREY FANTAIL

MEDIUM-SIZED BIRDS WITH WHITE FACIAL MARKINGS
POSSIBILITIES

EURASIAN COOT *Fulica atra* 37 cm
Almost tailless aquatic bird; overall dark slate-grey; **white bill and head shield.** Open sheets of deep fresh water.

COMMON BRONZEWING
Phaps chalcoptera 34 cm
Rare, large, plump pigeon; overall brownish; **white stripe below eye;** metallic green and bronze patches in wings. Open dry woodland. *May be confused with:* Perhaps SQUATTER PIGEON, but look for white stripe below eye and no black about face.

EASTERN WHIPBIRD
Psophodes olivaceus (Adult) 27 cm
Dark olive-green body; black head; **white cheek patches; small black crest** sometimes carried flat on back of head; **long tail.** Lower stratum of rainforest at higher altitudes, occasionally adjacent eucalypt forest. Sometimes coastal.

MAGPIE-LARK
Grallina cyanoleuca (Female and Juvenile) 34 cm
Common distinctive **black and white bird; short white bill;** white eye; white forehead and throat. Juvenile: dark bill; brown eye. **Walks on ground with head-nodding movement.** Usually in vicinity of water in open areas, creeks, swamps, farmland, parks and gardens.

LARGE BIRDS WITH WHITE FACIAL MARKINGS
POSSIBILITIES

WHITE-FACED HERON
Egretta novaehollandiae 67 cm
Overall medium-grey wading bird; long thin neck; **white face and throat;** long sharp black bill; **yellow legs.** Shallow fresh water, short wet grassland, mudflats, parks and gardens. *May be confused with:* Grey phase of EASTERN REEF EGRET but look for white face and throat.

SQUARE-TAILED KITE *Lophoictinia isura* 53 cm
Rare, brown bird of prey; whitish face; long wings extend beyond tail at rest; in flight, **wings are upswept with dull whitish 'window' towards tip.** Open forest and woodland and over rainforest. *May be confused with:* Other birds of prey. See Diurnal Birds of Prey, pp. 175–81.

BUSH STONE-CURLEW
Burhinus grallarius 55 cm
Nocturnal; streaked greyish plumage; streaked buffy underparts; **whitish forehead and eyebrow; large yellow eyes;** long legs; ground-dwelling. Moves slowly and deliberately when disturbed by day. Open forest, open lightly timbered areas, often urban areas.

BEACH STONE-CURLEW *Esacus neglectus* 55 cm
Large, long-legged, ground-dwelling shorebird; brownish; **darker patch on shoulder, white bars surrounding it; black patch through eye with white stripe above and below;** heavy dark bill with yellow base; yellow eye. Undisturbed beaches, but moreso sandy mouths of creeks and rivers.

SMALL BIRDS WITH YELLOW FACIAL MARKINGS
POSSIBILITIES

STRIATED PARDALOTE
Pardalotus striatus 10 cm
Tiny, short-tailed bird; black wings; **white wing stripe; black crown;** buff rump; yellow throat; yellow spot in front of eye. Eucalypt forest and woodland, parks and gardens. *May be confused with:* Other pardalotes, but look for black crown, yellow spot in front of eye and white wing-stripe.

YELLOW-THROATED SCRUBWREN
Sericornis citreogularis 14 cm
Brown bird of the rainforest floor; **fine yellow eyebrow; yellow throat;** wide dark mark through eye; longish pink legs. Female: duller. Upland rainforest above 600 m, sometimes down to 300 m. *May be confused with:* FERNWREN and WHITE-BROWED SCRUBWREN, but look for yellow eyebrow and throat.

LEWIN'S HONEYEATER *Meliphaga lewinii* 20 cm
Overall olive-green bird; **pale yellow ear patch;** pale yellow line from bill to under eye. Rainforest and adjacent forest above about 450 m. *May be confused with:* YELLOW-SPOTTED and GRACEFUL HONEYEATERS. See pp. 201–2.

YELLOW-SPOTTED HONEYEATER
Meliphaga notata   18 cm
Similar to LEWIN'S HONEYEATER and difficult to
separate. Rainforest, adjacent eucalypt forest,
woodland and gardens, usually below about 600 m.
May be confused with: LEWIN'S and GRACEFUL
HONEYEATERS. See pp. 201–2.

GRACEFUL HONEYEATER
Meliphaga gracilis   15 cm
Similar to LEWIN'S HONEYEATER and difficult to
separate. Rainforest, gallery forest, adjacent eucalypt
forest and woodland, mostly below about 400 m.
May be confused with: LEWIN'S and YELLOW-
SPOTTED HONEYEATERS. See pp. 201–2.

BRIDLED HONEYEATER
Lichenostomus frenatus   20 cm
Appears as a brown bird with a **dark head;** dark
throat; yellow and white lines along dark bill to small
white patch behind eye; **small yellow tuft on ear;**
pale buff patch on side of neck. Active, aggressive and
noisy. Rainforest above 600 m. but to coast in winter.
May be confused with: Perhaps YELLOW-FACED
HONEYEATER. Facial pattern distinguishes each
species.

YELLOW-FACED HONEYEATER
Lichenostomus chrysops   16 cm
Olive-brown; **thick yellow line below eye from bill
to ear;** black face. Mostly eucalypt forest at higher
altitudes. *May be confused with:* Perhaps BRIDLED
HONEYEATER which has a dark head. Facial pattern
distinguishes each species.

VARIED HONEYEATER
Lichenostomus versicolor   19 cm
Olive-brown above; yellow underparts faintly streaked
brown; **thick black line through eye and down side
of neck, with yellow below black line, ending in a
white patch below ear.** Mangroves, sometimes
adjacent forest and gardens, north from about
Cardwell. *May be confused with:* MANGROVE
HONEYEATER which is similar; has barred yellow
throat and grey underparts; note range. Perhaps the
rather plain YELLOW HONEYEATER, but VARIED is
more brightly marked about the face and breast.

MANGROVE HONEYEATER
Lichenostomus fasciogularis   19 cm
Similar to VARIED HONEYEATER, but with **barred
yellow throat and grey underparts.** Mangroves,
sometimes adjacent forest and gardens, south from
about Cardwell. *May be confused with:* VARIED
HONEYEATER. Note range.

WHITE-STREAKED HONEYEATER

Trichodere cockerelli 17 cm
Olive-brown above; whitish below; **well-streaked white on light grey throat and breast;** dark grey head and sides of face; yellow edges to wing and tail feathers; **yellow ear-coverts.** Eucalypt forest, heathland and paperbark swamps. *May be confused with:* NONE. WHITE-CHEEKED HONEYEATER has large white cheek patch.

FURTHER POSSIBILITIES
SINGING HONEYEATER — vagrant.

MEDIUM-SIZED & LARGE BIRDS WITH YELLOW FACIAL MARKINGS

POSSIBILITIES

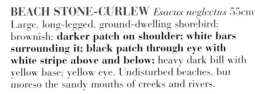

BEACH STONE-CURLEW *Esacus neglectus* 55cm
Large, long-legged, ground-dwelling shorebird; brownish; **darker patch on shoulder; white bars surrounding it; black patch through eye with white stripe above and below;** heavy dark bill with yellow base; yellow eye. Undisturbed beaches, but moreso the sandy mouths of creeks and rivers.

MASKED LAPWING *Vanellus miles* 37 cm
Common, large, ground or wading bird; grey-brown back and wings; black cap, sometimes sides of neck; white underparts; pinkish legs; **large yellow wattle about face and eye.** Grassland, edges of swamps, tidal flats, farmland and city parks.

COCKATIEL *Nymphicus hollandicus* 32 cm
Medium-sized, long-tailed parrot; **upright yellow crest; large white shoulder patch.** Male: large yellow cheek patch; orange ear patch. Female: much duller. Open drier woodland and lightly timbered country.

NOISY MINER *Manorina melanocephala* 27 cm
Pesky; **black mask about eye and over crown;** white forehead and throat; yellow spot behind eye; yellow bill; **grey rump.** Open drier eucalypt forest.
May be confused with: YELLOW-THROATED MINER which has yellow forehead and crown and white rump.

YELLOW-THROATED MINER

Manorina flavigula 27 cm
Similar to NOISY MINER, but with a **white rump; yellow forehead and crown.** Open drier eucalypt forest. *May be confused with:* NOISY MINER, but white rump of YELLOW-THROATED is conspicuous and diagnostic.

FURTHER POSSIBILITIES
AUSTRALASIAN GREBE
PIED and GREAT CORMORANTS
GREY GOSHAWK has yellow cere.
Introduced COMMON MYNA has yellow bill and yellow behind eye.

POSSIBILITIES

AUSTRALIAN BRUSH-TURKEY
Alectura lathami 70 cm
Large black bird; **bare red head; tail flattened
sideways.** Male: large yellow wattles during breeding
season Aug.–Feb. Rainforest at all altitudes but mainly
upland rainforest.

SARUS CRANE *Grus antigone* 115 cm
Migrant, present May–Dec.; long-legged; stately;
overall grey; **red on rear of head and nape
extending well down neck; small dewlap; pinkish
legs and feet.** Shallow swamps, grassland, pasture and
bare farmland. *May be confused with:* BROLGA, but
look for pinkish legs.

BROLGA
Grus rubicunda 115 cm
Almost identical to SARUS CRANE, but red does not
extend as far down neck; **dark grey legs; heavy
dewlap.** Similar habitat. *May be confused with:*
SARUS CRANE, but look for grey legs.

PIED OYSTERCATCHER
Haematopus longirostris 50 cm
Distinctive large black and white shorebird; black
head, back, wings and tail; white breast, belly and
under tail-coverts; conspicuous **red bill, eye-ring,
legs and feet.** Mostly sandy beaches, also mudflats
and estuaries.

SOOTY OYSTERCATCHER
Haematopus fuliginosus 50 cm
Similar to PIED OYSTERCATCHER, but **overall
sooty-black.** Rocky coastlines, exposed reef flats —
mostly on offshore islands.

CHANNEL-BILLED CUCKOO
Scythrops novaehollandiae 64 cm
Migrant, present Sept.–Apr.; overall grey; **large,
heavy, pale, curved bill; red about eye.** In flight, the
long wings and tail give it a distinctive hawk-like
appearance. Eucalypt forest, rainforest edges, gallery
forest and farmland, wherever figs abound.

FURTHER POSSIBILITIES
PURPLE SWAMPHEN

POSSIBILITIES

WHITE-BROWED CRAKE *Porzana cinerea* 19 cm
Aquatic; stubby tail; black and brown upperparts; grey
throat, neck and breast; white belly; **dark stripe
through eye with white eyebrow and white stripe
below eye.** Freshwater swamps, especially those with
reedbeds and water-lilies, rice fields and sometimes
about sugar-cane fields. Moreso in the lowlands.
May be confused with: The smaller BAILLON'S
CRAKE which lacks white stripes about eye. WHITE-
BROWED shows buff flanks in flight.

SPOTTED PARDALOTE
Pardalotus punctatus 9 cm
Tiny, well-spotted, short-tailed bird; black crown
spotted white; yellow throat; red rump; **lines of white
spots on black wings.** Open forest and wet sclerophyll
mostly at higher altitudes. *May be confused with:* Other
pardalotes which have a wing-stripe and yellow or buff
rump. Look for much spotting and red rump.

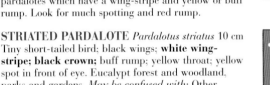

STRIATED PARDALOTE *Pardalotus striatus* 10 cm
Tiny short-tailed bird; black wings; **white wing-
stripe; black crown;** buff rump; yellow throat; yellow
spot in front of eye. Eucalypt forest and woodland,
parks and gardens. *May be confused with:* Other
pardalotes, but look for black crown, yellow spot in
front of eye and white wing-stripe.

FERNWREN *Oreoscopus gutturalis* (Adult) 13 cm
Rich olive-brown upperparts; slightly paler below;
**white eyebrow and throat, margined below by
small black 'bib';** longish bill. Upland rainforest,
usually above 600 m, sometimes lower. *May be
confused with:* YELLOW-THROATED and WHITE-
BROWED SCRUBWRENS, but look for dark eye and
black 'bib'.

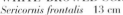

WHITE-BROWED SCRUBWREN
Sericornis frontalis 13 cm
Small; brown above; paler below; **white eyebrow over
a pale yellow eye; two small white markings on
shoulder.** Female: duller than male. Denser eucalypt
forest and rainforest edges in upland areas. *May be
confused with:* FERNWREN and YELLOW-
THROATED SCRUBWREN but look for pale eye and
white throat without 'bib'.

BROWN GERYGONE *Gerygone mouki* 10 cm
Small, plain, active, greyish bird; paler below. Mostly
upland rainforest above 250 m. *May be confused with:*
Other grey gerygones. See p. 200.

MANGROVE GERYGONE
Gerygone levigaster 10 cm
Small, plain, active, greyish bird of mangroves and
adjacent forest. *May be confused with:* Other grey
gerygones. See p. 200.

JACKY WINTER *Microeca fascinans* 13 cm
Small; grey-brown bird; paler below; **restlessly wags
tail from side to side; conspicuous white sides to
tail;** pale whitish eyebrow. Drier, open, sparsely
timbered areas. *May be confused with:* Perhaps female
and juvenile WHITE-WINGED TRILLER, but look for
white-sided tail, restlessly wagged. LEMON-BELLIED
FLYCATCHER has lemon underparts and plain tail.
Tail wagging in JACKY WINTER is diagnostic.

WHITE-BROWED ROBIN
Poecilodryas superciliosa 17 cm
Small brown and white bird with **prominent white
eyebrow; white bar across base of flight feathers;**
white tail tip. **Frequently cocks tail.** Gallery forest.
May be confused with: NONE, but sometimes the
juvenile GREY-HEADED ROBIN of true rainforest is
misidentified as WHITE-BROWED ROBIN. Note
cocking of tail and habitat.

GREY FANTAIL *Rhipidura fuliginosa* 16 cm
Small dark-grey bird; very active; **large fanned tail;**
white tip and white shafts to each tail feather; white
throat; short white eyebrow. Resident race *keasti* from
upland rainforest is **darker** and slightly smaller than
wintering southern race which inhabits open forest,
woodland, mangroves and denser parks and gardens.
May be confused with: NORTHERN FANTAIL. Look
for short, thick white eyebrow and white mark behind
eye. NORTHERN has a fine eyebrow only.

WILLIE WAGTAIL *Rhipidura leucophrys* 20 cm
Small, active, common bird; black upperparts; **black
throat; white eyebrow;** white underparts; tail partly
spread and **twitched frequently.** Lightly timbered
country, farmland and urban areas. *May be confused
with:* RESTLESS FLYCATCHER, but look for black
throat.

VARIED TRILLER *Lalage leucomela* 19 cm
Small; blackish crown and nape, back and tail; white
to off-white underparts from chin to belly; prominent
white eyebrow; grey rump; **buff lower belly and
under tail-coverts.** Female: lightly barred underparts.
Rainforest, gallery forest, denser eucalypt forest and
paperbark woodland, sometimes mangroves. *May be
confused with:* NONE. Buff lower belly and under tail-
coverts separate it from all other species.

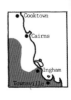

WHITE-BROWED WOODSWALLOW
Artamus superciliosus 19 cm
Rare, medium-sized bird; deep blue-grey; **chestnut lower breast and underparts; prominent white eyebrow; bluish bill;** dark grey face; grey tail tipped white. Wags tail. Female and juvenile: duller. Usually in noisy flocks. Drier, open lightly timbered country.

YELLOW WAGTAIL *Motacilla flava* 18 cm
Rare summer visitor, present usually Nov.–Feb.; small, mostly terrestrial; **constantly teeters long tail;** overall greyish with whitish eyebrow; **blackish legs; olive-green rump.** Larger open areas of short grass on bare ground, sometimes swamp margins and open wetlands in coastal lowlands. *May be confused with:* GREY WAGTAIL, but look for olive-green rump and black legs. Note habitat.

GREY WAGTAIL *Motacilla cinerea* 20 cm
Rare summer visitor, Nov.–Mar.; small bird similar to YELLOW WAGTAIL; **constantly teeters long tail up and down;** greyish; yellowish underparts; brighter under tail-coverts; white eyebrow; **yellowish-green rump; pale legs.** Mostly terrestrial. Open areas in rainforest at high altitudes. *May be confused with:* YELLOW WAGTAIL, but look for yellowish-green rump and pale legs. Note habitat.

TAWNY GRASSBIRD *Megalurus timoriensis* 19 cm
Brownish bird; brown upperparts **streaked dark grey and black;** unstreaked fawn underparts; longish brown tail; **plain rufous crown; pale eyebrow.** Tall rank grassland, pastures, crops, grassy roadsides and swampland. *May be confused with:* SINGING BUSHLARK, RICHARD'S PIPIT, CLAMOROUS REED-WARBLER, LITTLE GRASSBIRD, RUFOUS SONGLARK and female BROWN SONGLARK, but look for plain rufous crown and longish tail.

FURTHER POSSIBILITIES
BUFF-BANDED RAIL has a pale grey eyebrow.
LITTLE GRASSBIRD has a pale eyebrow.

BIRDS WITH A PROMINENT EYE-RING
POSSIBILITIES

PAINTED SNIPE *Rostratula benghalensis* 24 cm
Rare; medium-sized; overall greyish-brown but with blackish-brown head and breast; **bold white eye-ring leading back to nape; whitish line down middle of crown; curved white bar on side of breast bordering wing,** changing to buff as it continues down back; long grey pinkish-tipped bill slightly drooped at tip. Female: larger; more boldly marked. Male: duller; striated throat. Teeters rear of body up and down. Shallow freshwater swamps.

PIED OYSTERCATCHER
Haematopus longirostris   50 cm
Distinctive large black and white shorebird; black head, back, wings and tail; white breast, belly and under tail-coverts; **conspicuous red bill, eye-ring, legs and feet.** Mostly sandy beaches, also mudflats and estuaries.

SOOTY OYSTERCATCHER
Haematopus fuliginosus   50 cm
Similar to PIED OYSTERCATCHER, but **overall sooty-black.** Rocky coastlines, exposed reef flats — mostly on offshore islands.

BLACK-FRONTED DOTTEREL
Elseyornis melanops   17 cm
Small freshwater wader; greyish-brown above; white below; **black forehead; black band through eye connecting with black breastband** which when viewed from the front forms a **bold 'Y'** on breast; large white throat patch; **red eye-ring.** Riverbeds, muddy margins of freshwater swamps, lakes, dams and sewage ponds. *May be confused with:* Perhaps RED-KNEED DOTTEREL, but look for red eye-ring and greyish crown.

WHITE-HEADED PIGEON
Columba leucomela   40 cm
Medium-sized; white head and underparts; **black back, wings and tail; red bill; red about eye.** Rainforest at all altitudes, but moreso in higher areas.

CRESTED PIGEON *Ocyphaps lophotes*   33 cm
Overall grey medium-sized bird; **erect dark crest; red about eye; red legs;** iridescent bronze and green patch on wings. Feeds on ground. Open sparsely timbered areas and about farmhouses.

SQUATTER PIGEON *Geophaps scripta*   30 cm
Medium-sized, dull brown bird; broad white stripe bordering wings to flanks and belly; **prominent black and white facial pattern;** tan eye-ring. Drier, open grassy woodland and open forest. *May be confused with:* Perhaps COMMON BRONZEWING which lacks the strong facial pattern and coloured eye-ring.

DIAMOND DOVE *Geopelia cuneata*   20 cm
Rare, small grey bird similar to PEACEFUL DOVE, but without barring; **white spotting on wings; red eye-ring.** Mostly dry open forest.
May be confused with: PEACEFUL DOVE, but look for red eye-ring and absence of barring.

PEACEFUL DOVE *Geopelia striata* 20 cm
Small grey bird; long narrow tail; **fine black barring on breast, hind neck and wings; blue eye-ring.** Often sitting on powerlines. Eucalypt woodland, lightly timbered grassland, open forest, parks and gardens. *May be confused with:* DIAMOND DOVE, but look for blue eye-ring and extensive barring.

ORIENTAL CUCKOO
Cuculus saturatus (Adult) 31 cm
Long-tailed greyish bird; **boldly barred lower breast and belly;** yellow eye-ring and feet; long wings and long tail give it a hawk-like appearance in flight. Eucalypt forest and woodland, paperbark swamps, sometimes about rainforest clearings, moreso at lower altitudes. *May be confused with:* Perhaps BARRED CUCKOO-SHRIKE which has similar barring, but refolds its wings on alighting, has yellow eye, no eye-ring and black legs and feet.

PALLID CUCKOO *Cuculus pallidus* (Adult) 31 cm
Medium-sized overall greyish bird; long tail 'notched' white; **small spot on nape; faint darker curved line through eye and down to shoulder;** yellow eye-ring; dark feet. Open woodland.

CHESTNUT-BREASTED CUCKOO
Cacomantis castaneiventris (Adult) 24 cm
Rare; medium-sized; blue-grey above; **rich chestnut underparts; lower tail 'notched' at sides;** yellow eye-ring and feet. Rainforest at both high and low altitudes. *May be confused with:* FAN-TAILED CUCKOO. See p. 197.

FAN-TAILED CUCKOO
Cacomantis flabelliformis (Adult) 26 cm
Medium-sized slender bird; slate-grey above; **pale rufous underparts; fairly long tail markedly 'notched' white down each side; yellow eye-ring;** yellowish feet. Rainforest and denser eucalypt forest. *May be confused with:* CHESTNUT-BREASTED and BRUSH CUCKOOS. See pp. 197–8.

LITTLE BRONZE-CUCKOO
Chrysococcyx minutillus 16 cm
Small; dull bronze-green above; whitish below; bold barring from chin to tail. Male: **red eye-ring.** Female: **tan eye-ring.** Rainforest, open forest, paperbark forest, tropical woodland, gallery forest, moreso to the west of the region. *May be confused with:* Other Bronze-Cuckoos. See pp. 198–9.

GOULD'S BRONZE-CUCKOO
Chrysococcyx russatus 17 cm
Similar to LITTLE BRONZE-CUCKOO and difficult to separate. Mostly coastal. Rainforest, open forest, paperbark woodland, gallery forest, also mangroves. *May be confused with:* Other Bronze-Cuckoos. See pp. 198–9.

CHOWCHILLA *Orthonyx spaldingii*   27 cm
Medium-sized darkish bird of the rainforest floor;
conspicuous white eye-ring. Male: all-white
underparts. Female: **rufous throat and breast; white
belly.** Rainforest, moreso in upland areas.

VARIED SITTELLA
Daphoenositta chrysoptera   11 cm
A small, short-tailed, dark, **heavily striated bird
living on tree trunks and limbs;** small **white
wingbar;** slightly upturned bill; yellow eye-ring, legs
and feet. Male: dark crown. Female: dark head, throat
and upper breast. Dry woodland and eucalypt forest,
especially where Ironbark *Eucalyptus* spp. grow.

PIED MONARCH *Arses kaupi*   14 cm
Small; white collar; erectile frill on nape; **wide black
breastband on white underparts; blue eye-ring.**
Female: broader breastband; incomplete collar.
Rainforest, moreso at lower altitudes.

SILVEREYE
Zosterops lateralis   12 cm
Small; yellow-green, paler below; **prominent white
ring around eye;** greyish breast and back. Rainforest
margins, gallery forest, mangroves, parks and gardens.

MEDIUM-SIZED BIRDS WITH WHITE OR YELLOW EYE
POSSIBILITIES

MAGPIE-LARK *Grallina cyanoleuca*   27 cm
Common distinctive **black and white bird; short
white bill;** white eye; **walks on ground with a head-
nodding movement.** Usually in vicinity of water in
open areas, creeks, swamps, farmland, parks and
gardens.

BARRED CUCKOO-SHRIKE
Coracina lineata   27 cm
Immaculate; grey with **fine barring from lower
breast to under tail-coverts; yellow eye;** black wing
and tail tips; **refolds wings on alighting.** Rainforest
at all altitudes. *May be confused with:* Perhaps adult
ORIENTAL CUCKOO which has similar barring, dark
eye, yellow eye-ring and feet and long 'notched' tail.

GROUND CUCKOO-SHRIKE
Coracina maxima   36 cm
Rare; greyish with **black wings which it refolds on
alighting; long black forked tail;** paler underparts,
barred on lower breast and belly; **white faintly
barred back and rump conspicuous in flight;** white
eye. Drier open forest and open woodland.

Female

Male

POSSIBILITIES

BUSH STONE-CURLEW
Burhinus grallarius 55 cm
Nocturnal; streaked greyish plumage; long legs; streaked buffy underparts; **whitish forehead and eyebrow; large yellow eye.** Moves slowly and deliberately when disturbed by day. Ground-dwelling. Open forest, open lightly timbered areas, often in urban localities.

BEACH STONE-CURLEW
Esacus neglectus 55 cm
Long-legged ground-dwelling shorebird; brownish; **darker patch on shoulder, white bars surrounding it; black patch through eye with white stripe above and below;** heavy bill with yellow base; yellow eye. Undisturbed beaches; moreso the sandy mouths of creeks and rivers.

BLUE-WINGED KOOKABURRA
Dacelo leachii 43 cm
Whitish streaked head; faintly barred whitish underparts; heavy stout bill; **large blue patch on wings; blue rump;** white eye. Male: blue tail. Female: tail reddish-brown barred darker. Eucalypt forest and paperbark woodland. *May be confused with:* LAUGHING KOOKABURRA which has dark eye. Look for blue rump, pale head and crown and white eye.

PIED CURRAWONG *Strepera graculina* 46 cm
Predominantly black when perched; black and white in flight; some white in wing; white tail tip, under tail-coverts and rump; **prominent yellow eye;** heavy black bill. Hillside eucalypt forest, rainforest canopy and open woodland. Lowlands in winter.

AUSTRALIAN RAVEN
Corvus coronoides 52 cm
Totally black; heavy black bill; black legs. Adult: white eye. Juvenile: brown eye. Open, lightly timbered areas and farmland. *May be confused with:* TORRESIAN CROW. See p. 203.

TORRESIAN CROW
Corvus orru 50 cm
Similar to AUSTRALIAN RAVEN. *May be confused with:* AUSTRALIAN RAVEN. See p. 203.

FURTHER POSSIBILITIES
HARDHEAD
RUFOUS and BARKING OWLS
TAWNY FROGMOUTH
Species of EGRET, HERON and BITTERN have yellow eyes which are not a prominent feature.

POSSIBILITIES

COMMON KOEL *Eudynamys scolopacea* 43 cm
Migrant, present Sept.–Apr.; medium-sized rather shy long-tailed bird. Male: **entirely black with pale bill.** Female: brown back and wings **heavily spotted white; black head;** brown tail barred white; whitish underparts barred brown. Denser open forest, woodland, gallery forest, dense trees in farmland, parks and gardens. *May be confused with:* Male: SPANGLED DRONGO which has fish tail and dark bill. Look for long straight tail and pale bill. Female: NONE.

SPANGLED DRONGO *Dicrurus bracteatus* 30 cm
Noisy, medium-sized black bird; **fish tail; red eye;** shrugs shoulders and flicks tail somewhat 'crazily' while calling. Mostly edges of rainforest and adjacent woodland throughout, but moreso at lower altitudes, sometimes in mangroves. *May be confused with:* Male COMMON KOEL, but look for fish tail. Occasionally a SPANGLED DRONGO with outer tail feathers moulted or abraded has been mistaken for the TRUMPET MANUCODE, a rainforest bird of northern Cape York Peninsula.

YELLOW ORIOLE *Oriolus flavocinctus* (Adult) 28 cm
Medium-sized **yellow-green** bird with some striations; **red bill and eye; edges of wing feathers and tail tip yellow.** Rainforest, gallery forest at low altitudes and mangroves. *May be confused with:* OLIVE-BACKED ORIOLE, but look for overall yellow-green colouration and yellow tips and edges to wing feathers.

OLIVE-BACKED ORIOLE
Oriolus sagittatus (Adult) 27 cm
Medium-sized; olive-green back; dusky-grey or brownish wings; white underparts with **'teardrop' shaped markings; red eye and bill.** Eucalypt forest and tropical woodland. *May be confused with:* YELLOW ORIOLE, but look for white underparts with 'teardrop' striations. Female FIGBIRD has dark eye, bare skin about eye, short thickish black bill and brownish back.

SPOTTED CATBIRD *Ailuroedus melanotis* 28 cm
A medium-sized bird with deep-green back and wings; paler underparts spotted buffy-white; **brownish crown and throat heavily spotted white; dark ear-coverts.** Rainforest at all altitudes.

METALLIC STARLING *Aplonis metallica* 24 cm
Medium-sized gregarious bird; plumage appears **glossy-black** but with purple and green iridescence. **Prominent, bulging red eye;** long, sharply pointed tail. Immature: white, striated underparts. Rainforest and remnants of rainforest, mostly at lower altitudes. Sometimes mangroves.

FURTHER POSSIBILITIES
SPOTLESS CRAKE
PAPUAN FROGMOUTH

POSSIBILITIES

BLUE-FACED HONEYEATER
Entomyzon cyanotis   28 cm
Medium-sized; olive-green back and wings; white
underparts; **narrow dark smudgy mark on throat
and breast; large area of blue skin about eye**
(green in juvenile); shows large whitish patch in each
wing in flight. Dry woodland and eucalypt forest.

BLACK-CHINNED HONEYEATER
Melithreptus gularis   16 cm
Small; olive-green back, wings and tail; white
underparts washed grey; black head; **white line across
nape; pale blue crescent above eye; bright
yellowish-brown legs and feet; dark chin extending
to throat.** Eucalypt forest and tropical woodland. *May
be confused with:* WHITE-THROATED and WHITE-
NAPED HONEYEATERS, but look for dark chin and
throat and bright yellowish-brown legs.

WHITE-THROATED HONEYEATER
Melithreptus albogularis   14 cm
Similar to BLACK-CHINNED HONEYEATER, but with
white chin and throat and dull flesh-brown legs and
feet. Eucalypt forest and tropical woodland, moreso in
lowlands. *May be confused with:* BLACK-CHINNED
and WHITE-NAPED HONEYEATERS, but look for
white chin and throat and blue crescent above eye.

WHITE-NAPED HONEYEATER
Melithreptus lunatus   14 cm
Similar to BLACK-CHINNED HONEYEATER but with
red crescent above eye; dull flesh-brown legs and
feet. Eucalypt forest and edge of rainforest, e.g. where
stands of Flooded Gum *Eucalyptus grandis* are present
at higher altitudes. *May be confused with:* BLACK-
CHINNED and WHITE-THROATED HONEYEATERS
which have blue crescent above eye.

MEDIUM-SIZED BIRDS WITH GREEN WINGS
POSSIBILITIES

EMERALD DOVE *Chalcophaps indica*   26 cm
Plump ground-feeding small pigeon; brown head and
body; **deep green iridescent wings;** red bill and legs;
white shoulder patch; **two white bars on lower back**
obvious in flight. Immature: dull-green wings;
lacks white shoulder patch; head and body brown
barred and scalloped. Rainforest at all altitudes.

POSSIBILITIES

GREAT CRESTED GREBE
Podiceps cristatus   50 cm
Large brown and white aquatic bird appearing tailless;
**rufous black-tipped ruff or frill about neck; long
crest-like ear tufts** in breeding plumage (Sept.–Mar.);
ruff and ear tufts somewhat subdued in non-breeding
plumage; shows large white patches in surface of
upperwing and white underwing in flight. Lakes and
larger areas of fresh water.

WHITE-NECKED HERON *Ardea pacifica* 87 cm
Very large wading bird; blackish body; **white head
and neck; black bill and legs;** conspicuous white
patch on leading edge of wing in flight. Shallow
freshwater swamps, dams, stream and lake edges,
sometimes open grassland. *May be confused with:*
NONE in flight, though sometimes resembles a bird of
prey when seen at a height.

BUSH STONE-CURLEW *Burhinus grallarius* 55 cm
Nocturnal; streaked greyish plumage; streaked buffy
underparts; **whitish forehead and eyebrow; large
yellow eyes;** long legs; white patches in surface of
upperwing, mostly white underwing in flight. Moves
slowly and deliberately when disturbed by day. Open
forest, open lightly timbered areas, often urban localities.

BEACH STONE-CURLEW *Esacus neglectus* 55 cm
Large, long-legged, ground-dwelling shorebird; brownish
in colour; **darker patch on shoulder, white bar
surrounding it; black patch through eye with white
stripe above and below;** heavy dark bill with yellow
base; yellow eye; white patches in surface of upperwing,
white underwing in flight. Undisturbed beaches, but
moreso the sandy mouths of creeks and rivers.

FOREST KINGFISHER
Todiramphus macleayii   21 cm
Small immaculate-looking bird; two-toned blue
upperparts; white underparts; **white collar** (not entire
in female); large black bill; two prominent white spots
on forehead; **white 'window' in each wing in flight.**
The common kingfisher of the Wet Tropics region.
Open areas, farmland and gardens. *May be confused
with:* NONE in flight. No other kingfisher shows white
'windows' in wings.

DOLLARBIRD *Eurystomus orientalis*   29 cm
Migrant, present late Sept.–Apr./May; medium-sized;
plump; short tail; overall dark greyish to greenish-blue;
thin blue stripe along edge of wing; **broad red bill;
red feet; shows large white spot in each wing in
flight.** Sparsely timbered areas, especially along
watercourses, open woodland and farmland.

BLUE-FACED HONEYEATER
Entomyzon cyanotis 28 cm
Medium-sized; olive-green back and wings; white
underparts; **narrow dark smudgy mark on throat
and breast; large area of blue skin about eye**
(green in juvenile); shows pale patch in each wing in
flight. Dry woodland and eucalypt forest.

GREY-HEADED ROBIN
Heteromyias albispecularis 17 cm
Small; deep olive-brown above; rufous rump; **grey head
and breast; white throat; conspicuous white double
bars on dark wing** in flight. Often seen flying low over
roadways. Lower stratum of upland rainforest.
Sometimes in lowland rainforest. *May be confused with:*
NONE. The only rainforest species which shows bars in
wing. Juvenile sometimes misidentified as WHITE-
BROWED ROBIN which inhabits a much drier habitat.

VARIED SITTELLA
Daphoenositta chrysoptera 11 cm
Small, short-tailed, dark, **heavily striated bird living
on tree trunks and limbs; small white wingbar**
conspicuous in flight; slightly upturned bill; yellow
eye-ring, legs and feet. Male: dark crown. Female:
dark head, throat and upper breast. Dry woodland and
eucalypt forest, especially where Ironbark *Eucalyptus*
spp. grow.

WHITE-EARED MONARCH
Monarcha leucotis 13 cm
Small, active; black, white and grey bird; **greyish-
white underparts;** black tail tipped white; **three
white patches about eye in black head;** white
shoulder patch in wing. Coastal rainforest, sometimes
upland rainforest. *May be confused with:* Generally
NONE. VARIED TRILLER has buff lower belly and
under tail-coverts.

WHITE-WINGED CHOUGH
Corcorax melanorhamphos 45 cm
A large nearly all-black bird; **white patch in each
wing conspicuous in flight;** small curved bill; red
eye. **Feeds on ground in family groups.** Noisy when
alarmed. Note range. Open dry forest. *May be
confused with:* PIED CURRAWONG which has yellow
eye and stout bill.

COMMON MYNA *Acridotheres tristis* 24 cm
Introduced; medium-sized; cinnamon-brown; darker
wings, tail and head; paler on underparts; large white
wing patch conspicuous in flight; yellow eye; **bare
yellow skin about eye; yellow legs, feet and bill.**
Open farmland and urban areas.

FURTHER POSSIBILITIES
BLACK SWAN
NIGHTJARS
See also SHOREBIRDS, pp. 182–9.
See also Diurnal Birds of Prey, pp. 175–81.

POSSIBILITIES

SWAMP HARRIER
Circus approximans   Male 54 cm Female 58 cm
Large, graceful, brown, slow-flying bird of prey; long
upswept wings; **distinct owl-like facial disc; whitish
rump;** streaked underparts; long yellow legs. Male:
wings washed grey; **plain greyish tail.** Female: **faintly
barred** grey-brown tail. Swamps, reedbeds, sometimes
pastures and crops. *May be confused with:* Other birds
of prey. See Diurnal Birds of Prey, pp. 175–81.

ORIENTAL PRATINCOLE
Glareola maldivarum   24 cm
Rare summer visitor; medium-sized; long-winged;
olive-brown; buffish to white underparts; **buff throat
edged with broken black line; long forked tail** with
white sides and wide black margin at base; white
upper tail-coverts; **chestnut underwing;** graceful and
tern-like in flight. Open short-grassed plains, claypans
and sandflats. *May be confused with:* AUSTRALIAN
PRATINCOLE, but look for broken edging to buff
throat when on ground, chestnut underwings and long
forked tail in flight. AUSTRALIAN teeters, ORIENTAL
does not. AUSTRALIAN has grey rump and white
upper tail-coverts.

WHITE-RUMPED SWIFTLET
Collocalia spodiopygius   11 cm
Small, dark grey aerial bird; **small greyish-white
patch on rump; stiff-winged flight;** usually in flocks,
often low to the ground. Appears over most habitats at
all altitudes.

FORK-TAILED SWIFT *Apus pacificus*   17 cm
Migrant, present Oct.–Apr.; small to medium-sized
dark aerial bird; **long swept-back wings;** pale throat;
long deeply forked tail; fork in tail often not
discernible; most obvious feature is **white rump.**
Appears over all habitats at all altitudes.
May be confused with: The smaller HOUSE SWIFT,
but look for long thin tail. WHITE-THROATED
NEEDLETAIL has no white rump.

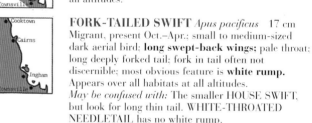

HOUSE SWIFT *Apus affinis*   15 cm
Rare summer visitor; aerial; mostly blackish; **small
and stocky; pale throat; slightly forked tail
becomes square when fanned;** underside of wings
two-toned. *May be confused with:* Other swifts,
swiftlets, swallows and martins, but mostly FORK-
TAILED SWIFT. Look for slight fork in squarish tail,
pale throat and stocky appearance.

BANDED HONEYEATER
Certhionyx pectoralis 13 cm
Small bird with black upperparts; white underparts; **thin black band across breast.** Dry open forest and woodland, especially where eucalypts and paperbarks are blossoming.

GROUND CUCKOO-SHRIKE
Coracina maxima 36 cm
Rare, medium-sized greyish bird; **black wings which it refolds on alighting; long black forked tail;** paler underparts, barred on lower breast and belly; **white faintly barred back and rump conspicuous in flight;** white eye. Drier, open forest and open woodland.

WHITE-BREASTED WOODSWALLOW
Artamus leucorynchus 17 cm
Medium-sized; dark grey; **white underparts sharply demarcated by dark grey upper breast; bluish bill.** Wags tail. Often about water, swamps, lakes, mangroves, seashore. Ever present on powerlines.

DOUBLE-BARRED FINCH
Taeniopygia bichenovii 10 cm
Small; brown back; white face and underparts; **two thin black bars across breast;** black wings heavily spotted white; black tail. Taller grassy woodland, open forest, parks and gardens.

BLACK-THROATED FINCH
Poephila cincta 10 cm
Small; brownish; grey head; **black throat and upper breast;** pale apricot-chestnut lower breast and belly; white under tail-coverts; short tail; short, thick **black bill.** Dry open woodland. Two races occur in the Wet Tropics region — black-rumped north from about Townsville; white-rumped from Townsville southward.

TREE MARTIN
Hirundo nigricans 12 cm
Small aerial bird; dark back and wings; whitish underparts; white rump appears dirty; **square tail; dark crown.** Open areas and farmland, often perches with other aerial birds on powerlines. *May be confused with:* FAIRY MARTIN, which has rusty crown.

FAIRY MARTIN
Hirundo ariel 12 cm
Small aerial bird similar to TREE MARTIN, but with cleaner white rump and **rusty crown.** Open areas, open farmland and open grassland. *May be confused with:* TREE MARTIN, but look for rusty crown.

POSSIBILITIES

RED-BACKED KINGFISHER
Todiramphus pyrrhopygia 22 cm
Rather dull kingfisher; upper back, wings and tail pale blue and whitish blue; **streaked crown; reddish-orange rump.** Open woodland and sparsely timbered areas. *May be confused with:* Perhaps other kingfishers, but look for rump colour and streaked crown.

RED-BACKED FAIRY-WREN
Malurus melanocephalus (Male) 12 cm
Spectacular; black head and body; **brilliant red back and rump; long cocked tail.** Long grass in and adjacent to woodland, grassy areas in farmland.

SPOTTED PARDALOTE
Pardalotus punctatus 9 cm
Tiny; short-tailed; well-spotted; black crown spotted white; yellow throat; red rump; **lines of white spots on black wings.** Open forest and wet sclerophyll, mostly at higher altitudes. *May be confused with:* Other pardalotes, but look for profuse spotting and red rump.

RED-BROWED PARDALOTE
Pardalotus rubricatus 11 cm
Rare; tiny short-tailed predominantly fawn-grey bird; yellowish breast; yellow rump; **black crown spotted white; yellow edges to wing feathers; small orange-red eyebrow.** Dry open forest. *May be confused with:* Other pardalotes, but look for spotted crown, orange-red eyebrow and yellow wing-stripe.

STRIATED PARDALOTE *Pardalotus striatus* 10cm
Tiny, short-tailed bird; black wings; **white wing-stripe; black crown;** buff rump; yellow throat; yellow spot in front of eye. Eucalypt forest and woodland, parks and gardens. *May be confused with:* Other pardalotes, but look for black crown, yellow spot in front of eye and white wing-stripe.

MOUNTAIN THORNBILL
Acanthiza katherina 10 cm
Greenish-brown bird of upland rainforest; **chestnut rump; whitish eye; indistinct scalloping on forehead.** Rainforest above 600 m.

BUFF-RUMPED THORNBILL
Acanthiza reguloides 11 cm
Greenish-olive upperparts; yellow underparts; **buff-yellow rump;** forehead and face scalloped yellowish-cream; tail tipped pale yellow with broad black band; dark bill; white eye. Dry open eucalypt forest and casuarina thickets. *May be confused with:* WEEBILL, FAIRY-GERYGONE, juvenile WHITE-THROATED GERYGONE and YELLOW THORNBILL, but buff-yellow rump is diagnostic.

EASTERN YELLOW ROBIN
Eopsaltria australis 15 cm
Medium-grey upperparts; **bright yellow underparts
and rump;** grey face. Tropical woodland with some
understorey, wet sclerophyll.

YELLOW-BREASTED BOATBILL
Machaerirhynchus flaviventer 12 cm
Black and yellow flycatcher; short disproportionately-
wide bill. Cocks tail. Male: prominent **yellow
eyebrow; white throat; yellow underparts;** yellow
rump. Female duller. Rainforest at all altitudes.

RUFOUS FANTAIL
Rhipidura rufifrons 16 cm
Active, brown fantail: **conspicuous rufous rump and
base of large fanned tail.** Rainforest at higher
altitudes in summer, but lowland rainforest and open
forest in winter.

RED-BROWED FINCH
Neochmia temporalis 11 cm
Olive-green and grey; **red rump, bill and eyebrow.**
Juvenile: black bill; lacks red eyebrow. Usually
gregarious. Margins of rainforest, regrowth, and
adjacent shrubby and grassy areas.

RED-RUMPED SWALLOW
Hirundo daurica 18 cm
Scarce summer visitor Dec.–Mar.; aerial; **deeply
forked long tail; conspicuous rufous rump; pale
buffy underparts striated darker;** black upperparts.
Immature: duller. Rests on powerlines with other
swallows and martins. Open areas and open farmland.

RUFOUS SONGLARK
Cincloramphus mathewsi 16 cm
Overall brown with patterned upperparts; paler below;
rich rufous rump; pale fawn eyebrow. Juvenile: dark
spots on throat and breast. Usually shy and retiring.
Grassy woodland. *May be confused with:* Female and
juvenile WHITE-WINGED TRILLER, SINGING
BUSHLARK, RICHARD'S PIPIT, TAWNY
GRASSBIRD, female and juvenile BROWN
SONGLARK. Only TAWNY GRASSBIRD has a rufous
rump (pale), but crown is rufous.

POSSIBILITIES

LOVELY FAIRY-WREN
Malurus amabilis 15 cm
Male: **bluish tail; blue head and ear-coverts;** black throat and breast; chestnut rump. Female: **dull blue head, back and tail; pale blue ear-coverts;** white throat and underparts. Denser tropical woodland, coastal paperbark swamps and mangroves.
May be confused with: NONE. Sometimes misidentified as the VARIEGATED FAIRY-WREN.

RED-BACKED FAIRY-WREN
Malurus melanocephalus 12 cm
Male: **black tail;** black body and head; **brilliant red back and rump.** Female: overall plain brown; brown tail. Long grass in and adjacent to woodland, grassy areas in farmland.

FURTHER POSSIBILITIES
VARIEGATED FAIRY-WREN *Malurus lamberti* 15 cm
A possibility that it may eventually reach the south-western corner of the region. Male resembles male LOVELY FAIRY-WREN but with less white in tail. Female is brown, paler below, tail washed blue, chestnut between bill and eye.

BIRDS THAT SOMETIMES COCK THEIR TAIL
POSSIBILITIES

BUFF-BREASTED PARADISE-KINGFISHER
Tanysiptera sylvia 34 cm
Migrant, present Nov.–early Apr.; **distinctively spectacular;** thick red bill; brilliant blue and black above; rufous-orange below; centre of back and rump white; **two very long, stiff, white tail feathers** which are sometimes broken-off during or after the breeding season. Raises and lowers tail when perched. Mostly lowland rainforest.

EASTERN YELLOW ROBIN
Eopsaltria australis 15 cm
Small bird; medium-grey upperparts; **bright yellow underparts and rump; grey face.** Tropical woodland with some understorey, wet sclerophyll.

WHITE-BROWED ROBIN
Poecilodryas superciliosa 17 cm
Small brown and white bird with **prominent white eyebrow; white bar across base of flight feathers;** white tail tip. Frequently cocks tail. Gallery forest.

GREY-CROWNED BABBLER
Pomatostomus temporalis   25 cm
Medium-sized, noisy bird, usually in small groups; dark brown upperparts; **pale crown;** white throat and breast; brown belly; longish **white-tipped tail, partly spread and often cocked;** long curved bill. Drier forest and open woodland.

YELLOW-BREASTED BOATBILL
Machaerirhynchus flaviventer   12 cm
Small black and yellow flycatcher; short disproportionately-wide bill. Male: prominent **yellow eyebrow; white throat; yellow underparts;** yellow rump. Female duller. Frequently cocks tail. Rainforest at all altitudes.

FURTHER POSSIBILITIES
Some PIGEONS and DOVES cock and spread their tail in courtship display or when alighting, e.g. CRESTED PIGEON and PEACEFUL DOVE. The male BROWN SONGLARK cocks its tail frequently during the breeding season, but it is only an uncommon to rare winter visitor to the Wet Tropics. Some text books indicate that the WHITE-GAPED HONEYEATER sometimes cocks its tail, but it is 'flicked' rather than cocked.

BIRDS WITH A LARGE FANNED TAIL
POSSIBILITIES

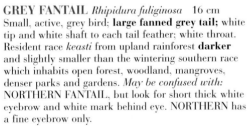

RUFOUS FANTAIL *Rhipidura rufifrons*   16 cm
Small, active, brown fantail; **conspicuous rufous rump and base of large fanned tail.** Rainforest at higher altitudes in summer, but in lowland rainforest and open forest in winter.

GREY FANTAIL *Rhipidura fuliginosa*   16 cm
Small, active, grey bird; **large fanned grey tail;** white tip and white shaft to each tail feather; white throat. Resident race *keasti* from upland rainforest **darker** and slightly smaller than the wintering southern race which inhabits open forest, woodland, mangroves, denser parks and gardens. *May be confused with:* NORTHERN FANTAIL, but look for short thick white eyebrow and white mark behind eye. NORTHERN has a fine eyebrow only.

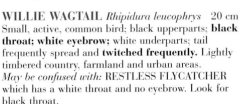

WILLIE WAGTAIL *Rhipidura leucophrys*   20 cm
Small, active, common bird; black upperparts; **black throat; white eyebrow;** white underparts; tail frequently spread and **twitched frequently.** Lightly timbered country, farmland and urban areas.
May be confused with: RESTLESS FLYCATCHER which has a white throat and no eyebrow. Look for black throat.

POSSIBILITIES

SPANGLED DRONGO *Dicrurus bracteatus* 30 cm
Noisy, medium-sized black bird; **fish tail; red eye;**
shrugs shoulders and flicks tail somewhat 'crazily' while
calling. Mostly edges of rainforest and adjacent woodland
throughout, but moreso at lower altitudes, sometimes in
mangroves.

BIRDS THAT FREQUENTLY FLICK THEIR TAIL INCLUDING AQUATIC BIRDS
POSSIBILITIES

RED-NECKED CRAKE
Rallina tricolor 30 cm
Medium-sized; initially appearing dark brown; **rich
chestnut head, neck and breast;** dark brown body;
short tail often flicked. Rainforest floor, especially close
to water, mostly at lower altitudes.

BUFF-BANDED RAIL *Gallirallus philippensis* 31cm
Medium-sized, shy ground bird; short tail; chestnut
crown and stripe through eye; **grey eyebrow; chestnut
patch on breast; extensive fine barring** on
underparts. Dense damp grassland, vegetation about
swamps and streams. *May be confused with:* The rare
LEWIN'S RAIL, but look for grey eyebrow and
chestnut on breast.

LEWIN'S RAIL *Rallus pectoralis* 22 cm
Rare, medium-sized shy ground bird; short tail; dark
upperparts; **rich chestnut head and nape** with black
streaks; **slate-grey throat and breast;** barred wings,
belly and under tail-coverts; **long black-tipped pink
bill.** Damp grassland and reedy swamps.
May be confused with: BUFF-BANDED RAIL, but
look for long bill, no eyebrow and slate-grey extending
from throat to upper belly.

BUSH-HEN *Amaurornis olivaceus* 26 cm
Medium-sized, **plain,** secretive ground bird; short
stubby tail; olive-brown and greyish; **buff lower belly
and under tail-coverts;** dull yellow legs; develops red
base to green bill during breeding season
approximately Nov.–Mar. Dense shrubby or grassy
creeks and dense wet grassland. *May be confused with:*
NONE. Distinct, with buff belly and under tail-coverts.

BAILLON'S CRAKE *Porzana pusilla* 15 cm
Small aquatic bird; stubby tail; olive back streaked
black; **plain grey face, throat and breast; olive-
brown legs; green bill;** barred belly and under tail-
coverts. Freshwater swamps and lagoons with reeds
and tussocks. *May be confused with:* Possibly other
small crakes, but BAILLON'S CRAKE distinct. Look
for plain grey face, olive-brown legs and all-green bill.

AUSTRALIAN SPOTTED CRAKE
Porzana fluminea 20 cm
Rare, small aquatic bird with stubby tail; olive back spotted white; barred black and white belly; **plain dark grey throat and breast; pure white under tail-coverts; olive-green bill with red base;** olive-green legs. Mostly well-vegetated freshwater swamps. *May be confused with:* Possibly other small crakes, but fairly distinct. Look for white under tail-coverts and olive-green bill with red base.

SPOTLESS CRAKE *Porzana tabuensis* 18 cm
Small aquatic bird; stubby tail; dark slate-grey head and underparts; chocolate-brown upperparts; **black bill; red legs; red eye.** Mostly very dense well-vegetated freshwater swamps.

WHITE-BROWED CRAKE *Porzana cinerea* 19cm
Small aquatic bird; stubby tail; black and brown upperparts; grey throat, neck and breast; white belly; **dark stripe through eye with white eyebrow and white stripe below eye.** Freshwater swamps, especially those with reedbeds and water-lilies, also rice fields and sometimes about sugar-cane fields. Moreso in the lowlands. *May be confused with:* The smaller BAILLON'S CRAKE which lacks white stripes about eye. WHITE-BROWED shows buff flanks in flight.

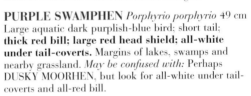

PURPLE SWAMPHEN *Porphyrio porphyrio* 49 cm
Large aquatic dark purplish-blue bird; short tail; **thick red bill; large red head shield; all-white under tail-coverts.** Margins of lakes, swamps and nearby grassland. *May be confused with:* Perhaps DUSKY MOORHEN, but look for all-white under tail-coverts and all-red bill.

DUSKY MOORHEN *Gallinula tenebrosa* 39 cm
A medium-sized aquatic bird; short tail; dark olive-brown; **red head shield; red bill tipped yellow; two white markings under tail** distinguish it from all other aquatic birds. Freshwater swamps, lakes, creeks, dams, especially those with open aquatic vegetation. *May be confused with:* PURPLE SWAMPHEN, which has heavier all-red bill and all-white under tail-coverts.

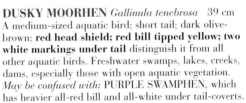

FERNWREN *Oreoscopus gutturalis* 13 cm
Small dark bird of the rainforest floor; rich olive-brown upperparts; slightly paler below; **white eyebrow and throat, margined below by small black 'bib';** longish bill. Juvenile: plain; **long thin buff eyebrow.** Occasionally flicks tail as it feeds. Upland rainforest, usually above 600 m, sometimes lower. *May be confused with:* Adult: YELLOW-THROATED and WHITE-BROWED SCRUBWRENS, but look for dark eye and black 'bib'. Juvenile: ATHERTON and LARGE-BILLED SCRUBWRENS. Look for long, thin buff eyebrow. Only the FERNWREN flicks its tail.

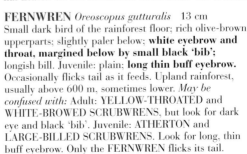

SPANGLED DRONGO *Dicrurus bracteatus* 30 cm
Noisy, medium-sized black bird; **fish tail; red eye;**
shrugs shoulders and flicks tail somewhat 'crazily'
while calling. Mostly edges of rainforest and adjacent
woodland throughout, but moreso at lower altitudes,
sometimes in mangroves. *May be confused with:* Male
COMMON KOEL, BLACK BUTCHERBIRD and male
SATIN BOWERBIRD. Look for fish tail. Only the
DRONGO flicks its tail. Occasionally the DRONGO
with outer tail feathers moulted or abraded has been
mistaken for the TRUMPET MANUCODE, a rainforest
bird of northern Cape York Peninsula.

CRIMSON FINCH *Neochmia phaeton* 13 cm
Small, long-tailed bird. Male: **deep crimson face,
bill, rump and underparts;** black belly; brown tail
washed crimson. Female: greyish-brown; **dull crimson
face, throat, rump and tail.** Flicks tail up and down
or sideways. Coastal paperbark swamps, rank grass
and about the edges of sugar-cane fields.
May be confused with: Male: NONE. Female:
sometimes misidentified as STAR FINCH, but look for
unspotted face and breast.

NUTMEG MANNIKIN *Lonchura punctulata* 11 cm
Introduced, small brown bird; dark bill; dark brown
face; yellowish rump; **finely-patterned 'scaly'
underparts.** Juvenile: overall brown, but more
yellowish below. Flicks tail from side to side.
Gregarious. Grassland, farmland, roadsides and fringes
of towns. *May be confused with:* Adult: NONE.
Juvenile: juvenile PLUM-HEADED FINCH which has
longer black tail, barred rump and white spots on
wing. Juvenile CHESTNUT-BREASTED MANNIKIN
has black under tail-coverts and paler underparts.

TAWNY GRASSBIRD *Megalurus timoriensis* 19 cm
Small brownish bird; brown upperparts **streaked
dark grey and black;** unstreaked fawn underparts;
longish brown tail often flicked; **plain rufous crown.**
Tall rank grassland, pastures, crops, grassy roadsides
and swampland. *May be confused with:* SINGING
BUSHLARK, RICHARD'S PIPIT, CLAMOROUS
REED-WARBLER, LITTLE GRASSBIRD, RUFOUS
SONGLARK and female BROWN SONGLARK. Look
for rufous crown and longish tail. Only the TAWNY
GRASSBIRD flicks its tail.

FURTHER POSSIBILITIES
WHITE-GAPED HONEYEATER
SHINING FLYCATCHER sometimes flicks tail.
Some FINCHES flick their tails when agitated.

POSSIBILITIES

BROWN CUCKOO-DOVE
Macropygia amboinensis 40 cm
A medium-sized **coppery-brown** bird without
distinctive markings. Usually allows a close approach.
Rainforest and its margins, lantana and Wild Tobacco
Solanum mauritianum thickets at all altitudes.

DIAMOND DOVE *Geopelia cuneata* 20 cm
Rare, rather plain small grey bird similar to PEACEFUL
DOVE; **white spotting on wings; red eye-ring.**
Juvenile: white bars in place of spots. Mostly dry open
forest. *May be confused with:* PEACEFUL DOVE, but
look for red eye-ring and absence of barring.

PEACEFUL DOVE *Geopelia striata* 20 cm
Small grey bird; **fine black barring on breast, nape,
hind neck and wings; blue eye-ring;** long narrow
tail; often sitting on powerlines. Eucalypt woodland,
lightly timbered grassland, open forest, parks and
gardens. *May be confused with:* DIAMOND DOVE, but
look for blue eye-ring and extensive barring.

AUSTRALIAN KING-PARROT
Alisterus scapularis 42 cm
Striking, medium-sized bird. Male: **brilliant red head
and underparts; dark green back and wings;** long
dark bluish tail. Female and immature: **dark green
head, back and wings;** red lower breast and belly.
Mostly upland rainforest and nearby eucalypt forest.

CRIMSON ROSELLA *Platycercus elegans* 33 cm
A medium-sized, striking bird; **blood-red head and
underparts;** long dark blue tail; **blue cheeks and
broad edges to wings.** Upland rainforest and nearby
eucalypt forest.

PALE-HEADED ROSELLA
Platycercus adscitus 30 cm
A colourful medium-sized bird; **pale yellow to white
head and throat; red under tail-coverts;** greenish-
blue belly, blue edges to wings; yellow and black back;
long greenish-blue tail. Eucalypt forest, tropical
woodland and lightly timbered grassland.

ORIENTAL CUCKOO *Cuculus saturatus* 31 cm
A long-tailed greyish bird; long wings and long tail give it
a hawk-like appearance in flight; **boldly barred lower
breast and belly;** yellow eye-ring and feet. Juvenile: dark
brown barring from throat to tail. Eucalypt forest and
woodland, paperbark swamps, sometimes about rainforest
clearings, moreso at lower altitudes. *May be confused
with:* Adult: perhaps BARRED CUCKOO-SHRIKE which
has similar barring, but refolds its wings on alighting and
has shorter tail. Juvenile and immature: juvenile and
immature PALLID, BRUSH and FAN-TAILED
CUCKOOS. See pp. 197–8.

PALLID CUCKOO *Cuculus pallidus* 31 cm
A medium-sized, overall greyish bird; long tail 'notched' white; **small white spot on nape; faint darker curved line through eye and down to shoulder;** yellow eye-ring, grey feet. Immature: **mottled brown and buff** on back and wings; lightly barred underparts heavier on breast; **streaked crown.** Open woodland. *May be confused with:* Adult: NONE. Juvenile and immature: juvenile and immature ORIENTAL, BRUSH and FAN-TAILED CUCKOOS. See pp. 197–8.

CHESTNUT-BREASTED CUCKOO
Cacomantis castaneiventris 24 cm
Rare; medium-sized. Adult: blue-grey above; **rich chestnut underparts;** yellow eye-ring and feet; **lower tail 'notched' white at sides.** Juvenile: pale reddish-brown above, paler below. Rainforest at high and low altitudes. *May be confused with:* Adult: FAN-TAILED CUCKOO. See p. 197. Juvenile: NONE.

FAN-TAILED CUCKOO
Cacomantis flabelliformis 26 cm
A medium-sized, slender bird; slate-grey above with **pale rufous underparts; yellow eye-ring** and yellowish feet; fairly long tail markedly 'notched' white **down each side.** Juvenile: brownish, tail 'notched' buff and dull barring on underparts. Rainforest and denser eucalypt forest. *May be confused with:* Adult: BRUSH and CHESTNUT-BREASTED CUCKOOS. See p. 197. Juvenile and immature: juvenile and immature ORIENTAL, PALLID and BRUSH CUCKOOS. See p. 198.

COMMON KOEL *Eudynamys scolopacea* 43 cm
Migrant, present Sept.–Apr.; rather shy medium-sized long-tailed bird. Male: **entirely black with pale bill.** Female: brown back and wings **heavily spotted white; black head;** brown tail barred white; white underparts barred brown. Juvenile: similar; more chestnut; no black crown. Denser open forest, woodland, gallery forest, dense trees in farmland, parks and gardens. *May be confused with:* Male: SPANGLED DRONGO, BLACK BUTCHERBIRD and male SATIN BOWERBIRD, but only KOEL has long tail. Female: NONE.

BUFF-BREASTED PARADISE-KINGFISHER
Tanysiptera sylvia 34 cm
Migrant, present Nov.–early Apr.; **distinctively spectacular;** thick red bill; brilliant blue and black above; rufous orange below; centre of back and rump white; **two very long, stiff, white tail feathers** which are sometimes broken-off during or after the breeding season. Mostly lowland rainforest.

121

EASTERN WHIPBIRD
Psophodes olivaceus 27 cm
Medium-sized. Adult: dark olive-green body; black head; **white cheek patches; small black crest** sometimes carried flat on back of head; long broad tail. Juvenile: plain brownish without cheek patches. Lower stratum of rainforest at higher altitudes, sometimes adjacent eucalypt forest. Sometimes coastal.

YELLOW WAGTAIL
Motacilla flava 18 cm
Rare summer visitor, present Nov.–Feb.; mostly terrestrial; **constantly teeters long tail;** overall greyish with whitish eyebrow; **blackish legs; olive-green rump.** Larger open areas of short grass on bare ground, sometimes swamp margins and open wetlands in coastal lowlands. *May be confused with:* GREY WAGTAIL, but look for greenish-grey rump and black legs. Note habitat.

GREY WAGTAIL
Motacilla cinerea 20 cm
Rare summer visitor, Nov.–Mar.; small; **constantly teeters tail;** greyish; yellowish underparts, brighter under tail-coverts; white eyebrow; **yellow-green rump; pale legs;** mostly terrestrial. Open areas in rainforest at high altitudes. *May be confused with:* YELLOW WAGTAIL, but look for yellowish-green rump and pale legs. Note habitat.

CRIMSON FINCH
Neochmia phaeton 13 cm
Small bird. Male: **deep crimson face, bill, rump and underparts;** black belly; long brown tail washed crimson. Female: greyish-brown, **dull crimson face, throat, rump and tail.** Coastal paperbark swamps, rank grass and about the edges of sugar-cane fields. *May be confused with:* Male: NONE. Female is sometimes misidentified as the STAR FINCH, but look for unspotted face and breast.

METALLIC STARLING
Aplonis metallica 24 cm
Medium-sized, gregarious bird; plumage appears **glossy black** but with purple and green iridescence. **Prominent, bulging red eye;** long, sharply pointed tail. Immature: white, striated underparts. Juvenile: similar; blackish eye. Rainforest and remnants of rainforest, sometimes mangroves, mostly at lower altitudes.

FURTHER POSSIBILITIES
BAR-SHOULDERED DOVE
GROUND CUCKOO-SHRIKE
TAWNY GRASSBIRD

POSSIBILITIES

RED-TAILED TROPICBIRD
Phaethon rubricauda 56 cm
An uncommon to rare white seabird; **red bill;** black eyebrow; black flank markings; **two long red tail streamers.** Waters and islands of Great Barrier Reef.

GREAT FRIGATEBIRD
Fregata minor 92 cm
Mostly black aerial seabird with **long slender wings and deeply forked tail.** Female has **white throat and breast.** Juvenile: brownish head. Lacks white 'armpits' of LESSER FRIGATEBIRD. Soars high on motionless wings. Offshore waters and islands of Great Barrier Reef, sometimes over coastal shorelines.
May be confused with: LESSER FRIGATEBIRD, but look for absence of white 'armpits' in both male and female, and also white throat in female.

LESSER FRIGATEBIRD
Fregata ariel 75 cm
Very similar to GREAT FRIGATEBIRD inhabiting similar oceanic areas. **White 'armpits' in flight. Female: all-black head and throat** and white underparts. Juvenile: brownish head.
May be confused with: GREAT FRIGATEBIRD, but look for white 'armpits' and all-black head in female.

CHANNEL-BILLED CUCKOO
Scythrops novaehollandiae 64 cm
Migrant, present Sept.–Apr.; overall grey; **large heavy pale curved bill; red about eye.** In flight, the **long wings and tail** give it a distinctive hawk-like appearance. Eucalypt forest, rainforest edges, gallery forest and farmland, wherever figs abound.

PHEASANT COUCAL
Centropus phasianinus 70 cm
Clumsy-looking; outsized tail; skulking; brownish in non-breeding plumage Apr.–Aug.; head and body **heavily streaked;** in breeding plumage head and body **black;** long broad dark tail with paler barring. Lives mostly on the ground in tall grassy areas in open forest and farmland.

FURTHER POSSIBILITIES
WHITE-TAILED TROPICBIRD — rare.

123

POSSIBILITIES

BLACK KITE *Milvus migrans* 52 cm
Generally abundant; large dark dull-brown bird of
prey; mostly seen flying or soaring on **slightly
drooped wings; tail continuously twisted and
turned;** tail squarish in flight but appears forked when
closed. Open areas. *May be confused with:* Other birds
of prey. See Diurnal Birds of Prey, pp. 175–81.

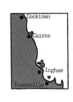

JACKY WINTER *Microeca fascinans* 13 cm
Small; grey-brown; paler below; **restlessly wags tail
from side to side; conspicuous white sides to tail;**
pale whitish eyebrow. Juvenile: well-striated. Drier open
sparsely timbered areas. *May be confused with:* Perhaps
female and juvenile WHITE-WINGED TRILLER which
have fairly plain tails. LEMON-BELLIED
FLYCATCHER has lemon underparts and plain tail. Tail
wagging in JACKY WINTER is diagnostic.

BROAD-BILLED FLYCATCHER
Myiagra ruficollis 15 cm
Rare small bird almost identical to female LEADEN
FLYCATCHER. Mangroves. *May be confused with:*
Female LEADEN and female SATIN FLYCATCHERS.
See p. 202.

LEADEN FLYCATCHER *Myiagra rubecula* 15 cm
Small bird; **constantly quivers its tail.** Male: blue-
grey upperparts; glossy-leaden head and upper breast
distinctly demarcated by white underparts.
Female: dull leaden-grey above; rusty-buff throat and
upper breast; white underparts. Eucalypt forest,
woodland, parks and gardens. *May be confused with:*
SATIN FLYCATCHER. Female LEADEN
FLYCATCHER may be confused with BROAD-
BILLED FLYCATCHER. See p. 202.

SATIN FLYCATCHER *Myiagra cyanoleuca* 16 cm
Rare passage migrant usually seen Aug.–Sept. and
Mar.–Apr.; almost identical to female LEADEN
FLYCATCHER. *May be confused with:* LEADEN
FLYCATCHER. Female SATIN may be confused with
BROAD-BILLED FLYCATCHER. See p. 202.

RESTLESS FLYCATCHER
Myiagra inquieta 20 cm
Small bird with black upperparts; white underparts
from throat to under tail; **faint buff on breast;** longish
straight tail which it sweeps from side to side;
frequently hovers. Open forest and woodland, often
near water and sometimes about farmhouses.
May be confused with: WILLIE WAGTAIL, but look
for white throat.

WILLIE WAGTAIL *Rhipidura leucophrys* 20 cm
Small, active, common fantail; black upperparts; **black throat; white eyebrow;** white upperparts. Tail partly spread and **twitched frequently.** Lightly timbered areas, farmland and urban areas. *May be confused with:* RESTLESS FLYCATCHER, but look for black throat.

WHITE-BREASTED WOODSWALLOW
Artamus leucorynchus 17 cm
Medium-sized; dark grey; **white underparts sharply demarcated by dark grey upper breast; bluish bill;** frequently wags tail. Often about water, swamps, lakes, mangroves and seashore. Ever present on powerlines.

MASKED WOODSWALLOW
Artamus personatus 19 cm
Rare, medium-sized bird; mid-grey; paler below; **bluish bill;** grey tail tipped white; frequently wags tail. Male: **large black face edged white.** Female: **subdued dusky-grey face.** Drier, open, lightly timbered country. *May be confused with:* Male: NONE. Female and juvenile: BLACK-FACED WOODSWALLOW, but look for large dusky-grey face and grey tail.

WHITE-BROWED WOODSWALLOW
Artamus superciliosus 19 cm
Rare, medium-sized bird; deep blue-grey; **chestnut lower breast and underparts; prominent white eyebrow; bluish bill;** dark grey face; grey tail tipped white; frequently wags tail. Female and juvenile duller. Usually in noisy flocks. Drier, open, lightly timbered country.

BLACK-FACED WOODSWALLOW
Artamus cinereus 18 cm
Medium-sized; smoky-grey; **small black face; bluish bill; black tail tipped white;** under tail-coverts white; frequently wags tail. Open, lightly timbered areas and almost treeless grassland. *May be confused with:* Female and juvenile MASKED WOODSWALLOW, but look for small black face and black tail.

DUSKY WOODSWALLOW
Artamus cyanopterus 18 cm
Small; overall dark smoky-brown; bluish-black wings; **bluish bill;** black tail tipped white; frequently wags tail; **thin white wing-stripe.** Open woodland and open areas with dead timber. *May be confused with:* LITTLE WOODSWALLOW which has no wing-stripe.

LITTLE WOODSWALLOW *Artamus minor* 14 cm
Rare; small; dark chocolate-brown; deep blue-grey wings; **bluish bill;** blackish-grey tail tipped white; frequently wags tail; **no wing-stripe.** Open and grassy woodland. *May be confused with:* DUSKY WOODSWALLOW, but look for plain wing without white wing-stripe.

FURTHER POSSIBILITIES
SQUARE-TAILED KITE and LITTLE EAGLE sometimes twist the tail in flight.
See Birds that Teeter, pp. 137–8.

POSSIBILITIES

ORIENTAL PRATINCOLE
Glareola maldivarum 24 cm
Rare summer visitor; medium-sized; long-winged;
olive-brown; buffish to white underparts; **buff throat
edged with broken black line; long forked tail** with
white sides and wide black margin at base; white
upper tail-coverts. Does not teeter. In flight, graceful
and tern-like; **chestnut underwing.** Open, short-
grassed plains, claypans and mudflats. *May be
confused with:* AUSTRALIAN PRATINCOLE, but look
for broken edging to buff throat when on ground, and
chestnut underwing and long forked tail in flight.

AUSTRALIAN PRATINCOLE *Stiltia isabella* 23 cm
Similar to ORIENTAL but has no throat patch; **square
tail, deep rufous belly patch;** longer legs; brownish
rump; white upper tail-coverts; white tail with broad,
black subterminal band. Frequently teeters rear of
body. Open, treeless, short-grassed and bare plains,
bare fallowed farmland and turf farms. *May be
confused with:* ORIENTAL PRATINCOLE which does
not teeter. Look for plain throat, rufous belly patch
and teetering when on ground. Square tail and
blackish underwing in flight.

TOPKNOT PIGEON *Lopholaimus antarcticus* 43 cm
Large overall-grey pigeon; **black tail with whitish
band; prominent chestnut 'bun' on back of head.**
Often flies above canopy, sometimes high. Rainforest,
moreso at higher altitudes. *May be confused with:*
NONE. Look for white tail band in flight.

LOVELY FAIRY-WREN *Malurus amabilis* 15 cm
Spectacular small bird with long **cocked bluish tail**
and prominent white tips to each feather forming
broad white edge to tail. Male: blue head and ear-
coverts; black throat and breast; chestnut rump.
Female: **dull-blue head, back and tail; pale-blue
ear-coverts;** white throat and underparts. Denser
tropical woodland, coastal paperbark swamps and
mangroves. *May be confused with:* NONE. Sometimes
misidentified as VARIEGATED FAIRY-WREN which
does not occur in the Wet Tropics.

EASTERN SPINEBILL
Acanthorhynchus tenuirostris 15 cm
Small active honeyeater; blackish head; rufous belly;
rufous patch in white throat; long fine curved bill;
shows much white in tail in flight; frequently hovers at
blossom. Rainforest and nearby eucalypt forest at
higher altitudes.

JACKY WINTER *Microeca fascinans* 13 cm

Small grey bird; paler below; **conspicuous white sides to tail;** pale whitish eyebrow; **restlessly wags tail from side to side.** Juvenile: well-striated. Drier open sparsely timbered areas. *May be confused with:* Perhaps female and juvenile WHITE-WINGED TRILLER which have fairly plain tails. LEMON-BELLIED FLYCATCHER has lemon underparts and plain tail. Tail wagging in JACKY WINTER is diagnostic.

GREY-CROWNED BABBLER

Pomatostomus temporalis 25 cm
Noisy, medium-sized bird usually in small groups; dark brown upperparts; pale crown; white throat and breast; brown belly; **longish tail prominently tipped white; tail partly spread and often cocked;** long curved bill. Drier forest and open woodland.

SPECTACLED MONARCH

Monarcha trivirgatus 16 cm
Small; grey back; **rufous breast; white belly;** black forehead and throat; black mask about eye; **black tail with conspicuous broad white corners.** Juvenile: lacks black about face. Rainforest at all altitudes. *May be confused with:* BLACK-FACED MONARCH which has all-grey tail. BLACK-WINGED MONARCH has all-black tail.

WHITE-EARED MONARCH

Monarcha leucotis 13 cm
Small; black, white and grey bird; **greyish white underparts; black tail conspicuously tipped white with white sides; three white patches about eye in black head.** Coastal rainforest, sometimes upland rainforest. *May be confused with:* Generally NONE. VARIED TRILLER has buff lower belly and under tail-coverts.

GREY FANTAIL *Rhipidura fuliginosa* 16 cm

Small active dark grey bird; **large fanned grey tail;** white tip and white shafts to each feather; white throat; short white eyebrow. Resident race *keasti* from upland rainforest **darker** and slightly smaller than wintering southern race which inhabits open forest, woodland, mangroves and denser parks and gardens. *May be confused with:* NORTHERN FANTAIL, but look for short thick white eyebrow and white mark behind eye. NORTHERN has a fine eyebrow only and little white in fairly straight tail.

FIGBIRD *Sphecotheres viridis* (Male) 28 cm

Medium-sized; deep olive-green back and wings; bright yellow (northern race) or green (southern race) underparts; black head; black tail with white edges and broad white corners; **large patch of red skin about eye.** Rainforest edges and remnants, gallery forest, nearby open forest, parks and gardens.

127

PIED CURRAWONG
Strepera graculina 46 cm
Large black and white bird; predominantly black when perched but black and white in flight; some white in wings; broad white tail tip; white rump and under tail-coverts; **prominent yellow eye;** heavy black bill. Hillside eucalypt forest, rainforest canopy and open woodland. Lowlands in winter.

RICHARD'S PIPIT *Anthus novaeseelandiae* 16 cm
Small brown ground bird; well-striated; prominent white sides to longish tail clearly visible in flight; **teeters tail up and down.** Open grassland and farmland. *May be confused with:* SINGING BUSHLARK, TAWNY GRASSBIRD, RUFOUS SONGLARK, female BROWN SONGLARK, but look for much white in tail and tail-teetering habit.

YELLOW WAGTAIL *Motacilla flava* 18 cm
Rare summer visitor, present usually Nov.–Feb.; small long-tailed ground bird; overall greyish with whitish eyebrow; **blackish legs; olive-green rump;** fairly broad white sides to tail; **constantly teeters tail up and down.** Larger, open areas of short grass on bare ground, sometimes swamp margins and open wetlands in coastal lowlands. *May be confused with:* GREY WAGTAIL, but look for olive-green rump and blackish legs. Note habitat.

GREY WAGTAIL *Motacilla cinerea* 20 cm
Rare summer visitor, Nov.–Mar.; similar to YELLOW WAGTAIL; yellowish underparts; brighter under tail-coverts; **yellow-green rump; pale legs.** Open areas in rainforest at high altitudes.
May be confused with: YELLOW WAGTAIL, but look for yellowish-green rump and pale legs. Note habitat.

RUSSET-TAILED THRUSH
Zoothera heinei 27 cm
Medium-sized brown bird with paler underparts; prominent 'scaly' pattern from throat to belly; white sides to tail seen only when tail spread in flight. Rainforest at higher altitudes. *May be confused with:* BASSIAN THRUSH and difficult to separate. BASSIAN has small white corners in tail. See p. 204.

FURTHER POSSIBILITIES
A number of birds have slight tail tips or an insignificant amount of white in the tail.
Some black and white birds have white patches in the tail, overwhelmed by the black and white pattern.
Male NANKEEN KESTREL has prominent black band in a greyish-white tail.

POSSIBILITIES

COMB-CRESTED JACANA
Irediparra gallinacea   22 cm
Medium-sized aquatic bird: brown back and wings:
whitish face, throat, breast and belly: black
breastband: pink or red comb on top of head:
disproportionately-long toes enable it to walk across
lily pads and floating vegetation. Freshwater swamps,
lagoons and dams.

SMALL & MEDIUM-SIZED BIRDS THAT FEED IN FRUITING TREES
POSSIBILITIES

SUPERB FRUIT-DOVE *Ptilinopus superbus* 23cm
A plump, medium-sized bird of the rainforest canopy.
Male: multicoloured: mid-green above: vivid **purple
crown: orange hind neck: blue-black breastband:
white belly:** red feet. Female: mostly green: white
belly: **bluish patch on rear of crown: greyish feet.**
Juvenile: overall greenish: underparts flecked or
mottled with yellow. Rainforest at all altitudes. *May be
confused with:* ROSE-CROWNED FRUIT-DOVE
which has yellow belly. Look for white belly in adult.
Juveniles of both species almost impossible to separate.

Male

Female

ROSE-CROWNED FRUIT-DOVE
Ptilinopus regina   22 cm
A plump, medium-sized bird or small pigeon: **rose-
pink crown:** pink across lower breast: **yellow belly
and broad yellow tail tip:** grey feet. Juvenile: overall
greenish: underparts flecked or mottled with yellow.
Male and female similar. Rainforest, moreso on coast,
especially offshore islands. *May be confused with:*
SUPERB FRUIT-DOVE which has white belly. Look
for yellow belly and tail tip. Juveniles of both species
almost impossible to separate.

Adult

Juvenile

DOUBLE-EYED FIG-PARROT
Cyclopsitta diophthalma   14 cm
Small mostly all-green parrot: very short tail: **thick
dark bill:** colourful facial pattern. Male: **red cheek
and forehead: blue about eye.** Female: similar, but
face mainly blue with buffy cheek patch. Rainforest at
most altitudes but mainly in the lowlands, often
breeding in nearby paperbark swamps. *May be
confused with:* LITTLE LORIKEET which has red
forehead and throat. Does not usually feed in fruiting
trees.

COMMON KOEL *Eudynamys scolopacea*   43 cm

Migrant, present Sept.–Apr.; rather shy, medium-sized, long-tailed bird. Male: **entirely black with pale bill.** Female: brown back and wings **heavily spotted white; black head;** brown tail barred white; whitish underparts barred brown. Juvenile: similar to female; more chestnut; no black crown. Denser, open forest, woodland, gallery forest, dense trees in farmland, parks and gardens. *May be confused with:* Male: SPANGLED DRONGO which has fish tail and dark bill. Male SATIN BOWERBIRD which has short tail, longish pale legs and violet eye. Look for long tail and pale bill. Female: NONE.

BARRED CUCKOO-SHRIKE

Coracina lineata   27 cm

Immaculate medium-sized grey bird; **refolds wings on alighting; grey fine barring from lower breast to under tail; yellow eye;** black wing and tail tips. Rainforest at all altitudes. *May be confused with:* Perhaps adult ORIENTAL CUCKOO which has similar barring, yellow eye-ring and feet, long 'notched' tail and does not usually inhabit fruiting trees.

YELLOW ORIOLE *Oriolus flavocinctus*   28 cm

Medium-sized **yellow-green bird with some striations; red bill and eye;** yellow edges to wing feathers and tail tip. Juvenile: well-striated, bill and eye brownish. Rainforest, gallery forest at low altitudes, and mangroves. *May be confused with:* OLIVE-BACKED ORIOLE, but look for overall yellow-green colouration and yellow tips and edges to wing feathers.

OLIVE-BACKED ORIOLE *Oriolus sagittatus* 27cm

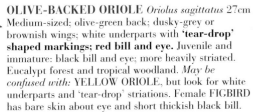

Medium-sized; olive-green back; dusky-grey or brownish wings; white underparts with **'tear-drop' shaped markings; red bill and eye.** Juvenile and immature: black bill and eye; more heavily striated. Eucalypt forest and tropical woodland. *May be confused with:* YELLOW ORIOLE, but look for white underparts and 'tear-drop' striations. Female FIGBIRD has bare skin about eye and short thickish black bill.

FIGBIRD *Sphecotheres viridis*   28 cm

Northern race

Female

Southern race

Medium-sized. Male: deep olive-green back and wings; bright yellow underparts (north of Townsville) or variable green to yellow (about Townsville); black head; black tail with white edges; **large area of red skin about eye.** Female: brownish, with paler, **heavily striated underparts; grey eye patch;** thickish black bill. Rainforest edges and remnants, gallery forest, parks and gardens. *May be confused with:* Male: NONE. Female: juvenile YELLOW ORIOLE, OLIVE-BACKED ORIOLE and TOOTH-BILLED BOWERBIRD, but look for bare grey skin about eye and thickish black bill.

VICTORIA'S RIFLEBIRD *Ptiloris victoriae* 24 cm
Medium-sized, short-tailed bird with **long, curved, black bill.** Male: velvety-black; iridescent green crown; triangular patch on throat. Female: greyish-brown above; rufous-buff below with darker flecking. Rainforest at all altitudes.

SPOTTED CATBIRD *Ailuroedus melanotis* 28 cm
Medium-sized bird with deep-green back and wings; paler underparts spotted buffy-white; **brownish crown and throat heavily spotted white; dark ear-coverts; red eye.** Rainforest at all altitudes.

TOOTH-BILLED BOWERBIRD
Scenopoeetes dentirostris 26 cm
Medium-sized; olive-brown; paler below; **coarse striations on breast and belly; robust dark bill.** Fast, direct flight, quick movements. Upland rainforest above 600 m, sometimes lower. *May be confused with:* Female FIGBIRD which has bare grey skin about eye, smaller bill and usually inhabits more open habitat. Juvenile and immature OLIVE-BACKED ORIOLES which have finer bill, greenish head and back and grey tail. Mostly open forest.

GOLDEN BOWERBIRD
Prionodura newtoniana 24 cm
Medium-sized; short bill; yellow eye. Male: striking; **golden-olive above; golden-yellow below.** Female: plain; olive back with ash-grey underparts. Upland rainforest, usually above 900 m, sometimes lower.

SATIN BOWERBIRD *Ptilonorhynchus violaceus* 24 cm
Medium-sized. Male: **glossy blue-black; shortish tail; pale bill; violet eye.** Female: olive-green; paler underparts with **darker 'scaly' pattern from throat to belly;** blue eye; longish, pale legs. Rainforest margins and adjacent open forest at higher altitudes. *May be confused with:* Male: male COMMON KOEL, SPANGLED DRONGO and male VICTORIA'S RIFLEBIRD, but look for short tail, short pale bill and violet eye. Female: NONE.

GREAT BOWERBIRD *Chlamydera nuchalis* 34 cm
Medium-sized; brownish back, wings and rump with feathers **margined greyish-white; plain grey head and underparts.** Male and some females have lilac nape crest, hidden when not displaying. Drier eucalypt forest and woodland, sometimes parks and gardens.

SILVEREYE *Zosterops lateralis* 12 cm
Small; yellow-green; paler below; **prominent white ring around eye;** greyish breast and back. Feeds on smaller fruits. Rainforest and margins, gallery forest, mangroves, parks and gardens.

METALLIC STARLING *Aplonis metallica* 24 cm
Medium-sized gregarious bird; plumage appears glossy-black but with purple and green iridescence.
Prominent, bulging red eye; long, sharply pointed tail.
Immature: white striated underparts. Juvenile: similar;
blackish eye. Rainforest and remnants of rainforest,
sometimes mangroves, mostly at lower altitudes.

LARGE BIRDS THAT FEED IN FRUITING TREES
POSSIBILITIES

WHITE-HEADED PIGEON
Columba leucomela 40 cm
Large pigeon with white head and underparts; **black
back, wings and tail; red bill; red about eye.**
Rainforest at all altitudes, but moreso in higher areas.

WOMPOO FRUIT-DOVE
Ptilinopus magnificus 37 cm
Large colourful pigeon of mid and upper strata of
rainforest; green upperparts; **greyish-white head;
purple breast; yellow belly.** Rainforest at all
altitudes, occasionally in tropical woodland.

PIED IMPERIAL-PIGEON *Ducula bicolor* 42 cm
Migrant, present Aug.–Apr.; predominantly white
pigeon; **black flight feathers and lower half of tail;**
head may be soiled brownish from fruit stains.
Rainforest and mangroves on coastal lowlands and
offshore islands.

TOPKNOT PIGEON *Lopholaimus antarcticus* 43cm
Overall-grey pigeon; red bill; **prominent chestnut
'bun' on back of head; black tail with whitish
band near tip;** often flies above canopy, sometimes
high. Rainforest, moreso at higher altitudes.
May be confused with: NONE. Look for white tail
band in flight.

CHANNEL-BILLED CUCKOO
Scythrops novaehollandiae 64 cm
Migrant, present Sept.–Apr.; overall grey; **large,
heavy, pale, curved bill; red about eye.** In flight,
long wings and tail give it a distinctive, hawk-like
appearance. Eucalypt forest, rainforest edges, gallery
forest and farmland, wherever figs abound.

PIED CURRAWONG *Strepera graculina* 46 cm
Large black and white bird; predominantly black when
perched but black and white in flight; some white in
wing; broad white tail tip; white rump and under tail-
coverts; **prominent yellow eye;** heavy black bill.
Hillside eucalypt forest, rainforest canopy and open
woodland. Lowlands in winter.

POSSIBILITIES

WHITE-THROATED TREECREEPER
Cormobates leucophaeus 14 cm
Small; brownish above; paler below; **small white throat patch; heavily streaked underparts from lower breast to tail.** Hops up tree trunks. Upland rainforest and adjacent wet sclerophyll. *May be confused with:* BROWN TREECREEPER which has prominent whitish eyebrow and inhabits dry open forest.

BROWN TREECREEPER
Climacteris picumnus 17 cm
Small to medium-sized; **blackish-brown upperparts** (paler in southern Wet Tropics); grey breast; **underparts lightly but prominently streaked white with black edging; pale throat; prominent whitish eyebrow.** Drier woodland and eucalypt forest, especially where Poplar Gum *Eucalyptus platyphylla* grows. *May be confused with:* WHITE-THROATED TREECREEPER, but look for eyebrow.

VARIED SITTELLA
Daphoenositta chrysoptera 11 cm
A small short-tailed dark **heavily striated** bird; small **white wingbar;** slightly upturned bill; yellow eye-ring, legs and feet. Male: dark crown. Female: dark head, throat and upper breast. Dry woodland and eucalypt forest, especially where Ironbark *Eucalyptus* spp. grow.

PIED MONARCH
Arses kaupi 14 cm
Small; white collar; erectile frill on nape; **wide black breastband on white underparts; blue eye-ring.** Female: broader breastband; incomplete collar; greyish nape. Rainforest, moreso at lower altitudes.

VICTORIA'S RIFLEBIRD
Ptiloris victoriae 24 cm
A medium-sized short-tailed bird with **long, curved, black bill.** Male: velvety-black; iridescent green crown and triangular patch on throat. Female: greyish-brown above; rufous-buff below with darker flecking. Rainforest at all altitudes.

FURTHER POSSIBILITIES
Some birds, such as LARGE-BILLED SCRUBWREN, occasionally feed on tree trunks.

POSSIBILITIES

PALE-YELLOW ROBIN *Tregellasia capito* 13 cm
Small; unobtrusive; greenish-grey upperparts; **greenish-yellow** underparts; **buff from bill to eye; white throat.** Rainforest at all altitudes.

EASTERN YELLOW ROBIN
Eopsaltria australis 15 cm
Small; medium-grey upperparts; **bright yellow underparts and rump; grey face.** Tropical woodland with some understorey, wet sclerophyll.

GREY-HEADED ROBIN
Heteromyias albispecularis 17 cm
Small; deep olive-brown above; rufous rump; **grey head and breast; whitish throat; conspicuous white double bars on dark wings** in flight. Often seen flying low over roadways. Lower stratum of upland rainforest. Sometimes in lowland rainforest. *May be confused with:* NONE, but juvenile sometimes misidentified as WHITE-BROWED ROBIN which inhabits a much drier habitat.

FURTHER POSSIBILITIES
LESSER SOOTY OWL

BIRDS THAT FREQUENTLY HOVER
POSSIBILITIES

BLACK-SHOULDERED KITE
Elanus axillaris 36 cm
Medium-sized immaculate bird or small bird of prey, appearing white at a distance but with grey back, wings and tail; **black shoulder patches;** red eye; frequently hovers with tail down and legs dangling. Open grassland and farmland. *May be confused with:* NONE, but LETTER-WINGED KITE sometimes appears as a vagrant.

BROWN FALCON
Falco berigora Male 45 cm Female 55 cm
A large bird with variable plumage — pale brown to near black; underparts sometimes paler; **paler throat and cheek; darker 'moustache' below eye; lightly-barred underwing and tail;** hovers clumsily. Open woodland, farmland, often on roadside power poles. *May be confused with:* NONE. No other large brown birds of prey hovers frequently.

NANKEEN KESTREL *Falco cenchroides* 33 cm
Medium-sized bird or small bird of prey; **pale rufous upperparts; whitish underparts; black flight feathers;** frequently hovers on flat wings. Open grassland and farmland.

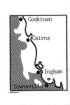

BROWN GERYGONE
Gerygone mouki   10 cm
Small, active, plain greyish bird; paler below; white
eyebrow; hovers outside foliage. Mostly upland
rainforest above 250 m. *May be confused with:* Other
grey gerygones. See p. 200.

LARGE-BILLED GERYGONE
Gerygone magnirostris   11 cm
Small, plain, active, greyish bird similar to BROWN
GERYGONE. Along streams, about paperbark swamps
and mangroves, mostly in lowlands. *May be confused
with:* Other grey gerygones. See p. 200.

MANGROVE GERYGONE
Gerygone levigaster   10 cm
Small, plain, active, greyish bird of mangroves and
adjacent forest. Similar to BROWN GERYGONE. *May
be confused with:* Other grey gerygones. See p. 200.

WESTERN GERYGONE
Gerygone fusca   10 cm
Rare; small active greyish bird similar to BROWN
GERYGONE. Dry open forest and woodland. *May be
confused with:* Other grey gerygones. See p. 200.

FAIRY GERYGONE *Gerygone palpebrosa*   11 cm
Small; greenish above; lemon underparts. Male north
of about Innisfail has blackish-brown throat; prominent
white 'whisker' down each side of face from bill.
South of Innisfail, male resembles female with only a
small black chin and trace of white 'whisker'. Female:
whitish throat merging into pale lemon breast.
Sometimes hovers about foliage. Lowland rainforest,
gallery forest, coastal vine scrub and mangroves.
Usually below 500 m. *May be confused with:*
WEEBILL has a short pale bill and white eye. WHITE-
THROATED GERYGONE has a well-demarcated white
throat. (Female FAIRY is difficult to separate from
juvenile WHITE-THROATED which lacks white
throat.) BUFF-RUMPED THORNBILL has a buff-
yellow rump. YELLOW THORNBILL has striations
behind eye. None occur in the denser habitats preferred
by the FAIRY.

*Male
(northern)*

*Male
(southern)*

Female

WHITE-THROATED GERYGONE
Gerygone olivacea   11 cm
Small; brown back; **yellow breast and belly; well-
demarcated white throat.** Juvenile: lacks white
throat. Hovers about foliage. Eucalypt forest and
woodland. *May be confused with:* WEEBILL, FAIRY
GERYGONE, BUFF-RUMPED and YELLOW
THORNBILLS. In adult, look for demarcated white
throat. Juvenile is difficult to separate from juvenile
and female FAIRY, but habitat should give some
indication.

EASTERN SPINEBILL
Acanthorhynchus tenuirostris   15 cm
Small active bird; blackish head; dark back and wings; **rufous patch in white throat; long, fine, curved bill;** rufous belly; shows much white in tail in flight. Frequently hovers at blossom. Rainforest and nearby eucalypt forest at higher altitudes.

JACKY WINTER *Microeca fascinans*   13 cm
Small; grey-brown; paler below; **restlessly wags tail from side to side; conspicuous white sides to tail;** pale whitish eyebrow; often hovers over grass. Juvenile: well-striated. Drier open sparsely timbered areas. *May be confused with:* Perhaps female and juvenile WHITE-WINGED TRILLER, but look for white-sided tail restlessly wagged. LEMON-BELLIED FLYCATCHER has lemon underparts and plain tail.

RESTLESS FLYCATCHER *Myiagra inquieta* 20cm
Small; black upperparts; white underparts from throat to under tail; **faint buff on breast;** longish, straight tail which it **sweeps from side to side;** frequently hovers. Open forest and woodland, often near water and sometimes about farmhouses.
May be confused with: Perhaps WILLIE WAGTAIL which does not hover.

BLACK-FACED WOODSWALLOW
Artamus cinereus   18 cm
Medium-sized; smoky-grey; **small black face; bluish bill; black tail tipped white;** white under tail-coverts; tail frequently wagged. Often hovers to take prey. Open, lightly timbered areas and almost treeless grassland. *May be confused with:* Female and juvenile MASKED WOODSWALLOW but look for black tail and small black face.

SINGING BUSHLARK *Mirafra javanica*   13 cm
Small; well-striated; paler below; **reddish patches on shoulders distinctive in flight; jerky, fluttering and hovering flight** low over grass or high in the air in courtship display. Drier grassland, farmland and crops.
May be confused with: RICHARD'S PIPIT, TAWNY GRASSBIRD, RUFOUS SONGLARK and female BROWN SONGLARK, none of which hovers.

FURTHER POSSIBILITIES
A number of species hover less frequently, others rarely, e.g.
OSPREY
PACIFIC BAZA
SWAMP HARRIER
Some TERNS
WEEBILL
Some THORNBILLS
EASTERN SPINEBILL
BROWN-BACKED and RUFOUS-THROATED HONEYEATERS
LEMON-BELLIED FLYCATCHER
SPECTACLED MONARCH
BLACK-FACED CUCKOO-SHRIKE
WHITE-WINGED TRILLER

POSSIBILITIES

WOOD SANDPIPER *Tringa glareola*   22 cm

Medium-sized shorebird; grey-brown above with **profuse white spotting;** whitish below; washed grey across breast; white rump; mostly white tail, finely barred black; straight black bill; prominent white eyebrow; long **greenish-yellow legs** protrude beyond tail in flight. Nervously active. Shallow freshwater swamps often with some timber, and muddy edges of waterholes. *May be confused with:* MARSH SANDPIPER but look for well-spotted darker upperparts and white eyebrow.

COMMON SANDPIPER *Actitis hypoleucos* 20 cm

Small shorebird; bronze-brown above; white below; brownish on sides of breast; **white above shoulder;** faintly barred wing-coverts; white eyebrow; tail longer than folded wings; shortish green legs; fine, white eye-ring; **constant nervous teetering;** white wingbar in flight. Mudbanks, creeks, swamps and mangrove channels. *May be confused with:* NONE. Look for white eye-ring, white above shoulder and constant teetering.

GREY-TAILED TATTLER
Heteroscelus brevipes   27 cm

A plump, medium-sized shorebird; **plain grey above;** whitish below; washed grey across breast; yellow legs; grey bill. Teeters body while feeding. Tidal flats, mangroves, reefs and rocky shorelines. *May be confused with:* WANDERING TATTLER. Can be difficult to separate but wing tips of GREY-TAILED **are the same length as or only slightly longer than the tail,** whereas those of WANDERING **extend 1 cm or more beyond tail.** WANDERING appears more brownish overall. Length of the nasal groove is only useful when in the hand. Calls are quite distinct. GREY-TAILED has a double-note call; WANDERING a trill of 6-10 notes.

WANDERING TATTLER
Heteroscelus incanus   27 cm
Similar to GREY-TAILED TATTLER but generally appears more brownish. Rocky shores, coral reefs, beaches. Mostly on offshore islands.
May be confused with: GREY-TAILED TATTLER.

PAINTED SNIPE *Rostratula benghalensis* 24 cm

Rare; medium-sized; overall greyish-brown but with blackish-brown head and breast; **bold white ring about eye leading back to nape; whitish line down middle of crown; curved white bar on side of breast bordering wing** changing to buff as it continues down back; long, grey, pinkish-tipped bill slightly drooped at tip. Female: larger; more boldly marked. Male: duller; striated throat. Teeters rear of body up and down. Shallow freshwater swamps.

AUSTRALIAN PRATINCOLE
Stiltia isabella   23 cm
Medium-sized, long-winged, cinnamon-brown bird; **deep rufous belly patch; square tail; brownish rump;** white upper tail-coverts; white tail with black subterminal band; black legs. Graceful and tern-like in flight. Frequently teeters rear of body. Open, short-grassed plains, aerodromes, fallowed paddocks, sometimes mudflats. *May be confused with:* ORIENTAL PRATINCOLE which does not teeter. ORIENTAL has broken black edging to buff throat patch and chestnut underwings.

RICHARD'S PIPIT
Anthus novaeseelandiae   16 cm
Small, well-striated light-brown bird; **teeters longish tail up and down.** Open grassland and farmland. *May be confused with:* SINGING BUSHLARK, TAWNY GRASSBIRD, RUFOUS SONGLARK and female BROWN SONGLARK, none of which teeter.

YELLOW WAGTAIL
Motacilla flava   18 cm
Rare summer visitor, present usually Nov.–Feb.; small bird; mostly terrestrial; overall greyish with white eyebrow; **blackish legs; olive-green rump; constantly teeters long tail.** Larger, open areas of short grass on bare ground, sometimes swamp margins and open wetlands in coastal lowlands. *May be confused with:* GREY WAGTAIL, but look for olive-green rump and black legs. Note habitat.

GREY WAGTAIL   *Motacilla cinerea*   20 cm
Rare summer visitor, Nov.–Mar.; small, mostly terrestrial bird similar to YELLOW WAGTAIL; greyish; yellowish underparts; brighter under tail-coverts; white eyebrow; **yellowish-green rump; pale legs;** constantly teeters long tail. Open areas in rainforest at high altitudes. *May be confused with:* YELLOW WAGTAIL, but look for yellowish-green rump and pale legs. Note habitat.

SMALL BROWN BIRDS OF THE RAINFOREST
POSSIBILITIES

WHITE-THROATED TREECREEPER
Cormobates leucophaeus   14 cm
Brownish above; paler below; **small white throat patch; heavily streaked underparts from lower breast to tail.** Hops up tree trunks. Upland rainforest and adjacent wet sclerophyll forest. *May be confused with:* BROWN TREECREEPER which inhabits dry open forest.

ATHERTON SCRUBWREN *Sericornis keri* 13 cm
A **plain nondescript** bird of the lower stratum of
upland rainforest above 750 m; dark eye in a pale,
brown face. *May be confused with:* Juvenile
FERNWREN which is rich olive-brown above with
long thin buff eyebrow, dark face and eye and longish
bill. LARGE-BILLED SCRUBWREN. See p. 200.

LARGE-BILLED SCRUBWREN
Sericornis magnirostris 13 cm
A plain nondescript bird mostly of the mid stratum of
rainforest almost identical to ATHERTON
SCRUBWREN. Rainforest at all altitudes, but mostly
below 1000 m. *May be confused with:* Juvenile
FERNWREN which is rich olive-brown above with
thin buff eyebrow, dark face and eye. ATHERTON
SCRUBWREN. See p. 200.

TROPICAL SCRUBWREN
Sericornis beccarii   11cm
Plain bird; **red eye; two small white marks on
shoulder;** white broken eye-ring. Mostly lowland
rainforest, dune scrub and similar dense habitat. *May
be confused with:* LARGE-BILLED SCRUBWREN, but
look for red eye and shoulder markings.

MOUNTAIN THORNBILL
Acanthiza katherina   10 cm
Greenish-brown with pale greenish-yellow underparts;
**chestnut rump; whitish eye and indistinct
scalloping on forehead** distinguish it from all other
rainforest birds. Upland rainforest above 600 m.
May be confused with: Perhaps BROWN GERYGONE
which is overall grey.

MACLEAY'S HONEYEATER
Xanthotis macleayana   20 cm
Stocky; initially appearing brownish; **boldly streaked;
black cap; patch of orange skin about eye.**
Rainforest, gallery forest, sometimes nearby eucalypt
forest and gardens at all altitudes.

BRIDLED HONEYEATER
Lichenostomus frenatus   20 cm
Often appears as a brownish bird with a **dark head;**
dark throat; yellow and white lines along dark bill;
**small white area behind eye; small yellow tuft on
ear;** pale buff patch on side of neck. Active, aggressive
and noisy. Rainforest above 600 m but to coast in
winter. *May be confused with:* YELLOW-FACED
HONEYEATER which has thick yellow line below eye
from bill to ear. YELLOW-FACED usually does not
inhabit rainforest.

DUSKY HONEYEATER *Myzomela obscura* 13 cm
Plain, dark brown nondescript bird with longish curved bill. Very active. Rainforest at all altitudes, gallery forest, mangroves, and open forest.
May be confused with: BROWN HONEYEATER and female SCARLET HONEYEATER with which it sometimes associates. Look for plain dark-brown bird.

GREY-HEADED ROBIN
Heteromyias albispecularis 17 cm
Deep olive-brown above; rufous rump; grey **head and breast; whitish throat; conspicuous white double bars on dark wings** in flight. Often seen flying low over roadways. Inhabits lower stratum of upland rainforest, occasionally lowland rainforest.
May be confused with: NONE, but juvenile sometimes misidentified as WHITE-BROWED ROBIN which inhabits a much drier habitat.

FURTHER POSSIBILITIES
See also Small Brown Birds of the Rainforest Floor, pp. 141–2.
Juvenile BUFF-BREASTED PARADISE-KINGFISHER is brownish with short tail.
Juvenile PALE YELLOW ROBIN is brownish for a short time after fledging.

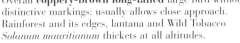

MEDIUM-SIZED & LARGE BROWN BIRDS OF THE RAINFOREST
POSSIBILITIES

BROWN CUCKOO-DOVE
Macropygia amboinensis 40 cm
Overall **coppery-brown long-tailed** large bird without distinctive markings; usually allows close approach. Rainforest and its edges, lantana and Wild Tobacco *Solanum mauritianum* thickets at all altitudes.

BRUSH CUCKOO
Cacomantis variolosus 24 cm
Medium-sized. Adult: initially appearing brownish; **grey eye-ring; fairly plain square tail tipped white;** grey head; buff-grey breast; buff belly. Juvenile: mottled and barred brown. Rainforest at most altitudes and most other forested habitats. *May be confused with:* Perhaps FAN-TAILED CUCKOO. See pp. 197–8.

LITTLE SHRIKE-THRUSH
Colluricincla megarhyncha 18 cm
Medium-sized **plain** bird; slightly striated on throat and upper breast; **pinkish-brown** bill; shortish tail. Rainforest moreso at lower altitudes, gallery forest and mangroves. *May be confused with:* BOWER'S SHRIKE-THRUSH which has dark grey back and head and black bill.

BOWER'S SHRIKE-THRUSH
Colluricincla boweri   20 cm
Medium-sized bird initially appearing dark-brownish;
short-tailed; **dark grey back and head; black bill;**
rufous underparts striated grey on throat and upper
breast. Upland rainforest, usually above 400 m.
May be confused with: LITTLE SHRIKE-THRUSH
which has pinkish-brown bill and is overall brown.

BLACK BUTCHERBIRD
Cracticus quoyi   (Juvenile) 36 cm
Medium-sized; rufous; streaked upperparts and paler
underparts; **thick, finely hooked blue-grey bill
tipped black.** Usually in the company of black adults.
Rainforest, moreso at lower altitudes, mangroves, and
all denser habitats.

VICTORIA'S RIFLEBIRD
Ptiloris victoriae   (Female) 24 cm
Medium-sized short-tailed bird; **long curved black
bill;** greyish-brown above; rufous-buff below with
darker flecking. Rainforest at all altitudes.

TOOTH-BILLED BOWERBIRD
Scenopoeetes dentirostris   26 cm
Medium-sized; olive-brown; paler below; **coarse
streaking on breast and belly; robust dark bill.**
Fast direct flight. Quick movements. Upland rainforest
above 600 m, sometimes lower. *May be confused with:*
Female FIGBIRD which has bare grey skin about eye,
smaller bill and usually inhabits more open habitat.
Juvenile and immature OLIVE-BACKED ORIOLE
have finer bill, greenish head and back, grey tail and
inhabit mostly open forest.

GOLDEN BOWERBIRD
Prionodura newtoniana   (Female) 24 cm
Medium-sized; **plain;** appears grey-brown; **olive back;
ash-grey underparts;** yellow eye; short bill. Upland
rainforest, usually above 900 m, sometimes lower.

FURTHER POSSIBILITIES
See also Medium-sized and Large Birds of the Rainforest Floor,
pp. 142–3.

SMALL BROWN BIRDS OF THE RAINFOREST FLOOR
POSSIBILITIES

FERNWREN   *Oreoscopus gutturalis* 13 cm
Rich olive-brown upperparts; slightly paler below;
**white eyebrow and throat, margined below by
small black 'bib';** longish bill. Juvenile: plain, but with
long, thin, buff eyebrow. Upland rainforest, usually
above 600 m, sometimes lower. *May be confused with:*
Adult: YELLOW-THROATED and WHITE-BROWED
SCRUBWRENS, but look for dark eye and black 'bib'.
Juvenile: ATHERTON and LARGE-BILLED
SCRUBWRENS, but look for long, thin, buff eyebrow;
darker face and eye and longish bill.

YELLOW-THROATED SCRUBWREN
Sericornis citreogularis   14 cm
Fine yellow eyebrow; yellow throat, wide, dark marking through eye; longish pink legs. Female: duller. Upland rainforest above 600 m, sometimes down to 300 m. *May be confused with:* FERNWREN and WHITE-BROWED SCRUBWREN. Look for yellow eyebrow and throat.

WHITE-BROWED SCRUBWREN
Sericornis frontalis   13 cm
Brown above; paler below; **white eyebrow over a pale yellow eye; white throat; two small white markings on shoulder.** Female: duller. Denser eucalypt forest and rainforest edges in upland areas. *May be confused with:* FERNWREN and YELLOW-THROATED SCRUBWREN but look for white throat without black 'bib', and pale eye.

ATHERTON SCRUBWREN *Sericornis keri* 13 cm
A plain nondescript bird of the lower stratum of upland rainforest above 750 m; dark eye in a pale-brown face. *May be confused with:* Juvenile FERNWREN which is rich olive-brown with long, thin, buff eyebrow, darker face and eye and longish bill. LARGE-BILLED SCRUBWREN. See p. 200.

FURTHER POSSIBILITIES
The GREY-HEADED ROBIN often takes food from the rainforest floor.

MEDIUM-SIZED & LARGE BROWN BIRDS OF THE RAINFOREST FLOOR
POSSIBILITIES

AUSTRALIAN BRUSH-TURKEY
Alectura lathami   70 cm
Large black bird; **bare red head; tail flattened sideways.** Male: large yellow wattles during breeding season Aug.–Feb. Rainforest at all altitudes, but mainly upland rainforest.

ORANGE-FOOTED SCRUBFOWL
Megapodius reinwardt   40 cm
Large plain bird; dark slate-grey head, neck and upperparts; chestnut-brown above; prominent **crest on back of head;** powerful **orange legs and feet.** Rainforest, moreso at lower altitudes, coastal vine scrubs, also mangroves.

RED-NECKED CRAKE *Rallina tricolor*   30 cm
Medium-sized; initially appearing dark-brown; **rich-chestnut head, neck and breast;** dark-brown body; short tail, often flicked. Rainforest, especially close to water. Mostly at lower altitudes.

LARGE-TAILED NIGHTJAR
Caprimulgus macrurus 26 cm

Nocturnal; medium-sized; dark-coloured with intricately-patterned plumage; thin, white crescent on each side of throat: **white bristles about bill. In flight, shows small white patch in underwing and white corners to tail.** Rainforest edges, adjacent woodland, and mangroves. Mostly in lowland areas. *May be confused with:* WHITE-THROATED and SPOTTED NIGHTJARS, which usually inhabit drier habitat. Look for white bristles when at rest or white in wings and tail corners in flight.

CHOWCHILLA
Orthonyx spaldingii 27 cm

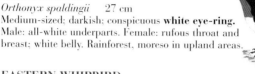

Medium-sized; darkish; conspicuous **white eye-ring.** Male: all-white underparts. Female: rufous throat and breast; white belly. Rainforest, moreso in upland areas.

EASTERN WHIPBIRD
Psophodes olivaceus 27 cm
Medium-sized; often appearing dark-brown; dark olive-green body; black head; **white cheek patches; small black crest** sometimes carried flat on back of head; **long tail.** Juvenile: plain brownish without cheek patches. Lower stratum of rainforest at higher altitudes and adjacent eucalypt forest. Sometimes coastal.

BASSIAN THRUSH
Zoothera lunulata 28 cm
Medium-sized; paler underparts; prominent **'scaly' pattern from throat to belly.** Rainforest at higher altitudes. *May be confused with:* RUSSET-TAILED THRUSH. See p. 204.

RUSSET-TAILED THRUSH
Zoothera heinei 27 cm
Very similar to BASSIAN THRUSH and difficult to separate in the field. Rainforest at higher altitudes. *May be confused with:* BASSIAN THRUSH. See p. 204.

FURTHER POSSIBILITIES
Juvenile EMERALD DOVE
BROWN CUCKOO-DOVE sometimes feeds in clearings and on paths in rainforest.
During the breeding season (usually Sept.–Jan.) the male TOOTH-BILLED BOWERBIRD maintains a display court on the rainforest floor.

POSSIBILITIES

RED-BACKED FAIRY-WREN
Malurus melanocephalus (Female) 12 cm
Plain; **long, cocked tail** distinguishes it from all other species. Long grass in and adjacent to woodland, grassy areas in farmland.

YELLOW-FACED HONEYEATER
Lichenostomus chrysops 16 cm
Olive-brown; **thick yellow line below eye from bill to ear;** black face. Mostly eucalypt forest at higher altitudes. *May be confused with:* BRIDLED HONEYEATER which has a dark head. Facial pattern distinguishes each species.

WHITE-GAPED HONEYEATER
Lichenostomus unicolor 19 cm
Plain grey-brown nondescript bird; **small white mark between eye and bill** (pale-yellow in immature). Gallery forest and adjacent woodland, suburban gardens and about farmhouses.
May be confused with: Perhaps the smaller BROWN HONEYEATER which is sometimes misidentified as the WHITE-GAPED. Note position and colour of small mark. BROWN has yellowish wash on flight and tail feathers.

FUSCOUS HONEYEATER
Lichenostomus fuscus 16 cm
Grey-brown; **yellowish face,** flight feathers and tail; **black plume over yellow** on ear. Tropical woodland, especially where Swamp Mahogany and Bloodwood *Eucalyptus* spp. grow. *May be confused with:* NONE, but sometimes misidentified as YELLOW-TINTED HONEYEATER which does not occur in the Wet Tropics.

BROWN HONEYEATER
Lichmera indistincta 12 cm
Overall brown; nondescript; **triangular yellowish spot behind eye;** yellowish wash on flight feathers; longish, curved black bill. Juvenile: lacks yellowish spot, but has dark face and yellow wash on flight and tail feathers. Open forest, parks and gardens, mangroves and paperbark swamps. *May be confused with:* WHITE-GAPED, DUSKY and female SCARLET HONEYEATERS, but look for triangular spot behind eye and yellow wash on flight feathers. Juvenile can be difficult to separate from juvenile RUFOUS-THROATED HONEYEATER but has darker face and is usually loudly vocal.

BROWN-BACKED HONEYEATER

Ramsayornis modestus   12 cm
Dark brown with off-white underparts: **indistinct brown barring on breast; thin whitish line under eye; pinkish-brown bill and feet.** Mostly paperbark swamps and waterways, sometimes in open forest and woodland. *May be confused with:* Perhaps immature BAR-BREASTED HONEYEATER which has 'tear-drop' striations on breast. Juvenile RUFOUS-THROATED HONEYEATER has yellow margins to flight feathers.

RUFOUS-THROATED HONEYEATER

Conopophila rufogularis   (Juvenile) 12 cm
Overall brown, nondescript bird; **yellow edges to wing and tail feathers.** Open forest, parks and gardens, paperbark swamps. *May be confused with:* Adult BROWN HONEYEATER which has triangular yellowish spot behind eye. (difficult to separate from juvenile BROWN which has darker face and is usually more loudly vocal), DUSKY HONEYEATER which is very dark brown, and female SCARLET HONEYEATER which has reddish wash on chin.

DUSKY HONEYEATER

Myzomela obscura   13 cm
Plain: **very dark-brown; nondescript; longish, curved bill.** Rainforest, gallery forest, mangroves and open forest. *May be confused with:* BROWN and female SCARLET HONEYEATERS with which it sometimes associates. Look for plain dark-brown bird.

SCARLET HONEYEATER

Myzomela sanguinolenta   (Female) 11 cm
Plain brown: paler below; **reddish wash on chin;** longish, curved bill. Flowering trees and shrubs, eucalypts, bottlebrush, paperbarks, sometimes rainforest canopy, sometimes mangroves.
May be confused with: BROWN and DUSKY HONEYEATERS, but look for reddish wash on chin. In more extensive areas of mangroves, it is possible that the RED-HEADED HONEYEATER may occur. Female is similar but has reddish wash on **both chin and forehead.** Usually with the distinct males.

JACKY WINTER *Microeca fascinans*   13 cm

Sometimes appears brownish, but overall grey-brown: paler below; **conspicuous white sides to tail;** pale, whitish eyebrow. **Restlessly wags tail from side to side.** Active. Drier open sparsely timbered areas. *May be confused with:* Perhaps LEMON-BELLIED FLYCATCHER and female and juvenile WHITE-WINGED TRILLER, but look for white-sided tail, restlessly wagged.

WHITE-WINGED TRILLER

Lalage sueurii (Female and juvenile) 18 cm
Female: plain brown; darker wings and tail; **thin, buff eyebrow.** Juvenile: similar to female, but with greyish-brown striations on breast and head. Male: black and white; develops brown head and back in non-breeding plumage. Open eucalypt forest and woodland.
May be confused with: RUFOUS SONGLARK which has rufous rump. Perhaps JACKY WINTER which has white sides to tail; wags tail.

DUSKY WOODSWALLOW

Artamus cyanopterus 18 cm
Smoky-brown; **bluish bill;** black tail tipped white; frequently wags tail; **thin, white wing-stripe.** Open areas and open woodland with dead timber.
May be confused with: LITTLE WOODSWALLOW which has no wing-stripe.

LITTLE WOODSWALLOW *Artamus minor* 14 cm

Rare; dark chocolate-brown; deep blue-grey wings **without white stripe; blue bill;** white-tipped, blackish-grey tail; frequently wags tail. Open, grassy woodland. *May be confused with:* DUSKY WOODSWALLOW which has a thin white wing-stripe.

RUFOUS SONGLARK

Cincloramphus mathewsi 16 cm
Overall brown with patterned upperparts; **rich rufous rump;** paler below; pale-fawn eyebrow. Juvenile: dark spots on throat and breast. Usually shy and retiring. Grassy woodland. *May be confused with:* Female and juvenile WHITE-WINGED TRILLER, SINGING BUSHLARK, RICHARD'S PIPIT, TAWNY GRASSBIRD and female and juvenile BROWN SONGLARK. Only TAWNY GRASSBIRD has a rufous rump (pale) but also a rufous crown.

BROWN SONGLARK

Cinclorhamphus cruralis Male 24 cm Female 21 cm
Rare, small to medium-sized bird; overall plain brown; **longish tail.** Male: much larger and darker than female; more uniform in colour. Female: paler below; faint, whitish eyebrow. Open, sparsely timbered grassland. *May be confused with:* Overall dark brown colour of male distinguishes it from all other species. Female can be confused with SINGING BUSHLARK which has a peculiar, jerky flight; RICHARD'S PIPIT which teeters its tail; TAWNY GRASSBIRD which has rufous crown and pale rufous rump and RUFOUS SONGLARK which has rufous rump.

FURTHER POSSIBILITIES

SPINY-CHEEKED and STRIPED HONEYEATERS are vagrants to the extreme south of the region.
Juvenile EASTERN YELLOW ROBIN is brown after fledging.
Some juvenile FINCHES and MANNIKINS are brownish but are usually in the company of the coloured adults.
HOUSE SPARROW — mostly about urban areas.

POSSIBILITIES

COLLARED SPARROWHAWK
Accipiter cirrhocephalus Male 31 cm Female 37 cm
A small hawk; usually appears quite brown; greyish-brown upperparts; finely barred **pale-rufous underparts;** rufous collar; longish yellow legs; longish **square tail.** Juvenile: overall brown; heavily streaked throat and upper breast, barred lower breast and belly. Open eucalypt forest and woodland. *May be confused with:* BROWN GOSHAWK which is almost identical in all stages, but larger with a rounded tail.

COMMON BRONZEWING *Phaps chalcoptera* 34 cm
Rare, large plump pigeon; overall brownish; **white stripe below eye;** metallic green and bronze patches on wings. Open, dry woodland. *May be confused with:* Perhaps SQUATTER PIGEON, but look for overall brown bird with fairly plain face without black markings.

SQUATTER PIGEON *Geophaps scripta* 30 cm
Dull brown; **broad, white stripe bordering wings to flanks and belly; prominent black and white facial pattern** and **tan eye-ring.** Drier, open, grassy woodland and open forest. *May be confused with:* Perhaps COMMON BRONZEWING, but look for strong facial pattern, tan eye-ring and white flanks.

BAR-SHOULDERED DOVE
Geopelia humeralis 28 cm
Back, wings and rump brown, barred blackish in a 'scaly' pattern; **chestnut patch on back of neck with dark 'scaly' pattern;** long tail. Rainforest edges, eucalypt forest with denser understorey, farmland and mangroves. *May be confused with:* In urban areas: SPOTTED TURTLE-DOVE, which has a black patch spotted white on back of neck.

BRUSH CUCKOO *Cacomantis variolosus* 24 cm
Plain grey-brown; often appearing brownish; **grey eye-ring; near plain square tail tipped white;** grey head; buffy-grey breast; buff belly. Juvenile: mottled and barred brown. Rainforest at most altitudes and most other forested habitats. *May be confused with:* Perhaps FAN-TAILED CUCKOO. See pp. 197–8.

SOUTHERN BOOBOOK
Ninox novaeseelandiae 32 cm
Nocturnal, small brown owl; **dark 'goggles' around yellow eyes** focused forward; white spots on wings; whitish underparts with thick, blotchy, brown streaks. All forested habitats. *May be confused with:* Perhaps the larger BARKING OWL which is more greyish and lacks dark 'goggles' about eyes.

SPOTTED NIGHTJAR *Eurostopodus argus* 30 cm

Rather rare, nocturnal, intricately-patterned brown bird; white crescent on throat. In flight, shows **large white patch in underwing with plain tail.** Drier woodland in western areas of the Wet Tropics.
May be confused with: LARGE-TAILED and WHITE-THROATED NIGHTJARS, but look for reddish-brown upperparts, no white bristles about bill when at rest; white in wings and plain tail in flight.

LARGE-TAILED NIGHTJAR
Caprimulgus macrurus 26 cm

Nocturnal; dark brown with intricately-patterned plumage; thin white crescent on each side of throat; **white bristles about bill.** In flight, shows **small white patch in underwing and white corners to tail.** Rainforest edges, adjacent woodland and mangroves. Mostly in lowland areas. *May be confused with:* WHITE-THROATED and SPOTTED NIGHTJARS, but look for white bristles when at rest, or white in wings and tail corners in flight.

BROWN TREECREEPER
Climacteris picumnus 17 cm

Hops up tree trunks; **blackish-brown upperparts** (paler in southern parts of the Wet Tropics); grey breast; **underparts lightly but prominently streaked white with black edging;** pale throat; **prominent whitish eyebrow.** Drier woodland and eucalypt forest, especially where Poplar Gum *Eucalyptus platyphylla* grows. *May be confused with:* WHITE-THROATED TREECREEPER which usually inhabits denser forest. Look for whitish eyebrow.

HELMETED FRIARBIRD
Philemon buceroides 34 cm

Overall brown; paler below; prominent **bare, black face; black bill with backward-sloping knob on top;** rather grotesque. Eucalypt forest, paperbark woodland, mangroves, cities and towns. Mostly coastal.
May be confused with: SILVER-CROWNED and NOISY FRIARBIRDS. See p. 201.

SILVER-CROWNED FRIARBIRD
Philemon argenticeps 29 cm

Paler below with prominent **bare black face; black knob on black bill; silvery-white crown;** silvery-white frill, nape and throat. Eucalypt forest and woodland. *May be confused with:* HELMETED and NOISY FRIARBIRDS. See p. 201.

NOISY FRIARBIRD *Philemon corniculatus* 28 cm
Paler below; conspicuous **bare black head** distinguishes it from other friarbirds; **upright knob on bill.** Eucalypt forest, sometimes paperbark woodland and gardens, moreso inland. *May be confused with:* Possibly HELMETED and SILVER-CROWNED FRIARBIRDS. See p. 201.

LITTLE FRIARBIRD
Philemon citreogularis 26 cm
Paler below; **patch of bare blue-grey facial skin from bill to under eye; lacks knob on bill.** Eucalypt forest and tropical woodland. *May be confused with:* NONE. Look for blue-grey facial skin.

GREY-CROWNED BABBLER
Pomatostomus temporalis 25 cm
Noisy; usually in small groups; dark-brown upperparts; pale crown; white throat and breast; brown belly; longish **white-tipped tail, partly spread and often cocked;** long curved bill. Drier forest and woodland.

CICADABIRD *Coracina tenuirostris* (Female) 25 cm
Migrant, present Oct.–Mar./Apr.; mid-brown with paler creamy-buff underparts **barred dark brown.** Fast flight. Usually wary. Does not refold wings as do other cuckoo-shrikes. Eucalypt forest, vine thickets, paperbark woodland, mangroves and canopy of lowland rainforest. *May be confused with:* Perhaps juvenile FAN-TAILED CUCKOO which has long, 'notched' tail.

GREAT BOWERBIRD *Chlamydera nuchalis* 34 cm
Brownish back, wings and rump with feathers **margined greyish-white; plain grey head and underparts;** lilac nape crest, hidden when bird is not displaying. Drier eucalypt forest and woodland, sometimes parks and gardens.

FURTHER POSSIBILITIES
FLOCK BRONZEWING — vagrant.
Perhaps juvenile GREY and PIED BUTCHERBIRDS, but these are usually in the company of the distinctive adults.

LARGE & VERY LARGE BROWN BIRDS OF OPEN FOREST & WOODLAND
POSSIBILITIES

SQUARE-TAILED KITE *Lophoictinia isura* 53 cm
Rare; large brown bird of prey; whitish face; long wings extend beyond tail at rest. In flight: **wings upswept with dull whitish 'window' towards tip.** Open forest and woodland, and over rainforest. *May be confused with:* Other large brown birds of prey. See Diurnal Birds of Prey, pp. 175–81.

BLACK KITE *Milvus migrans* 52 cm
Generally abundant; large **dark brown** bird of prey; mostly seen flying and soaring **on slightly drooped wings; tail continuously twisted and turned;** tail squarish in flight, but appears forked when closed. Open areas. *May be confused with:* Other large brown birds of prey. See Diurnal Birds of Prey, pp. 175–81.

WHISTLING KITE *Haliastur sphenurus* 53 cm

Common; large brown bird of prey; usually soaring effortlessly on **slightly drooped wings; long, rounded tail;** streaked head, back and breast; distinctive underwing pattern. Open areas, lightly timbered country, and about lakes, swamps, estuaries and tidal flats. *May be confused with:* Other large brown birds of prey. See Diurnal Birds of Prey, pp. 175–81.

BROWN GOSHAWK

Accipter fasciatus Male 42 cm Female 50 cm
Greyish-brown, medium-sized bird of prey; **finely barred pale rufous underparts;** rufous collar; longish yellow legs; **long rounded tail.** Juvenile: overall brown with heavily streaked throat and upper breast, barred lower breast and belly. Open eucalypt forest and woodland. *May be confused with:* The smaller COLLARED SPARROWHAWK which is almost identical in all stages, but look for rounded tail.

WEDGE-TAILED EAGLE

Aquila audax Male 91 cm Female 100 cm
Huge dark eagle ranging from brown to near black; thickly-feathered legs; heavy, hooked, pale bill; **longish wedge-shaped tail.** In flight, has upswept wings; wedge-shaped tail obvious. Mountainous forest to lowland tropical woodland. Generally avoids rainforest. *May be confused with:* Other large brown birds of prey. See Diurnal Birds of Prey, pp. 175–81.

LITTLE EAGLE

Hieraaetus morphnoides Male 47 cm Female 54 cm
Rather rare large bird of prey or small eagle. Two colour phases occur — dark brown and light brown; short, square tail often twisted in flight; **partial crest on nape; legs fully feathered to feet; glides on flat wings upturned slightly at tip.** Open forest and woodland, timber along watercourses. *May be confused with:* Other large brown birds of prey. See Diurnal Birds of Prey, pp. 175–81.

BROWN FALCON

Falco berigora Male 45 cm Female 55 cm
A medium-sized to large bird of prey with variable plumage — pale brown to near-black; underparts sometimes paler; **paler throat and cheek; darker 'moustache' below eye; lightly barred underwing and tail.** Open woodland, farmland, often on roadside power poles. *May be confused with:* Other large brown birds of prey. See Diurnal Birds of Prey, pp. 175–81.

PHEASANT COUCAL *Centropus phasianinus* 70 cm

Large, clumsy-looking bird with outsized tail; skulking. In breeding plumage Sept.–Mar./Apr. **black head and body** which becomes **streaked-brown** in non-breeding plumage; brown wings; long, broad, dark tail has paler barring. Lives mostly on the ground in tall grassy areas in open forest and farmland.

WHITE-THROATED NIGHTJAR
Eurostopodus mystacalis   34 cm

Nocturnal; **intricately-patterned** dark bird; white crescent on each side of throat. At rest, surface of wings and back **appear greyish**; in flight, shows **plain underwing and tail.** Rests on ground by day; flushes suddenly from underfoot. Drier tropical woodland. *May be confused with:* SPOTTED and LARGE-TAILED NIGHTJARS, but look for greyish upperparts when at rest, or plain underwing and tail in flight.

FURTHER POSSIBILITIES
TAWNY and PAPUAN FROGMOUTHS and BARKING OWL sometimes appear brownish.
BRAHMINY KITE sometimes occurs well inland — juvenile is overall striated-brown.

SMALL BIRDS OF DENSE GRASSLAND, REEDBEDS & AQUATIC VEGETATION
POSSIBILITIES

RED-BACKED FAIRY-WREN
Malurus melanocephalus   12 cm

Small bird with long cocked tail. Male: black body, head and tail: **brilliant red back and rump.** Female: plain brown. Long grass in and adjacent to woodland; grassy areas in farmland.

SINGING BUSHLARK *Mirafra javanica*   13 cm
Well-striated; paler below; **reddish patches on shoulders distinctive in flight;** has peculiar **jerky, fluttering and hovering flight** low over grass or high in the air in courtship display. Drier grassland, farmland and crops. *May be confused with:* RICHARD'S PIPIT, TAWNY GRASSBIRD, RUFOUS SONGLARK and female BROWN SONGLARK, but the jerky flight and reddish shoulders of SINGING BUSHLARK distinguish it.

RICHARD'S PIPIT *Anthus novaeseelandiae* 16 cm
Well-striated brown bird; **teeters longish tail up and down.** Open grassland and farmland. *May be confused with:* SINGING BUSHLARK, TAWNY GRASSBIRD, RUFOUS SONGLARK and female BROWN SONGLARK, but look for teetering habit.

PLUM-HEADED FINCH *Neochmia modesta* 11 cm
Rare; brownish; short, thick, black bill; black tail; **prominent brown barring on underparts; shoulders spotted white: barred white rump;** gregarious. Juvenile: lacks barred underparts. Taller grassland and lightly timbered grassy areas often close to streams. *May be confused with:* Adult: NONE. Juvenile: juveniles of CHESTNUT-BREASTED and NUTMEG MANNIKINS. Both have yellowish-brown rump and tail. Look for black tail.

RED-BROWED FINCH
Neochmia temporalis 11 cm
Olive-green and grey; **red rump, bill and eyebrow.**
Juvenile: black bill; lacks red eyebrow. Usually
gregarious. Margins of rainforest, regrowth and
adjacent shrubby and grassy areas.

NUTMEG MANNIKIN *Lonchura punctulata* 11 cm
Introduced; brown; dark brown face; yellowish rump;
finely-patterned 'scaly' underparts; gregarious;
flicks tail from side to side. Grassland, farmland,
roadsides, fringes of towns. *May be confused with:*
Adult: NONE. Juvenile: juvenile CHESTNUT-
BREASTED MANNIKIN has dark under tail-coverts
and paler underparts. Juvenile PLUM-HEADED
FINCH has longer black tail, barred rump and white
spots on wings.

CHESTNUT-BREASTED MANNIKIN
Lonchura castaneothorax 10 cm
Appears brownish; **large black mask extending to
throat; chestnut breast with a black band below;**
creamy belly; yellowish-brown rump and tail; gregarious.
Juvenile: plain brownish; dark under tail-coverts; paler
below. Grassland, reedy areas, roadsides, sugar-cane
fields and farmland. *May be confused with:* Adult:
NONE. Juvenile: juvenile PLUM-HEADED FINCH which
has black tail. Juvenile NUTMEG MANNIKIN has pale
under tail-coverts and is overall browner.

BLUE-FACED PARROT-FINCH
Erythrura trichroa 12 cm
Rare; **rich grass-green; blue face; dark reddish-
brown rump.** Face mid-blue in male, duller in female
and green in juvenile. Mostly rainforest and adjacent
tall grass at higher altitudes.

CLAMOROUS REED-WARBLER
Acrocephalus stentoreus 17 cm
Small brownish bird of reedbeds; paler underparts; **pale
eyebrow.** Rather elusive. Reedbeds in freshwater
swamps and streams. *May be confused with:*
ORIENTAL REED-WARBLER which is extremely
difficult to distinguish from CLAMOROUS. See p. 203.

TAWNY GRASSBIRD *Megalurus timoriensis* 19 cm
Brownish; brown upperparts **streaked dark grey and
black;** unstreaked fawn underparts; longish brown tail
often flicked; **plain rufous crown;** shy. Tall rank
grassland, pastures, crops, grassy roadsides and
swampland. *May be confused with:* SINGING
BUSHLARK, RICHARD'S PIPIT, RUFOUS
SONGLARK and female BROWN SONGLARK, but
look for rufous crown and longish tail.

LITTLE GRASSBIRD *Megalurus gramineus* 14 cm
A greyish-brown bird; paler below; heavily striated upperparts; fine streaks on throat and breast. Skulking. Reedbeds, dense swamp vegetation. *May be confused with:* TAWNY GRASSBIRD which has a rufous crown.

ZITTING CISTICOLA *Cisticola juncidis* 10 cm
Tiny brownish bird with creamy white underparts; **heavily streaked dusky-black back and crown;** dark brown tail tipped white. Almost identical to non-breeding male GOLDEN-HEADED CISTICOLA. Coastal saline grassland. *May be confused with:* GOLDEN-HEADED CISTICOLA. See p. 204.

GOLDEN-HEADED CISTICOLA
Cisticola exilis 10 cm
Tiny; golden-buff: heavily streaked back and crown. Male: develops **golden crown** through breeding season approximately Sept.–Apr. Elusive and inconspicuous in non-breeding season.
May be confused with: ZITTING CISTICOLA which is confined to a specific habitat. See p. 204.

FURTHER POSSIBILITIES
Several species of QUAIL and BUTTON-QUAIL. See pp. 158–9. Several FINCHES, e.g. CRIMSON, ZEBRA, DOUBLE-BARRED and the very rare STAR inhabit either reedy and swampy areas, grassy woodland or edges of sugar-cane fields.
The rare BROWN SONGLARK.

MEDIUM-SIZED & LARGE BIRDS OF DENSE GRASSLAND, REEDBEDS & AQUATIC VEGETATION

POSSIBILITIES

BUFF-BANDED RAIL *Gallirallus philippensis* 31cm
Medium-sized; shy brownish ground bird; chestnut crown and stripe through eye: **grey eyebrow; chestnut patch on breast; extensive fine barring** on underparts. Dense damp grassland, vegetation about swamps and streams. *May be confused with:* The rare LEWIN'S RAIL, but look for grey eyebrow and chestnut on breast.

LEWIN'S RAIL *Rallus pectoralis* 22 cm
Rare; medium-sized; shy ground bird; dark upperparts; **rich chestnut head and nape** with black streaks; **slate-grey throat and breast;** barred wings, belly and under tail-coverts; **long black-tipped pink bill.** Damp grassland and reedy swamps.
May be confused with: BUFF-BANDED RAIL, but look for long bill, no eyebrow and slate-grey extending from throat to upper belly.

BUSH-HEN *Amaurornis olivaceus* 26 cm
Medium-sized; **plain;** secretive ground bird; olive-brown and greyish; **buff lower belly and under tail-coverts;** dull yellow legs; develops red base to green bill during breeding season approximately Nov.–Mar. Dense shrubby or grassy creeks and dense wet grassland. *May be confused with:* NONE. Distinct with buff belly and under tail-coverts.

PHEASANT COUCAL *Centropus phasianinus* 70 cm
Large, clumsy-looking bird with outsized tail; skulking; brownish in non-breeding plumage Apr.–Aug.; head and body **heavily streaked.** In breeding plumage: **black** head and body; long broad dark tail with paler barring. Lives mostly on the ground in tall grassy areas in open forest and farmland.

GRASS OWL *Tyto capensis* Male 34 cm Female 37 cm
Nocturnal; large short-tailed bird; plumage variable; chestnut upperparts; whitish underparts **washed chestnut with sparse spotting; triangular facial disc;** relatively small eyes; **noticeably long legs which project beyond tail or dangle in flight.** Rests by day in dense grass, sometimes harvested sugar-cane fields and young pine plantations. *May be confused with:* BARN and MASKED OWLS. See p. 199.

AERIAL BIRDS — SWIFTS, SWALLOWS & MARTINS
POSSIBILITIES

WHITE-RUMPED SWIFTLET
Collocalia spodiopygius 11 cm
Small dark grey aerial bird; **small greyish patch on rump; stiff-winged flight;** usually in flocks, often low to ground. Appears over most areas at all altitudes. *May be confused with:* NONE. Distinctive flight separates it from all other aerial birds.

WHITE-THROATED NEEDLETAIL
Hirundapus caudacutus 20 cm
Migrant, present Oct.–Apr.; medium-sized dark bird; **long slender swept-back wings;** white throat; short square tail, **white underneath.** Swift flight. Appears over most areas at all altitudes. *May be confused with:* FORK-TAILED and HOUSE SWIFTS, but look for large swift with short squarish tail, white underneath.

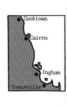

FORK-TAILED SWIFT *Apus pacificus* 17 cm
Migrant, present Oct.–Apr.; medium-sized dark bird; **long swept-back wings;** long deeply forked tail, but fork in tail is often not discernible; pale throat; **white rump;** flight is slower than that of NEEDLETAIL. Appears over most areas at all altitudes. *May be confused with:* WHITE-THROATED NEEDLETAIL and HOUSE SWIFT. Look for a large swift with white rump and longish tail.

HOUSE SWIFT *Apus affinis* 15 cm

Rare summer visitor; **small and stocky swift;** pale throat and white rump; **slightly forked tail becomes square when fanned;** underside of wings two-toned. *May be confused with:* Other swifts, swiftlets, swallows and martins. Look for slight fork in squarish tail, white rump and stocky appearance.

WHITE-BACKED SWALLOW

Cheramoeca leucosternus 14 cm
Rare; distinct black and white bird; **white throat, breast, crown and back;** plain deeply forked tail. Open woodland.

BARN SWALLOW *Hirundo rustica* 16 cm

Summer visitor present Nov.–Mar.; small; blue-black upperparts; **whitish underparts; black breastband; rusty-red throat and forehead;** long deeply forked tail. The BARN SWALLOW is in moult when it first arrives in Australia, and has a scruffy appearance and often no tail streamers. Attains full adult plumage before departing; often associates with WELCOME SWALLOW. Rests on powerlines in open areas and open farmland. *May be confused with:* NONE. Even in moult has distinct whitish underparts.

WELCOME SWALLOW *Hirundo neoxena* 15 cm

Small; blue-black upperparts; grey below; **rusty crown, throat and face;** deeply forked tail. Juvenile: almost no rust colour about head; short tail. Open areas, farmland, urban areas, often resting on powerlines. *May be confused with:* PACIFIC SWALLOW which has a shorter tail and different tail pattern. See p. 203.

PACIFIC SWALLOW *Hirundo pacifica* 13 cm

Almost identical to WELCOME SWALLOW with which it sometimes associates. Similar habitat. Juvenile: pale throat. *May be confused with:* WELCOME SWALLOW which has longer tail and different tail pattern. See p. 203.

RED-RUMPED SWALLOW *Hirundo daurica* 18 cm

Scarce summer visitor Dec.–Mar.; black upperparts; **striated pale buffy underparts; deeply forked long tail; conspicuous rufous rump.** Immature: duller. Rests on powerlines with other swallows and martins. Open areas and farmland. *May be confused with:* NONE. Striated underparts and rufous rump are distinctive.

TREE MARTIN *Hirundo nigricans* 12 cm

Small; dark back and wings; whitish underparts; **white rump appears dirty; square tail; dark crown.** Open areas and farmland, often perches on powerlines with other aerial birds. *May be confused with:* FAIRY MARTIN which has rusty crown.

FAIRY MARTIN *Hirundo ariel* 12 cm
Small aerial bird similar to TREE MARTIN, but with cleaner white rump; **rusty crown.** Open areas, open farmland and open grassland. *May be confused with:* TREE MARTIN, but look for rusty crown.

FURTHER POSSIBILITIES
GLOSSY SWIFTLET *Collocalia esculenta* 10 cm
Possibly a vagrant to the Wet Tropics region from New Guinea. Glossy dark blue upperparts, grey chin and throat, **white lower breast and belly.** Unmistakable. In New Guinea mostly occurs singly or in pairs, sometimes in small groups. **Flies at a low level,** never at a great height, hunting about clearings and gaps in the forest. Flight is rather slow and erratic with frequent changes of direction, consisting of fluttering followed by a short glide. Wing tips are pointed with wings slightly swept back.

UNIFORM SWIFTLET *Collocalia vanikorensis* 13 cm
Possibly a vagrant to the Wet Tropics region from New Guinea. **Nondescript;** dark grey above, slightly paler below. **Nearly always in flocks of varying size, feeding high,** often with other swifts and swiftlets. Sometimes comes low to the ground to hunt over open areas or water. Flight is relatively fast.

BIRDS THAT SPEND MUCH TIME IN THE AIR
EXCLUDING SWIFTS, SWALLOWS & MARTINS
POSSIBILITIES

GREAT FRIGATEBIRD *Fregata minor* 92 cm
Mostly black aerial seabird with **long slender wings and deeply forked tail;** lacks white 'armpits' of LESSER FRIGATEBIRD. Female: **white throat and breast.** Juvenile: brownish head. Soars high on motionless wings. Offshore waters and islands of Great Barrier Reef, sometimes over coastal shorelines. *May be confused with:* LESSER FRIGATEBIRD, but look for absence of white 'armpits', and white throat in female.

LESSER FRIGATEBIRD *Fregata ariel* 75 cm
Similar to GREAT FRIGATEBIRD and inhabits similar oceanic areas. **White 'armpits' in flight.** Female: **all-black head and throat** and white underparts. Juvenile: brownish head. *May be confused with:* GREAT FRIGATEBIRD, but look for white 'armpits', and all-black head in female.

BLACK KITE *Milvus migrans* 52 cm
Generally abundant; large dark brown bird of prey; mostly seen flying or soaring **on slightly drooped wings; tail continuously twisted and turned;** squarish tail in flight, but appears forked when closed. Open areas. *May be confused with:* Other birds of prey. See Diurnal Birds of Prey, pp. 175–81.

WHISTLING KITE *Haliastur sphenurus* 53 cm
Common; large dark brown bird of prey; usually soaring effortlessly on **slightly drooped wings; long and rounded tail;** streaked head, back and breast; distinctive underwing pattern. Open areas, lightly timbered habitats, and about lakes, swamps, estuaries and tidal flats. *May be confused with:* Other birds of prey. See Diurnal Birds of Prey, pp. 175–81.

WEDGE-TAILED EAGLE
Aquila audax Female 91 cm Female 100 cm
A huge dark eagle ranging from brown to near-black; thickly-feathered legs; heavy hooked pale bill; **longish wedge-shaped tail.** Soars on upswept wings. Mountainous forest to lowland tropical woodland. Generally avoids rainforest. *May be confused with:* Other large brown birds of prey. See Diurnal Birds of Prey, pp. 175–81.

ORIENTAL PRATINCOLE
Glareola maldivarum 24 cm
Rare summer visitor; medium-sized; long-winged; olive-brown; buffish to white underparts; **buff throat edged with broken black line; long forked tail** with white sides and wide black margin at base; white upper tail-coverts; **chestnut underwing;** does not teeter. In flight, graceful and tern-like. Open short-grassed plains, claypans and mudflats. *May be confused with:* AUSTRALIAN PRATINCOLE, but look for broken edging to buff throat when on ground and chestnut underwing and long forked tail in flight.

AUSTRALIAN PRATINCOLE
Stiltia isabella 23 cm
Similar to ORIENTAL PRATINCOLE, but with no throat patch; **square tail, deep rufous belly patch;** longer legs; brownish rump; white upper tail-coverts; white tail with broad black subterminal band. Teeters rear of body up and down. Open, treeless, short-grassed and bare plains, bare fallowed farmland and turf farms. *May be confused with:* ORIENTAL PRATINCOLE which does not teeter. Look for plain throat, rufous belly patch and teetering when on ground and square tail and black underwings in flight.

FURTHER POSSIBILITIES
TERNS
RAINBOW BEE-EATER
DOLLARBIRD
Other birds of prey.

POSSIBILITIES

STUBBLE QUAIL *Coturnix pectoralis* 18 cm
Large well-streaked brownish quail; whitish streaks
down back; **well-streaked black and white
underparts heavy on breast and forming blackish
patch in male; whitish eyebrow.** Male: chestnut throat
patch. Female: white throat patch. In flight, appears
overall brownish. Flight is fast and direct, low over grass
and often for several hundred metres. Wings appear long
and pointed; rapid wingbeats. Rank and dry grassland,
farmland and crops. *May be confused with:* Most other
quail and button-quail. Probably black patch on breast
of male responsible for occasional misidentifications as
BLACK-BREASTED BUTTON-QUAIL. At rest, look for
streaking; white eyebrow; dark bill; throat patch in
male. Long-winged flight distinctive.

BROWN QUAIL *Coturnix ypsilophora* 18 cm
Common large brownish quail; fine white streaks down
back; **fine wavy black barring on underparts.** In
flight, looks overall brownish. **Rises higher than
other quail,** to about 2 m, arching over and away.
Generally utters a 'squeak' as it rises. Usually flies for
some distance. Rank grassland, pasture, rice stubble,
grassy woodland. *May be confused with:* Most other
quail and button-quail, but look for plain overall
brown colour, barring on underparts and high-rising
habit when flushed. Smaller female KING QUAIL has
similar barring but buff-brown on face and throat.

KING QUAIL *Coturnix chinensis* 13 cm
Small quail. Male: dark brown back; **blue-grey breast
and flanks; chestnut belly; black and white throat
pattern.** Female: dark brown back; buff-brown
underparts with fine dark barring; **buff-brown face
and throat.** In flight, appears small and dark. When
flushed, will rise above the grass with a **weak, tail-
heavy flight and flop down a short distance away.**
Facial markings of the male usually seen in flight.
Farmland and open grassy areas, also grassy casuarina
forest and sometimes wetter grassland about swamps.
May be confused with: Male: NONE. Female: other
quail and button-quail, but look for barring on
underparts and buff-brown about face and throat.

RED-BACKED BUTTON-QUAIL
Turnix maculosa 14 cm
Small button-quail; well-patterned chestnut, brown
and black upperparts; generally buff below. Female:
**rich chestnut sides of neck and hind neck. Yellow
legs, eyes; fine, yellow or yellow-grey bill.** Male:
lacks chestnut sides to neck and hind neck; yellow-
grey bill; pale yellow eye. In flight, appears as a small
brownish quail with dark back and rump; paler wings;
small amount of buff on flanks. If close, one can
usually see the bill colour. Grassy woodland, about
wetlands, also pastures and crops. *May be confused
with:* Other quail and button-quail, but look for bill
colour, pale eye and yellow legs.

LITTLE BUTTON-QUAIL   *Turnix velox*   13 cm

Rare; small; **reddish-brown** above narrowly streaked white; **whitish throat and belly;** yellow-buff breast; white eye; stout, bluish-grey bill. In flight, appears slightly reddish above and usually shows white flanks. *May be confused with:* Other quail and button-quail, but look for white throat and belly, reddish-brown upperparts and white flanks in flight.

RED-CHESTED BUTTON-QUAIL

Turnix pyrrhothorax   14 cm

Medium-sized brownish button-quail; **rufous breast;** stout, grey bill; pink legs; white eye. In flight, shows **rufous flanks,** richer in female than male. Woodland, grassland, crops and pastures. *May be confused with:* Other quail and button-quail, but look for rufous breast, white eye, stout grey bill and rufous flanks in flight.

BUFF-BREASTED BUTTON-QUAIL

Turnix olivii   19 cm

Rare; large, rather plain, brownish button-quail; cinnamon shoulders; fine, almost indistinctly-spotted white face; plain cream to whitish underparts; **buff upper breast; yellow eye; large, thick, horn-coloured bill.** In flight, appears rather plain mid-brown without distinguishing features, though wings appear darker than tail, rump and back. Sparsely grassed open forest on gravelly hillsides. *May be confused with:* Other quail and button-quail, but note special habitat. Most likely to be confused with PAINTED BUTTON-QUAIL, but look for yellow eye, large horn-coloured bill and generally plain bird. Inhabits less dense habitats than PAINTED, and often adjacent.

PAINTED BUTTON-QUAIL *Turnix varia*   19 cm

Large, brownish button-quail; heavily mottled chestnut, black, white and grey; **well-spotted face, throat and breast; chestnut shoulder patch and sides of breast** (less so in male); grey underparts striated white; black bill; yellow legs; **red eye.** When flushed flies well away, at which time it appears fairly plain, but sometimes shows some chestnut on body. Open, grassy woodland on hillsides usually at higher altitudes. *May be confused with:* Other quail and button-quail. Most likely to be confused with BUFF-BREASTED BUTTON-QUAIL which is quite plain. Look for spotting about head, red eye and chestnut shoulders and upperparts.

POSSIBILITIES

SOUTHERN GIANT-PETREL
Macronectes giganteus 90 cm
A large petrel with **huge pale-yellow bill and single nostril tube.** Two colour phases — mostly dark brown with pale head, and white, but probably brown immatures only in the Wet Tropics. In flight, resembles a small ungainly albatross with a hunched-back appearance. *May be confused with:* NORTHERN GIANT-PETREL which probably does not reach this region. NORTHERN has dark reddish bill tip contrasting with rest of bill. SOUTHERN has pale greenish bill tip with no contrast.

WEDGE-TAILED SHEARWATER
Puffinus pacificus 43 cm
Medium-sized petrel; overall dark brown; dark grey hooked bill; **wedge-shaped tail which appears pointed in flight and extends beyond wing tips at rest;** pink feet. Distinctive, buoyant, drifting flight. Offshore coastal waters and islands. *May be confused with:* Usually NONE, but SHORT-TAILED SHEARWATER is accidental to the Wet Tropics. SHORT-TAILED has stiff, rapid, flapping flight, while that of WEDGE-TAILED is lazy, graceful and buoyant.

HUTTON'S SHEARWATER
Puffinus huttoni 38 cm
Rare winter visitor; medium-sized shearwater; **blackish head and upperparts; greyish chin and throat;** long thin grey bill; pinkish-brown feet; mostly dusky underwing. Oceanic, sometimes closer inshore. *May be confused with:* NONE in the Wet Tropics.

WILSON'S STORM-PETREL
Oceanites oceanicus 17 cm
Rare winter visitor; small dark brown seabird; **white rump and flanks; black feet with yellow webs;** fluttering flight, low over surface when feeding, otherwise resembles that of a swallow. Oceanic, but sometimes close to shore.

RED-TAILED TROPICBIRD
Phaethon rubricauda 56 cm
Uncommon to rare; large white seabird; black flank markings; black eyebrow; **two long, red tail streamers; red bill.** Juvenile: extensively barred black back and upperwings; blackish bill; no tail streamers. Waters and islands of Great Barrier Reef. *May be confused with:* Adult: NONE. However, when tail feathers are missing, resembles a tern. Look for white upperparts, black flank markings and shorter, broader wings. Juvenile RED-TAILED and WHITE-TAILED TROPICBIRDS difficult to separate.

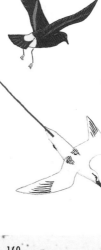

WHITE-TAILED TROPICBIRD
Phaethon lepturus 59 cm
Rare. Similar to RED-TAILED TROPICBIRD but smaller bodied. Black patch in flight feathers; **white tail streamers.** Juvenile: similar to juvenile RED-TAILED TROPICBIRD. *May be confused with:* NONE. Resembles a tern when tail streamers missing.

MASKED BOOBY *Sula dactylatra* 85 cm
Large seabird; overall white with part black wings (primaries and secondaries); **black tail; black facial mask; yellow bill; grey legs and feet.** Immature: brown and whitish. Oceanic, occasionally coming closer to shore. *May be confused with:* Adult: NONE. Immature: possibly dark form of RED-FOOTED BOOBY which has red legs and feet, and adult BROWN BOOBY which has sharply demarcated white belly.

RED-FOOTED BOOBY *Sula sula* 70 cm
Large seabird; longish tail; longish narrow wings; colour varies from entirely brown to white with black flight feathers; thick, pointed blue bill; **bright red legs and feet.** Oceanic, rarely closer to shore. *May be confused with:* NONE. Look for red legs and feet.

BROWN BOOBY *Sula leucogaster* 70 cm
Large seabird; overall brown but with **sharply demarcated white belly; yellow legs and feet;** yellow bill (bluish base in male). Juvenile: greyish-white belly and bluish bill. Offshore coastal waters and islands. *May be confused with:* usually NONE, but perhaps immature MASKED BOOBY.

GREAT FRIGATEBIRD *Fregata minor* 92 cm
Mostly black aerial seabird; **long slender wings; deeply forked tail;** lacks white 'armpits' of LESSER FRIGATEBIRD. Female: **white throat and breast.** Juvenile: brown head. Soars high on motionless wings. Offshore waters and islands of Great Barrier Reef, sometimes over coastal shorelines. *May be confused with:* LESSER FRIGATEBIRD, but look for absence of white 'armpits', and white throat in female.

LESSER FRIGATEBIRD *Fregata ariel* 75 cm
Very similar to GREAT FRIGATEBIRD and inhabits similar oceanic areas. Smaller; **white 'armpits' in flight.** Female: **all-black head and throat,** white underparts. Juvenile: brownish head. *May be confused with:* GREAT FRIGATEBIRD, but look for white 'armpits', and all-black head in female.

SILVER GULL *Larus novaehollandiae* 41 cm
Large familiar bird. Adult: immaculate white with silver-grey upperparts; **red legs, bill and eye-ring.** Juvenile and immature: no coloured eye-ring, black legs and bill later turning dull yellow-brown, finally turning red. Coastal shores, offshore islands, sometimes larger lakes and seaside suburbs.

161

FURTHER POSSIBILITIES

TAHITI PETREL *Pseudobulweria rostrata* 39 cm Large petrel; brown head and upperparts; brown breast **sharply demarcated from white belly.** Distinctive. A bird of tropical and subtropical Pacific Ocean reaching the Coral Sea and probably the outer Great Barrier Reef.

PROVIDENCE PETREL *Pterodroma solandri* 40 cm Large petrel; overall dark grey with **whitish face and white patches on underwings.** Distinctive. A bird of the western Pacific Ocean which may wander to the outer Great Barrier Reef.

HERALD PETREL *Pterodroma arminjoniana* 36 cm Medium-sized petrel with variable plumage. Varies from grey-brown upperparts with whitish underparts usually with a **broad dusky breastband,** to overall brown with **white patch at base of flight feathers on underwing. White or pale leading edge of inner wing** in all forms. Pale and intermediate forms distinctive in the Wet Tropics region but dark form could be confused with PROVIDENCE and BULWER'S PETRELS and some dark SHEARWATERS. Look for pale patch near the tip of the underwing and pale leading edge to inner wing. A bird of the tropical and subtropical Pacific Ocean reaching the Coral Sea. Breeding recorded Raine Island. A recent probable record near Michaelmas Cay.

BULWER'S PETREL *Bulweria bulwerii* 27 cm A small dark petrel with **pale bar across upperwing.** Long tail, usually held folded in a narrow point but **wedge-shaped when spread.** Long narrow pointed wings. Distinctive. A bird of tropical oceans wandering to the Coral Sea. One record from the outer Great Barrier Reef.

STREAKED SHEARWATER *Calonectris leucomelas* 48 cm A large shearwater with grey-brown upperparts and white underparts; **white face, conspicuously streaked nape.** Mostly white underwing with narrow black margin; pink feet. A visitor to the Coral Sea, Oct.–Mar. from the north-west Pacific. To date, not recorded from the Wet Tropics region but little doubt that it reaches the outer Great Barrier Reef. One record Raine Island.

SOOTY SHEARWATER *Puffinus griseus* 43 cm A large dark brown shearwater. **Whitish streak down centre of underwing** is diagnostic but difficult to separate in flight from SHORT-TAILED SHEARWATER some of which have a white underwing. Widespread through Pacific and Atlantic oceans. Vagrant to the Wet Tropics region.

SHORT-TAILED SHEARWATER *Puffinus tenuirostris* 42 cm A large dark brown shearwater, very similar to SOOTY SHEARWATER and difficult to distinguish from that species. SHORT-TAILED has **shorter** bill. Has shorter tail and bill than WEDGE-TAILED SHEARWATER with stiff, rapid, flapping flight. WEDGE-TAILED has lazy, graceful, bouyant flight. A species breeding in southern Australia and migrating to the northern Pacific. Accidental to the Wet Tropics region.

AUDUBON'S SHEARWATER *Puffinus lherminieri* 30 cm A medium-sized shearwater with dark upperparts and white underparts, resembling HUTTON'S SHEARWATER but separated by **black under tail-coverts and under tail giving a dark rear-end appearance.** Flight is easier, more gliding than most other shearwaters, resembling that of a WEDGE-TAILED SHEARWATER. Inhabits tropical and subtropical regions of Atlantic, Indian and Pacific oceans. Probably wanders to the Coral Sea.

WHITE-FACED STORM-PETREL *Pelagodroma marina*
19 cm Greyish-brown with rounded wings, **white face,
forehead and underparts.** Broad dark mark through eye.
Long legs with yellow webs between toes, projecting well
beyond tail in flight. Distinctive. A species of southern oceans,
moving into subtropical and tropical waters in winter. Possible
on outer Great Barrier Reef May-Sept.

BLACK-BELLIED STORM-PETREL *Fregetta tropica* 20 cm
Head and upperparts sooty-black; white rump and underparts;
broad black band down centre of belly; small white chin.
Distinctive, but black belly often difficult to see. Breeds in Southern
Ocean, moving into subtropical and tropical oceans in non-breeding
season. Possible on outer Great Barrier Reef June–Sept.

AUSTRALASIAN GANNET *Morus serrator* 90 cm Similar to
MASKED and RED-FOOTED BOOBIES but with **head tinged
yellow;** blue-grey bill; blackish legs and feet. A species of
southern Australia and New Zealand. Accidental to the Wet
Tropics region.

POMARINE JAEGER *Stercorarius pomarinus* 51 cm Its flight
resembles that of a falcon's. Plumage variable. Light phase: grey-
brown above; white below; black cap. Dark phase: uniform dark
brown. Whitish at base of flight feathers. **Central pair of tail
feathers or streamers, twisted and blunt and protrude from
tail.** Streamers diagnostic but may be missing, when it is difficult
to separate from ARCTIC JAEGER. Breeds mostly Arctic Circle,
wandering to southern oceans, and reaching the Coral Sea.

ARCTIC JAEGER *Stercorarius parasiticus* 48 cm Similar to
POMARINE JAEGER in plumage and movements but with
longer, more pointed tail streamers. Difficult to distinguish
from POMARINE when tail streamers missing. Wanders to
Coral Sea.

AQUATIC BIRDS FRESHWATER SWIMMING
POSSIBILITIES

AUSTRALASIAN GREBE
Tachybaptus novaehollandiae 25 cm
Medium-sized, grey-brown bird; usually with rufous tinge
to flanks; looks like a young duck; appears tailless. In
breeding plumage: develops black head and neck, **yellow
spot between eye and bill, yellow eye.** Non-breeding
plumage: no yellow spot between eye and bill. Frequently
dives. Still fresh water with an abundance of aquatic
vegetation. *May be confused with:* NONE in breeding
plumage. In non-breeding plumage: the rare HOARY-
HEADED GREBE which is difficult to separate. Line of
the dark cap passes **through** the eye in AUSTRALASIAN,
and **just under** the eye in HOARY-HEADED.

Non-breeding

Breeding

HOARY-HEADED GREBE
Poliocephalus poliocephalus 27 cm
Rare in the Wet Tropics. Seen in this region in non-
breeding plumage which closely **resembles the
plumage of non-breeding** AUSTRALASIAN GREBE.
'Brushed-hair' look about head in breeding plumage.
Lakes, swamps, larger areas of fresh water.
May be confused with: AUSTRALASIAN GREBE.

Breeding

Non-breeding

GREAT CRESTED GREBE
Podiceps cristatus 50 cm
Large brown and white bird appearing tailless.
Breeding plumage Sept.–Mar. **rufous, black-tipped
ruff or frill about neck, long crest-like ear tufts.**
Non-breeding plumage: ruff and ear tufts somewhat
subdued. Lakes and larger areas of fresh water.

DARTER
Anhinga melanogaster 90 cm
Large bird with **long thin neck; sharp yellow bill.**
Swims with body submerged with only slender head
and neck visible above surface. Male: overall blackish.
Female: dark greyish upperparts; off-white underparts.
Deeper fresh water, sometimes river estuaries.

LITTLE PIED CORMORANT
Phalacrocorax melanoleucos 52 cm
Large black and white bird; black upperparts; white
underparts; **shortish yellow hooked bill;** white face;
lacks black flank. Mostly freshwater lakes, swamps,
rivers, creeks, also estuaries and mangroves. *May be
confused with:* PIED CORMORANT, but look for white
face, shorter yellow bill and absence of black flank.

PIED CORMORANT
Phalacrocorax varius 72 cm
Similar to LITTLE PIED CORMORANT but larger;
**horn-coloured hooked bill; orange-yellow facial
and throat skin; black flank.** Dives for fish.
Estuaries and bays, larger lakes and lagoons.
May be confused with: LITTLE PIED CORMORANT,
but look for orange-yellow facial skin and black flank.

LITTLE BLACK CORMORANT
Phalacrocorax sulcirostris 62 cm
Large black bird; **black face;** dark hooked bill. Lakes,
rivers, swamps, sometimes estuaries and bays.
May be confused with: GREAT CORMORANT, but
look for black face.

GREAT CORMORANT *Phalacrocorax carbo* 82 cm
Similar to LITTLE BLACK CORMORANT but larger;
yellowish face; hooked, dark, horn-coloured bill.
Breeding: develops white patch on flank and white
chin. Larger areas of deeper water, rivers, lakes, bays,
estuaries. *May be confused with:* LITTLE BLACK
CORMORANT, but look for yellowish face.

AUSTRALIAN PELICAN
Pelecanus conspicillatus 165 cm
Well-known, huge black and white bird; **enormous
flesh-coloured bill;** black flight feathers, shoulders,
rump and tail; white head and underparts. Larger
areas of deeper fresh water, also along foreshore.

DUSKY MOORHEN *Gallinula tenebrosa* 39 cm
Medium-sized, short-tailed bird; dark olive-brown; **red head shield; red bill tipped yellow; two white markings under tail** distinguish it from all other aquatic birds. Freshwater swamps, lakes, creeks, dams, especially those with open aquatic vegetation. *May be confused with:* PURPLE SWAMPHEN which has heavier all-red bill and all-white under tail-coverts.

EURASIAN COOT *Fulica atra* 37 cm
Medium-sized; almost tailless; overall dark slate-grey; **white bill; white head shield.** Open sheets of deep fresh water, sometimes at edge.

AQUATIC BIRDS
FRESHWATER WADERS
POSSIBILITIES

WHITE-FACED HERON
Egretta novaehollandiae 67 cm
Large, overall medium-grey bird; long thin neck; **white face and throat; yellow legs;** long sharp black bill. Shallow fresh water, short wet grassland, mudflats, parks and gardens.
May be confused with: NONE in freshwater habitat.

LITTLE EGRET *Egretta garzetta* 56 cm
Large white bird or small egret; **long thin neck;** long legs; long sharp **black** bill. Stalks prey in shallow water. Freshwater swamps, sometimes about mangroves and foreshore. *May be confused with:* Other egrets. See pp. 196–7.

WHITE-NECKED HERON *Ardea pacifica* 87 cm
Very large bird with long thin neck; glossy black body; white head and neck; **black bill and legs; conspicuous white patch on leading edge of each wing in flight.** Juvenile: duller with much spotting down front of neck. Shallow freshwater swamps, dams, edges of streams and lakes. Sometimes open grassland. *May be confused with:* The smaller juvenile PIED HERON, but look for dark bill and legs.

PIED HERON *Ardea picata* 46 cm
Rare; large; blue-black body; long thin neck; white cheeks, throat and neck; **black crown and crest;** long thin sharp **yellow bill; yellow legs.** Juvenile: lacks black crown and crest. Freshwater swamps and lagoons, pasture, mudflats, mangroves and tidal rivers.
May be confused with: Adult: NONE. Juvenile: the larger WHITE-NECKED HERON, but look for yellow legs and bill.

GREAT EGRET
Ardea alba 83 cm
Similar to LITTLE EGRET, but larger. Usually utters a guttural croak when it takes flight. Inhabits similar habitat. *May be confused with:* Other egrets. See p. 196–7.

INTERMEDIATE EGRET
Ardea intermedia 65 cm
Similar to LITTLE EGRET, but larger. Inhabits similar habitat. *May be confused with:* Other egrets. See p. 196–7.

GLOSSY IBIS *Plegadis falcinellus* 55 cm
Large bird appearing black at a distance but is **reddish-brown;** purple-green sheen on wings; **long black curved bill.** Shallow freshwater swamps, sometimes mangroves and mudflats. *May be confused with:* Generally NONE, but can be confused with LITTLE BLACK CORMORANT in flight. Look for drooping, extended neck and more downcurved wings.

AUSTRALIAN WHITE IBIS
Threskiornis molucca 70 cm
Large, mostly white; **bare black head; black tail; long curved black bill;** plumage often soiled. Shallow fresh water, grassland, tidal flats, mangroves and city parks.

STRAW-NECKED IBIS
Threskiornis spinicollis 70 cm
Large; black back; white neck and underparts; **bare black head; long curved black bill.** Adult: yellow straw-like plumes on neck. Wet or dry grassland, pasture, swamps and city parks.

ROYAL SPOONBILL *Platalea regia* 77 cm
Large white bird; **long black bill spoon-shaped at tip; black legs;** black face. Develops long white tuft on back of head during breeding season, usually Sept.–Mar. Fresh, brackish or saltwater swamps, mudflats and mangroves.

YELLOW-BILLED SPOONBILL
Platalea flavipes 83 cm
Similar to ROYAL SPOONBILL, but with **pale yellow bill and legs.** Does not develop breeding tuft. Similar habitat.

BLACK-NECKED STORK
Ephippiorhynchus asiaticus (Adult) 120 cm
Huge black and white bird with long red legs; black head and neck; large heavy black bill. In flight, appears mostly white with black wingbar; flies with neck outstretched. Usually freshwater swamps, sometimes estuaries and mangroves.

BLACK-NECKED STORK
Ephippiorhynchus asiaticus (Immature) 120 cm
Huge, long-legged **grey-brown** bird; long, heavy bill;
grey face; black eye. Flies with neck extended. Usually
freshwater swamps, sometimes estuaries and mangroves.
May be confused with: GREAT-BILLED HERON which
is smaller, has pale throat, yellow eye and flies with neck
folded. Look for heavy bill, long legs and black eye when
standing and extended neck in flight.

SARUS CRANE
Grus antigone 115 cm
Migrant, present Dec.–May; huge, long-legged, stately,
overall grey; **red on rear of head and nape,
extending well down neck; small dewlap; pinkish
legs and feet.** Shallow swamps, grassland, pasture and
bare farmland. *May be confused with:* BROLGA, but
look for pinkish legs.

BROLGA *Grus rubicunda* 115 cm
Almost identical to SARUS CRANE, but red does not
extend as far down neck; **dark grey legs; heavy
dewlap.** Similar habitat. *May be confused with:*
SARUS CRANE, but look for grey legs.

PURPLE SWAMPHEN *Porphyrio porphyrio* 49 cm
Large; dark purplish-blue; **thick red bill; large red
frontal shield; all-white under tail-coverts.** Margins
of lakes, swamps and nearby grassland.
May be confused with: Possibly DUSKY MOORHEN
which has two white markings under tail. Look for all-
white under tail-coverts.

LATHAM'S SNIPE *Gallinago hardwickii* 25 cm
Asiatic summer visitor; medium-sized; plump; **long
straight bill; upperparts boldly patterned brown,
cream and black;** creamy-white throat and upper
breast flecked black; barred flanks; short legs; wary.
Grassy edges of freshwater swamps and wet grassland.
May be confused with: Distinct from other wading
birds although SWINHOE'S SNIPE probably reaches
the Wet Tropics in small numbers. See FURTHER
POSSIBILITIES below.

MARSH SANDPIPER *Tringa stagnatilis* 22 cm
Medium-sized; greyish upperparts; white underparts;
white forehead; resembles a small COMMON
GREENSHANK, but has **a more needle-like
straight, black bill.** The yellow-green legs are
proportionately longer, **trailing well beyond the tail
in flight.** Freshwater swamps and tidal mudflats.
May be confused with: COMMON GREENSHANK and
WOOD SANDPIPER, but look for paler colour without
spotting and fine straight bill. In flight, shows a long
tapered white back and rump.

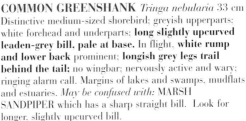
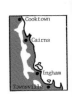

COMMON GREENSHANK *Tringa nebularia* 33 cm

Distinctive medium-sized shorebird; greyish upperparts; white forehead and underparts; **long slightly upcurved leaden-grey bill, pale at base.** In flight, **white rump and lower back** prominent; **longish grey legs trail behind the tail;** no wingbar; nervously active and wary; ringing alarm call. Margins of lakes and swamps, mudflats and estuaries. *May be confused with:* MARSH SANDPIPER which has a sharp straight bill. Look for longer, slightly upcurved bill.

WOOD SANDPIPER *Tringa glareola* 22 cm

Medium-sized; grey-brown above with **profuse white spotting;** whitish below; washed grey across breast; white rump; tail mostly white finely barred black; straight black bill; prominent white eyebrow; long **greenish-yellow legs** which protrude beyond tail in flight; nervously active; bobs head. Shallow freshwater swamps often with some timber, and muddy edges of waterholes. *May be confused with:* MARSH SANDPIPER, but look for well-spotted darker upperparts and white eyebrow.

RED-NECKED STINT *Calidris ruficollis* 15 cm

Tiny shorebird; active; streaked and mottled grey-brown above; **white forehead, eyebrow, cheeks and underparts;** greyish-brown smudge on side of breast; **short stout bill;** black legs. **Shows broad white wingbar and dark centre to rump and tail in flight.** Muddy edges of swamps and lakes, also tidal flats, and beaches.

SHARP-TAILED SANDPIPER

Calidris acuminata 21 cm

Small, abundant shorebird; upperparts **boldly mottled** with brownish, buff and black; streaked breast and flanks; white belly; **rufous crown;** short, straight black bill; green legs. **No obvious wingbar in flight,** but rump and tail dark brown in the centre with white sides. Immature: rufous-pink breast; bright rufous crown; black feathers edged chestnut and white on back. Freshwater swamps and lakes, also mudflats and estuaries. *May be confused with:* PECTORAL and CURLEW SANDPIPERS, both of which have slightly downcurved bills. Look for rufous crown with streaked breast grading into white belly, and short straight black bill.

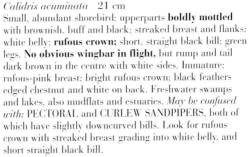

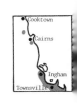

PAINTED SNIPE *Rostratula benghalensis* 24 cm

Rare; medium-sized; overall greyish-brown but with blackish-brown head and breast; **bold white ring about eye leading back to nape; whitish line down middle of crown; curved white bar on side of breast bordering wing** changing to buff as it continues down back; long, grey, pinkish-tipped bill slightly drooped at tip. Female: larger; more boldly marked. Male: duller; striated throat. Teeters rear of body up and down. Shallow freshwater swamps.

BLACK-WINGED STILT

Himantopus himantopus 37 cm
Distinctive, boldly marked, medium-sized wader; white
head and body; black nape and wings; longish needle-
like bill; **extremely long pink legs;** often 'yaps' like a
small dog. Shallow freshwater lakes, swamps and
riverbeds, sometimes estuaries and mudflats.

RED-NECKED AVOCET

Recurvirostra novaehollandiae 44 cm
Distinctive, large black and white wader; **rufous head
and upper neck; long upcurved fine black bill.**
Freshwater swamps, sometimes riverbeds, estuaries,
mudflats and other saline areas.

RED-CAPPED PLOVER

Charadrius ruficapillus 15 cm
Tiny shorebird; greyish-brown upperparts; white
underparts; incomplete breastband; **white forehead;
rufous cap and nape in breeding plumage;** short
black bill; black legs. Female: duller. Immature:
resembles female, but is mottled above; greyish forehead.
Margins of lakes and swamps, tidal flats and beaches.
May be confused with: Usually NONE in freshwater
habitat. RED-NECKED STINT is more mottled-grey
with smaller head and longer tapering bill.

BLACK-FRONTED DOTTEREL

Elseyornis melanops 17 cm
Small wader; greyish-brown above; white below; **black
forehead; black band through eye connecting with
black breastband** which when viewed from the front
forms a **bold 'Y'** on breast; large white throat patch;
red eye-ring. Riverbeds, muddy margins of freshwater
swamps, lakes, dams and sewage ponds. *May be
confused with:* Perhaps RED-KNEED DOTTEREL,
but look for red eye-ring and greyish crown.

RED-KNEED DOTTEREL

Erythrogonys cinctus 18 cm
Small greyish wader: **prominent black head and
breastband separated by large white throat patch;**
chestnut flanks; bobs head. Mainly muddy edges of
lakes and swamps — fresh and brackish.
May be confused with: Perhaps BLACK-FRONTED
DOTTEREL, but look for black head, broad black
breastband and absence of eye-ring.

MASKED LAPWING

Vanellus miles 37 cm
Common, large, ground or wading bird; grey-brown
back and wings; black cap, sometimes sides of neck;
white underparts; pinkish legs; **large yellow wattle
about face and eye.** Grassland, edges of swamps,
tidal flats, farmland and city parks.

FURTHER POSSIBILITIES
GREAT-BILLED HERON sometimes inhabits freshwater creeks.
LITTLE RINGED PLOVER — vagrant.
LONG-TOED STINT — rare.
PECTORAL SANDPIPER — rare.
CURLEW SANDPIPER
BANDED LAPWING — rare.

SWINHOE'S SNIPE *Gallinago megala* 24 cm Extremely
difficult to separate from LATHAM'S SNIPE without extensive
experience. SWINHOE'S is slightly smaller than LATHAM'S
with a more squat appearance giving a fairly distinctive
silhouette. Eye stripe in SWINHOE'S is usually bolder, legs
and feet more yellowish (olive-grey in LATHAM'S). When
flushed LATHAM'S usually utters one or more rasping notes;
SWINHOE'S is mostly silent. It is suspected LATHAM'S may
be mostly a passage migrant only, through the Wet Tropics —
Sept.–Oct. and Mar.–Apr. Birds present Dec.–Feb. may be
SWINHOE'S.

AQUATIC BIRDS
GEESE, DUCKS & SWANS
POSSIBILITIES

MAGPIE GOOSE
Anseranas semipalmata 80 cm
Very large black and white bird; black head, neck,
rump and tail; fleshy-grey bill and part of face; yellow
legs; **black knob on top of head.** Juvenile: dark grey
without knob on head. Coastal wetlands, especially
those with dense reeds.

PLUMED WHISTLING-DUCK
Dendrocygna eytoni 57 cm
Large **mid-brown** duck; pale brown belly; rufous breast
with black barring at sides; **long upswept cream flank
plumes; pinkish bill, legs and feet;** legs and feet trail
in flight. Freshwater swamps, dams and lakes, feeding
out into grassland by night. *May be confused with:*
WANDERING WHISTLING-DUCK, but look for pinkish
bill, legs and feet, and long flank plumes.

WANDERING WHISTLING-DUCK
Dendrocygna arcuata 58 cm
Large, **rich chestnut and brown** duck; chestnut
underparts; short buff plumes along flanks; **black bill,
legs and feet.** Legs and feet trail in flight. Well-vegetated
lagoons and swamps, also flooded grassland. *May be
confused with:* PLUMED WHISTLING-DUCK, but look
for black bill, legs and feet, and short flank plumes.

BLACK SWAN *Cygnus atratus* 125 cm
Well-known, very large, distinctive and graceful bird;
black; **long neck; bright red bill;** shows white wing
feathers in flight. Larger expanses of open water,
mostly fresh water.

RADJAH SHELDUCK
Tadorna radjah   54 cm
Rare; large duck; brown back; completely white head
and underparts; **thin chestnut breastband.** Lagoons,
swamps, river margins, tidal creeks and mudflats.

AUSTRALIAN WOOD DUCK
Chenonetta jubata   48 cm
Large grey duck; **brown head; black along middle
of back.** Female: duller than male; **white line above
and below eye.** Freshwater lagoons, swamps and
farm dams.

COTTON PYGMY-GOOSE
Nettapus coromandelianus 35 cm
Small, whitish duck; glossy greenish-black back and
crown. Male: **white face; black band on breast.**
Female: **long thin black line through eye; white
eyebrow.** Freshwater lakes and lagoons and sometimes
paperbark swamps with abundant water-lilies. *May be
confused with:* Perhaps female GREEN PYGMY-
GOOSE, but look for white face and breastband in
male, and black line through eye in female.

GREEN PYGMY-GOOSE *Nettapus pulchellus* 33 cm
Small, greenish-black duck; patterned greyish
underparts: **well-barred breast and flanks.** Male:
oval, white cheek patch. Female: **white cheek
below eye.** Freshwater lakes and lagoons with
abundant water-lilies. *May be confused with:* Male:
NONE. Female: perhaps COTTON PYGMY-GOOSE,
but look for black cap extending to below eye.

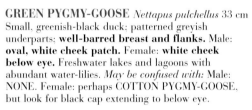

PACIFIC BLACK DUCK *Anas superciliosa* 54 cm
Common, large **brown** duck; pale face; **long black
stripe through eye;** pale eyebrow; grey bill; wary.
Most fresh water, but sometimes brackish and salt
water. *May be confused with:* GREY TEAL, female
CHESTNUT TEAL, female and non-breeding male
GARGANEY and female and non-breeding male
AUSTRALASIAN SHOVELER, but look for long black
stripe through eye and long pale eyebrow.

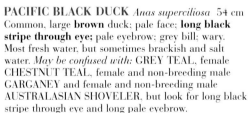

AUSTRALASIAN SHOVELER
Anas rhynchotis   49 cm
Rare, large duck; **heavy spatulate bill; sloping
forehead.** Breeding male: dark back; chestnut
underparts; glossy blue-grey head; white facial
crescent; orange legs and feet. Female and non-
breeding male: overall mottled brownish; pale chestnut
underparts; dull blue shoulders. Female has yellow-
brown legs and feet. Male retains orange legs and feet
in non-breeding plumage. Larger areas of fresh water
with extensive cover, but also brackish water.
May be confused with: Generally other brown ducks,
but look for distinctive bill shape.

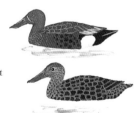

GREY TEAL *Anas gracilis* 42 cm

Medium-sized plain brown duck **without distinctive markings;** pale throat. Larger areas of fresh water, but sometimes brackish and salt water. *May be confused with:* The larger BLACK DUCK which has long black stripe through eye. Female CHESTNUT TEAL is slightly darker with dark throat and slightly higher forehead. AUSTRALASIAN SHOVELER has heavy spatulate bill and low, sloping forehead. GARGANEY has short stripe through eye and pale blue-grey shoulder patch. Look for nondescript brown duck with pale throat.

CHESTNUT TEAL *Anas castanea* 43 cm

Rare, medium-sized duck. Male: rich chestnut body; **deep green head; white flanks;** black rear end. Female: plain overall brown; similar to GREY TEAL but overall slightly darker with darker throat and slightly higher forehead. Larger areas of fresh water, but sometimes brackish and salt water. *May be confused with:* Male: NONE. Female: GREY TEAL, but look for dark throat.

GARGANEY *Anas querquedula* 38 cm
Rare summer visitor from Northern Hemisphere; medium-sized duck; overall brownish; **dark line from bill through eye; blue-grey wing patch.** Can occur on any fresh water. *May be confused with:* Other brownish ducks, but look for shoulder patch and dark line through eye.

PINK-EARED DUCK

Malacorhynchus membranaceus 41 cm
Medium-sized duck appearing brown at a distance; darker upperparts; whitish underparts; **heavily barred flanks, sides of body and breast; large grey square-tipped bill;** pink ear. Larger areas of open fresh water, lagoons and swamps, also muddy water and flood water.

HARDHEAD *Aythya australis* 49 cm

Large, plain **rich dark brown duck; white tip to bill; white patch under tail.** Male: conspicuous white eye. Female: brown eye. Larger expanses of freshwater lagoons, dams and swamps.

FURTHER POSSIBILITIES
SPOTTED WHISTLING-DUCK *Dendrocygna guttata* 43 cm
Similar to other whistling-ducks but with **spotting** on flanks, sides of neck and breast. **No flank plumes.** Widespread to the north of Australia. Numbers recently recorded from northern Cape York.

BLUE-BILLED DUCK *Oxyura australis* 39 cm Small duck; dumpy, low set in water, stiff pointed tail feathers; **top of bill quite concave;** bill pale blue in breeding male, dull grey in non-breeding male and female. Vagrant from southern Australia.

MUSK DUCK *Biziura lobata* Male 66 cm Female 41 cm
Large dark grey duck with **short wedge-shaped bill.** Male
has **large lobe under bill.** Low set in water. Vagrant from
southern Australia.

FRECKLED DUCK *Stictonetta naevosa* 54 cm
A plain dark grey duck with no obvious markings, but
plumage freckled pale buffy-white. **Large head with crown
peaked at rear.** Vagrant from southern Australia.

NORTHERN SHOVELER *Anas clypeata* 49 cm Similar to
AUSTRALASIAN SHOVELER (male in winter plumage when
in Australia) and extremely difficult to distinguish. Best field
mark is **broad white edges to tail** visible at close range.
NORTHERN has varying amount of orange on sides of bill —
AUSTRALASIAN has dark bill, occasionally with small area of
orange at junction of mandibles only. Widespread through the
Northern Hemisphere, wintering southward. Vagrant to
Australia, not recorded from Wet Tropics.

AQUATIC BIRDS
OF REEDBEDS & STREAM MARGINS
POSSIBILITIES

NANKEEN NIGHT HERON
Nycticorax caledonicus 60 cm
Large **cinnamon** wading bird; **black cap;** yellow legs;
black bill; two white plumes from back of head. Juvenile:
heavily striated brownish; greenish legs; paler
underparts well-striated. Nocturnal; rests by day in thick
foliage. Freshwater swamps, lakes and creeks. *May be
confused with:* Adult: NONE. Juvenile: STRIATED
HERON, but look for well-striated head and body;
greenish legs. Juvenile often misidentified as a bittern.

LITTLE BITTERN *Ixobrychus minutus* 24 cm
Rare; small bittern. Male: blackish back and crown,
chestnut sides of head and neck; **large chestnut
shoulder patch; yellow legs, yellow bill with black
ridge.** Female: duller than male. Juvenile: streaked
brown. Dense tall reeds, but at times other dense
grassy habitats. *May be confused with:* Generally
NONE. STRIATED HERON sometimes misidentified
as a LITTLE BITTERN. STRIATED is blue-grey and
occupies a different habitat. Look for chestnut and
brown colouration.

BLACK BITTERN *Ixobrychus flavicollis* 60 cm
Large **dark sooty** bird; yellowish streaked breast and
sides of neck; **yellowish plume on neck; olive-brown
legs; dark bill.** Female: duller. Juvenile: sooty-brown;
paler edging to feathers; pale neck plume; yellow-brown
legs. Feeds at dusk and dawn. Freshwater swamps,
especially paperbark swamps, well-vegetated streamsides
and sometimes mangroves. *May be confused with:* Perhaps
STRIATED HERON which has black cap and yellow to
orange legs, but look for neck plume and olive-brown legs.

BUFF-BANDED RAIL
Gallirallus philippensis   31 cm
Medium-sized, brownish; chestnut crown and stripe through eye; **grey eyebrow; chestnut patch on breast; extensive fine barring on underparts.** Dense, damp grassland and vegetation about swamps and streams. *May be confused with:* The rare LEWIN'S RAIL, but look for grey eyebrow and chestnut on breast.

LEWIN'S RAIL   *Rallus pectoralis*   22 cm
Rare; medium-sized; dark upperparts; **rich chestnut head and nape** with black streaks; **slate-grey throat and breast;** barred wings, belly and under tail-coverts; **long black-tipped pink bill.** Damp grassland and reedy swamps. *May be confused with:* Perhaps BUFF-BANDED RAIL, but look for long bill, absence of eyebrow and slate-grey extending from throat to upper belly.

BUSH-HEN   *Amaurornis olivaceus*   26 cm
Medium-sized; **plain; olive-brown and greyish; buff lower belly and under tail-coverts;** dull yellow legs; develops red base to green bill during breeding season approximately Nov.–Mar. Stubby tail often flicked. Dense shrubby or grassy creeks and dense wet grassland. *May be confused with:* NONE. Distinct, with buff belly and under tail-coverts.

BAILLON'S CRAKE   *Porzana pusilla*   15 cm
Small bird; olive back streaked black; **pale grey face, throat and breast; olive-green legs; green bill;** barred belly and under tail-coverts; stubby tail often flicked. Freshwater swamps and lagoons with reeds and tussocks. *May be confused with:* Possibly other small crakes, but look for pale grey face, olive-brown legs and all-green bill.

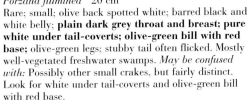

AUSTRALIAN SPOTTED CRAKE
Porzana fluminea   20 cm
Rare; small; olive back spotted white; barred black and white belly; **plain dark grey throat and breast; pure white under tail-coverts; olive-green bill with red base;** olive-green legs; stubby tail often flicked. Mostly well-vegetated freshwater swamps. *May be confused with:* Possibly other small crakes, but fairly distinct. Look for white under tail-coverts and olive-green bill with red base.

SPOTLESS CRAKE   *Porzana tabuensis*   18 cm
Small; dark slate-grey head and underparts; chocolate-brown upperparts; **black bill; red legs; red eye;** stubby tail often flicked. Mostly very dense, well-vegetated freshwater swamps.

WHITE-BROWED CRAKE *Porzana cinerea* 19 cm
Small; black and brown upperparts; grey throat, neck and breast; white belly; **dark stripe through eye with white eyebrow and white stripe below eye;** stubby tail often flicked. Freshwater swamps, especially those with reedbeds and water-lilies, also rice fields and sometimes sugar-cane fields. Moreso in the lowlands. *May be confused with:* BAILLON'S CRAKE, but look for white eyebrow and white below eye. Shows buffy flanks in flight.

BLACK-TAILED NATIVE-HEN
Gallinula ventralis 34 cm
Rare; medium-sized, short-tailed **bantam-like** bird; plain dark olive-brown above; slate-grey below; **bright red legs, several white spots on flanks and green and red bill** distinguish it from other aquatic birds. Margins of lakes and swamps.

LATHAM'S SNIPE *Gallinago hardwickii* 25 cm
Asiatic summer visitor; medium-sized; plump; **long straight bill; upperparts boldly patterned brown, cream and black;** creamy-white throat and upper breast flecked black; barred flanks; short legs; wary. Grassy edges of freshwater swamps and wet grassland. *May be confused with:* Distinct from other wading birds although SWINHOE'S SNIPE probably reaches the Wet Tropics in small numbers. See p. 170.

PAINTED SNIPE *Rostratula benghalensis* 24 cm
Rare; medium-sized; overall greyish-brown but with blackish-brown head and breast; **bold white ring about eye leading back to nape; whitish line down middle of crown; curved white bar on side of breast bordering wing** changing to buff as it continues down back; long, grey, pinkish-tipped bill slightly drooped at tip. Female: larger; more boldly marked. Male: duller; striated throat. Teeters rear of body up and down. Shallow freshwater swamps.

DIURNAL BIRDS OF PREY
POSSIBILITIES

OSPREY *Pandion haliaetus* Male 53 cm Female 63 cm
Large fishing hawk; dark brown back, wings and tail; white head and underparts; **heavy dark line through eye and down neck; brownish, varying broken band across breast** generally heavier in female. Juvenile: larger band across breast. Coastal waters, estuaries, offshore islands, sometimes larger rivers and lakes. *May be confused with:* Usually NONE, but juvenile and immature WHITE-BELLIED SEA-EAGLE sometimes mistaken for OSPREY in flight. Look for squarish dark tail and breastband.

PACIFIC BAZA
Aviceda subcristata   Male 37 cm Female 44 cm
Medium-sized grey hawk: **reddish-brown barring on belly; small upright crest on back of head; large yellow eye.** Open forest, rainforest (especially the edges), riverside vegetation and forested farmland.

BLACK-SHOULDERED KITE
Elanus axillaris   36 cm
Immaculate-looking, small, grey and white bird of prey: **black shoulder patch;** orange-yellow legs and feet; red eye. **Frequently hovers.** Immature: brownish head. Open grassland and farmland. *May be confused with:* The vagrant LETTER-WINGED KITE which has black 'W' under wings. GREY GOSHAWK lacks black shoulder patch and inhabits denser forest.

LETTER-WINGED KITE   *Elanus scriptus*   36 cm
Vagrant: similar to BLACK-SHOULDERED KITE, but with **thick black 'W' on underwings;** larger eyes; **pale yellow or cream legs and feet;** flight more tern-like, more swooping.
May be confused with: BLACK-SHOULDERED KITE.

SQUARE-TAILED KITE   *Lophoictinia isura*   53 cm
Rare, large brown bird: **whitish face.** At rest, long wings extend beyond tail. In flight, **harrier-like with long, upswept wings showing dull white 'windows' towards tip;** tail square and well-spread: two-toned brown colour to upper surfaces. Open forest and woodland, and over rainforest. *May be confused with:* Mostly harriers, but look for whitish face and wing 'windows' in adult. Juvenile: usually rich rufous and difficult to identify. Look for a combination of upswept wings without teetering, fairly plain squarish tail and reddish rump in flight.

BLACK-BREASTED BUZZARD
Hamirostra melanosternon   Male 55 cm Female 60 cm
Rare; large, robust, short-tailed dark bird: **black head, breast and back;** prominent **white 'windows' in broad wings** in flight. Soars high with **upswept wings; wings frequently teetered from side to side.** Juvenile and immature: rich rufous to brownish without black breast; 'window' in wing indistinct. Drier, open woodland and open forest. *May be confused with:* Mostly SQUARE-TAILED KITE, immature WHITE-BELLIED SEA-EAGLE and WEDGE-TAILED EAGLE. Adult: distinctive with black head and breast. Juvenile and immature: difficult to distinguish, but in flight look for upswept, teetering wings with indistinct 'windows' and short tail.

Juvenile

BLACK KITE

Milvus migrans 52 cm

Most common bird of prey; large; fairly uniform dull-brown; mostly seen flying and soaring leisurely on **slightly drooped wings with tail frequently twisted and turned;** tail often appears quite square in flight — forked when closed. Open areas, open woodland, farmland, about homesteads, cities and towns. *May be confused with:* SQUARE-TAILED, WHISTLING and juvenile BRAHMINY KITES and LITTLE EAGLE. In flight, look for near-square tail, tail twitching and slightly drooped wings, or dull dark brown colour and well-forked tail when perched.

WHISTLING KITE

Haliastur sphenurus 53 cm

Common, large, brown bird of prey; usually soaring effortlessly on **slightly drooped wings; long rounded tail;** streaked head, back and breast; **distinct pale 'wedge' in underwing in flight;** distinctive musical call. Open areas, lightly timbered country, and about lakes, swamps, estuaries and tidal flats. *May be confused with:* BLACK and juvenile BRAHMINY KITES and light form of LITTLE EAGLE. Look for long rounded tail, slightly drooped wings and 'wedge' in underwing in flight.

BRAHMINY KITE

Haliastur indus 48 cm

Large; deep chestnut back, wings, lower body and tail; **white head and breast;** short, rather rounded tail. Juvenile: brown head and breast, well-streaked with pale 'window' in underwing. Mangroves, estuaries, larger rivers, sometimes open forest and open areas some kilometres inland. *May be confused with:* Adult: NONE. Juvenile: BLACK and WHISTLING KITES and pale form of LITTLE EAGLE, but look for short, fairly rounded tail.

WHITE-BELLIED SEA-EAGLE

Haliaeetus leucogaster Male 76 cm Female 83 cm

Huge grey and white fishing eagle; **grey** back, wings and base of tail; graceful flight with **upswept wings; white, broad, short, rather rounded tail.** Juvenile and immature: dark brown with **pale 'half moon'** near tip of underwing; pale tail. Estuaries, bays, larger lakes and rivers and offshore islands. *May be confused with:* Adult: NONE. Juvenile and immature: mostly WEDGE-TAILED EAGLE, but look for pale, short, broad tail and pale 'half moon' in wings. Juvenile and immature WHITE-BELLIED in flight sometimes mistaken for OSPREY, which has squarish dark tail and breastband.

Juvenile

Immature

Adult

Juvenile

Female

Male

SPOTTED HARRIER

Circus assimilis   Male 53 cm Female 59 cm
Large, graceful, slow-flying hawk with long **black-tipped** upswept wings; smoky-grey above; distinct chestnut **owl-like facial disc; rich chestnut underparts finely spotted white; tail slightly wedge-shaped at tip;** long yellow legs. Adult: grey tail with darker barring. Juvenile: reddish-brown, sometimes pale; brown barred tail; pale buff rump. Immature: similar to adult, but with well-streaked underparts; tail similar to adult's; pale buff rump. During first moult, juvenile often appears 'dark-hooded' with pale underparts as it moults into immature plumage.
May be confused with: Adult: NONE. Juvenile and immature: can be mistaken for SQUARE-TAILED KITE and SWAMP HARRIER (which also has pale rump). Juvenile 'dark-hooded' SPOTTED has been mistaken for subadult male PAPUAN HARRIER, but look for heavily barred tail slightly wedge-shaped at tip and black-tipped wings.

SWAMP HARRIER

Circus approximans   Male 54 cm Female 58 cm
Large, graceful, brown hawk with upswept wings; **owl-like facial disc; whitish rump;** streaked underparts; yellow legs. Male: wings washed grey; **long plain greyish tail.** Female: **faintly barred brown tail.** Juvenile: dark brown; **orange-brown rump.** Swamps, reedbeds, sometimes pastures and crops. *May be confused with:* SQUARE-TAILED KITE and juvenile and immature SPOTTED HARRIER, but look for whitish or pale rump and plain or lightly barred squarish tail.

BROWN GOSHAWK

Accipiter fasciatus   Male 42 cm Female 50 cm
Medium-sized bird of prey; greyish-brown; **finely barred pale rufous underparts;** rufous collar; longish yellow legs; yellow eye; **long rounded tail.** Juvenile: overall brown, heavily streaked throat and upper breast, barred lower breast and belly. Open eucalypt forest and woodland. *May be confused with:* The smaller COLLARED SPARROWHAWK in all stages, but look for rounded tail. Sometimes tail shape can be difficult to discern and can appear rounded in certain positions in the SPARROWHAWK.

GREY GOSHAWK

Accipiter novaehollandiae   Male 38 cm Female 52 cm
Medium-sized bird of prey. Two colour phases: plain grey upperparts with white underparts and faint grey barring; or pure white. Rather **long, powerful yellow legs and feet;** yellow cere; red eye. Rainforest and adjacent tall eucalypt forest of higher areas, sometimes in coastal woodland and on rainforested offshore islands. *May be confused with:* In flight, can be overlooked for SULPHUR-CRESTED COCKATOO. GOSHAWK usually circles, COCKATOO has direct flight.

COLLARED SPARROWHAWK

Accipiter cirrhocephalus   Male 31 cm Female 37 cm
Almost identical to BROWN GOSHAWK but smaller
with a **square tail** sometimes difficult to discern.
Juvenile: almost identical to juvenile BROWN
GOSHAWK. Open eucalypt forest and woodland.
May be confused with: BROWN GOSHAWK.

RED GOSHAWK

Erythrotriorchis radiatus   Male 49 cm Female 59 cm
Very rare; large, powerful reddish hawk; long wings
and tail; **head and breast boldly streaked black;**
plain bright rufous 'trousers'; **underwings and tail
prominently barred grey; massive yellow legs and
feet.** Open forest and tree-lined watercourses.
May be confused with: Mostly reddish juveniles of
similar-sized birds of prey, but look for barred wings
and tail, black streaked breast and massive yellow legs.

WEDGE-TAILED EAGLE

Aquila audax   Male 91 cm Female 100 cm
A **huge dark eagle** ranging from brown to near-black;
thickly-feathered legs; heavy, hooked, pale bill;
**longish wedge-shaped tail; upswept wings in
flight.** Mountainous open forest to lowland tropical
woodland. Generally avoids rainforest. *May be
confused with:* Juvenile and immature WHITE-
BELLIED SEA-EAGLE which has shorter, pale, more
rounded tail and more upswept wings. BLACK-
BREASTED BUZZARD teeters wings in flight; short
tail. Watch for GURNEY'S EAGLE. See p. 181.

LITTLE EAGLE

Hieraaetus morphnoides   Male 47 cm Female 54 cm
Rare large hawk or small eagle. Two colour phases:
dark brown and light brown. Short square tail often
twisted in flight; **partial crest on nape; legs fully-
feathered to feet; glides in tight circles on flat
wings slightly upturned at tip.** Initially one of the
more difficult birds of prey to identify, especially the
dark phase. Open forest and woodland, often along
watercourses. *May be confused with:* Generally other
similar-sized, brownish birds of prey. Look for fully-
feathered legs and partial crest when perched, and flat
wings and shortish square tail in flight.

BROWN FALCON

Falco berigora   Male 45 cm Female 55 cm
A medium-sized hawk with variable plumage — pale
brown to near-black; underparts sometimes paler;
**paler throat and cheek; darker 'moustache' below
eye; lightly barred tail. Wings upswept in flight.**
Hovers clumsily. Open woodland, farmland, often on
roadside power poles. *May be confused with:*
Sometimes other similar-sized birds of prey, but look
for paler throat and cheek markings and lightly barred
tail. BLACK FALCON is sometimes confused with
dark-plumaged BROWN.

Dark

Light

Light

AUSTRALIAN HOBBY *Falco longipennis* 33 cm

Small hawk resembling a small PEREGRINE FALCON but more slender; dark slate-blue above; rufous underparts streaked blackish; black crown and cheeks; **small buffy-white forehead; partial buffy-white rear collar** which continues around and up side of head. Sparsely timbered country, open forest, watercourses and over cities and towns.
May be confused with: PEREGRINE FALCON, but look for buffy-white forehead, yellowish-grey eye-ring; partial buffy-white collar; long slender wings in flight.

GREY FALCON

Falco hypoleucos Male 34 cm Female 42 cm
Vagrant; medium-sized grey bird of prey; paler below with fine, dark streaks; **black faintly barred tail; yellow cere, eye-ring and feet.** A bird of the arid inland. *May be confused with:* NONE. BLACK-SHOULDERED and LETTER-WINGED KITES have black shoulder patches. GREY GOSHAWK has long legs and faint barring on breast.

BLACK FALCON

Falco subniger Male 49 cm Female 55 cm
Rare; medium-sized bird of prey; dark sooty-brown; faint, **pale chin and face;** longish tail. Older birds: white speckled throat, developing into an extensive white 'bib' with age; **plain tail.** Distinctive flight with shallow wingbeats. Wings do not move above horizontal plane. Open grassland and open woodland. *May be confused with:* The dark-plumaged BROWN FALCON, but look for pale chin and face without 'moustache'; plain tail and distinctive wingbeats. Sometimes passed over as a TORRESIAN CROW.

PEREGRINE FALCON

Falco peregrinus Male 39 cm Female 48 cm
Medium-sized bird of prey; stocky; slate-grey back; **dark hood about head and face; buff throat and breast; yellow cere and eye-ring. Very fast, powerful flight.** Mountainous forest, open forest and woodland, sometimes over open grassland and swamps. *May be confused with:* AUSTRALIAN HOBBY, but look for black forehead, yellow eye-ring and cere.

NANKEEN KESTREL

Falco cenchroides 33 cm
A small bird of prey; **pale rufous upperparts; whitish underparts; black flight feathers.** Male: grey tail. Female: brown-barred tail. Shows dark subterminal band in tail in flight. Frequently hovers on flat wings. Open grassland and farmland.

FURTHER POSSIBILITIES

LONG-TAILED BUZZARD *Henicopernis longicauda*
Male 54 cm Female 58 cm Large brownish-black bird of prey
with long broad wings. **Striking light and dark bands in tail
and flight feathers.** Head with whitish streaks. Underparts
pale buff, streaked black. Distinctive. Endemic to New Guinea
and some islands. Not yet recorded for Australia but expected.

PAPUAN HARRIER *Circus spilonotus spilothorax* Male 48 cm
Female 53 cm Similar to other harriers in habits. Fully adult
male unmistakable — mostly black with white breast and belly
and plain grey tail. The female is similar to female SWAMP
HARRIER but has a **more heavily barred tail** (only **slightly**
barred in SWAMP). Some female PAPUAN have white about
the head, which is lacking in female SWAMP. Juveniles of both
species are chocolate-brown in colour but the PAPUAN has
**variable patches of pale near-white on back of crown and
face.** Juvenile SWAMP has **whitish streaks only, on nape.**
Endemic to New Guinea but a number of probable sightings
from the Wet Tropics region in recent times. Some reports of
subadult male PAPUAN may have been dark-hooded juvenile
SPOTTED HARRIER which is more grey and white with dark
streaking and spotting on the breast, flanks and underwings.
The juvenile SPOTTED can be easily eliminated by heavily
barred tail, slightly wedge-shaped at tip.

NEW GUINEA GREY-HEADED GOSHAWK *Accipiter
poliocephalus* Male 30 cm Female 38 cm Adult similar to
GREY GOSHAWK, but smaller with pale **unbarred
underparts**, reddish-orange cere, legs and feet, **dark eye.**
Juvenile and immature slaty-grey above, white below,
sparingly marked with **bold blackish streaks on breast;
underside of tail barred.** Endemic to New Guinea and
adjacent islands. A probable juvenile seen by the author at Mt
Molloy Feb. 1993.

GURNEY'S EAGLE *Aquila gurneyi* Male 75 cm
Female 84 cm Similar to WEDGE-TAILED EAGLE but
soars on **horizontal** wings. Tail is more **rounded** rather than
wedge-shaped. A New Guinea species, with one confirmed
record from Torres Strait. Easily overlooked because of
similarity to WEDGE-TAILED.

ORIENTAL HOBBY *Falco severus* 28 cm Similar to
AUSTRALIAN HOBBY but smaller and darker, with **dark
reddish underparts, plain tail, yellow eye-ring,** orange-
yellow legs and feet. Immature has heavily streaked underparts
and barred tail almost identical to AUSTRALIAN. Widespread
in New Guinea; not yet recorded for Australia but expected.

Gurney's

Wedge-tailed

POSSIBILITIES

RUDDY TURNSTONE *Arenaria interpres* 23 cm
Thickset, medium-sized shorebird; dark grey-brown
above; **white throat; blackish upper breast;** white
belly; **short orange legs.** In flight, shows two
prominent white bars in each wing — one bar shorter
than the other; white rump and middle of back.
Pebbly shores with debris, coral reefs, usually avoiding
mudflats.

SANDERLING
Calidris alba 20 cm
Small active shorebird; pale grey above; white below;
head almost white; dark shoulder patch; **the palest
shorebird.** Juvenile: black back spotted white. In
flight, shows the **largest white wingbar of any
sandpiper.** Mostly open sandy beaches.

RED-NECKED STINT *Calidris ruficollis* 15 cm
Tiny common shorebird; active; streaked and mottled
grey-brown above; **white forehead, eyebrow, cheeks
and underparts;** greyish-brown smudge on side of
breast; **short stout bill;** black legs. **Shows broad
white wingbar and dark centre to rump and tail in
flight.** Tidal flats, beaches and swamps.

LONG-TOED STINT *Calidris subminuta* 15 cm
Rare; small shorebird, somewhat similar to RED-
NECKED STINT with which it associates, but slightly
darker with **greenish-yellow legs; shows no wingbar
in flight.** Muddy margins of shallow fresh water,
occasionally mudflats. *May be confused with:* The
larger SHARP-TAILED SANDPIPER which has rufous
crown and green, brown or yellow legs.

SHARP-TAILED SANDPIPER
Calidris acuminata 21 cm
Small abundant shorebird; upperparts **boldly mottled**
with brownish, buff and black; streaked breast and
flanks; white belly; **rufous crown;** short, straight
black bill; green, brown or yellow legs. **No obvious
wingbar in flight** but rump and tail dark brown in
centre with white sides. Immature: rufous-pink breast;
bright rufous crown; black feathers edged chestnut and
white on back. Mudflats, freshwater swamps and
lakes. *May be confused with:* Mostly PECTORAL
SANDPIPER which has slightly downcurved bill. Look
for rufous crown with streaked breast grading into
white belly and short straight black bill.

RUFF *Philomachus pugnax* Male 30 cm Female 25 cm
Rare; medium-sized shorebird; resembles a very large
**erect SHARP-TAILED SANDPIPER. Appears 'pot-
bellied' with slender neck and small head; no
rufous cap;** dark greyish 'scaly' upperparts; paler
greyish underparts; head and neck light grey-brown
slightly streaked darker; shortish brown bill; yellowish
legs. In flight, shows white wingbar and distinctive **large
oval white patch on each side of a dark rump.** Male:
larger than female. Associates with SHARP-TAILED
SANDPIPER. Tidal flats and freshwater swamps. *May
be confused with:* Perhaps SHARP-TAILED and
PECTORAL SANDPIPERS which are much smaller.
RUFF has distinctive silhouette and mannerisms.

PACIFIC GOLDEN PLOVER *Pluvialis fulva* 26cm
Medium-sized shorebird; overall mottled **greyish;
darker above;** whitish belly; large head; dark eye; short
black bill; **pale buff forehead, face and upper
breast.** In flight, shows **dark rump, faint wingbar
and buff-grey 'armpits'.** Breeding plumage
(sometimes seen Sept. and Apr.): black underparts;
spangled golden-black above. Tidal flats, saltmarsh,
short grass and freshwater swamps. *May be confused
with:* GREY PLOVER, but look for more buffy
appearance and dark rump.

GREY PLOVER *Pluvialis squatarola* 27 cm
Similar to PACIFIC GOLDEN PLOVER; shows
**whitish rump; white wingbar and black 'armpits'
in flight.** Tidal flats. *May be confused with:* PACIFIC
GOLDEN PLOVER, but look for more grey
appearance, whitish rump and wingbar.

LITTLE RINGED PLOVER
Charadrius dubius 15 cm
Vagrant. Similar to female RED-CAPPED PLOVER
but with **thin whitish collar, yellow eye-ring and
pinkish or yellow legs.** Narrow band over forehead.
Dark band or partial band across breast. Mostly
margins of freshwater lakes and swamps.
May be confused with: Perhaps juvenile RED-CAPPED
and DOUBLE-BANDED PLOVERS, and juvenile
BLACK-FRONTED DOTTEREL, but look for eye-ring
and band over forehead.

RED-CAPPED PLOVER
Charadrius ruficapillus 15 cm
Tiny shorebird; common resident; greyish-brown
upperparts; white underparts; incomplete breastband;
**white forehead; rufous cap and nape in breeding
plumage;** short black bill; black legs. Female: duller.
Immature: resembles female, but is mottled above;
greyish forehead. Beaches, estuaries, mudflats and
sometimes margins of lakes. *May be confused with:*
Fairly distinctive, but perhaps DOUBLE-BANDED
PLOVER which has no white forehead. RED-
NECKED STINT is more mottled-grey above with
smaller head and longer tapering bill.

DOUBLE-BANDED PLOVER
Charadrius bicinctus 18 cm
Rare; small shorebird similar to LESSER SAND
PLOVER. Tidal sandflats and beaches.
May be confused with: LESSER SAND PLOVER and
other small shorebirds, but look for a **combination of
buff tinge to head and nape, no prominent white
patch on forehead, faint eyebrow** and sometimes a
suggestion of double breastbands at sides of breast.

LESSER SAND PLOVER
Charadrius mongolus 20 cm
Rather plain; small shorebird; grey upperparts; white
underparts; **grey-brown breastband usually
confined to sides of breast; whitish forehead and
throat; dark mark through eye.** Handsome breeding
plumage (sometimes seen Sept. and Apr.); black mask;
white forehead; **broad chestnut breastband
extending to flanks.** Tidal flats, estuaries, sandy bays.
May be confused with: DOUBLE-BANDED PLOVER,
but look for white forehead and more prominent
eyebrow. GREATER SAND PLOVER, but look for
shorter, thinner bill.

GREATER SAND PLOVER
Charadrius leschenaultii 23 cm
Medium-sized shorebird similar to LESSER SAND
PLOVER. Breeding plumage (sometimes seen Sept.
and Apr.) similar to LESSER SAND PLOVER but
with more **narrow chestnut breastband.** Tidal flats
and beaches. *May be confused with:* LESSER SAND
PLOVER and other small shorebirds, but look for
longer heavier bill which almost equals the length of
the head, and lighter grey underparts.

ORIENTAL PLOVER *Charadrius veredus* 23 cm
Overall greyish, **long-legged, elegant,** medium-sized
bird; pale buff to white face, throat and eyebrow;
white belly; resembles small PACIFIC GOLDEN
PLOVER but plainer with yellowish legs. Open dry
ground, farmland, aerodromes and occasionally
mudflats.

SHOREBIRDS WITH MEDIUM-LENGTH STRAIGHT BILLS
POSSIBILITIES

COMMON REDSHANK *Tringa totanus* 28 cm
Rare; medium-sized shorebird; resembles COMMON
GREENSHANK but with straight bill; browner
upperparts; **red legs; red base to bill.** In flight, shows
**white trailing edge to wings; white rump and
lower back.** Flight is swift with frequent tilting from
side to side. Wary. Associates with other shorebirds.
Mudflats. *May be confused with:* NONE. Red legs and
red base to bill distinctive.

COMMON SANDPIPER *Actitis hypoleucos* 20 cm

Small: bronze-brown above; white below; brownish on sides of breast; **white above shoulder;** faintly barred wing-coverts; tail longer than folded wings; **white eye-ring;** shortish green legs; **constant nervous teetering; stiff-winged flight; white wingbar** in flight. Mudbanks, creeks, swamps, mangrove channels, watercourses and edges of lakes. *May be confused with:* NONE. Look for white eye-ring, white above shoulder and teetering.

WOOD SANDPIPER *Tringa glareola* 22 cm

Medium-sized; grey-brown above with **profuse white spotting;** whitish below; washed grey across breast; white rump; tail mostly white finely barred black; straight black bill; prominent white eyebrow; long **greenish-yellow legs** which protrude beyond tail in flight; nervously active; bobs head. Shallow freshwater swamps often with some timber, and muddy edges of waterholes. *May be confused with:* MARSH SANDPIPER, but look for well-spotted darker upperparts and white eyebrow. GREEN SANDPIPER is sometimes reported but none has been confirmed. Most likely misidentified WOOD.

GREY-TAILED TATTLER

Heteroscelus brevipes 27 cm

A plump, medium-sized shorebird; **plain grey above;** whitish below; washed grey across breast; yellow legs; grey bill. In Mar. and Apr. begins to assume breeding plumage which consists of flecks and barring on throat, face, breast and flanks. Teeters body while feeding. Tidal flats, mangroves, reefs and rocky shorelines. *May be confused with:* WANDERING TATTLER. Can be difficult to separate, but wing tips of GREY-TAILED **are the same length as or only slightly longer than the tail,** whereas those of WANDERING **extend 1 cm or more beyond the tail.** The WANDERING appears more brownish overall. Length of the nasal groove is only useful when in the hand. Calls are quite distinct; the GREY-TAILED has a double note call, the WANDERING a trill of 6–10 notes.

WANDERING TATTLER

Heteroscelus incanus 27 cm

Similar to GREY-TAILED TATTLER, but generally appears **more brownish.** Teeters body continuously while feeding. Rocky shores, coral reefs, beaches. Mostly on offshore islands.
May be confused with: GREY-TAILED TATTLER.

GREAT KNOT *Calidris tenuirostris* 29 cm
A thickset medium-sized shorebird; grey mottled above; paler below with darkish spots on breast and flanks; **black bill longer than head;** shortish olive legs. In flight, shows **faint white wingbar,** whitish rump; greyish-brown tail. Tidal mudflats and beaches. *May be confused with:* RED KNOT, but look for whiter rump and rather inconspicuous wingbar. GREAT KNOT is larger with relatively longer, more slender bill. Tattlers are plain grey without mottling and have grey rumps.

RED KNOT *Calidris canutus* 25 cm
Similar to GREAT KNOT with which it associates. Bill is shorter, thick and tapering and the **same length as the head.** In flight, shows a narrow white wingbar and barred greyish rump. *May be confused with:* GREAT KNOT.

SHOREBIRDS WITH LONG STRAIGHT BILLS
POSSIBILITIES

LATHAM'S SNIPE *Gallinago hardwickii* 25 cm
Medium-sized plump shorebird; **boldly patterned brown, cream and black upperparts;** creamy-white throat and upper breast flecked black; barred flanks; short legs; wary. Grassy edges of freshwater swamps and wet grassland. *May be confused with:* Distinct from other shorebirds although SWINHOE'S SNIPE probably reaches the Wet Tropics in small numbers. See p. 170.

BLACK-TAILED GODWIT *Limosa limosa* 40 cm
Large; overall greyish; paler below; long, **straight, bicoloured bill.** In flight, shows **white rump; black tail; broad white wingbar;** white underwing with black flight feathers. Tidal mudflats, sandspits, shallow fresh and brackish water. *May be confused with:* BAR-TAILED GODWIT with which it associates. BAR-TAILED has upcurved bill. Look for black tail, straight bill and white wingbar.

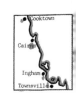

MARSH SANDPIPER *Tringa stagnatilis* 22 cm
Medium-sized; greyish upperparts; white underparts; white forehead; resembles a small COMMON GREENSHANK, but has a **more needle-like straight, black bill.** The yellow-green legs are proportionately longer, **trailing well beyond the tail in flight.** Fresh or brackish swamps, sometimes tidal mudflats. *May be confused with:* COMMON GREENSHANK and WOOD SANDPIPER, but look for paler colour without spotting and fine straight bill. In flight, shows a long tapered white patch in back and white rump.

ASIAN DOWITCHER
Limnodromus semipalmatus 34 cm
Rare; medium-sized shorebird; overall greyish; paler below; **long straight black bill slightly swollen at tip;** resembles a small BAR-TAILED GODWIT but is darker brown above; barred greyish rump. Tidal flats. *May be confused with:* BAR-TAILED GODWIT which has upcurved bill.

POSSIBILITIES

BAR-TAILED GODWIT *Limosa lapponica* 42 cm
Large; overall greyish, paler below; **slightly upcurved bill; barred whitish rump and tail.** No white wingbar. Tidal flats, shallow fresh and brackish water. *May be confused with:* BLACK-TAILED GODWIT, but look for slightly upcurved bill, barred tail and lack of wingbar.

COMMON GREENSHANK *Tringa nebularia* 33 cm
Distinctive medium-sized shorebird; greyish upperparts; white forehead and underparts; **long slightly upcurved leaden-grey bill, pale at base.** In flight, **white rump and lower back** are prominent and the **longish grey legs trail behind the tail;** no wingbar; nervously active and wary; ringing alarm call. Tidal flats, margins of lakes and swamps.
May be confused with: MARSH SANDPIPER which has a sharp straight bill. Look for longer, slightly upcurved bill. Records of the rare NORDMANN'S (SPOTTED) GREENSHANK have never been confirmed. Probably misidentified COMMON.

TEREK SANDPIPER *Xenus cinereus* 22 cm
Distinctive small shorebird; greyish above; white below; faintly streaked on breast; dark patch on shoulder; **long slightly upcurved black bill; short orange legs.** In flight, prominent **white trailing edge to wings;** feeds in a **distinctive, crouched, darting manner.** Tidal mudflats and estuaries, rarely freshwater swamps.

SHOREBIRDS WITH DOWNCURVED BILLS
POSSIBILITIES

LITTLE CURLEW *Numenius minutus* 33 cm
Well-streaked **long-legged** shorebird of medium-size; shortish downcurved bill; **face, throat and eyebrow whitish to pale buff; dark rump;** legs light blue-grey. Short grassy areas, margins of drying swamps; dry open grassland, aerodromes and sometimes tidal mudflats.

WHIMBREL *Numenius phaeopus* 41 cm
A large, well-streaked brownish shorebird resembling a small EASTERN CURLEW; **stripe over eye; whitish rump.** Tidal flats, mangroves and beaches.
May be confused with: The larger EASTERN CURLEW, but look for eye stripe and rump colour.

EASTERN CURLEW

Numenius madagascariensis 58 cm

Large, dark, well-streaked brown coastal shorebird;
**buff rump and lower back; very long downcurved
bill four to five times the length of its head;** loudly
vocal in flight. Tidal flats, sandy beaches.
May be confused with: The smaller WHIMBREL, but
look for buff rump and no stripe over eye.

PECTORAL SANDPIPER *Calidris melanotos* 22 cm

Small shorebird similar to SHARP-TAILED
SANDPIPER, but striated breast is **sharply
demarcated from white belly;** bill slightly downcurved; brownish crown. Associates with SHARP-
TAILED SANDPIPER and easily overlooked. Mostly
grassy margins of shallow fresh water, also mudflats.
May be confused with: SHARP-TAILED SANDPIPER,
but look for downcurved bill and sharply demarcated
breast striations.

CURLEW SANDPIPER *Calidris ferruginea* 21 cm

Small, active shorebird; grey-brown above; whitish
below; faintly streaked darker on breast; **broad white
eyebrow; longish, slim, black bill downcurved at
tip;** longish black legs. In flight, shows **white rump**
and white wingbar. Newly-arrived birds (Aug.–Sept.)
have a 'scaly' chestnut pattern to back. Tidal flats and
margins of freshwater swamps. *May be confused with:*
BROAD-BILLED SANDPIPER which has dark centre
line on crown, margined with white. DUNLIN is
difficult to separate but CURLEW SANDPIPER is
more grey-brown, more slender in build with bill more
curved. In flight, all-white rump separates it from both
BROAD-BILLED and DUNLIN, both of which have
white rumps with a dark centre.

DUNLIN *Calidris alpina* 20 cm

Vagrant, very similar to CURLEW SANDPIPER and
difficult to separate. Tidal flats and beaches. *May be
confused with:* CURLEW SANDPIPER, but look for
white rump with dark centre in flight. DUNLIN is
more grey in colour with shorter, straighter bill.

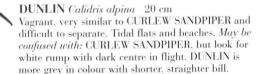

BROAD-BILLED SANDPIPER

Limicola falcinellus 18 cm

Small active shorebird; greyish, often heavily mottled
above; white below; breast streaked darker; dark
shoulder patch; **dark centre line on crown
margined by white stripe; longish black bill,
broad and downcurved near tip.** In flight, shows
white wingbar; dark centre to rump; dark shoulder.
Juvenile: black, buff and white back. Tidal flats.
May be confused with: NONE. Crown stripe and bill
shape set it apart from other shorebirds.

COX'S SANDPIPER 21 cm

Originally thought to be an unknown species, but now known to be a hybrid. Similar to PECTORAL SANDPIPER, but with longer, darker bill; dark legs.

FURTHER POSSIBILITIES

BRISTLE-THIGHED CURLEW *Numenius tahitiensis* 42 cm
Similar to WHIMBREL but darker above, with pale chestnut rump and barred tail. Unconfirmed record Cairns Esplanade.
EURASIAN CURLEW *Numenius arquata* 56 cm
Similar to EASTERN CURLEW but with white rump and lower back. Unconfirmed record Cairns Esplanade.

GULLS

POSSIBILITIES

KELP GULL *Larus dominicanus* 57 cm

Vagrant; large black and white gull; white body; slate-black wings; **all-white tail;** yellow bill with **red spot at tip of lower mandible;** yellowish legs. Juvenile and immature: mottled grey-brown, paler on head and underparts. Coastal shores. *May be confused with:* PACIFIC GULL from southern Australia which is unrecorded from the Wet Tropics. Look for all-white tail. PACIFIC has a narrow black band across the tail, and a much larger yellow bill with both mandibles tipped orange. Juvenile and immature of each species difficult to separate.

SILVER GULL *Larus novaehollandiae* 41 cm

Medium-sized, familiar bird. Adult: immaculate white with silver-grey back and wings, **red legs, bill and eye-ring.** Juvenile and immature: no eye-ring; black bill and legs, later dull yellowish-brown before turning red. Coastal shores, offshore islands, sometimes larger lakes and seaside suburbs.

LAUGHING GULL *Larus atricilla* 40 cm

Vagrant; medium-sized gull; **rather long, heavy bill and flat forehead; conspicuous, broken, white eye-ring; black wing tips.** In non-breeding plumage: white and grey; white head, underparts, rump and tail and trailing edge of wing; dusky-grey mottling on sides and back of head; grey bill tinged red; blackish legs. In breeding plumage: black head; red bill and legs. Juvenile and immature: similar to non-breeding adult, but with heavier mottling on head; black band in tail; breast and sides of body washed grey. Coastal shores. *May be confused with:* Mostly FRANKLIN'S GULL, but look for sloping forehead, all-black wing tips and heavy bill. Juvenile and immature have less distinct dusky-grey about sides of head, nape and crown than FRANKLIN'S.

FRANKLIN'S GULL *Larus pipixcan* 35 cm
Vagrant; similar to LAUGHING GULL in all
plumages, but has **rounded forehead, black wing
tips edged white and smaller bill.** Juvenile and
immature: resemble non-breeding adult.
May be confused with: LAUGHING GULL. Juvenile
and immature FRANKLIN'S have more dusky-grey on
sides of head, nape and crown than LAUGHING.
Perhaps also BLACK-HEADED and SABINE'S
GULLS.

FURTHER POSSIBILITIES

BLACK-TAILED (Japanese) GULL *Larus crassirostris* 47 cm
Large gull, slightly larger than SILVER GULL, white with
dark grey back and wings, **broad black band near tip of
tail, pale yellow bill with red tip followed by black line.**
Eastern Asia, migrating south, recorded Darwin NT, and
Melbourne Vic. Unrecorded in the Wet Tropics.

BLACK-HEADED GULL *Larus ridibundus* 40 cm Resembles
FRANKLIN'S GULL in all plumages, but **hood is smaller**
extending from nape to throat. In winter plumage: dusky-grey
spot **only behind eye** and **two dusky bands over crown;**
pale red bill and legs. Ranges through Europe and Asia,
wintering southward. Recorded Broome WA, but unrecorded in
the Wet Tropics.

SABINE'S GULL *Larus sabini* 34 cm Small white gull similar
to FRANKLIN'S GULL in all plumages. Breeding plumage:
black bill tipped bright yellow; black legs; red eye-ring;
distinctive wing pattern with black wedge in forewing and white
triangle in rear of wing. In non-breeding plumage: **black bill
tipped dull yellow.** Breeding within the Arctic Circle,
wintering to South America. Recorded Darwin NT, Wollongong
NSW and Port McDonnell SA. Unrecorded in the Wet Tropics.

TERNS

Terns are not difficult to distinguish from other birds but some
species can be difficult to separate individually. Most have
breeding and non-breeding plumages which, together with juvenile
and immature plumages, can cause considerable confusion.

POSSIBILITIES

GULL-BILLED TERN *Sterna nilotica* 39 cm
Medium-sized; pale tern; grey back, wings and tail;
white underparts; black bill. In breeding plumage: **neat
black cap, the edge of which follows the curve of
head and does not dip below eye.** Non-breeding
plumage: **white head; blackish smudge through and
behind eye.** Immature: similar to non-breeding adult,
but mottled above. At rest, wings extend beyond short
tail. In flight, looks almost pure white with dark-tipped
broad wings; short white forked tail. Tidal flats,
freshwater swamps. *May be confused with:* COMMON
TERN, but look for line of black cap in breeding
plumage, and smudge about eye and absence of black
bar on shoulders in non-breeding plumage.

CASPIAN TERN *Sterna caspia* 56 cm
The largest tern; pale-grey above; white below; short
tail. In breeding plumage: **massive red bill; black
cap.** In non-breeding plumage: cap streaked black
and white. Immature: similar to non-breeding birds,
but with black-tipped, orange-red bill. In flight, shows
long, slender, blackish-tipped wings; slightly forked
tail. Coastal and inland swamps, estuaries. Sometimes
beaches and tidal mudflats.

LESSER CRESTED TERN
Sterna bengalensis 39 cm
Similar to CRESTED TERN, but smaller and paler.
Distinguished by **orange bill** at all stages. Islands and
cays of Great Barrier Reef, ocean beaches. *May be
confused with:* CRESTED TERN which has yellow bill.

CRESTED TERN *Sterna bergii* 47 cm
Large marine tern; grey wings, back and tail; white
underparts; **yellow bill.** In breeding plumage: **black
crown with shaggy black crest on nape.** In non-
breeding plumage: whitish forehead; top of crown
mottled blackish; **no crest.** Juvenile: blackish sides of
head, face and crown; yellowish-grey bill. Bays, tidal
rivers, inlets, sandy beaches and offshore islands.
May be confused with: The smaller LESSER
CRESTED TERN which has orange bill.

ROSEATE TERN *Sterna dougallii* 37 cm
Medium-sized oceanic tern; grey above; white below;
**white tail streamers extend well beyond wings at
rest.** In breeding plumage: long black cap reaches **black
scarlet-based bill; very pale pink-tinged
underparts;** red legs. In non-breeding plumage: white
forehead; black hind crown; black bill; dull shoulder
bar; orange-brown legs and feet; often retains **rosy tinge
on breast.** Immature: similar to non-breeding; black in
front of eye; freckled dark brown and white forehead.
Offshore waters, coral reefs, sand cays and islands of
Great Barrier Reef. *May be confused with:* In breeding
plumage: NONE. In non-breeding plumage: mostly
COMMON TERN which is usually more coastal. Look
for longer tail streamers, less white on forehead, duller
shoulder bar and possible faint rose tinge on breast.

BLACK-NAPED TERN *Sterna sumatrana* 31 cm
Medium-sized, elegant, **mostly white; black nape
extending in a wide line to just in front of eye;**
black legs; deeply forked tail. Juvenile: feathers on
back mottled grey and brown; streaked grey back of
head merging into black nape. Mostly offshore waters,
about islands and cays of Great Barrier Reef,
sometimes reaching the mainland. *May be confused
with:* Adult: NONE. Juvenile: perhaps non-breeding
LITTLE TERN, but larger with mottled back. Usually
with adults.

COMMON TERN *Sterna hirundo*   35 cm

Summer visitor, but some birds remain throughout the year; medium-sized; grey upperparts; white underparts; black crown; **white forehead; black bar on shoulder;** grey rump; black bill and feet; moderately forked tail. **At rest, wings extend beyond tail.** Coastal tidal flats, estuaries and ocean beaches. *May be confused with:* GULL-BILLED and non-breeding ROSEATE TERNS. Look for line of black cap on white forehead and black shoulder bar to separate from GULL-BILLED; less white forehead, dark shoulder bar, shorter tail streamers and plain white breast to separate from ROSEATE.

LITTLE TERN *Sterna albifrons*   22 cm

Summer visitor; small, pale grey and white tern. In breeding plumage: black crown and nape; white forehead; black line from eye to bill; **yellow bill tipped black; yellow legs.** In non-breeding plumage: white forehead and nape; black crown mottled white; **darkish bar on shoulder;** black bill sometimes yellow at base; black legs and feet. Juvenile: similar to non-breeding adult, but upperparts mottled grey and buff. Coastal waters, bays, inlets, ocean beaches and coral reefs. *May be confused with:* Distinct from all terns except FAIRY TERN which occurs accidentally in Wet Tropics. Look for colour of bill and feet and shoulder bar.

FAIRY TERN *Sterna nereis*   23 cm

Accidental; small tern similar to LITTLE TERN, but with **paler back and upper wings.** Note different profile with bulkier body; larger head; thicker and shorter legs. In breeding plumage: **bill and legs richer orange-yellow; bill without black tip.** In non-breeding plumage: orange-brown bill, dark at tip and base; **no shoulder bar;** white on forehead more extensive. *May be confused with:* LITTLE TERN, but look for colour of bill and feet together with absence of shoulder bar.

BRIDLED TERN   *Sterna anaethetus*   39 cm

Resembles a small SOOTY TERN, but with **grey-brown upperparts** and white forehead **extending beyond eye as an eyebrow.** Juvenile: upperparts have pale edges to feathers; paler underparts; crown streaked white. Oceanic, breeding on offshore islands, rarely to mainland shores. *May be confused with:* SOOTY TERN, but look for eyebrow and grey-brown upperparts.

SOOTY TERN *Sterna fuscata*   44 cm

Large tern; **black above; white below; white forehead does not extend beyond eye;** black bill, legs and feet. Juvenile: distinctive **sooty-grey;** white scallops on back and wings. Oceanic, coming to coral cays to breed. *May be confused with:* The smaller BRIDLED TERN, but look for black upperparts; white forehead extending only to eye. Juvenile: NONE.

WHISKERED TERN *Chlidonias hybridus* 26 cm
Graceful, medium-sized grey tern with slightly forked
tail. In breeding plumage: **dark grey belly; black cap
ends abruptly at eye level;** white cheeks; **red bill
and legs.** In non-breeding plumage: grey above; white
below; faint shoulder bar; blackish bill; cap varies from
full to reduced to the nape, with streaked crown.
Juvenile: black bill; white forehead; black nape and
crown; brown-barred back. Mostly freshwater swamps,
sometimes over nearby grassland. *May be confused
with:* In breeding plumage: NONE. In non-breeding
plumage: the smaller WHITE-WINGED BLACK TERN
(in non-breeding plumage) with which it associates, but
look for black through eye, extending in a curved line
to nape, mainly white ear-coverts, white forehead and
crown with black streaking on rear of crown.

WHITE-WINGED BLACK TERN
Chlidonias leucopterus 23 cm
Summer visitor; medium-sized tern; grey wings; white
head and underparts; **white rump;** variable edge to
blackish band from eye to rear of crown: **round,
blackish patch on ear-coverts.** Juvenile: similar, but
with dark brownish-grey shoulders. Some birds may
attain breeding plumage about March, before departure:
distinctive black head and body; white wings. Mostly
coastal lakes and swamps, both fresh and brackish. *May
be confused with:* The larger WHISKERED TERN in
non-breeding plumage, but look for round, blackish
patch on ear-coverts; brownish shoulder bar and white
rump. WHITE-WINGED BLACK has a more fluttering
flight than the WHISKERED.

COMMON NODDY *Anous stolidus* 39 cm
Medium-sized; dark brown; greyish crown; white forehead;
**greyish underwing; upperwings have two-toned effect;
long wedge tail with shallow central notch.** Nests on
the ground. Oceanic, islands and cays of Great Barrier
Reef. The common noddy in the Wet Tropics. *May be
confused with:* BLACK NODDY. Difficult to separate.
BLACK has blackish body, darker underwing; shorter,
slimmer tail with wider fork, more slender bill.

BLACK NODDY *Anous minutus* 36 cm
Rare; similar to COMMON NODDY but with darker
body; dark underwing; **slim, short, 'notched' tail.
Lacks two-toned effect in upperwings.** Nests in
trees. Oceanic, islands and cays of Great Barrier Reef.
May be confused with: COMMON NODDY.

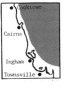

WHITE TERN *Gygis alba* 31 cm
Accidental. Usually a victim of cyclones. Small, **pure-
white** tern with **large dark eye, bill and feet.**
Unmistakable. Distributed through subtropical and
tropical oceans. Breeds on Lord Howe and Norfolk
islands off the central eastern Australian coast.

FURTHER POSSIBILITIES
TROPICBIRDS resemble TERNS when tail streamers missing.
ORIENTAL and AUSTRALIAN PRATINCOLES (birds of open
plains and farmland) have a tern-like flight.

POSSIBILITIES

NANKEEN NIGHT HERON
Nycticorax caledonicus 60 cm
Large **cinnamon wading bird with black cap;** yellow
legs; black bill; two white plumes from back of head.
Juvenile: **heavily-striated brownish; greenish legs;**
paler underparts well-striated. Rests by day in thick
foliage. Freshwater swamps, lakes and creeks. *May be
confused with:* Adult: NONE. Juvenile: STRIATED
HERON, but look for well-striated head and body and
greenish legs. Juvenile often misidentified as a bittern.

BUSH STONE-CURLEW *Burhinus grallarius* 55 cm
Large ground bird with streaked-greyish plumage;
streaked buffy underparts; **whitish forehead and
eyebrow; large yellow eyes;** long legs; moves slowly
and deliberately when disturbed by day. Open forest,
open lightly timbered areas, often in urban localities.

RUFOUS OWL *Ninox rufa* 51 cm
Large **rufous-brown owl** with large yellow eyes
focused forward; **narrow dense barring on
underparts; darker barring on upperparts;** tail
barred below; perches by day in dense foliage, e.g.
rainforest, gallery forest; hunting out over woodland by
night.

BARKING OWL *Ninox connivens* 40 cm
Large greyish-brown bird; **streaked grey underparts;
large staring yellow eyes** focused forward. Open
forest with some dense cover, rainforest margins,
paperbark swamps and woodland. *May be confused
with:* Perhaps the smaller, browner SOUTHERN
BOOBOOK which has distinct 'goggles' about eyes.

SOUTHERN BOOBOOK
Ninox novaeseelandiae 32 cm
Small brown owl; **dark 'goggles' around yellow eyes,**
focused forward; white spots on wings; whitish
underparts with thick blotchy brown streaks. All
wooded habitats. *May be confused with:* Perhaps the
larger BARKING OWL which is more greyish and
lacks the dark 'goggles' around eyes.
NOTE: A small dark distinct race *lurida* inhabits
rainforest, mostly at higher altitudes. 'Goggles' are
indistinct and underparts spotted white rather than
streaked.

LESSER SOOTY OWL
Tyto multipunctata Male 33 cm Female 37 cm
Elusive, medium-sized, short-tailed bird or small owl;
dark grey spotted upperparts; paler below; some fine
barring across breast; large prominent **pale grey facial
disc edged with black; very large black eyes** focused
forward. Rainforest at all altitudes, sometimes to edges
of mangroves. Often into adjacent open forest.

MASKED OWL
Tyto novaehollandiae   Male 37 cm Female 47 cm
Similar to BARN OWL but larger. Eucalypt forest,
farmland and about sugar-cane fields. *May be
confused with:* BARN and GRASS OWLS. See p. 199.

BARN OWL *Tyto alba*   34 cm
Medium-sized short-tailed bird; chestnut-grey
upperparts; white underparts lightly spotted on breast;
white heart-shaped facial disc with dark edging;
black eyes focused forward; sparsely-feathered legs.
Scattered eucalypt forest, open grassy areas and
farmland. *May be confused with:* MASKED and
GRASS OWLS. See p. 199.

GRASS OWL
Tyto capensis   Male 34 cm Female 37 cm
Similar to BARN OWL. Rests by day in dense grass,
sometimes harvested sugar-cane fields and young pine
plantations. *May be confused with:* MASKED and
BARN OWLS. See p. 199.

TAWNY FROGMOUTH *Podargus strigoides* 39 cm
Large grey or brownish bird; **short broad heavy bill;
tuft of plumes over bill;** black streaking on
underparts; long tail; **yellow eyes;** adopts stick-like
attitude by day. Eucalypt forest and woodland.
May be confused with: The larger PAPUAN
FROGMOUTH, but look for yellow eyes.

PAPUAN FROGMOUTH *Podargus papuensis* 49 cm
Large greyish bird; female more reddish; similar to
TAWNY FROGMOUTH, but underparts more speckled
or mottled with some streaking; **red eyes.** Gallery
forest and similar dense vegetation, paperbark
swamps, mangroves and sometimes upland rainforest.
May be confused with: The smaller TAWNY
FROGMOUTH, but look for red eyes.

WHITE-THROATED NIGHTJAR
Eurostopodus mystacalis   34 cm
A large, dark, intricately-patterned bird; white crescent
on each side of throat. At rest, upper surface of wings
and back **appear greyish.** In flight, shows **plain
underwing and tail.** Rests on ground by day in drier
tropical woodland. *May be confused with:* SPOTTED
and LARGE-TAILED NIGHTJARS, but look for
greyish upperparts and lack of white bristles about bill
when at rest and plain underwing and tail in flight.

SPOTTED NIGHTJAR *Eurostopodus argus* 30 cm
Similar to WHITE-THROATED NIGHTJAR, but smaller;
reddish-brown upperparts; white crescent on throat. In
flight, shows **large white patch in underwing and
plain tail.** Dry woodland in western areas of the Wet
Tropics. *May be confused with:* WHITE-THROATED and
LARGE-TAILED NIGHTJARS, but look for reddish-
brown upperparts and lack of white bristles about bill
when at rest. In flight, white in wings only.

LARGE-TAILED NIGHTJAR
Caprimulgus macrurus 26 cm
A medium-sized bird similar to WHITE-THROATED
NIGHTJAR; thin white crescent on each side of throat;
**white bristles about bill. In flight, shows small
white patch in underwing and white corners to
tail.** Rainforest edges, adjacent woodland and
mangroves, mostly in lowland areas. *May be confused
with:* WHITE-THROATED and SPOTTED
NIGHTJARS, but look for white bristles when at rest,
and white in wings and tail corners in flight.

AUSTRALIAN OWLET-NIGHTJAR
Aegotheles cristatus 22 cm
Small, moth-like greyish bird; **double collar on hind
neck;** large black eyes; bristles about bill; sometimes
flushed from hollows by day. Open forest and
woodland, occasionally rainforest.

DIFFICULT GROUPS OF BIRDS

EGRETS

Noting bill colour, in conjunction with some other features, is the easiest method of
distinguishing each species of egret. Bill colour changes in three species at the approach of the
breeding season, usually through spring. The two most difficult species to separate are the
GREAT and INTERMEDIATE EGRETS in non-breeding plumage. The REEF EGRET has a
different silhouette and manner of feeding.

YELLOW BILL
EASTERN REEF EGRET (White phase)
Sometimes has upper mandible slate-grey; olive-grey or yellow-green
legs; appears **shorter-legged and longer-billed than other egrets;**
adopts a more **crouched stance** when foraging. Marine habitat.

GREAT EGRET (In non-breeding plumage)
Bill tipped black; **gape colour extends past eye;** long kinked neck; no
plumes on back; blackish legs. The largest egret.

INTERMEDIATE EGRET (In non-breeding plumage)
Gape colour does not extend past eye; dark brown legs; plumes on
back and breast absent; shorter, less kinked neck than GREAT EGRET;
smaller.

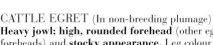

CATTLE EGRET (In non-breeding plumage)
Heavy jowl; high, rounded forehead (other egrets have flat
foreheads) and **stocky appearance.** Leg colour can be black or yellow.
Often **with cattle** in grassy paddocks.

ORANGE/RED BILL

INTERMEDIATE EGRET (In breeding plumage)
Plumes on back and breast; reddish legs down to knees, then black; green face.

CATTLE EGRET (In breeding plumage)
Develops distinctive **orange-buff head, breast and lower back; reddish legs.**

BLACK BILL

LITTLE EGRET (In all plumages)
Black bill and legs throughout the year. Two long plumes from back of head when breeding. The smallest egret.

GREAT EGRET (In breeding plumage)
Blackish legs; green facial skin; **gape colour extends past eye;** long kinked neck.

CATTLE EGRET (Juvenile)
Present for a few months in summer and autumn until acquiring yellow bill; dark legs; **heavy jowl; high rounded forehead** (other egrets have flat foreheads); **stocky appearance;** often about cattle.

CUCKOOS WITH PLAIN UNDERPARTS
EXCLUDING JUVENILE BRONZE-CUCKOOS

PALLID CUCKOO (Adult)
Overall greyish; medium-sized bird; tail longish and rounded, well-notched white on sides; yellow eye-ring; grey feet. Look for **faint darker curved line through eye and down shoulder, and small white spot on nape.**

BRUSH CUCKOO (Adult)
Appears overall greyish-brown; **paler buff-grey breast and belly;** tail plain above, rather square, tipped white; lacks yellow eye-ring of other cuckoos (grey and not obvious); grey feet.

CHESTNUT-BREASTED CUCKOO (Adult)
Very similar to FAN-TAILED CUCKOO, but with rich chestnut breast. Look for **smaller size; richer colour and less etching on tail.** Note restricted range which is also inhabited by the FAN-TAILED. Juvenile CHESTNUT-BREASTED is distinctive, plain, reddish-brown above; paler below.

FAN-TAILED CUCKOO (Adult)
Medium-sized bird; slate-grey above; **pale rufous underparts; yellow eye-ring; fairly long tail markedly 'notched' white down each side;** yellowish feet.

BLACK-EARED CUCKOO (Adult and juvenile)
Overall brownish-grey; paler below; thick white eyebrow, white tail tip. **Curved black mark through eye and down neck diagnostic.** Juvenile HORSFIELD'S BRONZE-CUCKOO is similar and sometimes misidentified as BLACK-EARED. HORSFIELD'S has faint barring on sides of breast and shows some rufous in tail.

CUCKOOS WITH BARRED UNDERPARTS

These comprise mostly juveniles and immatures of medium-sized cuckoos. Plumage can be variable as they change from juvenile through immature to adult, compounding identification difficulties.

ORIENTAL CUCKOO (Adult)
Medium-sized; grey above; grey head, throat and breast; **boldly barred lower breast and belly;** dark tail lightly spotted white on upper surface; yellow eye-ring; **yellow feet;** appears hawk-like in flight. Distinctive and unlikely to be mistaken for another cuckoo.

ORIENTAL CUCKOO (Juvenile)
Chestnut-brown above. **Heavy barring from throat to under tail,** white-tipped tail with **upper surface well-barred rufous** and hawk-like flight separate it from other cuckoos. Note that a rare reddish form is similarly marked, but with well-barred back and head.

PALLID CUCKOO (Immature)
Medium-sized. A combination of **heavily mottled-brown back and wings,** well-striated crown, **barred underparts most prominent on breast** and almost absent on belly, **yellow eye-ring** and grey feet distinguish it from other cuckoos. Often mistaken for ORIENTAL, but note colour of feet.

BRUSH CUCKOO (Juvenile)
Small to medium-sized cuckoo; overall brownish; **heavily mottled or barred brown and buff on upperparts; underparts barred from throat to tail;** squarish tail well-notched buff; grey feet and eye-ring. Mostly confused with juvenile FAN-TAILED CUCKOO which has less conspicuous barring on underparts and plainer upperparts. Feet are pinkish to yellow and eye-ring yellowish in FAN-TAILED.

FAN-TAILED CUCKOO (Juvenile)
A medium-sized cuckoo similar to the juvenile BRUSH CUCKOO. See above. Look for longer, more rounded tail; more obscure barring on underparts; plainer upperparts; **yellowish eye-ring; pinkish to yellow feet** in FAN-TAILED.

BRONZE-CUCKOOS
SMALL CUCKOOS WITH BARRED UNDERPARTS

These birds are initially difficult to separate, but habitat preference is important.

HORSFIELD'S BRONZE-CUCKOO
Prefers drier open forest, woodland and lightly timbered areas. Look for **broken** bars across underparts, **white eyebrow, dark line from eye to ear** and rufous edges of upper sides of tail.

SHINING BRONZE-CUCKOO
Inhabits upland rainforest. Look for **complete** copper-bronze bars across underparts and **iridescent golden-green upperparts.** Lacks colour or prominent markings about eyes or face; no rufous in tail.

LITTLE BRONZE-CUCKOO
Inhabits open, paperbark and gallery forests and tropical woodland, moreso in the west of the region. Look for **complete** greenish or bronze bars across **white** underparts; bronze-green upperparts; **prominent red eye-ring in male; tan in female.**

GOULD'S BRONZE-CUCKOO

Inhabits coastal rainforest, nearby open forest and gallery forest as well as mangroves. Almost identical to LITTLE. Look for **complete** greenish or bronze bars across **off-white underparts; variable rufous tinge on breast;** bronze-green upperparts; **prominent red eye-ring in male; tan in female.**

In the Wet Tropics, hybridisation between LITTLE and GOULD'S has been suggested, but this may be doubtful. See p. 242. The juvenile HORSFIELD'S, sometimes mistaken for the larger BLACK-EARED CUCKOO, has a distinctive dark mark through the eye to the ear and a rufous base to the tail feathers. Juveniles of SHINING, LITTLE and GOULD'S are almost impossible to separate. All four species have plain bodies with faint barring on sides of breast.

NOTE: In some field guides, undertail patterns of LITTLE and GOULD'S are illustrated quite differently from each other. However, both have white outer tail feathers with large black spots, GOULD'S often with a little rufous. Rufous on inner tail feathers of GOULD'S varies.

MASKED OWL, BARN OWL, GRASS OWL

Though initially difficult to distinguish, these three species can be separated with reasonable ease. The best feature is the **colour of the edging of the facial mask,** which can usually be ascertained from a reasonable distance. In the MASKED the edging is **heavy and black,** though in pale-coloured birds it is thinner, but black. That of the BARN is **thin and appears brownish,** being a mixture of fawn and black. The GRASS has **pale fawn to white edging.**

MASKED OWL   Appears as a thickset owl (female larger) with a **round face.** Plumage varies, some birds are pale but upperparts always appear **dark greyish** with distinctive **barring across the wings.** Some pale MASKED can resemble BARN but look for round facial mask **edged black** and barred pattern on wing. Degree of spotting on underparts, buff wash on breast and dark colour about eyes, as mentioned in some field guides, are not entirely reliable features on which to base identification though females are often heavily spotted. The feathering on the legs (to the feet) can only be discerned at close range. Usually seen on posts, in trees, and sometimes on the ground.

BARN OWL   Appears small and white with a rather **longish face,** looking almost like that of a monkey from a distance. Facing an observer, it stands 'knock-kneed'. **Upperparts have a chestnut appearance** being usually a mottled mixture of grey, fawn, buff and yellow-buff. **Legs are fairly bare,** appearing hairy rather than feathered. The most common *Tyto* owl, usually seen on fence posts or in trees and sometimes on the ground.

GRASS OWL   Appears **more upright** than other *Tyto* owls. Facial disc is **triangular, longish** and varies from **chestnut** to white with small eyes. Upperparts appear chestnut (actually a mixture of dark grey and orange) with **wings broadly barred chestnut.** Noticeably long legs which **project beyond tail or dangle in flight.** In birds with white faces which can be mistaken for BARN and MASKED, look for pale edging to mask. Terrestrial; almost invariably seen either on the ground, or in flight. Probably never perches on posts or in trees though recorded perching on tops of young introduced pine trees *Pinus* sp. (J. Young pers. comm.).

Masked   *Barn*   *Grass (white)*   *Grass (chestnut)*

ATHERTON SCRUBWREN, LARGE-BILLED SCRUBWREN, TROPICAL SCRUBWREN

With a little practice it is relatively easy to separate ATHERTON and LARGE-BILLED SCRUBWRENS. Habits, as well as rainforest strata are initially important in separating them. They do not appear to coexist to any great extent.
TROPICAL reaches the Wet Tropics only about Cooktown and Helenvale.

ATHERTON SCRUBWREN
Tends to be **solitary,** though sometimes in pairs **feeding quietly on or close to the rainforest floor. Slight yellowish tinge from throat to belly.** Faint shoulder markings. Appears slightly darker than LARGE-BILLED about the head and upperparts; obscure eyebrow. Eye colour at close range appears reddish-brown. Song closely resembles that of the WHITE-BROWED. Usually ignores a squeaking sound.

LARGE-BILLED SCRUBWREN
Usually found in **small parties,** sometimes pairs. **foraging on tree-trunks and in mid stratum foliage;** occasionally close to the rainforest floor. Flocks usually fairly vocal. **More fawnish underparts** than ATHERTON'S. No shoulder markings. Eye colour at close range appears near-black. Usually responds readily to a squeaking sound. Shares habitat with the TROPICAL in the north of the region. *There is no truth in the belief that a lemon-bellied form of the LARGE-BILLED inhabits high altitude rainforest.*

TROPICAL SCRUBWREN
Fairly easily identified by **red eye and two small white marks on shoulder.** Shares habitat with the LARGE-BILLED.

BROWN GERYGONE, MANGROVE GERYGONE, WESTERN GERYGONE, LARGE-BILLED GERYGONE

Differences between the four grey gerygones are slight. Each can be identified by song, eyebrow and tail tip differences, though the latter can be difficult to discern in these very active birds. Each generally occurs in a different habitat, though where the MANGROVE and LARGE-BILLED coexist in mangroves in southern parts of the Wet Tropics, the juvenile MANGROVE can be confusing. Face, sides of neck, throat and breast are washed lemon-yellow in juvenile MANGROVE which has no eyebrow, but a similar lemon eye-ring to that of the LARGE-BILLED.

BROWN GERYGONE
Widespread; inhabits mostly upland rainforest above 250 m. White eyebrow; white tail tip; repeated twittering.

MANGROVE GERYGONE
Mangroves and adjacent forest north to about Cardwell. White eyebrow; white tail tip; sweet rising and falling song resembles that of WHITE-THROATED.

WESTERN GERYGONE
Dry woodland; just reaches the south-western part of the region. Thin white eyebrow; much white on tip and base of tail; beautiful song which ends abruptly.

LARGE-BILLED GERYGONE
Several denser habitats, mostly lowlands. No eyebrow, but faint white divided eye-ring; no white tail tip; short, simple series of rising and falling notes uttered in succession. Where LARGE-BILLED and MANGROVE coexist, the LARGE-BILLED tends to inhabit the taller mangroves.

HELMETED FRIARBIRD, SILVER-CROWNED FRIARBIRD, NOISY FRIARBIRD

Only the HELMETED and NOISY are common throughout the Wet Tropics, the HELMETED being the common species of coastal areas, while the NOISY is generally common and widespread in drier forests to the west, but sometimes reaching the coast. The SILVER-CROWNED extends southward only to the vicinity of Cooktown and Shiptons Flat where it is moderately common, inhabiting similar drier open forest to that preferred by the NOISY. Distinguishing HELMETED and SILVER-CROWNED where both are present can be frustrating. The crown colour of the HELMETED varies from silver-grey to brown, sometimes appearing similar to that of the SILVER-CROWNED. The HELMETED has an overall grotesque appearance.

HELMETED FRIARBIRD
Appears darker brownish, larger and more grotesque than other friarbirds. Frill on throat and breast not prominent. Combination of **greyish-brown to silvery-grey crown, small blackish patch below ear**; rather scruffy-looking head and **no white tail tip** distinguishes it from the SILVER-CROWNED.

SILVER-CROWNED FRIARBIRD
Has a neater appearance than the HELMETED, especially about the head. Darker back and **narrow white tail tip.** Silvery feathers on crown obvious. Appears slightly smaller and slimmer. Look for **narrow silvery crown,** well-frilled silvery-white throat and breast, and tail tip.

NOISY FRIARBIRD
Distinct with all-black, wholly bare head and **white tail tip.** Frill on throat and breast is quite noticeable. Knob on bill is upright rather than sloped backward.

'YELLOW-SPOTTED' HONEYEATERS — LEWIN'S HONEYEATER, YELLOW-SPOTTED HONEYEATER, GRACEFUL HONEYEATER

Much has been written about separating these three honeyeaters, emphasis being placed on features such as bill shape, eye colour, facial pattern and gape stripe. Most attention has been given to shape of ear patch, but even this is not a reliable field mark. **All** of these differences are subtle and invariably difficult to assess.

The major problem is that some field guides depict the *southern* populations of LEWIN'S which have a large, nicely 'moon-shaped' ear patch quite distinct from that of the YELLOW-SPOTTED'S and GRACEFUL'S. However, the ear patch in *northern* populations of LEWIN'S is smaller and often variable, especially in the northern parts of the Wet Tropics where the ear patch can vary from 'moon-shaped' to roughly rounded. Frequently one can be observing a honeyeater with a rather rounded ear patch thinking it to be a YELLOW-SPOTTED, only to hear the bird utter the call of a LEWIN'S! The YELLOW-SPOTTED'S ear patch is frequently described as 'diamond-shaped' when roughly rounded is more accurate.

Altitude too is an unreliable guide as LEWIN'S sometimes wanders to coastal areas, while YELLOW-SPOTTED and GRACEFUL are occasionally found at higher altitudes. **Call is the most reliable characteristic to identify each species.** All three calls are faithfully reproduced on David Stewart's tapes, see p. 316.

LEWIN'S HONEYEATER
Upland rainforest, usually above 450 m, but sometimes in the lowlands; **loud staccato rattling call.** Adult: bluish eyes and grey face. Juvenile: brown eye.

YELLOW-SPOTTED HONEYEATER
Usually below 600 m, sometimes higher. Most common call is a series of **loud, slow notes descending in pitch.**

GRACEFUL HONEYEATER

The easiest of the three to identify; small honeyeater with slender bill and **quick movements** similar to those of other small honeyeaters; ear patch consistently small and rounded. Usually below 400 m, occasionally to 500 m. Most common call is a single 'tick' resembling a hiccup. The softest call of the three.

GOLDEN WHISTLER, MANGROVE GOLDEN WHISTLER

These yellow-breasted whistlers occupy different habitats. In the Wet Tropics, the MANGROVE GOLDEN WHISTLER appears to be restricted to an area about Hinchinbrook Channel. There is only a remote possibility that the two may occur together, and then only in winter.

GOLDEN WHISTLER

Rainforest at higher altitudes, sometimes to coastal regions in winter. Male: **clear yellow underparts; narrow yellow collar; olive edges to wing feathers.** Female: **all-grey with yellow under tail-coverts.** Juvenile: resembles female, but with **rufous edging to wings.**

MANGROVE GOLDEN WHISTLER

Mangroves and sometimes adjacent forest. Male: **rich mid-yellow underparts, broad rich mid-yellow collar; greyish-green edges** to wing feathers; more richly coloured than GOLDEN. Female: **yellow from breast to under tail.** Juvenile: resembles female, but with **rufous tinge to upperparts; whitish throat; buff underparts; bright yellow under tail-coverts.**

BROAD-BILLED FLYCATCHER, LEADEN FLYCATCHER, SATIN FLYCATCHER

The BROAD-BILLED is generally restricted to mangrove habitat in which the LEADEN, the most common flycatcher in the Wet Tropics is also found, and possibly the SATIN on occasions. The SATIN is a rare passage migrant. All quiver their tails.

THE 'BLUE-BLACK' MALES: LEADEN and SATIN

If one knows the LEADEN well, the SATIN appears more glossy, darker and slightly larger. Most birds seen will be LEADEN which has **glossy leaden head; rather dull leaden** back, wings and breast. The SATIN has **glossy blue-black** upperparts and breast.

'FEMALE-PLUMAGED' BIRDS: MALE and FEMALE BROAD-BILLED, FEMALE LEADEN, FEMALE SATIN

BROAD-BILLED FLYCATCHER

Even in the hand, this slightly more intensely coloured flycatcher is difficult to separate, especially from the female LEADEN. BROAD-BILLED has a more 'flattened' forehead and pale lores. The broader bill is not a reliable characteristic in the field, neither is white in the tail as stated in some publications. Juveniles have white in the tail — later lost with age. Where two 'female-plumaged' birds are seen together in mangroves, or close by, with one slightly brighter than the other, one should suspect BROAD-BILLED.

LEADEN FLYCATCHER

Look for dull leaden-grey upperparts; rusty-buff throat and upper breast.

SATIN FLYCATCHER

Look for slightly glossy blue-grey upperparts and rufous-buff throat and upper breast. Again, if one knows the LEADEN well, the female SATIN appears slightly larger and brighter.

AUSTRALIAN RAVEN, TORRESIAN CROW

With some close observation, both species can be separated fairly easily. Each has a distinctive call and distinct profile. Eyes are white in adults of both species.

AUSTRALIAN RAVEN
Long throat hackles, very obvious when bird is calling. Call, often given, is a **long drawn-out wailing. Grey** base to body feathers. Uncommon, reaching north to the Ingham and Mt Garnet areas.

TORRESIAN CROW
The more common and widespread of the two. **Short throat hackles.** Call, often given, is a series of **short, sharp 'arks'.** Also gives a drawn-out 'bleating', sometimes mistaken for the wailing call of the RAVEN. Base of body feathers **white.**

WELCOME SWALLOW, PACIFIC SWALLOW

The PACIFIC is not easy to separate from the WELCOME, though any short-tailed adult swallow should be suspected as a PACIFIC. However, the WELCOME has a short tail during moult. One of the best methods is to watch a bird in flight. When it turns and spreads its tail, one can briefly see the **row of spots** in the PACIFIC'S tail as distinct from the **broader white which forms a bar** across the WELCOME'S.
Under tail-covert pattern is a fairly reliable guide in adults. Juveniles lack this pattern. The PACIFIC has **a wide solid black subterminal bar with smaller bars above.** In the WELCOME, the markings are much less pronounced, being smaller and more dusky.

WELCOME SWALLOW
Tail slightly splayed with long outer tail feathers reaching well beyond wings when sitting. When outer tail feathers moulted, tail is same length as folded wings. Grey underdown in hand.

Welcome

PACIFIC SWALLOW
Tail more slender than WELCOME'S; roughly same length as folded wings. Juvenile often shows paler edging to inner web of tail fork. Throat usually paler than juvenile WELCOME'S. PACIFIC tends to flock together though will associate with WELCOME. White underdown in hand.

Pacific

CLAMOROUS REED-WARBLER, ORIENTAL REED-WARBLER

These two reed-warblers are almost impossible to separate in the field by plumage differences alone. Field characteristics such as rufous on the flanks and obscure greyish streaks on the upper breast in the ORIENTAL are variable and unreliable. Wing length differences are also impossible to discern in the field. The deeper and shorter bill of the ORIENTAL is reputed to be the most reliable characteristic to separate these birds in the field. Not only is this difficult to detect, but much experience with the CLAMOROUS is an essential prerequisite. Colour of the inside of the mouth has been given as a reliable characteristic when one has birds in the hand, but this is incorrect.

Song is the best aid to identification. Their songs differ slightly, but if one knows the call of the CLAMOROUS well, the ORIENTAL'S sounds lower in pitch and of a harsher quality.
The ORIENTAL breeds in Asia and migrates southward, reaching northern Australia during the southern summer months. During this period, CLAMOROUS numbers in the Wet Tropics are very low, with only a small breeding population, mostly in the southern parts. Any reed-warbler at this time is worth investigating.
See McKEAN, J.L. 1983, 'Some notes on the occurrence of the Great Reed Warbler *Acrocephalus arundinaceus* in the Northern Territory', *Northern Territory Naturalist* **6**, 3.

ZITTING CISTICOLA, GOLDEN-HEADED CISTICOLA

To separate the ZITTING from the non-breeding male and female GOLDEN-HEADED in the field is almost impossible unless calls are heard. Both have similar streaked crowns. A minor difference between the two, and one difficult to discern in the field, is the tail tip, which is **white** in the ZITTING and **buff** in the GOLDEN-HEADED.
Songs, heard only during the breeding season, are quite distinctive. ZITTING: a strange metallic clinking. GOLDEN-HEADED: a peculiar buzzing followed by a short double 'clink'.

ZITTING CISTICOLA

White tail tip. Restricted to **coastal saline grassland,** e.g. couch grass *Sporobolus* sp. close to mangroves. Recorded only from the southern part of the Wet Tropics — habitat which is also sometimes exploited by the GOLDEN-HEADED.

GOLDEN-HEADED CISTICOLA

Buff tail tip. Male: develops a distinctive **plain golden crown** during the breeding season in spring and summer. Abundant and widespread throughout various grassy habitats.

BASSIAN THRUSH, RUSSET-TAILED THRUSH

The call and extent of white in the sides of the tail (visible only when tail is spread, e.g. on alighting) are the most reliable features to separate these two thrushes.

Bassian

BASSIAN THRUSH
Only the corners of the outer tail feathers white. Appears plump with an olive-brown rump. Call, heard at dawn and dusk, is a sweet warble not unlike that of the introduced Common Blackbird *Turdus merula.*

Russet-tailed

RUSSET-TAILED THRUSH
White sides for the greater length of the slightly shorter tail. Appears slim with a russet rump. Call, heard at dawn and dusk, is a somewhat mournful, double-whistle 'pee-poo'.

Note: Square brackets denote unconfirmed sighting.

FAMILY CASUARIIDAE

SOUTHERN CASSOWARY *Casuarius casuarius*
Status Generally uncommon, but a widespread rainforest resident. Numbers have decreased markedly, especially at lower altitudes, because of extensive clearing of habitat and other factors.
Habits Usually seen singly. It is shy, but will often remain quite still when approached. If approached too closely, will give a form of threat display. Feeds on fallen fruit, sometimes snails and fungi. The sole disperser of the larger rainforest seeds.
Where to see it The most noted area is at Mission Beach. Walking the tracks of Licuala and Lacey Creek state forest parks is often productive. At Wallaman Falls and Lake Barrine, birds sometimes visit the picnic area. Sightings elsewhere are by chance.

EMU *Dromaius novaehollandiae*
Status Moderately common in the south-western part of the Wet Tropics about Hervey Range, west of Paluma, and westward from Mt Fox (breeding). Probably still present in the drier country west of the Normanby and Annan rivers. Previously present in open woodland on the western edge of the Atherton Tableland, sometimes wandering into farmland. Still occasionally recorded south-west of Ravenshoe.
Habits Usually singly, in pairs or small groups. Usually shy, but often attracted by some form of movement. Feeds on grasses, fruits, flowers, leaves and insects.
Where to see it Probably the greatest chance is in the vicinity of Mt Fox. Easily seen in inland Australia.

ORDER GALLIFORMES

FAMILY MEGAPODIIDAE

AUSTRALIAN BRUSH-TURKEY *Alectura lathami*
Status Mostly common and breeding in upland rainforest. Usually scarce below 300 m, but some birds wander down to sea level during autumn and winter. A small resident population about Cooktown; common in suitable habitat about Townsville. Absent from most offshore islands but a resident population on Dunk Island.
Habits Normally a wary bird, it has become tame about human habitation to the point of becoming a pest. Usually seen singly, but congregates into loose flocks about a food source such as picnic areas in national parks. Feeds on the ground but roosts in trees by night.
Where to see it Nowadays about picnic areas in national parks or state forest parks, e.g. Mt Whitfield, Lakes Barrine and Eacham, Dunk Island, Wallaman Falls and Mt Spec.

ORANGE-FOOTED SCRUBFOWL *Megapodius reinwardt*
Status A common, widespread breeding resident. Less common at higher altitudes. Rare or absent from some upland rainforest. Common on all rainforested islands.
Habits Usually seen in pairs, sometimes singly. When disturbed, will run away or fly heavily up to a low branch. An active bird, it is especially noisy during the night throughout the year. Feeds on the rainforest floor, scratching in leaf litter.
Where to see it In most lowland rainforest, e.g. Mt Whitfield, Mission Beach, Dunk Island. Easily seen about some of the lodges, e.g. Kingfisher Park Birdwatchers Lodge.

FAMILY PHASIANIDAE

STUBBLE QUAIL *Coturnix pectoralis*
Status Generally uncommon, but probably more common than records indicate. Reasonably common on the Atherton Tableland where numbers fluctuate. Breeding recorded Atherton Nov.–Jan. (Bravery 1970).
Habits Seen singly, in pairs or small coveys. Prefers to squat when disturbed, but will run or fly when pressed.
Where to see it About open grassland, crops and pastures, especially on the Atherton Tableland. Difficult to observe.

BROWN QUAIL *Coturnix ypsilophora*
Status Common and widespread. Present throughout the year and breeding. Since the introduction of Guinea and Panic grasses *Panicum* spp. and *Glycine javanica* on the Atherton Tableland, numbers have increased (Bravery 1970).
Habits Usually in pairs or small coveys often appearing at the edge of grassy roadsides. Flushes noisily, sometimes underfoot, and flies quickly away. Individuals fly off in all directions.
Where to see it The best places are along grassy roadsides, especially during early morning and late afternoon.

KING QUAIL *Coturnix chinensis*
Status A common breeding species about Ingham and the Atherton Tableland. Only a few records from other areas, but has been recorded from Cooktown to Townsville.
Habits In pairs or small coveys. A secretive bird and difficult to observe, which probably accounts for infrequent records from some areas. If disturbed, it will often squat or sometimes run.
Where to see it About farmland on the Atherton Tableland, although it has been seen regularly at Davies Creek National Park in casuarina *Allocasuarina* spp. forest and occasionally about Townsville Town Common.

ORDER ANSERIFORMES

FAMILY ANSERANATIDAE

MAGPIE GOOSE *Anseranas semipalmata*
Status Generally abundant throughout the year in most wetlands, especially about Ingham, Townsville and the Atherton Tableland. Numbers have increased considerably over the past 30 years. Bravery (1970) recorded the first bird at Atherton in 1960. By 1969 it was in 'good numbers' and breeding. Now, up to 3500 visit Hasties Swamp regularly during the Dry.
Habits Usually in small to large flocks. Feeds about muddy margins of swamps, searching for roots and tubers. Wades, swims and sometimes dabbles. Occasionally feeds out into crops and becomes a pest. Perches freely in trees.
Where to see it On most larger freshwater swamps throughout the wetlands and also about wet pastures and ploughed land on the Atherton Tableland. Hasties Swamp.

FAMILY ANATIDAE

PLUMED WHISTLING-DUCK *Dendrocygna eytoni*
Status Common to locally abundant. Nomadic.
Habits Usually in small to large flocks, sometimes numbering thousands. Flocks are quite noisy. Swims buoyantly, appearing quite clumsy. Usually roosts on the ground by day, rarely in trees. Settles with legs dangling and head lowered. Wings whistle in flight.
Where to see it Throughout wetlands, sometimes in large numbers at such places as Hasties Swamp, Tinaburra and the borrow pits at Ross River Dam.

WANDERING WHISTLING-DUCK *Dendrocygna arcuata*
Status Moderately common to abundant. Less common in the northern part of the Wet Tropics, but the most common duck about Ingham. Present throughout the year but nomadic. Breeding.
Habits Usually in small to large flocks resting by day on bare ground on margins of swamps and rivers. Feeds by dabbling, diving or swimming under water. In flight, wings whistle and legs and feet are lowered before settling.
Where to see it Throughout wetlands. Usually present at Hasties Swamp, Lake Barrine, Eubenangee Swamp, the borrow pits at Ross River Dam and many other places.

BLUE-BILLED DUCK *Oxyura australis*
Status Vagrant. A few records only, e.g. a pair at a swamp at Yorkeys Knob during Sept. and Oct. 1992 (J. Crowhurst pers.comm.) and a pair with a nest at Forrest Beach in 1977 (J. Young pers.comm.). A species of south-eastern and south-western Australia.
Habits Spends its time on water, rarely going ashore and seldom flying. Often dives.

MUSK DUCK *Biziura lobata*
Status Vagrant. A pair recorded breeding at Forrest Beach in 1977 (J. Young pers.comm.). A species of south-eastern and south-western Australia.
Habits Spends its time in water, rarely going ashore. Swims low and dives frequently.

FRECKLED DUCK *Stictonetta naevosa*
Status Vagrant. A few records from the Atherton Tableland, Ingham and Townsville. One record from Abattoir Swamp. A species of south-eastern and south-western Australia.
Habits Associates with other ducks. Perches on stumps or snags in water. Feeds by wading in shallow water or up-ending in deeper water. Quiet and inconspicuous.

BLACK SWAN *Cygnus atratus*
Status Uncommon to common. Most common on larger areas of water. Limited breeding.
Habits A graceful bird, usually seen singly or in loose gatherings sometimes numbering many birds. Flight is strong with long neck outstretched, wings whistling and accompanied by bugling calls.
Where to see it On larger areas of open water, e.g. Lakes Mitchell and Tinaroo, Nardello's Lagoon, Ross River Dam.

RADJAH SHELDUCK *Tadorna radjah*
Status Rare. A few records from Cooktown (mainly June–Mar.). Two records at Cairns Esplanade. One record of a small group Mareeba 1994. One bird Hasties Swamp 1995. Pair at Mt Carbine 1996. A small population to the west of Mt Fox in the Burdekin River catchment (J. Young pers.comm.).
Habits Spends much time wading on the edge of pools or resting on mudbanks and limbs of trees. Sometimes dabbles while feeding. Flight is strong and direct accompanied by much calling.
Where to see it Can appear anywhere on fresh water or even on muddy foreshores. Best chance in the Wet Tropics region is probably Keatings Lagoon near Cooktown.

AUSTRALIAN WOOD DUCK *Chenonetta jubata*
Status Uncommon to moderately common and widespread. More common about Ingham during the Wet, but in more northerly areas appears to be more common in the Dry. Present throughout the year and breeding.
Habits Mostly seen in pairs or small parties by day. Spends much time on dry land beside water. During late afternoon or at dusk, birds move onto herbage to graze. Perches in dead trees and on logs in water.
Where to see it About freshwater swamps, lagoons and farm dams. Fairly easily encountered.

COTTON PYGMY-GOOSE *Nettapus coromandelianus*
Status Scarce to moderately common over much of the Wet Tropics. Rare about Cooktown. Numbers fluctuate. In dry years when water levels drop and water-lilies die back around the shallow edges, numbers drop markedly. Breeds Lake Tinaroo.
Habits Usually in pairs or small groups. Rarely comes ashore, living amongst water-lilies and sometimes resting on partly submerged logs and snags. Feeds on aquatic plants. Flight is fast and low to the water.
Where to see it On any fresh water, mostly where water-lilies are present, but it can appear on other water, e.g. paperbark swamps. Best places are Rotary Park at Mareeba, Nardello's Lagoon, the backwaters of Lake Tinaroo, Tinaburra, the borrow pits at the Ross River Dam spillway and Ross River. Easily overlooked when amongst water-lilies.

GREEN PYGMY-GOOSE *Nettapus pulchellus*
Status Moderately common and widespread throughout the Wet Tropics. Present throughout the year and breeding. Numbers fluctuate and drop drastically in dry years to a point where it almost disappears.
Habits Similar to those of the Cotton Pygmy-goose.
Where to see it On any fresh water where water-lilies are present, but it can appear on other waters. Easily overlooked when amongst water-lilies. Most likely places are Keatings Lagoon, Rotary Park Mareeba, Hasties Swamp, the backwaters of Lake Tinaroo, Tinaburra, Centenary Lakes, Townsville Town Common and Ross River Dam.

PACIFIC BLACK DUCK *Anas superciliosa*
Status Common to abundant throughout the Wet Tropics. Numbers build up in many areas after the Wet. Up to 1500 birds are present at this time in most years on Nardello's Lagoon. Limited breeding.
Habits Usually seen sitting low in the water with a typical duck profile or resting at the water's edge, sometimes on partly submerged logs. Wary. Bursts noisily from the water when approached by an observer. Dabbles when feeding. Flight is strong with whistling wings.
Where to see it On any area of fresh water throughout the Wet Tropics.

AUSTRALASIAN SHOVELER *Anas rhynchotis*
Status A rare visitor to freshwater areas, probably coinciding with drought in southern parts of the continent.
Habits By day, usually rests well out from shore, often amongst cover. Feeds off the surface of the water by straining it with its specialised bill. Shy and alert, it takes to the air with whirring wings at the approach of an observer, often before other ducks.
Where to see it Can appear on any area of fresh water.

GREY TEAL *Anas gracilis*
Status Common to abundant, widespread. Mostly a dry season visitor.
Habits In small to large flocks. Feeds by dabbling. Flight is fast and direct. Prefers muddy edges of drying lakes and swamps. Highly nomadic.
Where to see it Throughout the wetlands.

CHESTNUT TEAL *Anas castanea*
Status A rare visitor, mostly to freshwater areas.
Habits Similar in habits to the Grey Teal with which it often associates.
Where to see it Turns up mostly on fresh water in this region, e.g. Hasties Swamp. Always worth checking through gatherings of Grey Teal.

GARGANEY *Anas querquedula*
Status A rare summer visitor from the Northern Hemisphere, but possibly more birds than records indicate because of its similarity to the Grey Teal. Five birds at Blakey's Crossing 1988.
Habits Prefers shallow water where it feeds by dabbling. Usually seen singly or in small flocks, often associating with other ducks.
Where to see it A possibility on any freshwater swamp. Always worth checking through groups of Grey Teal.

PINK-EARED DUCK *Malacorhynchus membranaceus*
Status Uncommon to rare visitor. Rare on the Atherton Tableland and parts of the coastal wetlands. Uncommon about the Townsville area but common when inland regions are drought-affected.
Habits Usually in small flocks, sometimes singly or in pairs. Seldom comes ashore, perching on fallen trees and snags. Often associates with Grey Teal. Filters water through its bill to feed, sometimes with head under water. Rarely up-ends. Usually easy to approach.
Where to see it Has been recorded from mine ponds about Mt Carbine; Lakes Mitchell and Tinaroo, Nardello's Lagoon, Hasties Swamp, Blakey's Crossing, Ross River Dam.

HARDHEAD *Aythya australis*
Status Common and widespread. Nomadic. Mostly a dry season visitor with numbers building up considerably in the latter half of the year. Limited breeding.
Habits Usually in pairs or small flocks. A wary species and difficult to approach. Feeds by up-ending, diving and swimming under water. Seldom comes ashore and never perches in trees.
Where to see it On larger expanses of fresh, deeper water throughout the Wet Tropics. At Lake Barrine some birds have become accustomed to people.

ORDER PODICIPEDIFORMES
FAMILY PODICIPEDIDAE

AUSTRALASIAN GREBE *Tachybaptus novaehollandiae*
Status Common and widespread throughout the area. Mostly a dry season visitor. Limited breeding.
Habits Usually seen singly, in pairs or small groups. It dives for food frequently, but also feeds from the surface of the water. Will dive at the approach of an observer and hide amongst aquatic vegetation. Spends all of its time in the water.
Where to see it On most freshwater lakes, dams and swamps.

HOARY-HEADED GREBE *Poliocephalus poliocephalus*
Status Rare visitor. Highly nomadic.
Habits Usually appears singly. Dives for food. When approached by an observer, often flies across the water to escape. Associates with the Australasian Grebe. Rarely comes ashore.
Where to see it Always a remote chance on larger expanses of water, e.g. Hasties Swamp, Lakes Mitchell and Tinaroo, and Ross River Dam.

GREAT CRESTED GREBE *Podiceps cristatus*
Status An occasional visitor in small numbers, moreso from early autumn until late spring, but sometimes present throughout the year. Flocks of 30–40 recorded from Lakes Barrine and Tinaroo. Numbers have increased over the past 40 years since the advent of large dams.
Habits Usually in flocks, sometimes singly. Spends its time on water, rarely flying. Feeds by diving under water for fish or other aquatic animals. Will dive to escape danger or skitter across the water.
Where to see it Best places are Lakes Barrine and Tinaroo, larger swamps about Ingham and Ross River Dam, but can appear on any areas of deeper water.

FAMILY PROCELLARIIDAE

SOUTHERN GIANT-PETREL *Macronectes giganteus*
Status Vagrant. A bird of Antarctic waters breeding along the coast of Antarctica and Subantarctic islands, moving northward in winter. One record of a juvenile from Magnetic Island in June 1987. A few records from Michaelmas Cay over recent years (J. Crowhurst pers.comm.). A bird banded as a nestling in South Shetlands, Antarctica, recovered five months later, 11139 km north at Upolu Cay, 34 km east of Cairns, Aug. 1993 (McLean 1994).

BULWER'S PETREL *Bulweria bulwerii*
Status Vagrant. A bird of tropical oceans. One record from the vicinity of Pith Reef on the outer Barrier Reef approximately 100 km east of Dunk Island (Cheshire 1989).

WEDGE-TAILED SHEARWATER *Puffinus pacificus*
Status Moderately common offshore, sometimes beach-washed. Probably migratory. Does not breed in the Wet Tropics, breeding only on Raine, Combe and Fife islands and Rocky Islets off Cape York Peninsula. Also breeds in the Capricorn and Bunker groups of islands in the southern part of the Great Barrier Reef.
Habits Usually seen singly or in small parties. Feeds on small fish, crustaceans and squid caught while swimming or from shallow dives in flight.
Where to see it Offshore, especially about some islands, e.g. Palm and Brook. Often seen on a trip to Michaelmas Cay.

[SOOTY SHEARWATER *Puffinus griseus*
Status Vagrant. One bird recorded off Townsville by several observers during abnormally cool and windy conditions Aug. 1995 (*Drongo* 21). Common in southern Australia and New Zealand.]

SHORT-TAILED SHEARWATER *Puffinus tenuirostris*
Status Accidental. Breeds in south-eastern Australia. Migrates northward well off the Queensland coast. A few records of birds blown ashore by cyclones and severe weather.

HUTTON'S SHEARWATER *Puffinus huttoni*
Status Rare. A few offshore records in north-eastern Queensland mostly Feb.–Aug., e.g. off Mission Beach and Townsville. Breeds in the South Island of New Zealand, dispersing into Australian seas.
Habits Forms flocks to feed on fish and crustaceans. Smaller than the other shearwaters which occur in the Wet Tropics. Flight is usually fast and low over water, with bursts of rapid stiff wingbeats followed by brief glides.
Where to see it A possibility well out to sea.

FAMILY HYDROBATIDAE

WILSON'S STORM-PETREL *Oceanites oceanicus*
Status Rare. Winter visitor. Breeds in Antarctica and on many Subantarctic islands, wintering into the Northern Hemisphere.
Habits Usually feeds by picking its food from the surface of the sea with legs dangling and wings held high, sometimes diving. Often follows ships, feeding in their wake.
Where to see it Offshore waters, moreso in the vicinity of the outer Great Barrier Reef. Sometimes around Michaelmas Cay.

FAMILY PHAETHONTIDAE

RED-TAILED TROPICBIRD *Phaethon rubricauda*
Status Uncommon about Great Barrier Reef. Accidental onshore and usually only a victim of cyclones. Breeds on Raine Island off northern Cape York Peninsula and on several cays well out in the Coral Sea.
Habits Usually seen as a solitary bird. Feeds in a manner similar to a gannet by diving for prey from heights up to 12 m or more. Rarely approaches ships.
Where to see it Always a chance anywhere along Great Barrier Reef. Sometimes occurs about Michaelmas Cay.

WHITE-TAILED TROPICBIRD *Phaethon lepturus*
Status A rare visitor to the Coral Sea and Great Barrier Reef. Has been recorded about Michaelmas Cay and on the outer Great Barrier Reef. Breeds in tropical Pacific Ocean.
Habits Similar to the Red-tailed Tropicbird, but follows ships more often.
Where to see it Always worth looking for when visiting the outer Great Barrier Reef. Sightings have been made about Michaelmas Cay in Oct. (J. Squire pers.comm.).

FAMILY SULIDAE

AUSTRALASIAN GANNET *Morus serrator*
Status Vagrant. A bird of south-eastern and southern Australia and New Zealand. A bird banded at a rookery on eastern coast of North Island, New Zealand recovered in the vicinity of Magnetic Island (Wodzicki & Stein 1958).

MASKED BOOBY *Sula dactylatra*
Status Generally uncommon. An oceanic species, occasionally to Michaelmas Cay and other cays along the inner Reef, but more common on the outer Great Barrier Reef.
Habits Usually seen singly, sometimes in small flocks. Takes fish by plunging into the sea from a height of 15–40 m, sometimes as high as 100 m. Strong flight. Roosts on coral cays, buoys and beacons.
Where to see it Offshore waters mainly about the outer Great Barrier Reef. Always worth watching for if visiting Michaelmas Cay.

RED-FOOTED BOOBY *Sula sula*
Status Uncommon oceanic species breeding on several coral cays of outer Great Barrier Reef, e.g. Raine and Wreck islands off northern Cape York Peninsula. Rare along the coast and usually a victim of cyclones. A few records from Michaelmas Cay.
Habits Generally seen singly. Sometimes follows ships, occasionally resting on masts and rigging. Feeds on fish, crustaceans and squid which it usually takes by plunging into the sea. Takes flying fish which it often catches in flight. Feeds both by day and night.
Where to see it About the Great Barrier Reef. Always worth watching for if visiting Michaelmas Cay.

BROWN BOOBY *Sula leucogaster*
Status Common oceanic species present throughout the year and breeding on coral cays of Great Barrier Reef. Sometimes comes close to the mainland, especially in rough weather.
Habits Usually seen singly or in small flocks. Takes fish by diving spectacularly into the sea or by plucking them from waves. Roosts on coral cays, buoys, beacons, trees and even ships.
Where to see it Easily seen about Great Barrier Reef, e.g. Michaelmas Cay, but usually about more inshore islands, e.g. Green, Dunk, Magnetic. One of the best places is on the channel marker posts out of Cairns Harbour.

FAMILY ANHINGIDAE

DARTER *Anhinga melanogaster*
Status Common and present throughout the year. Breeding.
Habits Takes fish and other aquatic animals under water by impaling them with its sharp bill. Opens its wings to dry while perched on dead branches, fallen limbs and snags in water. Wary and will writhe its neck at the approach of an intruder.
Where to see it On most larger expanses of fresh water, especially deeper water.

FAMILY PHALACROCORACIDAE

LITTLE PIED CORMORANT *Phalacrocorax melanoleucos*
Status Very common and widespread. Present throughout the year, some breeding in southern parts of the Wet Tropics.
Habits Similar to other cormorants and often solitary. Plumage is sometimes stained from the water. Penetrates farther up rivers and creeks than other cormorants.
Where to see it Wherever there is fresh water.

PIED CORMORANT *Phalacrocorax varius*
Status Generally uncommon to rare north of Ingham but moderately common on some parts of the coast in the south, e.g. mouth of the Ross River. Present throughout the year. Breeding colonies about Ross River mouth and at Ingham.
Habits Usually seen singly, or in small and sometimes larger groups. Takes fish by diving and spends much time resting on partly submerged logs, snags, piers, sandspits. Often holds its wings out to dry. Flight is strong and direct and flocks usually fly in long lines of 'V' formations.
Where to see it Along the coast, especially at the mouths of some rivers in south of region, occasionally on reef flats.

LITTLE BLACK CORMORANT *Phalacrocorax sulcirostris*
Status Common and widespread. Present throughout the year. Some breeding, mostly in the south of the region.
Habits Similar to other cormorants. Usually seen singly or in small to large flocks. Often feeds in compact flocks by herding shoals of fish. Often associates with pelicans when feeding.
Where to see it On most larger areas of fresh water, sometimes salt water in coastal areas.

GREAT CORMORANT *Phalacrocorax carbo*
Status Uncommon in coastal areas but usually common on Lake Tinaroo and other larger inland lakes. Present throughout the year. Limited breeding.
Habits Similar to other cormorants.
Where to see it Most larger areas of fresh water, especially the inland lakes.

FAMILY PELECANIDAE

AUSTRALIAN PELICAN *Pelecanus conspicillatus*
Status Common and widespread, but numbers fluctuate probably according to conditions farther inland. Present in most months.
Habits Seen singly, in pairs or flocks. Perches on partly submerged logs, pylons, piers, sandbanks and in dead trees. Has an attractive, easy flight and soars to great heights.
Where to see it Usually on any larger expanse of water, e.g. Lake Tinaroo, Ross River Dam. Nearly always present along Cairns Esplanade and at Centenary Lakes.

FAMILY FREGATIDAE

GREAT FRIGATEBIRD *Fregata minor*

Status Moderately common well offshore about the Great Barrier Reef but sometimes seen high over mainland beaches.

Habits Usually seen in small to larger loose groups soaring buoyantly and effortlessly for hours. Being unable to walk or swim, spends most of its time in the air. Roosts in shrubbery and trees on islands each evening. Feeds by harrying other seabirds until they disgorge or by snatching food from the surface of the sea. Associates with the Lesser Frigatebird.

Where to see it About the Great Barrier Reef, e.g. Michaelmas Cay. Close to shore in cyclonic weather.

LESSER FRIGATEBIRD *Fregata ariel*

Status Moderately common about Great Barrier Reef but occasionally patrolling mainland beaches. More common than the Great Frigatebird.

Habits Similar to the Great Frigatebird with which it associates.

Where to see it About the Great Barrier Reef, e.g. Michaelmas Cay, sometimes over mainland shore, especially when conditions are stormy or windy.

ORDER CICONIIFORMES

FAMILY ARDEIDAE

WHITE-FACED HERON *Egretta novaehollandiae*

Status Common and widespread. Present throughout the year and breeding.

Habits Mostly seen singly though numbers may gather where a food source is prevalent. Stalks prey in shallow water or over grassy paddocks, jabbing with its bill to take an insect, frog or other animal. Flight is slow with long neck usually folded.

Where to see it About most swamps, creeks, rivers and in open grassy paddocks. Often along the Cairns Esplanade.

LITTLE EGRET *Egretta garzetta*

Status Moderately common and widespread but with a noticeable drop in numbers through the Wet. Present throughout the year. Limited breeding.

Habits Usually solitary, foraging in the shallows of lakes and swamps, sometimes in association with other egrets and aquatic birds, taking prey which they disturb. Long neck folded in flight.

Where to see it On freshwater swamps throughout the Wet Tropics, sometimes on foreshore. Usually present about the Cairns Esplanade.

EASTERN REEF EGRET *Egretta sacra*

Status Uncommon to moderately common. Present throughout the year and breeding.

Habits Usually solitary but roosts communally. Searches for food on reefs exposed at low tide and along foreshore, creeping along with a crouched stance. Flight is direct with rather rapid wingbeats. The grey phase outnumbers the white phase.

Where to see it Along most foreshores and about islands. Easily encountered.

WHITE-NECKED HERON *Ardea pacifica*

Status Scarce to common. Widespread. Nomadic but present throughout the year. Breeding near Ingham where numbers increase through the Wet.

Habits Usually occurs singly, sometimes in loose flocks at a food source. Feeds in shallow water, stalking fish, frogs and other aquatic animals which it takes with a quick jab of the bill. Flight is easy with slow-beating wings, neck folded and long legs protruding beyond the tail.

Where to see it Wherever there is fresh water.

GREAT-BILLED HERON *Ardea sumatrana*
Status Scarce. Resident. Small numbers scattered throughout most areas of extensive mangroves and along the middle reaches of some rivers, e.g. Daintree.
Habits Usually solitary. Sometimes wary and secretive and difficult to approach. In tidal areas, feeds by stalking in shallows and over mudbanks. At high tide it rests on mangrove limbs and roots at the edges of channels. Flight is heavy with the long neck folded.
Where to see it Difficult to locate and sightings are by chance. Can appear anywhere along the larger rivers and about mangroves. The best chance is along the Daintree River where resident pairs are known.

PIED HERON *Ardea picata*
Status A rare but regular visitor to the entire wetland area. No record of breeding from the Wet Tropics region but a small colony breeds to the south in mangroves at the mouth of Barratta Creek. Occasional birds appear about Cooktown Nov.–Apr. (J. McLean pers.comm.). Townsville records are from Dec.–Feb. (A. Griffin pers.comm.).
Habits Usually seen singly, sometimes in small groups, often in the company of other aquatic birds. Captures prey by stalking. In deeper water, will stalk slowly, standing and waiting. Neck folded in flight.
Where to see it Can appear anywhere wherever there is shallow fresh water.

GREAT EGRET *Ardea alba*
Status Common and widespread but with a noticeable drop in numbers during the Wet. Present throughout the year. Limited breeding.
Habits Similar to those of the Intermediate Egret.
Where to see it Freshwater swamps throughout the Wet Tropics. Usually present about Cairns Esplanade.

INTERMEDIATE EGRET *Ardea intermedia*
Status Common and widespread but with a noticeable drop in numbers during the Wet. Present throughout the year. Limited breeding.
Habits Usually a solitary bird seen stalking prey in shallows of swamps and lakes, sometimes to a depth as far as its long legs will allow. Often seen on grassy fields. Will sometimes freeze for a considerable time and then make a lightning lunge to take prey. Long neck folded in flight.
Where to see it On freshwater swamps throughout the Wet Tropics. Usually present about Cairns Esplanade.

CATTLE EGRET *Ardea ibis*
Status Previously uncommon to rare but numbers presently increasing considerably especially about Townsville. Moderately common along the Daintree River, on the Atherton Tableland and about Ingham. A breeding colony on the Ross River and another near Innisfail.
Habits Mostly seen in small, scattered, loose flocks catching insects disturbed by cattle. Birds congregate at a communal roosting place each evening, usually a stand of trees in a swamp to which they may fly a long distance.
Where to see it In open grassy paddocks about cattle.

STRIATED HERON *Butorides striatus*
Status Moderately common along most of the coastline. Common about Ingham and the Hinchinbrook Channel. Uncommon about Townsville.
Habits Usually seen singly on exposed mud close to mangroves or along streams. Flies away quickly when disturbed but sometimes will freeze in a bittern-like manner with bill pointing skyward. Flight is moderately fast with quick wingbeats and always low to the water.
Where to see it About mangroves and nearby areas. Sometimes about the Cairns Esplanade. Easily seen from some cruises into mangrove habitat.

NANKEEN NIGHT HERON *Nycticorax caledonicus*
Status Moderately common and widespread throughout the Wet Tropics and present throughout the year. Nomadic. Only breeding colony recorded in the Wet Tropics is at the mouth of the Bohle River.
Habits Nocturnal. From dusk, feeds about the shallow margins of lakes, creeks and swamps. Daytime roost usually in adjacent densely-foliaged trees. At the approach of an intruder will burst out and fly off, then sometimes perch on an exposed branch.
Where to see it About freshwater streams and swamps throughout the region.

LITTLE BITTERN *Ixobrychus minutus*
Status Rare. Few acceptable records. Birds reported from mangroves appear to be Striated Herons. Migrant in southern parts of the continent. There is a suggestion that some birds are winter visitors to New Guinea from Australia. However, the few records from the Wet Tropics do not support this, but appear to coincide with drought in southern Australia.
Where to see it By chance about denser reedy swamps. Most unlikely about mangroves.

BLACK BITTERN *Ixobrychus flavicollis*
Status Uncommon to moderately common breeding summer visitor Nov.–Apr. Most (probably all) of the population appears to vacate the Wet Tropics by late Apr.
Habits Usually solitary, sometimes in pairs. Rests by day in waterside vegetation, sometimes in trees. Hunts at dusk and dawn for fish, frogs and other aquatic animals. Sometimes points bill skyward and freezes to escape detection.
Where to see it Always a chance about any larger watercourses and freshwater swamps, especially paperbark swamps. Sometimes seen beside roadside pools on the Kuranda to Mareeba road during the Wet. Frequently seen on the Daintree River Nov.–Apr.

FAMILY THRESKIORNITHIDAE

GLOSSY IBIS *Plegadis falcinellus*
Status Uncommon but widespread visitor throughout the Wet Tropics with the majority of records through the Dry.
Habits Usually seen as single birds or small flocks. Feeds by probing the ground or mud with its bill. Sometimes associates with other ibis and waterbirds. Perches in trees close to water. Flight is strong with shallow wingbeats, flocks flying in lines or 'V' formation.
Where to see it Always a possibility about larger freshwater swamps and lakes, especially where water is drying back.

AUSTRALIAN WHITE IBIS *Threskiornis molucca*
Status Common throughout the year in most areas. Breeding in coastal wetlands.
Habits Occasionally seen singly but mostly in small to large flocks. Often occurs at unusual places such as garbage tips and about farmyards. Flight is strong with quick shallow wingbeats and a glide.
Where to see it Throughout the wetlands, especially coastal. Common about the Cairns Esplanade, in Townsville gardens and other similar habitats.

STRAW-NECKED IBIS *Threskiornis spinicollis*
Status Common and widespread. Numbers fluctuate greatly throughout the year with a large influx in some years. More common during the Dry. Does not breed in the Wet Tropics.
Habits Usually in small to large well-scattered groups striding across open grassy areas, probing at the ground with its long bill. Often rests in large dead trees where it will also roost in flocks by night. Flight is strong with quick wingbeats and a glide. Highly nomadic. Sometimes flocks soar to a great height.
Where to see it On open wet grassland, dry cultivated fields, sports fields and gardens throughout the Wet Tropics.

ROYAL SPOONBILL *Platalea regia*
Status Scarce to moderately common throughout coastal wetlands. Uncommon on the Atherton Tableland. Regular at the Cairns Esplanade. Fewer birds during the Wet. Generally present throughout the year. Highly nomadic.
Habits Usually seen singly or in small groups. Forages in shallow water by sweeping its bill from side to side. Rests in dead trees and on banks of dams and swamp edges. Flight is strong with steady wingbeats.
Where to see it Throughout the wetlands.

YELLOW-BILLED SPOONBILL *Platalea flavipes*
Status Uncommon to rare throughout the Wet Tropics.
Habits Similar to those of the Royal Spoonbill.
Where to see it A possibility anywhere in freshwater wetlands, moreso about Townsville.

FAMILY CICONIIDAE

BLACK-NECKED STORK *Ephippiorhynchus asiaticus*
Status Moderately common throughout the coastal wetlands. Probably more common about the Ingham wetlands than elsewhere, where 15 breeding pairs have been located within a 30 km radius of the town (J. Young pers.comm.). Scarce on the Atherton Tableland. Present throughout the year.
Habits Usually seen singly or in pairs in shallow water, stalking prey. Often strides through water, sweeping bill from side to side or dashes about erratically chasing fish, including eels.
Where to see it Likely on any freshwater swamp and along the edges of larger rivers, on coastal saltwater inlets and foreshores.

ORDER FALCONIFORMES

FAMILY ACCIPITRIDAE

OSPREY *Pandion haliaetus*
Status Common about the entire coastal strip and nearby islands. Perhaps most common about Hinchinbrook Channel. Present throughout the year and breeding. A few inland breeding pairs at Lakes Tinaroo and Mitchell.
Habits Usually seen singly or in pairs. It takes fish by either plunging into the water or snatching them from the surface. Flight is rather slow, consisting of flaps and glides. Perches conspicuously on pylons, channel markers and dead trees. Frequently uses power pylons for nest building, especially in the Cardwell to Townsville area.
Where to see it Anywhere along the coastline or about islands. Easily encountered.

PACIFIC BAZA *Aviceda subcristata*
Status Uncommon to moderately common. Common about Ingham. Widespread, present throughout the year and breeding.
Habits Usually seen singly or in pairs. In spring it performs spectacular courtship displays with an aerial tumbling high in the air over its breeding territory, uttering loud 'wee-chew' notes. Takes insects from the foliage of trees as well as frogs and small reptiles. Normally quiet and unobtrusive.
Where to see it Can appear almost anywhere in forested country. Easily overlooked. Usually seen while one is searching for other species.

BLACK-SHOULDERED KITE *Elanus axillaris*

Status Widespread but generally uncommon. Moderately common on the Atherton Tableland.
Single birds appear in winter at Cooktown (J. McLean pers.comm.).
Habits Hovers over open grassland or crops, dropping down to take prey (mostly rodents)
from the ground. Hunts early morning and late afternoon, but often crepuscular. Often glides on
stiff wings held in a 'V'. Perches conspicuously in dead tree tops and on telephone poles where
it sits upright. Mostly seen singly or in pairs.
Where to see it About open areas, especially about farmland.

LETTER-WINGED KITE *Elanus scriptus*

Status Vagrant. A species of the Barkly Tableland and Lake Eyre drainage in central Australia,
its normal distribution generally coinciding with that of the Long-haired Rat *Rattus
villosissimus* on which it preys. When rat colonies collapse following bountiful seasons, it irrupts
to all parts of the continent, e.g. 12 birds at Halifax in 1977 (J. Young pers.comm.); two birds
at Mt Carbine in July 1994 and another at West Barron Reserve (K. & L. Fisher pers.comm.);
numbers south of Townsville at Toonpan 1995.
Habits Similar to those of the Black-shouldered Kite, though within its normal range it is a
nocturnal hunter.

SQUARE-TAILED KITE *Lophoictinia isura*

Status Rare, thinly distributed but widespread. West of Ingham breeds in tall Flooded Gums
Eucalyptus grandis towering over upland rainforest. Mostly a winter visitor to northern parts of
the Wet Tropics. Seen regularly about Atherton throughout the year.
Habits Usually seen singly, sweeping close above the treetops in search of prey which it takes
from the outer foliage. Sometimes rides an air current to a great height. Each pair holds a huge
territory.
Where to see it Always a slight chance anywhere. Birds have been seen occasionally at the
Bloomfield River, Mt Molloy, Julatten, Hasties Swamp, along the Mareeba to Dimbulah road,
Herberton, Broadwater Creek State Forest Park, Wallaman Falls, and Paluma. One record
Admiralty Island (J. Crowhurst pers.comm.).

BLACK-BREASTED BUZZARD *Hamirostra melanosternon*

Status Rare. An inland species which just reaches the Wet Tropics. Mostly a winter visitor to
the western edge of the Atherton Tableland. Two sightings over the Cairns Esplanade (J.
Crowhurst pers.comm.). Others from the Palmer River (regular), Mt Carbine, Big Mitchell
Creek, Mareeba, Tinaburra and Paluma. A breeding pair at Mt Fox used the same nest for
12 years (J. Young pers.comm.).
Habits Usually seen as a solitary bird. Spends much of its time soaring and circling high in the
air. Takes most of its prey from the ground. Often sits quietly for hours on an exposed perch.
Where to see it Usually seen as a rare chance sighting. More easily seen in inland Australia.

BLACK KITE *Milvus migrans*

Status Generally abundant and widespread. Less common north of Cairns. Rare north of the
Daintree River but fairly common about Cooktown, mostly Mar.–Nov. The population fluctuates
with numbers dropping considerably at the onset of the Wet, then becoming abundant during
the Dry. The most common bird of prey in the Wet Tropics.
Habits Seen singly or in large loose flocks flying leisurely or soaring at a great height. It is
mainly a scavenger feeding on carrion on the ground, but also takes rodents, small reptiles and
insects. Attracted to fires, taking small animals and insects flushed by the flames. Patrols roads
at daybreak.
Where to see it Throughout the Wet Tropics. One of the first birds encountered.

WHISTLING KITE *Haliastur sphenurus*
Status Common and widespread. Often close to water. Present throughout the year and breeding.
Habits Usually seen singly or in pairs gliding at a low height or soaring high in the air. Often perches on a dead branch of a large tree. It has a pleasant and distinctive call. Patrols roads at daybreak.
Where to see it Throughout the more open areas. One of the first species encountered.

BRAHMINY KITE *Haliastur indus*
Status Common and widespread along the coast. Sometimes recorded some distance inland, e.g. Julatten, Mareeba, Atherton, Lakes Barrine and Tinaroo. Present throughout the year and breeding.
Habits Usually seen singly, sometimes in pairs, gliding and circling usually quite low, or perched in the dead top of a mangrove or other tree. Takes its prey from the ground. Unwary and easily approached.
Where to see it About mangroves and estuaries along the coast. Often close to roadsides. Usually easily encountered.

WHITE-BELLIED SEA-EAGLE *Haliaeetus leucogaster*
Status Common. Present throughout the year and breeding.
Habits Usually seen singly or in pairs soaring majestically, often high, on upturned wings or hunting over water where it dives for fish or snatches them from the surface. Also takes waterfowl and freshwater turtles. Each pair commands a large territory.
Where to see it Along the coast, about larger lagoons, dams and islands. Fairly easily encountered.

SPOTTED HARRIER *Circus assimilis*
Status Generally uncommon and irregular but locally common about Atherton Tableland where there may be a half dozen breeding pairs (J. Squire pers.comm.). Numbers fluctuate about Ingham where there are normally about three breeding pairs but this builds up to about 20 pairs when rodent numbers increase (J. Young pers.comm.). Rare about Cooktown and Townsville.
Habits Usually seen singly or in pairs. Sails low over grassland on broad upturned wings with head down, searching for prey. Sometimes perches on a fence post or stump. Does not soar to great heights as do many other raptors though often seen above canopy level.
Where to see it Over open grassland and farmland. Best place is probably the Atherton Tableland. Quite conspicuous.

SWAMP HARRIER *Circus approximans*
Status Generally uncommon. A regular non-breeding visitor mostly during the autumn and winter months but occasional birds seen throughout the year, especially on the Atherton Tableland.
Habits Sails low on upswept wings over reedbeds, sometimes farmland, gliding gracefully with only an occasional wingbeat. Feeds and rests on the ground, but sometimes will perch on fence posts and stumps. Preys on waterfowl but takes a variety of ground-dwelling animals.
Where to see it Moreso about larger swamps and areas of reeds, e.g. Nardello's Lagoon, Hasties Swamp, Blakey's Crossing.

[PAPUAN (EASTERN MARSH) HARRIER *Circus spilonotus*
Status Widespread through Asia with an endemic race *spilothorax* in New Guinea. A number of reports from the Wet Tropics mostly from the Atherton Tableland over recent years, but none has been accepted officially. However, there is little doubt that it is a rare but probably regular visitor to this region. *See* Mackay, R. 1991, 'Papuan Harrier in North Queensland', *The Australian Bird Watcher* **14**, 146.]

BROWN GOSHAWK *Accipiter fasciatus*

Status Common and widespread and breeds throughout the Wet Tropics. Most records in winter on Dunk Island (K. Uhlenhut pers.comm.). Mostly seen towards the end of the year about Kuranda and the Atherton Tableland (J. Squire pers.comm.). Less common north of Cairns.
Habits Usually seen singly. It hunts by stealth through the forest, circling and gliding through and over the trees to dislodge prey. Its flight can be quite fast, flying with quick wingbeats and glides.
Where to see it Can appear anywhere in open forest and woodland. Rather secretive and sometimes difficult to observe.

GREY GOSHAWK *Accipiter novaehollandiae*

Status Uncommon to moderately common. Present throughout the year and breeding.
Habits Mostly seen singly. Hunts through taller timber and can be seen occasionally gliding and circling above rainforest, often favouring gorges. Wary and usually difficult to approach. The grey phase far outnumbers the white phase; Gill (1970) estimated the ratio at about 6:1.
Where to see it Throughout rainforest. Generally not an easy species to locate. Mostly sighted when one is looking for other birds.

COLLARED SPARROWHAWK *Accipiter cirrhocephalus*

Status Widespread but generally rare. However, moderately common about Mts Molloy and Carbine. Present throughout the year and breeding.
Habits Similar to those of the Brown Goshawk.
Where to see it Can appear anywhere in open forest and woodland.

RED GOSHAWK *Erythrotriorchis radiatus*

Status Very rare. The few records are well-scattered, e.g. Bloomfield River, Daintree, Mts Carbine and Molloy; Julatten, Big Mitchell Creek, Yungaburra, Ingham, Bluewater State Forest, Townsville.
Habits Usually solitary, it is secretive and hunts stealthily under the forest canopy for a variety of birds, sometimes mammals and reptiles. It is a powerful predator taking birds as large as ducks, herons, cockatoos and kookaburras. Sometimes circles to a great height.
Where to see it The chance of seeing a Red Goshawk is extremely remote but it can occur anywhere, especially about well-vegetated watercourses through open woodland.

WEDGE-TAILED EAGLE *Aquila audax*

Status Widespread and common in some areas but rather rare in many areas such as parts of the coastal lowlands and north from Mareeba.
Habits Usually seen soaring at great heights. Perches in dead trees or on bare branches of large living trees. Animals up to the size of small kangaroos are taken as prey. Will feed on the carcasses of animals such as cattle when the opportunity arises. Rather clumsy on the ground. When disturbed takes off laboriously with legs dangling.
Where to see it Can appear anywhere over wooded areas right to the coast. Best places are the Atherton Tableland and Townsville Town Common. Easily seen in inland Australia.

LITTLE EAGLE *Hieraaetus morphnoides*

Status Rare but widespread. Breeding pairs are well-scattered. Only two pairs are known about Ingham (J. Young pers.comm.).
Habits Usually seen singly, sometimes in pairs. Spends much time soaring in tight circles over wooded areas, searching for prey. Sometimes perches high in a tree for long periods or will ride air currents to a great height. Preys mostly on mammals and reptiles, sometimes birds.
Where to see it Can appear in any open forest or woodland. More easily seen in inland southern Australia.

FAMILY FALCONIDAE

BROWN FALCON *Falco berigora*
Status Common, widespread and breeding. Numbers build up during the winter months, but fluctuate from year to year. Sometimes becomes abundant in places such as the Atherton Tableland.
Habits Usually seen singly or in larger loose groups when influxes occur. Perches on telephone poles, fence posts, termite mounds and dead trees. Flight is rather slow as it soars and circles on upswept wings with tail fanned. Sometimes hovers clumsily to take prey from the ground.
Where to see it In open and lightly timbered country and farmland, often by roadsides. Not difficult to locate.

AUSTRALIAN HOBBY *Falco longipennis*
Status Generally uncommon but widespread with sightings throughout the year. Appears to be more common about Ingham, Townsville and south and west towards Charters Towers where it frequently breeds in old nests of Torresian Crows, built in power pylons. Seen moreso in winter about Tully.
Habits Usually seen singly, sometimes in pairs. Flies swiftly, occasionally soaring and circling. Preys on small birds which it takes in mid-air, also flying insects such as dragonflies. Flushes small birds by flying about treetops.
Where to see it Usually appears unexpectedly in open areas or open forest. Often seen about Centenary Lakes.

GREY FALCON *Falco hypoleucos*
Status Vagrant to the Wet Tropics. Several records from Atherton 1962–69 (Bravery 1970). Two birds at Ingham Sept. 1990; another at Townsville Mar. 1995. A rare species of the dry inland and desert areas.

BLACK FALCON *Falco subniger*
Status Rare. Absent from most of the Wet Tropics but regular in small numbers on the Atherton Tableland. Two pairs breeding at Ingham 1989–92 (J. Young pers.comm.). A bird of inland plains, grasslands and watercourses.
Habits Usually seen singly, sometimes in pairs. Preys mostly on birds which it takes in a stooping dive or by outright chase, snatching them in mid-air. Takes birds up to the size of ducks and galahs. Also takes small mammals.
Where to see it Sightings in the Wet Tropics are by chance but best chance is about Mareeba and Atherton. More easily seen in inland Australia.

PEREGRINE FALCON *Falco peregrinus*
Status Generally rare but widespread. Where sightings are regularly made, one will usually find a resident pair. Nesting sites known from ranges behind Mossman, Hinchinbrook Island and Townsville. Sometimes appears about the Cairns Esplanade (usually Sept.–Nov.) preying on shorebirds (J. Crowhurst pers.comm.).
Habits Usually seen singly, sometimes in pairs and occasionally small family groups when young have fledged. Perches in tall dead trees, on bare limbs of large living trees and on crags about cliff faces. Its flight can be rapid, wheeling and turning with ease at incredible speed in pursuit of prey. Has a loud cackling call.
Where to see it Can appear unexpectedly at any time but best chance is within the territory of a breeding pair, e.g. a pair breeding in 1995 at the old mine site at Mt Carbine.

NANKEEN KESTREL *Falco cenchroides*
Status Generally common but absent from some parts of coastal lowlands. A winter visitor only, to the Innisfail area (Gill 1970). Present throughout the year. Numbers often fluctuate especially in the Dry.
Habits Usually seen singly or in pairs. Perches in dead trees and on telephone poles and powerlines. Hovers to locate prey on the ground. Soars in circles. Feeds on insects and rodents.
Where to see it In lightly timbered areas and farmland, especially about Mt Carbine, Atherton Tableland and Townsville. Easily seen from the roadway.

FAMILY GRUIDAE

SARUS CRANE *Grus antigone*
Status Generally rare dry season visitor over most of the Wet Tropics, but common and regular to the Atherton Tableland May–Dec. The only breeding recorded is of one pair with a nest at Ingham 1978 (J. Young pers.comm.).
Habits In pairs or loose flocks sometimes numbering hundreds. Forages by day in smaller groups, congregating during late afternoon to roost in swamps. Similar to the Brolga in habits.
Where to see it Easily seen about swamps and farmland on the Atherton Tableland June–Dec. Large numbers roost at Bromfield Swamp; smaller numbers at Hasties Swamp.

BROLGA *Grus rubicunda*
Status Common about Ingham and Townsville where it is present throughout the year and breeding. Uncommon to rare north of Ingham, but a regular visitor to the Atherton Tableland May–Dec. where it has previously been recorded in good numbers. However, appears to be declining about Townsville (Wieneke 1988) and the Atherton Tableland (G. Holmes pers.comm.). Scarce about Cooktown.
Habits Usually seen singly, in pairs or flocks, sometimes very large at a food source. Gathers during the late afternoon to roost in groups in shallow swamps. The flight is graceful with outstretched neck. Sometimes soars to a great height. Occasionally an agricultural pest.
Where to see it Best places are in the south of the region, e.g. Townsville Town Common and often beside the highway at Blakey's Crossing. Also on Atherton Tableland and Lake Mitchell.

FAMILY RALLIDAE

RED-NECKED CRAKE *Rallina tricolor*
Status Common, present throughout the year and breeding. Moreso at lower altitudes.
Habits Usually shy and difficult to observe. Rests through the day, becoming active before dusk and feeding well into the night. Becomes noisy during the Wet when breeding takes place.
Where to see it In rainforest, moreso close to streams, especially during early morning and late afternoon. Kingfisher Park Birdwatchers Lodge and Cassowary House are noted for the ease and regularity with which this species can be observed.

BUFF-BANDED RAIL *Gallirallus philippensis*
Status Common and widespread in coastal areas. Abundant on the Atherton Tableland. Common on Hope Island and similar coral cays off Cooktown (J. McLean pers.comm.). Present throughout the year and breeding.
Habits Usually seen singly or in pairs. Lives on the ground, mostly keeping to cover. Rarely flies but runs to escape. Shy and secretive. Walks with a somewhat hunched stance.
Where to see it About wet grassland, especially early morning and late afternoon. Frequently beside roadways, especially after a shower of rain. Often bathes in roadside puddles. One of the better places is about the Cairns Crocodile Farm.

LEWIN'S RAIL *Rallus pectoralis*
Status Rare, but may be more than records indicate because of its secretive habits.
Habits Spends its time on the ground, skulking in dense vegetation. Feeds mostly at dawn and dusk. Rarely flies when disturbed but runs to escape. Flight is rather clumsy with legs trailing.
Where to see it About damp grassland and swamps. Has been recorded from Julatten, Centenary Lakes, Hasties Swamp and Ingham.

BUSH-HEN *Amaurornis olivaceus*

Status Generally common in suitable habitat. Scarce about Cooktown and Townsville. Very common about parts of the Atherton Tableland and Julatten during the breeding season, but appears to vacate these areas after the Wet. Recorded from some parts of coastal lowlands throughout the year, e.g. Daintree.

Habits A wary and secretive species which makes its presence known during the Wet when breeding takes place. Calls continuously and monotonously for lengthy periods throughout the night. Usually seen singly, sometimes in pairs.

Where to see it Tends to remain in dense cover and can be frustrating to observe. Walking quietly along grassy-sided roads, especially close to creeks during early morning or late afternoon is often productive. One should watch well ahead for birds feeding out from the grassy edge.

BAILLON'S CRAKE *Porzana pusilla*

Status Uncommon. Records are few but probably larger numbers present than indicated because of its secretive habits. Probably an erratic visitor — absent in some years, remaining to breed in others.

Habits A shy species, it forages along the edge of marshy ground and swamps. When disturbed, it sometimes flutters laboriously over vegetation with legs dangling for a short distance before dropping back to cover.

Where to see it Can appear about any freshwater swamps with a reedy cover. Has been recorded from Hasties Swamp, Lake Tinaroo, Centenary Lakes and about Ingham and Townsville. One of the better places is the Cairns Crocodile Farm.

AUSTRALIAN SPOTTED CRAKE *Porzana fluminea*

Status Rare. Probably an occasional visitor with more birds present than records indicate because of its secretive habits.

Habits A shy and secretive species occurring singly or in pairs. Will venture from cover to feed in shallow water and about margins of swamps. Feeds quietly, hesitantly creeping and darting to catch insects. Flight is laboured with legs dangling.

Where to see it A remote possibility about lakes and swamps with a reedy cover, especially where the water is brackish. Has been recorded from Innisfail, Ingham and Blakey's Crossing.

SPOTLESS CRAKE *Porzana tabuensis*

Status Uncommon. Nearly all records are from the Atherton Tableland where there may be an isolated resident population. However, single records from Mt Elliot and Paluma may suggest some migration (Nielsen 1992).

Habits A shy and secretive species of dense reeds and aquatic vegetation. Sometimes feeds in open, or beside dense aquatic vegetation.

Where to see it Best chance is about swamps and streams on the Atherton Tableland. Difficult to locate and observe.

WHITE-BROWED CRAKE *Porzana cinerea*

Status A common breeding species in the lowlands. In smaller numbers but common on parts of the Atherton Tableland and about Mareeba and Julatten.

Habits Usually seen singly, sometimes in pairs. Usually secretive in dense habitat, but during the Dry when swamps recede it feeds across water-lily pads in the same manner as the Comb-crested Jacana, taking little notice of an observer. It is an active feeder, rarely remaining still.

Where to see it About coastal freshwater swamps, e.g. Centenary Lakes, Eubanangee Swamp, Blakey's Crossing. One of the better places is about the Cairns Crocodile Farm. Sometimes about sugar-cane fields. Can be difficult to locate where cover is dense.

PURPLE SWAMPHEN *Porphyrio porphyrio*

Status Generally common and widespread. Common on the Atherton Tableland where sometimes 600 or more can be seen at Hasties Swamp. Present throughout the year and breeding.
Habits A conspicuous bird usually seen in scattered groups, sometimes singly. Spends much of its time on grassy areas out from the edges of freshwater swamps and lakes. Usually swims only when pressed and is quite a poor swimmer. Flies awkwardly with legs dangling.
Where to see it About most freshwater swamps with reeds and adjacent short grass.

DUSKY MOORHEN *Gallinula tenebrosa*

Status Uncommon in most areas but common on the Atherton Tableland and about Ingham. Present throughout the year and breeding.
Habits Usually seen singly or in pairs swimming close to the banks of streams or amongst aquatic vegetation in lakes and dams. Swims with a head-jerking movement and will sometimes skitter across the water.
Where to see it On freshwater swamps and streams with some aquatic vegetation, e.g. Lakes Barrine and Tinaroo; Centenary Lakes.

BLACK-TAILED NATIVE-HEN *Gallinula ventralis*

Status Rare. A highly nomadic species of inland Australia. Small flocks have been recorded during the Dry in the southern part of the Wet Tropics about Ingham and Townsville.
Habits Feeds about the drying edges of swamps, and runs about like a bantam fowl. Usually appears in flocks. Subject to erratic irruptions throughout its range.
Where to see it A remote chance about Ingham and Townsville during the Dry.

EURASIAN COOT *Fulica atra*

Status Common and widespread on larger areas of open fresh water through the Dry. The population decreases markedly when the Wet arrives. Limited breeding.
Habits A bird of open water. Sometimes comes ashore. Usually in small to large loose flocks spread across the water. When surprised by an observer it will often skitter across the surface to escape.
Where to see it On most larger expanses of fresh water, e.g. Lakes Tinaroo and Barrine, West Barron Reserve, Ross River Dam. Easily located and observed.

FAMILY OTIDIDAE

AUSTRALIAN BUSTARD *Ardeotis australis*

Status Rare or absent over much of the Wet Tropics but locally common in some areas, e.g. Mt Carbine and Townsville Town Common. Moderately common on open cultivation about Lakeland. A common winter visitor to parts of the Atherton Tableland. Breeds regularly about Mt Carbine.
Habits Usually seen singly or in pairs, sometimes in larger loose flocks. Spends its time on the ground, never perching. Mostly rests by day, moving out to feed during late afternoon. Has a slow stately walk with bill and head held high. Flight is powerful with legs trailing. When disturbed, will often freeze then walk slowly away.
Where to see it Best places are grasslands in the Mt Carbine area and Townsville Town Common. Also on open cultivation on the Atherton Tableland during winter.

ORDER TURNICIFORMES

FAMILY TURNICIDAE

RED-BACKED BUTTON-QUAIL *Turnix maculosa*

Status Common and widespread in many areas at most altitudes. Scarce in others. Breeding.
Habits Usually singly or in pairs, sometimes in small coveys. Shy and flushes only when pressed, flying only a short distance before dropping to cover again.
Where to see it Edges of clearings, beside roadways, on grassy tracks through open forest, especially during early morning and late afternoon. A difficult species to locate and observe.

LITTLE BUTTON-QUAIL *Turnix velox*
Status Vagrant. Four records to date at Mts Carbine, Lewis and Molloy; Paluma. A bird of the inland grasslands of Australia. Highly nomadic.

RED-CHESTED BUTTON-QUAIL *Turnix pyrrhothorax*
Status Generally rare to uncommon. An erratic visitor to the Atherton Tableland usually Nov.–Mar. (Bravery 1970) and to the Ingham/Townsville area where breeding has been recorded. Three birds at Mt Molloy Jan. 1994 appears to be the only record north of the Atherton Tableland. Numbers fluctuate greatly but probably more birds present than records indicate because of its secretive habits and reluctance to flush.
Habits Occurs singly, in pairs or in small coveys. When flushed, flies a short distance before dropping back to cover again. Flight is fast with rapid, whirring wings.
Where to see it Very difficult to locate and observe. The best chance may be in grassland about Townsville, e.g. Blakey's Crossing, and about Ingham.

BUFF-BREASTED BUTTON-QUAIL *Turnix olivii*
Status Rare and possibly endangered. Absent in some years. Squire (1990) noted that it only appeared in any numbers in two years out of ten. Recorded from Cooktown, south to Mareeba and Davies Creek National Park. Recently recorded from Broadwater State Forest Park (J. Young pers.comm.). Breeding recorded near Mt Molloy.
Habits Little is known of this button-quail. Usually flushed singly, in pairs, sometimes in small loose groups. Shy, preferring to run rapidly away at the approach of an intruder rather than fly. It seems to have a strong preference for very sparse grass. When the Wet arrives and the grass cover thickens it appears to vacate these areas almost entirely.
Where to see it Best places to date seem to be about Mt Molloy and Davies Creek National Park. Difficult to locate and observe. A good knowledge of habitat preference (patches of sparsely-grassed open forest on gently-sloping gravelly hillsides) is essential for success.

PAINTED BUTTON-QUAIL *Turnix varia*
Status Moderately common. Extends north to the vicinity of Cooktown. Appears to be present throughout the year and breeding.
Habits Usually seen in small coveys, sometimes singly or in pairs. Will burst out from underfoot when flushed. Flight is fast; a bird dodging between trees before dropping back to cover again.
Where to see it The best places are in open woodland on the Atherton Tableland, Davies Creek National Park and about Mareeba.

[BLACK-BREASTED BUTTON-QUAIL *Turnix melanogaster*
Status J. Young (pers.comm.) found a bird on a nest of four eggs at Mission Beach, Sept. 1977 and considered it to be an aviary escapee. A species of dry rainforest in southern Queensland. Bravery (1970) recorded what he took to be this species on a number of occasions on his property at Atherton.]

ORDER CHARADRIIFORMES

FAMILY SCOLOPACIDAE

LATHAM'S SNIPE *Gallinago hardwickii*
Status A generally uncommon but widespread non-breeding summer visitor from the Northern Hemisphere. Appears to be a passage migrant through the Wet Tropics region Sept.–Oct. and Mar.–Apr. Bravery (1970) suggested Willett's Swamp (several kilometres south of Atherton) was a flocking area before northward migration. Willett's Swamp has since been drained. Gill (1970) noted it as a numerous regular passage migrant about Innisfail during Sept. and Oct. and again in Mar. and Apr. K. Uhlenhut (pers.comm.) has made similar observations about Tully.

Habits Usually seen singly, sometimes in small loose flocks. Usually does not flush from its grassy habitat until almost trodden on, and then bursts up, startling the observer. Uttering a harsh single note, it zigzags away with a fast flight before dropping back to cover. Always wary. Feeds by probing the mud with its bill.

Where to see it Margins of grassy swamps, especially on the Atherton Tableland, e.g. Hasties Swamp, Lake Mitchell, Abattoir Swamp. Small parties sometimes occur at the Cairns Esplanade.

[SWINHOE'S SNIPE *Gallinago megala*

Status Breeds in Siberia and Mongolia, wintering southward to India, south-east Asia and Indonesia, with small numbers reaching northern Australia. Recently reported in the Wet Tropics (G. Holmes pers.comm.).]

BLACK-TAILED GODWIT *Limosa limosa*

Status A non-breeding summer visitor from the Northern Hemisphere Sept.–Apr. with some overwintering. Moderately common at the Cairns Esplanade, uncommon in other areas. Rare on the Atherton Tableland.

Habits Usually seen singly, in pairs, or small flocks. Feeds by probing its bill deep into the mud. Feeds leisurely, sometimes wading in water up to its belly. Has a swift flight, usually low to the water.

Where to see it On mudflats. Best place is Cairns Esplanade.

BAR-TAILED GODWIT *Limosa lapponica*

Status A common non-breeding summer visitor from the Northern Hemisphere Sept.–Apr. with some overwintering.

Habits Similar to those of the Black-tailed Godwit.

Where to see it On most tidal mudflats. Easily seen.

LITTLE CURLEW *Numenius minutus*

Status Small numbers appear regularly on turf farm at Edmonton Sept.–Mar./Apr. Rare south of about Innisfail. On the Atherton Tableland Bravery (1970) recorded large flocks regularly 1964–69. Up to 130 have been recorded at Innisfail aerodrome.

Habits Usually in small to large flocks, sometimes in pairs or singly. Associates freely with other shorebirds. Wary. Squats or freezes at the approach of an observer. Sometimes flushes, with shrill calls.

Where to see it A possibility on any open grassland, e.g. farming areas on the Atherton Tableland, about Lake Tinaroo and the turf farm at Edmonton.

WHIMBREL *Numenius phaeopus*

Status A common non-breeding summer visitor from the Northern Hemisphere Sept.–Apr. with some overwintering.

Habits Usually singly or in small flocks, often with other shorebirds. It is a wary species, flying off noisily, uttering rapid shrill notes. Feeds by probing the sand with its long bill. Often roosts in mangroves.

Where to see it On most tidal mudflats or estuaries. Obvious.

EASTERN CURLEW *Numenius madagascariensis*

Status A common non-breeding summer visitor from the Northern Hemisphere present Aug.–Apr. with some overwintering. The sewage outlet south of Ross River supports a large wintering population.

Habits Mostly seen as a single bird, sometimes in scattered groups. It is a wary species, flying off noisily at the approach of an observer. Locates prey by probing sand or mud with its long bill. Often roosts in mangroves.

Where to see it On most mudflats and estuaries. One of the most obvious shorebirds.

225

[**BRISTLE-THIGHED CURLEW** *Numenius tahitiensis*
Status Breeds in North America, wintering southward to Polynesia. A bird at Cairns Esplanade, Nov. 1990 (J. Crowhurst, J. Squire pers.comm.).]

[**EURASIAN CURLEW** *Numenius arquata*
Status Breeds through northern Europe and Asia, migrating southward during the northern winter to Japan, southern Asia, Africa and the Mediterranean. A bird at Cairns Esplanade, Nov. 1990 (J. Crowhurst pers.comm.) and another Oct. 1995 (A. Anderson pers. comm.). Both birds with 'conspicuous white rump and lower back.']

COMMON REDSHANK *Tringa totanus*
Status A rare non-breeding summer visitor from the Northern Hemisphere. Several sightings at Cairns Esplanade mostly Aug. and Mar.–Apr.
Habits Mostly seen singly in this region. Actively feeds over tidal flats, sometimes wading in shallow water.
Where to see it A remote chance at Cairns Esplanade, moreso during migration.

MARSH SANDPIPER *Tringa stagnatilis*
Status An uncommon to common summer visitor from the Northern Hemisphere, Sept.–Apr. Common about the Atherton Tableland and Townsville, uncommon elsewhere.
Habits Wades in shallow water up to its belly, sometimes swimming, taking prey from the surface. Sometimes darts back and forth to capture insects, or sweeps its bill back and forth through the water. Usually seen singly, sometimes in parties. Flight is fast with clipped wingbeats.
Where to see it Mostly about swamps, e.g. Lakes Mitchell and Tinaroo, Hasties Swamp, Blakey's Crossing, less often on tidal mudflats such as the Cairns Esplanade.

COMMON GREENSHANK *Tringa nebularia*
Status A common non-breeding summer visitor from the Northern Hemisphere Sept.–Apr. with some overwintering. Widespread.
Habits Often seen as a solitary bird but sometimes in small parties or flocks. Dashes about searching for prey, pecking and probing and wading in water up to its belly. Fast flight.
Where to see it On most mudflats and estuaries, sometimes freshwater swamps.

WOOD SANDPIPER *Tringa glareola*
Status A rare to uncommon non-breeding summer visitor from the Northern Hemisphere Sept.–Apr.
Habits Usually solitary, nervously active, bobbing its head and flicking its tail. When flushed usually zigzags high and fast, twisting about, accompanied by clear calls and rapid wingbeats. Perches on dead branches and fence posts.
Where to see it A possibility on any freshwater swamp, moreso on migration Sept.–Nov. and Mar.–Apr. Lake Mitchell, Hasties Swamp, Cairns Crocodile Farm, Blakey's Crossing are likely places.

TEREK SANDPIPER *Xenus cinereus*
Status A non-breeding summer visitor from the Northern Hemisphere Aug.–Apr. with some overwintering. Common on Cairns Esplanade but rare in southern parts of the Wet Tropics.
Habits An active bird which dashes about with body held low and horizontally and with head and bill forward, chasing prey. Sometimes probes the mud or sand. Bobs its head and flicks its tail. Usually singly or in pairs, sometimes loose flocks.
Where to see it On tidal mudflats. Cairns Esplanade is the best place in north-eastern Queensland to see Terek Sandpipers all year round.

COMMON SANDPIPER *Actitis hypoleucos*

Status A generally uncommon non-breeding summer visitor from the Northern Hemisphere Aug.–Apr. with some overwintering.

Habits Usually singly or in pairs feeding actively with body teetering up and down. Feeds by pecking rather than probing. Perches on rocks, snags, mangrove roots and branches. Has a distinctive flight with shallow wingbeats and glides on down-arched wings, skimming straight and low over water.

Where to see it Muddy areas about freshwater swamps, mangrove channels and mangrove-lined river mouths. Atherton Tableland, Centenary Lakes, Cairns Esplanade, Dunk Island, Hinchinbrook Channel.

GREY-TAILED TATTLER *Heteroscelus brevipes*

Status A common non-breeding summer visitor from the Northern Hemisphere Sept.–Apr. with some overwintering.

Habits Sometimes in flocks but often singly. It is an active feeder, appearing nervous, probing the mud while walking quickly, bobbing its head and teetering the rear of its body. Flight is usually low across the water with clipped wingbeats. On landing it raises its wings vertically before folding them. Perches on mangrove branches, rocks and snags at low tide.

Where to see it On most tidal mudflats and estuaries. One of the more common shorebirds.

WANDERING TATTLER *Heteroscelus incanus*

Status A rare non-breeding summer visitor from the Northern Hemisphere, but more common on islands and reefs, preferring stony beaches.

Habits It is a busy feeder running about rocks and associated pools probing for food. Head and body are bobbed up and down as it runs. Has a wing-flicking flight like the Common Sandpiper's when flying short distances.

Where to see it Moreso on islands, e.g. Green, Palm and Dunk.

RUDDY TURNSTONE *Arenaria interpres*

Status An uncommon non-breeding summer visitor from the Northern Hemisphere. Possibly more common on offshore islands. Mostly a passage migrant in the Wet Tropics. At Cairns it is common during the inward migration Sept.–Nov., but then disappears.

Habits Usually seen singly or in small groups. Associates with other shorebirds. Busy when feeding, walking and running, pecking at seaweed and debris with its bill. Pushes up seaweed and shells to expose food.

Where to see it Anywhere along the seashore or on islands of the Great Barrier Reef.

ASIAN DOWITCHER *Limnodromus semipalmatus*

Status A rare summer visitor to Australia from the Northern Hemisphere, wintering mostly in India and south-eastern Asia. Irregular at Cairns Esplanade with three or four birds appearing in some years.

Habits Feeds by pushing bill deep into soft mud, using a stiff action. Associates freely with other shorebirds, especially godwits.

Where to see it Always worth checking through flocks of godwits at the Cairns Esplanade.

GREAT KNOT *Calidris tenuirostris*

Status Generally a common non-breeding summer visitor from the Northern Hemisphere Sept.–Apr. with some overwintering.

Habits Usually in small to large flocks and often with other shorebirds, especially godwits. Feeds slowly with head bent over, thrusting bill deeply into the sand. Often feeds in compact flocks. Flight is strong and direct with members of a flock flying in unison.

Where to see it Tidal mudflats and estuaries. Easily overlooked.

RED KNOT *Calidris canutus*
Status A rare to uncommon non-breeding summer visitor from the Northern Hemisphere
Aug.–Apr.
Habits Associates with the more common Great Knot as well as other shorebirds. Feeds by
thrusting its bill rapidly and deeply into the sand. Rather easy to approach when feeding but
wary when resting on sand banks and other high tide roosts.
Where to see it Usually amongst Great Knots on tidal mudflats and estuaries.

SANDERLING *Calidris alba*
Status An uncommon non-breeding summer visitor from the Northern Hemisphere Sept.–Apr.
Habits Usually solitary, sometimes mingling with other shorebirds. It is a busy feeder with
head down, chasing insects and searching for marine organisms at the edge of waves. Has a fast
direct flight low over water.
Where to see it On ocean beaches. Appears occasionally at the Cairns Esplanade.

[TEMMINCK'S STINT *Calidris temminckii*
Status Breeds through northern Europe and Asia, migrating southward to tropics. One
recorded on freshwater swamp near Malanda Sept. 1995 (G. Holmes pers. comm.).]

RED-NECKED STINT *Calidris ruficollis*
Status A common non-breeding summer visitor from the Northern Hemisphere Sept.–Apr. with
some overwintering. Less common on the Atherton Tableland.
Habits Usually in flocks. Associates with other shorebirds. Feeds by busily jabbing its bill into
the mud. Runs about with body hunched. Forms compact flocks in flight, wheeling and turning
and alighting together.
Where to see it On tidal mudflats and margins of fresh water throughout the Wet Tropics.

LONG-TOED STINT *Calidris subminuta*
Status Vagrant. A non-breeding summer visitor to Australia from the Northern Hemisphere. A
few records from the Cairns Esplanade.

PECTORAL SANDPIPER *Calidris melanotos*
Status Generally a rare non-breeding summer visitor from the Northern Hemisphere
Sept.–Mar. Recorded regularly only at Cairns Esplanade, with a few sightings each year. Others
from Daintree, Atherton Tableland and a few from Blakey's Crossing.
Habits Usually seen as a solitary bird. Rather shy and wary. Cranes its neck or freezes when
approached. Flushes with a zigzag flight, like a snipe.
Where to see it Best chance is at the Cairns Esplanade.

SHARP-TAILED SANDPIPER *Calidris acuminata*
Status An abundant widespread visitor from the Northern Hemisphere Aug.–Apr. with some
overwintering in most years.
Habits Usually in small to large flocks. It is a busy feeder with head down, probing for food in
the mud. Often associates with other shorebirds. When flushed, birds fly in a compact flock in
unison, then split up and alight again.
Where to see it Mudflats and freshwater swamps throughout the Wet Tropics.

DUNLIN *Calidris alpina*
Status Breeds in the high Arctic region of the Northern Hemisphere, wintering in North
America, Europe and southern China. Accidental to Australia. One confirmed record from the
Cairns Esplanade (Roberts 1983). Several unconfirmed records.

CURLEW SANDPIPER *Calidris ferruginea*

Status A non-breeding summer visitor from the Northern Hemisphere Aug.–Apr. with some overwintering. Generally uncommon throughout the Wet Tropics but common at the Cairns Esplanade.

Habits Often seen in flocks feeding along the shore and wading in water up to its belly, plunging its head below the surface. Frequently feeds with Red-necked Stints. Flocks in flight are compact, wheeling and turning and then spreading out to alight. Individual flight is fast but easy.

Where to see it Mostly on tidal flats. Best place is the Cairns Esplanade.

BROAD-BILLED SANDPIPER *Limicola falcinellus*

Status A non-breeding summer visitor from the Northern Hemisphere Aug.–Apr. Rare along most of the coastline but usually present at the Cairns Esplanade.

Habits Usually seen singly, often feeding with other small shorebirds, e.g. Curlew Sandpiper and Red-necked Stint, where it can be easily overlooked. An active feeder, running rapidly. Feeds deliberately with a jabbing action of the bill, probing deeply into the mud, sometimes with its head under water.

Where to see it Best place is the Cairns Esplanade.

RUFF *Philomachus pugnax*

Status A rare non-breeding summer visitor from the Northern Hemisphere. Appears sometimes at the Cairns Esplanade. Other records from Hasties Swamp and Townsville.

Habits Usually seen singly. Feeds in a deliberate manner, probing and pecking at mud. The flight is strong with regular wingbeats and glides.

Where to see it The best chance is at Cairns Esplanade.

FAMILY ROSTRATULIDAE

PAINTED SNIPE *Rostratula benghalensis*

Status Rare. A visitor mostly to southern parts of the Wet Tropics generally north to about Ingham where breeding has been recorded. During winter 1994, nine birds were seen at a swamp at Mt Carbine over a period of three months.

Habits Mostly singly, sometimes in pairs and parties. Active through the night, resting by day under grass or in reeds. Skulks like a rail while feeding. Often freezes when disturbed.

Where to see it Best chance is freshwater swamps about Townsville and Ingham during the Wet, e.g. Blakey's Crossing.

FAMILY JACANIDAE

COMB-CRESTED JACANA *Irediparra gallinacea*

Status Common and widespread but erratic. Widespread movement, birds arriving at a suitable body of water (water-lily-covered), breeding, and departing when conditions become unsuitable.

Habits Spends its entire time on water-lily pads and other floating vegetation over which it walks with ease. Never ventures onto dry land. In flight the long legs and toes trail behind the body.

Where to see it On freshwater swamps and water-lilies or other floating vegetation. Easily located.

FAMILY BURHINIDAE

BUSH STONE-CURLEW *Burhinus grallarius*

Status Generally a common, widespread breeding species. Present throughout the year. Common on all offshore wooded islands. Common in some urban areas of Cairns and Townsville.

Habits Usually seen singly or in pairs, sometimes gathering into larger flocks. Shy. Rests by day on the ground under shady trees, relying on its cryptic plumage to escape detection. Feeds by night and often noisy.

Where to see it Not difficult to locate and observe. Best places are Cairns at Little Street Cemetery, Dunk and Magnetic islands and about Townsville.

BEACH STONE-CURLEW *Esacus neglectus*

Status Scarce. Pairs are well-dispersed along the coastline and about the islands. Present throughout the year and breeding.

Habits Usually seen singly or in pairs. A shy species, it runs or flies ahead of an observer. Flight is characterised by slow stiff wingbeats.

Where to see it Best areas are undisturbed beaches along the coast, e.g. about Mission Beach and the beach suburbs north of Cairns. Also on some islands such as Dunk or at the mouths of rivers and creeks.

FAMILY HAEMATOPODIDAE

PIED OYSTERCATCHER *Haematopus longirostris*

Status Common only about Townsville and farther south. Rare north of Townsville. Only one pair known from the Ingham area at Taylor's Beach. A pair occasionally visited the Cairns Esplanade 1991–93.

Habits Usually singly or in pairs, sometimes in small groups. Forages over sandy beaches and bars at low tide for molluscs which it locates by probing deeply with its bill. Flight is strong and direct and usually low to the sand or water. Has a loud piping call and is quite vocal.

Where to see it Best chance is on sandy beaches about Townsville.

SOOTY OYSTERCATCHER *Haematopus fuliginosus*

Status Rare on the mainland coast. Uncommon on offshore islands but present throughout the year and breeding.

Habits Similar to those of the Pied Oystercatcher with which it sometimes associates. Feeds mostly on mussels and limpets prised from rocks.

Where to see it On rocky coastlines of islands such as Frankland, Brook, Hinchinbrook, Magnetic.

FAMILY RECURVIROSTRIDAE

BLACK-WINGED STILT *Himantopus himantopus*

Status Common, widespread and nomadic. Mostly a dry season visitor to the Wet Tropics. Has appeared at the Cairns Esplanade. Limited breeding. Nests on sandbars in some larger rivers, e.g. Herbert.

Habits Usually seen singly, in pairs or small flocks wading in shallow water. Flight is rather slow with long legs trailing behind.

Where to see it About larger shallow freshwater lakes and swamps throughout the wetlands.

RED-NECKED AVOCET *Recurvirostra novaehollandiae*

Status An uncommon to rare nomadic visitor north to Cooktown. One breeding record — a pair nesting amongst Black-winged Stilts on the Herbert River Sept. 1978 (J. Young pers.comm.).

Habits Usually singly, in pairs or small flocks, sometimes with Black-winged Stilts. Wades in shallow water to feed, sweeping its bill from side to side or sometimes pecking at prey in clearer water. Flies with quick wingbeats and legs trailing.

Where to see it Can appear on any shallow swamp, e.g. Keatings Lagoon, Lake Tinaroo, Blakey's Crossing. Quite often saline areas, e.g. Giru.

FAMILY CHARADRIIDAE

PACIFIC GOLDEN PLOVER *Pluvialis fulva*

Status A common non-breeding summer visitor from the Northern Hemisphere to the coast and the Atherton Tableland Aug.–Apr. with some overwintering.

Habits Similar to those of the Grey Plover.

Where to see it On any extensive mudflat on the coastline. Easily seen at Cairns Esplanade and the turf farm at Edmonton.

GREY PLOVER *Pluvialis squatarola*
Status A non-breeding summer visitor from the Northern Hemisphere, present Sept.–Mar. Generally uncommon along the coastline. Rare on the Atherton Tableland.
Habits Usually seen singly or in small parties. Feeds mostly alone at low tide on sand and mudflats, but gathers with other shorebirds at resting points at high tide. Flight is swift and graceful.
Where to see it A chance anywhere along the coastline but the best area is Cairns Esplanade Sept.–Nov. when birds are moving southward.

LITTLE RINGED PLOVER *Charadrius dubius*
Status A vagrant to Australia from the Northern Hemisphere. First record for north-eastern Queensland Blakey's Crossing Feb. 1985 (Wieneke 1988). Another at Lake Tinaroo 1995 (G. Holmes pers.comm.).

RED-CAPPED PLOVER *Charadrius ruficapillus*
Status A common breeding species present throughout the year.
Habits Usually in pairs, sometimes small loose groups, occasionally forming flocks and frequently associating with other shorebirds. Runs quickly across sand or mud. Feeds on small insects taken from the surface.
Where to see it Present on most coastal beaches and sandflats.

DOUBLE-BANDED PLOVER *Charadrius bicinctus*
Status An uncommon to rare non-breeding winter visitor from late Apr.–Aug. Breeds in New Zealand, wintering on the Australian coast. In some years stragglers reach as far north as Cairns.
Habits Usually seen singly with other small shorebirds. Searches for insects along the shore and over damp ground. When feeding, it will stop abruptly and then suddenly run.
Where to see it The best chance is at Cairns Esplanade, but sometimes a chance on sandflats and estuaries farther south.

LESSER SAND PLOVER *Charadrius mongolus*
Status A common non-breeding summer visitor from the Northern Hemisphere Sept.–Apr. with some overwintering. Numbers build up during the inward passage Sept. and Oct. and again on the outward passage Mar. and Apr. when many birds are in full or partial breeding plumage.
Habits Usually seen singly or in small parties, but sometimes in large flocks. Feeds unobtrusively over wet sand or mud, running here and there to catch prey. Often associates with the Greater Sand Plover and gathers into flocks with other shorebirds when resting at high tide.
Where to see it On any extensive sandflat or mudflat, e.g. the Cairns Esplanade.

GREATER SAND PLOVER *Charadrius leschenaultii*
Status An uncommon to common non-breeding summer visitor from the Northern Hemisphere Aug.–May with some overwintering. Probably more common about Cairns Esplanade than elsewhere.
Habits Usually seen singly. Associates with other small shorebirds, especially the Lesser Sand Plover. Flight is swift and low, accompanied by trilling notes. Feeds unobtrusively over wet sand or mud.
Where to see it Usually on any extensive sand or mudflats.

ORIENTAL PLOVER *Charadrius veredus*
Status Scarce. A non-breeding summer visitor from the Northern Hemisphere to northern Australia, with small numbers reaching north-eastern Queensland annually.
Habits Usually seen in small flocks. Associates with pratincoles, rarely with other shorebirds. Has a graceful flight, strong but erratic.
Where to see it A chance on open plains, grassy aerodromes and tidal mudflats, moreso in the northern part of the Wet Tropics. The most reliable place is the turf farm at Edmonton. Has been recorded Lake Tinaroo, Cairns and Innisfail aerodrome.

BLACK-FRONTED DOTTEREL *Elseyornis melanops*
Status Common and widespread but numbers fluctuate. Numbers increase after the Wet. Present throughout the year and breeding. Sometimes visits the Cairns Esplanade through winter.
Habits Usually seen singly or in pairs. Runs rapidly across muddy and stony areas, feeding on insects and small aquatic life taken from the wet ground. Flight is rather easy, buoyant and undulating with jerky wingbeats.
Where to see it Fairly easily encountered about fresh water.

RED-KNEED DOTTEREL *Erythrogonys cinctus*
Status An uncommon, irregular but widespread dry season visitor over most of the Wet Tropics. Absent in some years. Records from Townsville are mostly Jan.–May.
Habits Usually occurs singly, sometimes as a loose group. Feeds in shallow water, probing into mud for insects. Runs quickly. Flight is fast, weaving back and forth low to the ground or water.
Where to see it A chance about muddy edges of any drying lake or swamp.

BANDED LAPWING *Vanellus tricolor*
Status Rare. Records from Mareeba, Atherton, Cairns, Ingham and Townsville. A breeding record from Ingham airport (J. Young pers.comm.). A small population Tinaroo Creek Road, Mareeba, Sept. 1996.
Habits Similar to those of the Masked Lapwing.
Where to see it A chance on any short-grassed area. Easily seen in southern Australia.

MASKED LAPWING *Vanellus miles*
Status Abundant and widespread. Indication of extensive movement, probably local, on the Atherton Tableland.
Habits Occurs in pairs, sometimes loose flocks. Walks with a hunched stance as it picks up insects from the ground. Often very noisy. The northern race *miles* is present throughout the Wet Tropics but intergrades with the race *novaehollandiae* in southern parts of the region.
Where to see it In all open short-grassed areas. One of the first birds encountered.

FAMILY GLAREOLIDAE

ORIENTAL PRATINCOLE *Glareola maldivarum*
Status Usually a rare, irregular non-breeding summer visitor to the Wet Tropics from the Northern Hemisphere, but larger numbers occur in some years, e.g. about Cairns in 1988 and 1992. A flock of 500 recorded from Dimbulah. Most records Nov.–Jan.
Habits Mostly occurs singly or in small flocks, sometimes associates with Australian Pratincole. Has a graceful flight and hawks flying insects. Nomadic while in Australia.
Where to see it Has been seen more regularly at the turf farm at Edmonton than elsewhere, but also worth looking for at the Innisfail aerodrome or Townsville Town Common.

AUSTRALIAN PRATINCOLE *Stiltia isabella*
Status Generally uncommon and erratic in most areas, but a common and usually regular visitor to the Atherton Tableland May--Jan. Breeding has been recorded from Innisfail, Ingham and Townsville. A species of the inland plains of Australia.
Habits Occurs singly or in pairs, but more commonly in small to large flocks. Spends much of its time on the ground. Near dusk, flocks hawk for flying insects, often quite high in the air. It is a graceful bird both on the wing and the ground. Has a sweet, whistling call.
Where to see it Always worth looking on any short-grassed areas, e.g. the turf farm at Edmonton, Innisfail aerodrome, Townsville Town Common. Also on bare fallowed farmland on the Atherton Tableland.

FAMILY LARIDAE

[JAEGER Sp. *Stercorarius* sp.
Status Both the Pomarine and Arctic Jaegers frequently winter to the Coral and Tasman seas from their Arctic breeding grounds. An immature dark-phased bird was present near the mouth of the Endeavour River for a week in Mar. 1991 (J. McLean pers.comm.).]

KELP GULL *Larus dominicanus*
Status A species with a circumpolar distribution which was unrecorded in Australia before 1939. It has since become established in south-eastern and south-western Australia. A vagrant to north-eastern Queensland. Several records from the Cairns Esplanade, Michaelmas Cay and Townsville.

SILVER GULL *Larus novaehollandiae*
Status Very common to abundant in marine and coastal areas in the south of the Wet Tropics where it is present throughout the year and breeding. Generally uncommon to rare north of Ingham. Breeding not recorded from Ingham (J. Young pers.comm.). Always a few about Cairns Esplanade. Small numbers about Cooktown. Usually small numbers about Lake Tinaroo. Large flocks recorded on the Atherton Tableland after cyclones. Common and breeding on some offshore islands.
Habits Occurs mostly in flocks, sometimes large. Scavenges human food scraps and often follows boats.
Where to see it Best places are about the Cairns Esplanade, Townsville and offshore islands. Conspicuous.

LAUGHING GULL *Larus atricilla*
Status A vagrant to Australia from the Northern Hemisphere. Breeds in southern North America, wintering southward into South America. Two birds at Cairns Esplanade remained for two years 1988–89.

FRANKLIN'S GULL *Larus pipixcan*
Status A vagrant to Australia from the Northern Hemisphere. Breeds in North America and winters along the west coast of South America. One record from Cairns Esplanade in 1989. Another from mid-Nov. 1993 — this bird later acquired full breeding plumage. Another record from Ross River, Townsville in late 1994.

GULL-BILLED TERN *Sterna nilotica*
Status A common visitor, but absent through the Wet. Very common about the Cairns Esplanade. Rare on the Atherton Tableland.
Habits Usually seen singly, in pairs or small groups. Searches for prey by hawking and skimming over the water, gliding swiftly down to take it from the surface. Seldom dives. Sometimes hawks out over nearby land for insects.
Where to see it Over coastal swamps and tidal flats. Usually easily located. Obvious at Cairns Esplanade.

CASPIAN TERN *Sterna caspia*
Status Generally present in small numbers throughout the year. Numbers decrease at Cooktown Nov.–Jan. No record of breeding in the Wet Tropics.
Habits Usually seen singly or in small loose groups. Patrols over open water, in search of prey. Flight easy with deliberate beating of wings. Plummets into the water on closed wings. Often rests with Gull-billed Terns.
Where to see it About coastal swamps and estuaries and the larger inland lakes. Usually fairly obvious.

LESSER CRESTED TERN *Sterna bengalensis*
Status Uncommon to common. More common about the islands of the Great Barrier Reef where it breeds. Present throughout the year. Occasionally about the Endeavour and Annan rivers, mainly Sept.–Apr. Small numbers visit the Cairns Esplanade between Sept. and Nov. Most Townsville records from Oct. and Nov. (A. Griffin pers.comm.).
Habits Similar to those of the Crested Tern. Associates freely with other terns.
Where to see it Moreso about offshore islands, but occasionally with other terns along the coastline. Often a few birds about Michaelmas Cay.

CRESTED TERN *Sterna bergii*
Status Common throughout the year and breeding. The most common tern.
Habits Singly, in pairs or flocks. Rests on coastal beaches, sandspits, inlets and reefs. Flight is graceful and leisurely. Feeds by flying back and forth over the water, bill pointing downwards, then plunging headlong to take small fish from the surface.
Where to see it Along the coast and offshore islands. Easily seen.

ROSEATE TERN *Sterna dougallii*
Status Uncommon to rare on the coast but fairly common and breeding about some of the islands of the Great Barrier Reef. Present throughout the year.
Habits Usually seen in flocks. Often associates with the Black-naped Tern. Has a very graceful flight with shallow wingbeats. Fishes with head down, occasionally dropping to the surface to take prey.
Where to see it About islands of the Great Barrier Reef such as Green, Barnard, Purtaboi, Dunk, Brook, and Michaelmas Cay.

BLACK-NAPED TERN *Sterna sumatrana*
Status Uncommon close to the coast but common about islands of the Great Barrier Reef. Present throughout the year and breeding.
Habits Mostly seen in small groups and sometimes with other terns, especially the Roseate. It flies with a distinctive short wingbeat, swooping to pick up prey from the surface of the water, sometimes submerging briefly. Flocks are usually noisy.
Where to see it About the islands of the Great Barrier Reef, e.g. Green, Barnard, Brook, Purtaboi, Dunk, and Michaelmas Cay.

COMMON TERN *Sterna hirundo*
Status An uncommon non-breeding summer visitor from the Northern Hemisphere Oct.–Apr. with some overwintering.
Habits Usually seen singly or in small groups, sometimes larger when migrating. Rests on mudflats, sandbars and jetties. Feeds on tidal flats and inshore waters. Flight is light and buoyant. Hovers and dips about 4–5 m above the water in search of prey which it either plunges to take or picks from the surface.
Where to see it About tidal mudflats and estuaries.

LITTLE TERN *Sterna albifrons*
Status A regular uncommon to common summer visitor Sept.–Apr. Breeding has been recorded from the mouth of the Daintree River and the Innisfail and Townsville areas.
Habits Usually in small loose flocks, sometimes larger. Flight is distinctive with deep rapid wingbeats as it flutters and hovers over water then plunges to take small fish.
Where to see it About inshore waters along the coastline and about the mouths of rivers, sometimes well upstream. Fairly easily seen.

FAIRY TERN *Sterna nereis*
Status Accidental. A few records from Cairns Esplanade, probably of the race *exsul* from New Caledonia. The few records seem to coincide with the passage of cyclones in the Coral Sea, e.g. several birds appeared Mar.–Apr. 1994 after cyclones off the north-eastern Queensland coast.

BRIDLED TERN *Sterna anaethetus*
Status A common oceanic tern about the islands of the Great Barrier Reef. Rare about the coast. More common than the Sooty Tern in the southern part of the Wet Tropics. Breeds on wooded and grassy islands.
Habits Will often hover over water, dipping down to pick up prey or plunging into the water to take small fish. Returns to islands to roost at night during the breeding season, but disperses far out to sea later in the year.
Where to see it Easily seen about the islands and along the Great Barrier Reef.

SOOTY TERN *Sterna fuscata*
Status Abundant oceanic species breeding on coral cays of the Great Barrier Reef, dispersing far out to sea after breeding. Rare in inshore waters. Generally more common than the Bridled Tern in the northern section of the Wet Tropics.
Habits Usually in flocks. Feeds by skimming small fish and crustaceans from the surface of the water. Does not dive into water as other terns do. Also feeds by night.
Where to see it About the Great Barrier Reef, Michaelmas Cay being the most noted area.

WHISKERED TERN *Chlidonias hybridus*
Status Generally common in suitable habitat, moreso during the Wet. Less common and often rare in the northern parts of the Wet Tropics. Widespread and nomadic. Limited breeding.
Habits Usually occurs singly or in small loose flocks. Flight is rather graceful as it flies back and forth over open water, sometimes dipping to the surface, sometimes hovering and circling. Occasionally will dive into the water to take prey.
Where to see it Over freshwater swamps. Easily observed.

WHITE-WINGED BLACK TERN *Chlidonias leucopterus*
Status A non-breeding summer visitor from the Northern Hemisphere Sept.–May. Locally moderately common at Cairns and Townsville. Rather rare elsewhere.
Habits Usually seen in groups resting on rocks, posts and sandspits. Feeds in groups, flying, wheeling and hovering low over the water, taking insects from the surface as well as from the air. Associates with the Whiskered Tern.
Where to see it About coastal lakes and swamps.

COMMON NODDY *Anous stolidus*
Status Abundant oceanic species about coral cays of the Great Barrier Reef. Present throughout the year. Rare inshore. Appears at the Cairns Esplanade only during rough weather.
Habits Usually seen in flocks. Feeds out to sea, roosting on islets and cays. Skims low over the waves, sometimes diving through the crests to take food from the surface of the water.
Where to see it In offshore waters. Michaelmas Cay is undoubtedly the best and easiest place. Sometimes seen about Green Island.

BLACK NODDY *Anous minutus*
Status A rare oceanic species in the Wet Tropics. More common farther north and south. Numerous at Rocky Islets (J. McLean pers.comm.). Breeds on a few islands off Cape York Peninsula, e.g. Wallace, Chapman and Quoin. A small breeding colony on Green Island some years ago constitutes the only breeding record for the region. A very common breeding species about the Capricorn and Bunker groups of islands in the southern Great Barrier Reef.
Habits Generally similar to those of the Common Noddy.
Where to see it Always a chance about the Great Barrier Reef. Can sometimes be seen at Michaelmas Cay and Green Island.

WHITE TERN *Gygis alba*
Status Accidental to the eastern Australian coast. Usually blown westward by cyclones and gales from the Pacific Ocean where it is a common breeding species. Single exhausted birds Ingham Feb. 1974; Mission Beach Apr. 1974; Tolga Dec. 1990.

FAMILY COLUMBIDAE

ROCK DOVE *Columba livia*
Status Introduced. Common in all cities and towns.

WHITE-HEADED PIGEON *Columba leucomela*
Status Scarce to moderately common. Locally common at Yungaburra and Malanda. Usually present throughout the year though numbers fluctuate. North nearly to Cooktown. Breeding.
Habits Usually seen singly, in pairs or small flocks. Has a deep double-note call which is often the first indication of its presence. A bird of the rainforest canopy, but will occasionally feed in lower trees and shrubbery and even on the ground on fallen fruits of introduced Camphor Laurel *Cinnamomum camphora*, e.g. at Yungaburra, Malanda and Atherton.
Where to see it Mostly in rainforest at higher altitudes, e.g. Mt Lewis and Paluma. The best place is about Yungaburra, especially during early morning and late afternoon.

SPOTTED TURTLE-DOVE *Streptopelia chinensis*
Status Introduced. Variable. Uncommon at Cooktown, common at Cairns. Resident throughout settled areas at Innisfail. Numbers increasing at Tully, a small population at Ingham. 'Died out' in Townsville (Wieneke 1988). Present about towns on the Atherton Tableland.

BROWN CUCKOO-DOVE *Macropygia amboinensis*
Status Scarce to very common and widespread. Numbers fluctuate but it is usually present throughout the year. Breeding.
Habits Usually seen singly or in pairs, sometimes flocks at a food source. Occasionally comes to the ground on gravelly paths and by roadsides. Often seen flying low across clearings with a strong but easy flight. Frequently feeds in shrubbery at the rainforest edge.
Where to see it Throughout rainforest or edges of rainforest at all altitudes. A fairly trusting species and easily approached.

EMERALD DOVE *Chalcophaps indica*
Status Common, locally nomadic. Present throughout the year and breeding.
Habits Mostly seen feeding on bare areas of the rainforest floor, such as walking tracks and roadways. When disturbed it rises with a loud whirr of the wings and flies rapidly away. Usually seen singly or in pairs.
Where to see it Throughout rainforest, often by roadways. Fairly easily encountered.

COMMON BRONZEWING *Phaps chalcoptera*
Status Rare in drier areas on the western edge of the Wet Tropics. A small population at Mt Carbine. Breeding. Appeared on Black Mountain Road during 1992.
Habits Usually seen singly or in pairs, sometimes gathering in larger numbers at a food source. It feeds on seed on the ground. When disturbed, flies off with a clatter of the wings. Flight is fast and direct.
Where to see it Always a chance in the Mts Carbine and Fox; Mareeba and Kaban areas.

FLOCK BRONZEWING *Phaps histrionica*
Status Vagrant. A record of three birds at Ingham Oct. 1991. Several records over the years from Townsville, including a flock of 50 at Toonpan south of Townsville Dec. 1994. A highly nomadic species of grassy plains, mostly of northern inland Australia.

CRESTED PIGEON *Ocyphaps lophotes*
Status Common in drier country on the south-western edges of the Wet Tropics about Mt Fox. Rare about Mt Carbine and Mareeba. Absent elsewhere. Breeding.
Habits Usually seen singly or in small flocks. When disturbed, flies off with a metallic whirr of the wings interspersed with glides. Upon alighting it tips its tail up. Mostly perches in dead trees, sometimes on powerlines. Feeds on the ground.

Where to see it Can sometimes be seen about Mt Carbine, Maryfarms and Mareeba. Best chance is about Mt Fox and Townsville. Common in inland Australia.

SQUATTER PIGEON *Geophaps scripta*
Status Common in the dry country along the western fringe of the Wet Tropics. Present throughout the year and breeding.
Habits Usually in small parties, sometimes in larger flocks. Spends much of its time on the ground. Feeds on seed. When alarmed it freezes or escapes by running. If pressed, it will burst up with a clatter of wings, flying off with a whirr interspersed with glides, only to settle again on the ground or limb of a tree.
Where to see it In dry woodland about Mts Carbine, Molloy and Fox; Mareeba, Hidden Valley, Hervey Range and Townsville.

DIAMOND DOVE *Geopelia cuneata*
Status A rare visitor. An inland bird which appears in dry periods, e.g. an irruption into the Wet Tropics region in 1986. Sometimes breeds when it arrives.
Habits Similar to those of the Peaceful Dove.
Where to see it The best chance is in the drier, open forest on the western edge of the Wet Tropics about Mt Carbine and Mareeba and on the western edge of the Atherton Tableland. Very occasionally about Townsville. Easily encountered in inland Australia.

PEACEFUL DOVE *Geopelia striata*
Status Abundant and widespread. Present throughout the year and breeding.
Habits Usually seen singly, in pairs or groups at a food source. Feeds on the ground and flushes with an audible beating of the wings. Has a distinctive habit of rising very steeply to overhead branches when flushed.
Where to see it Throughout open areas. One of the first birds encountered.

BAR-SHOULDERED DOVE *Geopelia humeralis*
Status Generally common and widespread. Abundant on Dunk Island. Breeding.
Habits Usually seen singly, in pairs or loose flocks. Feeds on seed on the ground. Flight is fast and direct.
Where to see it Throughout the Wet Tropics. Easily encountered. Often wary.

WONGA PIGEON *Leucosarcia melanoleuca*
Status Extinct. Records from late last century — status unknown. Sightings at Boar Pocket in the Danbulla area and Herbert River. Eggs collected at Cairns 1896 (Blakers *et al.* 1984).

WOMPOO FRUIT-DOVE *Ptilinopus magnificus*
Status A moderately common breeding species at all altitudes. Present throughout the year.
Habits Often feeds high in the rainforest canopy where it is difficult to see despite its bright colours. Its bubbly 'wompoo' call is often the only indication of its presence. Flight is swift and direct and nearly always below the canopy.
Where to see it Anywhere in rainforest.

SUPERB FRUIT-DOVE *Ptilinopus superbus*
Status A common breeding species, nomadic according to the abundance of fruit. Widespread, inhabiting rainforest at all altitudes. Status on the forested offshore islands varies, being absent or casual on some, and common on others, e.g. the islands off Ingham.
Habits Usually seen singly, in pairs, or small groups about a food source. It inhabits the upper foliage of the rainforest except when nesting when it will place its nest a few metres from the ground. Wary.
Where to see it Anywhere in the rainforest, but despite the brilliant colours of the male, it can be difficult to see. More often heard than seen. Regular sightings on some islands, e.g. Dunk, Hinchinbrook and Magnetic.

ROSE-CROWNED FRUIT-DOVE *Ptilinopus regina*

Status Moderately common but nomadic or migratory according to abundance of fruit. More common in the lowlands and on offshore islands. Rare on the Atherton Tableland.

Habits Similar to those of the Superb Fruit-Dove.

Where to see it The best places are on the offshore islands, e.g. Green, Fitzroy, Dunk, Brook, Hinchinbrook. Also about Mission Beach. Often difficult to see in the rainforest canopy.

PIED IMPERIAL-PIGEON *Ducula bicolor*

Status A moderately common to abundant breeding migrant, present Aug.–Apr., in coastal lowlands. Winters in New Guinea. Large numbers breed on various offshore islands with some birds breeding on the coast, mainly in mangroves. Breeds along the Cairns Esplanade and in mangroves beside Cairns airport. Breeding recorded at Abergowrie in Oct. 1992, 40 km up the Herbert River (J. Young pers.comm.).

Habits Usually seen in flocks, sometimes singly or small groups. It travels daily to and from the mainland where it feeds, to breeding colonies on offshore islands. Flight is fast and direct.

Where to see it Throughout lowland rainforest and on offshore islands. Easily seen, especially during late afternoon as flocks fly out to islands.

TOPKNOT PIGEON *Lopholaimus antarcticus*

Status Generally common but highly nomadic. Numbers can fluctuate greatly according to supply of rainforest fruit. Abundant in some years, almost absent in others. More common at higher altitudes but sometimes common at lower altitudes in winter.

Habits Usually in small to large flocks frequently seen high over the rainforest. This and the Pied Imperial-Pigeon are the only rainforest pigeons to consistently fly high above the canopy. Once feeding is finished, it will sometimes rest high in the open, dead top of a rainforest tree or nearby eucalypt.

Where to see it Mostly in upland rainforest, e.g. Mt Lewis, Atherton Tableland, Palmerston National Park, Paluma. Occasionally in lowland rainforest in winter, e.g. Cape Tribulation, Tully.

ORDER PSITTACIFORMES

FAMILY CACATUIDAE

RED-TAILED BLACK-COCKATOO *Calyptorhynchus banksii*

Status A moderately common nomadic species of the drier woodland on the western edge of the Wet Tropics and about Townsville. (Very common about Lakeland.) Usually moves to the drier parts of the coast in the non-breeding season, i.e. the late Dry. Breeding recorded in the Mts Carbine and Molloy areas to the west of the Great Dividing Range. Several pairs breeding about Ingham, June 1992 (J. Young pers.comm.).

Habits Usually in pairs or small groups, sometimes very large flocks. Feeds mostly on a variety of seed, especially eucalypts. The flight is slow with deep, slow wingbeats usually accompanied by its harsh, grating call.

Where to see it Can appear anywhere in open areas mostly to the west, e.g. Cooktown, Mts Carbine, Fox and Molloy; Julatten, Mareeba, Kaban, Townsville.

GALAH *Cacatua roseicapilla*

Status An inland bird which reaches the western edge of the Wet Tropics. Common about Mt Carbine. Uncommon on the Atherton Tableland. Occasional visitor to Ingham. Small numbers about Townsville. Absent from other areas.

Habits Usually in pairs or small flocks which are often noisy. Feeds on the ground. Has a habit of performing aerial acrobatics by hanging from telephone wires and the like by its bill and feet.

Where to see it Best places are about Mt Carbine and Maryfarms and outskirts of Townsville. Easily seen in inland Australia.

LITTLE CORELLA *Cacatua sanguinea*
Status A resident flock about Ross River, Townsville and another small flock about Mareeba. Uncommon visitor to Ingham and the western edge of the Atherton Tableland. Two birds at Cooktown Sept. 1993 (J. McLean pers. comm.).
Habits Usually seen in flocks which are often noisy. Feeds on the ground. Flight is swift and direct with individuals of a flock moving in unison.
Where to see it Best place is along the Ross River on south-eastern outskirts of Townsville. Easily seen in inland Australia.

SULPHUR-CRESTED COCKATOO *Cacatua galerita*
Status Abundant and widespread. Present throughout the year and breeding.
Habits Usually seen singly, in pairs or small flocks. Feeds on seeds of trees but sometimes feeds on the ground in open areas. Has a loud screeching call and is undoubtedly our noisiest bird.
Where to see it Throughout the Wet Tropics. Easily seen.

COCKATIEL *Nymphicus hollandicus*
Status Reaches the south-western region of the Wet Tropics north to Mt Garnet. Common south and west of Townsville. Vagrant to the drier western fringe of the Atherton Tableland. Eight birds at Mt Carbine Aug. 1996 (D. Richards pers.comm.).
Habits Usually occurs in pairs or small parties. Often perches very upright on a dead branch of a dead or living tree and can be difficult to see, its colours blending with the wood. It feeds mostly on the ground.
Where to see it West and south of Townsville, but common farther inland.

FAMILY PSITTACIDAE

RAINBOW LORIKEET *Trichoglossus haematodus*
Status Abundant, widespread and nomadic. Present throughout the year and breeding.
Habits Usually in small flocks, sometimes larger. Noisy and aggressive while feeding. Follows the blossoming of trees (mostly eucalypts) and also ripening of commercial fruits such as mangoes and lychees. Sometimes seen flying very high in the air as it moves to its feeding grounds. Flight is swift and direct.
Where to see it Throughout the Wet Tropics. Easily seen.

SCALY-BREASTED LORIKEET *Trichoglossus chlorolepidotus*
Status Common, widespread and nomadic. Present throughout the year and breeding.
Habits Similar to those of the Rainbow Lorikeet with which it often associates.
Where to see it Throughout open forest. Easily seen.

VARIED LORIKEET *Psitteuteles versicolor*
Status Vagrant. One record from Ingham in 1988 (J. Young pers.comm.). Another record from Lakeland. A species of tropical woodland from north and north-western Australia.

LITTLE LORIKEET *Glossopsitta pusilla*
Status Uncommon to common in eucalypt forest on the ranges. Very rare on the coastal plain.
Habits Follows the flowering of various tree species, mostly eucalypts. Usually in pairs or small flocks. Sometimes seen flying high as it moves to feeding areas, usually uttering a high-pitched 'zyt' in flight.
Where to see it In taller eucalypt forest on the ranges to the west, e.g. Kaban, Ravenshoe, Wallaman Falls, Paluma and Hervey Range.

DOUBLE-EYED FIG-PARROT *Cyclopsitta diophthalma*

Status Generally common from Ingham north. Rare at Paluma. Common at Wallaman Falls. Avoids more open forest on the coast in some areas but common in similar habitat in other areas, e.g. Cape Tribulation.
Habits A rather unobtrusive species. Quietly feeds on seeds of fruits, mostly figs. Often high in the rainforest canopy where it is difficult to locate. Flight is swift and direct just above and through the rainforest canopy.
Where to see it Throughout the rainforest, especially where native figs are plentiful. Also in paperbark forest where it often breeds from Aug. Birds are sighted regularly about Cape Tribulation, Daintree, Mossman, Palm Cove, Centenary Lakes, Palmerston National Park, Lacey Creek State Forest Park and Wallaman Falls.

AUSTRALIAN KING-PARROT *Alisterus scapularis*

Status Scarce to common in most upland areas. Uncommon at Mt Lewis and Paluma. Extends northward nearly to Cooktown. Breeds in rainforest and adjacent eucalypt forest. Some altitudinal migration in winter, birds appearing in some areas at the foot of the Great Dividing Range, e.g. Mossman Gorge, and the Seaview Range west of Ingham.
Habits Usually seen in pairs or small flocks with the green-headed females and juveniles predominating. It feeds mostly on seeds in the foliage of trees. Flight is fast with strong wingbeats.
Where to see it Best places are in upland rainforest, e.g. Lakes Eacham and Barrine, Kirrama State Forest, Wallaman Falls.

RED-WINGED PARROT *Aprosmictus erythropterus*

Status Moderately common and widespread. Common about Mts Molloy and Carbine. Common to the coast about Ingham. Absent from the wetter coastal strip north of Ingham. Scarce about Townsville where it is a dry season visitor May–Sept. Numbers fluctuate in most areas. Breeding.
Habits Usually seen singly or in pairs, sometimes small flocks. Flight is distinctive and somewhat erratic with deep wingbeats seemingly interspersed with brief pauses. Feeds on seed and fruits sometimes taken from the ground.
Where to see it In drier open forest about Cooktown, Mts Carbine and Molloy; Mareeba, Kaban and Ingham.

CRIMSON ROSELLA *Platycercus elegans*

Status Scarce to common resident in upland areas throughout the Wet Tropics. Scarce about Mt Lewis and Mts Windsor and Carbine tablelands.
Habits Feeds on seed and fruit in rainforest and adjacent eucalypts. Sometimes feeds on the ground in open areas. Mostly seen in pairs and small groups. Flight is undulating with a series of wingbeats then a pause on closed wings.
Where to see it In upland rainforest, e.g. Danbulla State Forest, Lake Eacham, The Crater, Ravenshoe State Forest, Wallaman Falls, Paluma.

PALE-HEADED ROSELLA *Platycercus adscitus*

Status Common and widespread in drier woodland. Present throughout the year and breeding. Generally absent from the coastal strip north from about Cardwell.
Habits Mostly seen in pairs, sometimes small groups. Flight is similar to that of other rosellas. Feeds on seeds taken on or close to the ground, but sometimes in foliage.
Where to see it In drier woodland about Helenvale, Mt Carbine, Atherton, Kaban, Ravenshoe, Ingham and Townsville.

BUDGERIGAR *Melopsittacus undulatus*

Status A rare, highly nomadic visitor in small numbers to the southern part of the Wet Tropics, usually appearing in dry years. A bird of inland Australia.
Habits A gregarious species, it is conspicuous when present, being both active and noisy. Flight is swift and direct. Feeds on grass seeds taken from the ground.
Where to see it Has occurred about Townsville and Ingham. More easily seen in inland Australia.

FAMILY CUCULIDAE

ORIENTAL CUCKOO *Cuculus saturatus*
Status A scarce to moderately common non-breeding summer visitor from the Northern Hemisphere Sept.–Mar./Apr. with some overwintering. Moderately common about Helenvale and Shiptons Flat.
Habits Usually a solitary bird but sometimes in pairs or small groups. Rather shy. Feeds on insects and caterpillars taken from foliage, sometimes from the ground.
Where to see it Can appear anywhere throughout eucalypt forest and open woodland, probably moreso about swampy areas. Sometimes in clearings in rainforest.

PALLID CUCKOO *Cuculus pallidus*
Status Generally rare over most of the Wet Tropics. Most are probably migratory; majority of records mid-autumn to late winter. Several small breeding populations at Mt Molloy, Atherton Tableland and Ingham.
Habits Usually seen singly. Feeds on caterpillars and insects. The flight is fast, slightly undulating and rather hawk-like. Tail is often raised and lowered on alighting.
Where to see it Can appear anywhere in open forest, woodlands and open areas, e.g. farmland. Easily overlooked unless calling.

BRUSH CUCKOO *Cacomantis variolosus*
Status Common and widespread. Mostly spring and summer breeding visitor. A few birds through winter. Present throughout the year at Helenvale and Shiptons Flat.
Habits Usually solitary but sometimes seen in pairs. A calling bird can be difficult to locate as it sits almost motionless on an open branch where it will call for a lengthy period. Very vocal through the breeding season, interspersed with an occasional agitated, frenzied call. Sometimes calls through the night.
Where to see it In most forested habitats. Favoured areas are paperbark swamps where one of its hosts, the Brown-backed Honeyeater breeds.

CHESTNUT-BREASTED CUCKOO *Cacomantis castaneiventris*
Status Rare. Seems to be confined to rainforest from Cooktown to Bloomfield River, and in the vicinity of Mt Lewis and Julatten where small, probably resident populations exist. Several probable sightings from Yungaburra.
Habits Usually seen singly. Mostly in the mid and lower strata of rainforest. Rather unobtrusive. Similar in habits to the Fan-tailed Cuckoo.
Where to see it Rainforest at Mt Lewis. Sometimes about Kingfisher Park Birdwatchers Lodge. Vocal through spring. Can be difficult to locate if not calling.

FAN-TAILED CUCKOO *Cacomantis flabelliformis*
Status Uncommon to common. Rare about Townsville. Widespread. Breeding north to at least Tully. Appears to be a winter visitor only, in the north of the region, e.g. Mareeba, Cooktown. A race *athertoni* from north-eastern Queensland, described by Matthews in 1912, has never been accepted by modern taxonomists.
Habits Usually seen singly, sometimes in pairs. Vocal through the breeding season when it will sit with upright posture on an open branch and call for some time. Can be quite unobtrusive.
Where to see it Always a good chance in most forested areas. Can be easily seen in the lowlands at such places as Centenary Lakes.

BLACK-EARED CUCKOO   *Chrysococcyx osculans*
Status Rare visitor reaching mostly the south-western part of the Wet Tropics about Townsville and Mt Fox. Bravery (1970) recorded single birds in June of most years at Atherton. Some records from the north of the Wet Tropics appear to be misidentified juvenile Horsfield's Bronze-cuckoos.
Habits Usually seen singly. A quiet and unobtrusive species with a swift and slightly undulating flight. Often feeds in low vegetation.
Where to see it A slight chance about Townsville and Mt Fox. More easily seen in inland Australia.

HORSFIELD'S BRONZE-CUCKOO   *Chrysococcyx basalis*
Status Moderately common in most coastal areas and on the Atherton Tableland where it is present throughout the year and breeding. Less common about Cairns and northwards. Possibly only a passage migrant about Townsville.
Habits Usually seen singly or in pairs. Feeds on insects and caterpillars. Calls frequently when breeding but quiet and unobtrusive for the rest of the year.
Where to see it Throughout open forest. A good chance where its favourite hosts, Red-backed and Lovely Fairy-wrens and cisticolas occur.

SHINING BRONZE-CUCKOO   *Chrysococcyx lucidus*
Status Common in upland rainforest above 300 m. Present throughout the year and breeding. The Mountain Thornbill is its favourite host. Rare at lower altitudes where it is probably a passage migrant only.
Habits Usually seen singly or in pairs. During the spring breeding months males call frequently from a high, open or dead branch where they may remain for a lengthy period. Quiet and unobtrusive during the non-breeding season.
Where to see it Throughout upland rainforest, e.g. Mt Lewis, Atherton Tableland, Kirrama State Forest, Wallaman Falls and Paluma.

LITTLE BRONZE-CUCKOO*   *Chrysococcyx minutillus*
Status Moderately common, moreso in the drier inland parts of the region. Appears to be present throughout the year and breeding.
Habits Similar to those of other bronze-cuckoos.
Where to see it About the drier western areas, e.g. Mt Carbine, Mareeba, and west of Ingham.

GOULD'S BRONZE-CUCKOO*   *Chrysococcyx russatus*
Status Common throughout coastal lowlands. Present throughout the year and breeding.
Habits Similar to those of other bronze-cuckoos.
Where to see it Throughout coastal lowlands.

---

* Ford (1981) attempted to combine *minutillus* and *russatus* as forms of a single species. He also suggested there was considerable hybridisation between the two in north-eastern Queensland where their ranges overlap. However, an examination of skins reveals quite distinct features between the two, while observations in the field strengthen the view that both are distinct species which probably do not hybridise. There seems to be considerable variation in colouration in the larger *russatus*, especially in the degree of rufous on the breast and in the tail. The smaller white-breasted *minutillus* appears to show no variation with barring consistently narrower and closer together.

Russatus appears to inhabit a wetter, denser coastal habitat than *minutillus*, parasitising mostly Large-billed Gerygone; *minutillus* inhabits drier, open forest on the western section of the Wet Tropics region, parasitising mostly White-throated Gerygone as well as Fairy Gerygone in adjoining gallery forest. There is considerable difference in egg colouration (J. Young pers.comm.) — consistent with my observations — those of coastal birds are dark-chocolate while those of inland birds are paler with very fine blackish spotting or peppering. M. Goddard (pers.comm.) noted a difference in skin and down colour of newly-hatched chicks, those from coastal habitats being blackish while those of inland birds were flesh-coloured.

COMMON KOEL *Eudynamys scolopacea*

Status A common and widespread breeding species Sept.–Mar., wintering in Indonesia.

Habits One of the two birds known as 'stormbird'. It has a loud 'coo-ee' call which is heard both by day and night during the breeding season when storms are frequent. It is a shy species and spends much of its time skulking and feeding in thick foliage.

Where to see it Throughout most denser woodland and adjacent forest. Often in urban areas near fruiting trees.

CHANNEL-BILLED CUCKOO *Scythrops novaehollandiae*

Status A common and widespread breeding species, present Sept.–Mar. Winters in islands to the north of Australia.

Habits Occurs singly, in pairs or small flocks. Its call is a loud raucous note often heard during early morning. Sometimes called 'stormbird', its calls are obvious during spring and early summer when storms are frequent. During Mar. flocks of up to 30 birds are seen flying north on outward migration, mostly during late afternoon.

Where to see it Throughout the more open areas. Often not an easy bird to locate and observe. Visiting a fruiting tree such as a large fig, *Ficus* sp. close to where birds have been heard, is often successful. One of the best places is about Daintree River where there is a large spring/summer population and where, in most years, one or two birds overwinter.

FAMILY CENTROPODIDAE

PHEASANT COUCAL *Centropus phasianinus*

Status A common and widespread resident both in the lowlands and on the Atherton Tableland.

Habits Skulks through grass and other low cover. Flies laboriously and perches on fence posts, small dead trees and other low vantage points. Usually drops to the ground when approached, or if in a tree will hop higher and finally fly out the other side, gliding to the ground to escape. Becomes secretive during the non-breeding season.

Where to see it In most grassy habitats where the grass is long enough to provide cover. Easily seen in spring and summer, more difficult during the non-breeding season.

ORDER STRIGIFORMES

FAMILY STRIGIDAE

RUFOUS OWL *Ninox rufa*

Status Widespread. Probably moderately common in suitable habitat and probably more common than records indicate. J. Young has located 25 breeding pairs about Ingham and it seems to be present in a similar density about Mt Molloy and Julatten.

Habits A nocturnal species. Usually seen singly or in pairs, sometimes as a family party of three or four birds. Roosts unobtrusively by day in a moderately densely foliaged tree, sometimes holding the previous night's kill in its talons. Wary and will often vacate a daytime roost at the approach of an observer, well before one is aware of its presence.

Where to see it Most sightings are by chance. Elusive and difficult to locate, even when a territory is known. Extremely difficult to spotlight at night. During the non-breeding season, birds tend to use many roosts for a short time and may never return to them. During the breeding season, the male roosts close to the nesting tree. Local birdwatchers, guides and lodges sometimes know a regular roosting site.

BARKING OWL *Ninox connivens*
Status Scarce to common widespread resident. Very common about Ingham and the Atherton Tableland. Moderately common about Julatten and Mt Molloy. Scarce about Townsville.
Habits Nocturnal, roosting by day in thick foliage. Usually seen singly or in pairs, sometimes small family groups. It has a distinctive call, a rapid 'wok wok' like the yapping of a small dog. It will often answer this call if imitated. Often begins calling an hour or so before dark.
Where to see it Throughout the open woodlands. Unless a roosting site is known, can be difficult to locate. Can sometimes be flushed by day. Listening for the distinctive call at dusk and tracking it to its source is most successful.

SOUTHERN BOOBOOK *Ninox novaeseelandiae*
Status Represented in the Wet Tropics by two distinct forms. The race *boobook* of open forest and woodland is common about Ingham and Townsville but scarce in the north of the region, e.g. the Atherton Tableland, Mt Molloy, Julatten, Cairns and Innisfail. The smaller and darker race *lurida* appears to be common in some areas of upland rainforest, usually above 400 m, e.g. Mt Lewis. There appears to be no hybridisation between the two forms each inhabiting distinct habitats. Further research may prove *lurida* to be a distinct species.
Habits A nocturnal species, it roosts by day in hollows and sometimes in dense foliage. Its familiar call 'boobook' or 'morepork' is sometimes uttered for long periods at night. Mostly seen singly, in pairs and sometimes small family groups.
Where to see it A possibility throughout the Wet Tropics in all habitats. Usually somewhat difficult to locate at night by spotlighting, though *lurida*, the smaller rainforest form, has proved less difficult. The larger open forest form is occasionally seen on fence posts in farming areas.

FAMILY TYTONIDAE

LESSER SOOTY OWL *Tyto multipunctata*
Status Common to abundant resident in rainforest from the vicinity of Cooktown to Paluma, at all altitudes. Endemic to the Wet Tropics.
Habits A nocturnal species roosting in hollows. Prey consists of rodents, small mammals, insects and birds, some of which are taken from the ground. Often hunts over clearings and tracks in the rainforest.
Where to see it Difficult to locate but worth looking for at night by spotlighting in any rainforest.

MASKED OWL *Tyto novaehollandiae*
Status Always considered a rare species, it was found to be moderately common about sugar-cane fields in some areas such as Ingham and Julatten. Over recent times numbers have plummeted. Poisoning of rodents in sugar-cane is suspected as the cause.
Habits A nocturnal species hunting over open grassland, farmland and especially sugar-cane fields. Sometimes hunts in heavier forest. Roosts by day in hollows.
Where to see it Very difficult without local knowledge. Spotlighting about sugar-cane fields may prove successful though this practice is often discouraged by local residents.

BARN OWL *Tyto alba*
Status Generally a common and widespread species, very common about Ingham. Numbers sometimes fluctuate according to food supply. Along with Masked and Grass Owls, numbers have plummeted in recent times.
Habits A nocturnal species, it hunts over open grassland and farmland. Sometimes sits on roadside fence posts or other vantage points, watching for prey. Roosts in hollows by day. If disturbed by day, it is instantly and ferociously mobbed by small birds.
Where to see it Throughout open, lightly timbered areas and farmland. A fairly easy species to spotlight at night. Usually allows a close approach.

GRASS OWL   *Tyto capensis*
Status Like the Masked Owl, which was considered a rare species, it was found to be moderately common in restricted habitat about sugar-cane fields, especially about Ingham. However, along with Masked and Barn Owls, numbers have plummeted in recent times.
Habits Nocturnal. Roosts and nests on the ground. Hunts for rodents over open grassy areas and about sugar-cane fields.
Where to see it Difficult to locate without local knowledge. Sometimes watching at dusk over grassy paddocks bordering sugar-cane can result in sightings.

ORDER CAPRIMULGIFORMES
FAMILY PODARGIDAE

TAWNY FROGMOUTH   *Podargus strigoides*
Status Uncommon to common widespread resident.
Habits Nocturnal. Sometimes seen sitting on posts by roads or flying across roadways.
Where to see it Throughout open forest areas, e.g. Mts Carbine and Fox; Atherton Tableland, Townsville. Sometimes unexpectedly flushed from daytime roost.

PAPUAN FROGMOUTH   *Podargus papuensis*
Status A moderately common and widespread resident, less common south of Ingham. Generally more common at lower altitudes but in reasonable numbers in some upland rainforests, e.g. Mt Lewis.
Habits Nocturnal. Usually seen singly, sometimes in pairs. Roosts in thick cover by day. Similar to the Tawny Frogmouth in habits.
Where to see it About rainforest or mangroves. Often difficult to locate by spotlighting, but along roads in upland rainforest can prove successful.

FAMILY CAPRIMULGIDAE

WHITE-THROATED NIGHTJAR   *Eurostopodus mystacalis*
Status Probably a migrating population through the Wet Tropics. Bravery (1970) recorded large numbers suddenly arriving at Atherton, staying a few months and disappearing. Wieneke (1988) considered it an uncommon passage migrant through Townsville. At Julatten, small numbers are seen only through winter. However, there is a large breeding population present in open woodland west of Ingham (J. Young pers.comm.).
Habits Nocturnal, it rests on the ground by day, usually amongst areas of shady leaf litter where the colour of its plumage blends perfectly. Will flush suddenly from under one's foot, fly a short distance and drop to the ground or perch on a low branch. When hawking insects at dusk, it flies with a peculiar, jerking flitting flight often low to the ground.
Where to see it Usually by spotlighting roads through open woodland during winter, and roads west of Ingham during spring and summer. Sometimes flushed by chance during the day.

SPOTTED NIGHTJAR   *Eurostopodus argus*
Status Reaches the dry western parts of the Wet Tropics where it is uncommon to rare. Breeding recorded. Probably some migration through the region by birds from southern Australia. Occurs at Julatten in small numbers through winter.
Habits Similar to those of the White-throated Nightjar.
Where to see it Spotlighting along roads through dry woodland in the Mts Carbine, Molloy and Fox, and Julatten, Herberton areas.

LARGE-TAILED NIGHTJAR   *Caprimulgus macrurus*
Status Generally a common and widespread breeding species throughout lowland areas. Less common on the Atherton Tableland and south of Ingham. A considerable breeding population in open woodland at Julatten, which appears to vacate the area during winter when it is replaced by White-throated and Spotted Nightjars.
Habits Similar to the White-throated Nightjar. Has a distinctive, loud monotonous call — a 'chop' repeated for long periods.
Where to see it Jourama Falls National Park at dusk is excellent. Also on some islands, e.g. Dunk. Spotlighting along roads through woodland in proximity of rainforested creeks, especially in the lowlands, is often productive.

FAMILY AEGOTHELIDAE

AUSTRALIAN OWLET-NIGHTJAR   *Aegotheles cristatus*
Status Generally moderately common and widespread, though less common in wetter habitats and sometimes absent. Present throughout the year and breeding.
Habits Nocturnal, it roosts by day in tree hollows, emerging at dusk to hunt for insects. Not often seen, but its double churring note is sometimes heard by day.
Where to see it Difficult to locate and difficult to spotlight by night. Sightings are often by chance when a bird flushes from a hollow by day. A possibility in open forest habitats at dusk when birds first emerge from daytime roosts.

ORDER APODIFORMES

FAMILY APODIDAE

WHITE-RUMPED SWIFTLET   *Collocalia spodiopygius*
Status Generally common and widespread, but less common over drier areas about Townsville. Present throughout the year and breeding.
Habits Spends its time on the wing hawking for insects. Has a leisurely flight, soaring and dipping and quickly changing direction, gliding on downswept wings.
Where to see it Throughout most of the Wet Tropics, especially over clearings. Fairly obvious and distinctive.

WHITE-THROATED NEEDLETAIL   *Hirundapus caudacutus*
Status A common to uncommon summer visitor Oct.–Mar./Apr. from the Northern Hemisphere. Uncommon about Townsville. Moderately common about Ingham and Innisfail. In some localities, e.g. Cairns and Atherton, it is common in passage but otherwise uncommon.
Habits Usually in small to large loose flocks. Often seen during unsettled weather hawking insects, sometimes low to the ground but normally high in the air. Often associates with the Fork-tailed Swift. Flight is swift but occasionally slow on fluttering wings.
Where to see it Moreso about the ranges, but can appear anywhere, often before a storm.

FORK-TAILED SWIFT   *Apus pacificus*
Status A non-breeding summer visitor from the Northern Hemisphere. Common in passage Oct.–Nov. and Feb.–Mar., less common Dec.–Jan. Less common than the White-throated Needletail in most areas. Somewhat irregular.
Habits Similar to those of the White-throated Needletail with which it often associates. It circles, turns and flutters in an easy style of flight, pursuing flying insects.
Where to see it Throughout the Wet Tropics.

HOUSE SWIFT *Apus affinis*

Status A rare summer visitor. Small numbers first recorded during late 1994 and again in early 1996 about Mossman, Cairns, Mt Molloy, Mareeba and Townsville. A flock of about 20 birds seen at Mt Molloy Jan.–Mar. 1996. Probably a regular visitor but until 1994, overlooked. A species of the Northern Hemisphere, ranging widely from southern Europe and Africa to south-eastern Asia.

Habits Similar to those of other swifts.

Where to see it Always worth checking flocks of needletails or swifts with which it sometimes associates.

ORDER CORACIIFORMES

FAMILY ALCEDINIDAE

AZURE KINGFISHER *Alcedo azurea*

Status A common resident. Less common at higher altitudes.

Habits Usually seen singly, either flying low and swiftly over the water, uttering a thin high single note, or perched on a low branch, flood debris or tree root over or beside the water. Dives into the water to take prey.

Where to see it Along freshwater streams in rainforest or about mangroves.

LITTLE KINGFISHER *Alcedo pusilla*

Status An uncommon to common breeding resident in its restricted habitat throughout the Wet Tropics. Single birds recorded from Hope Islands and Low Isles (J. McLean pers.comm.).

Habits Similar to those of the Azure Kingfisher.

Where to see it Mainly in mangroves and along rainforest streams in the lowlands. Some of the more reliable places are Cooper Creek, Daintree River, Centenary Lakes, Thomson Road, Hinchinbrook Channel and the Hull River.

FAMILY HALCYONIDAE

BUFF-BREASTED PARADISE-KINGFISHER *Tanysiptera sylvia*

Status Generally a common, widespread breeding species below 500 m but sometimes higher. Present Nov.–early Apr. Winters in New Guinea. A passage migrant through the Townsville area.

Habits Arrives on its breeding grounds overnight and soon becomes quite vocal as pairs re-establish territories. Preys on insects, lizards and frogs which are taken mostly from the ground.

Where to see it Throughout most lowland rainforest. Fairly easily located though sometimes wary.

LAUGHING KOOKABURRA *Dacelo novaeguineae*

Status A common widespread resident.

Habits Usually seen singly, in pairs or family parties. Birds congregate at daylight and dusk to perform a concert of 'laughter'. Mostly seen perched on a vantage point such as a dead branch or on powerlines where it may sit for a lengthy period watching the ground below for prey, occasionally pouncing down to take it.

Where to see it Throughout open, lightly timbered areas. Easily seen.

BLUE-WINGED KOOKABURRA *Dacelo leachii*

Status Uncommon or absent along northern coastal areas and about Cairns. Common about Cooktown and Townsville and the drier western areas. Abundant about Ingham.

Habits Similar to those of the Laughing Kookaburra with which it shares habitat. Sometimes less confiding than the Laughing Kookaburra. Has quite a startling call.

Where to see it In most open forest areas. Fairly easily seen.

[YELLOW-BILLED KINGFISHER *Syma torotoro*
A number of unconfirmed sightings in the Wet Tropics over recent years. It is doubtful if this sedentary species from northern Cape York Peninsula reaches the Wet Tropics region. Most reports have been at a time when juvenile Buff-breasted Paradise-Kingfishers are first on the wing (usually Feb.–Mar.). These may have been misidentified as Yellow-billed Kingfishers.]

FOREST KINGFISHER *Todiramphus macleayii*
Status Abundant and widespread. Resident.
Habits Usually seen singly or in pairs sitting quietly on a vantage point such as a dead branch, post or powerline, peering at the ground below for prey which it takes by pouncing on it. Similar in habits to other kingfishers.
Where to see it Throughout the Wet Tropics. Commonly seen on powerlines.

RED-BACKED KINGFISHER *Todiramphus pyrrhopygia*
Status An uncommon to common winter visitor, moreso to the drier areas in the west of the Wet Tropics but occasionally reaching the coast. Rare about Cooktown. Occasional and irregular to the Atherton Tableland. A single breeding record north of Mareeba (D. Magarry pers.comm.). One record from Dunk Island. Moderately common visitor about Ingham. Mostly a bird of dry inland Australia.
Habits Similar to those of the Forest Kingfisher. Perches readily on powerlines.
Where to see it Can occur in any open areas, moreso in drier localities. The most likely areas are Mt Carbine, Mareeba, Dimbulah and Ingham.

SACRED KINGFISHER *Todiramphus sanctus*
Status Generally uncommon but widespread. Mostly a passage migrant in the coastal lowlands, with some birds overwintering. Common about Cairns in winter but absent after Oct. Common winter visitor to Townsville. A substantial breeding population about Kaban and a small breeding population about Hasties Swamp. Sporadic breeding recorded from Atherton, Ravenshoe and Millaa Millaa.
Habits Similar to those of the Forest and Red-backed Kingfishers.
Where to see it In open forest and open areas, or on powerlines. During winter often seen on sandy beaches and about fringing mangroves. Kaban during spring and summer.

COLLARED KINGFISHER *Todiramphus chloris*
Status An uncommon to moderately common resident present throughout the year and breeding. Uncommon south of about Hinchinbrook. More common northward. Records from Hope Islands and Low Isles (J. McLean pers.comm.).
Habits Similar to those of Forest and Sacred Kingfishers. Call similar to that of the Sacred Kingfisher, but louder and slower.
Where to see it Usually fairly easily seen about the taller mangroves, but can be overlooked when not calling. Sometimes shows a preference for the zone where mangroves and paperbark swamps meet. Mangroves at the mouths of the major rivers offer the best chance. Can sometimes be seen in mangroves from Thomson Road and about Cooper Creek.

FAMILY MEROPIDAE

RAINBOW BEE-EATER *Merops ornatus*
Status A small scarce to common spring/summer breeding population, mostly in the south of the region, absent in the north. However, numbers increase greatly throughout the Wet Tropics with the arrival of a large wintering population from early autumn, with some flocks arriving as early as late Jan.
Habits Usually in pairs or small loose flocks. Sits on a vantage point from where it will fly out to take insects in mid-air. Flight is graceful, undulating and soaring. Occasionally flocks over rainforested hills. Breeds in tunnels dug into soft, sandy soil.
Where to see it Moreso throughout open and lightly forested areas. Conspicuous.

FAMILY CORACIIDAE

DOLLARBIRD *Eurystomus orientalis*
Status A common widespread breeding species arriving from its wintering grounds in New Guinea about late Sept. and departing Apr. and May.
Habits The first indication of its arrival in spring is its loud 'kak-kak-kak' notes. It perches conspicuously on high dead limbs from where it sallies forth to take insects. Most active during early morning and at dusk. Usually seen singly or in pairs.
Where to see it Throughout open and lightly timbered areas, especially about tall eucalypts. Conspicuous.

ORDER PASSERIFORMES

FAMILY PITTIDAE

NOISY PITTA *Pitta versicolor*
Status A scarce to moderately common breeding species. Less common at higher altitudes. Present on some rainforested islands throughout the year, e.g. Dunk (K. Uhlenhut pers.comm.). Movements little known, but seems to be absent from high altitude rainforest in winter.
Habits Lives on the rainforest floor, hopping over leaf litter and turning leaves aside with its bill as it searches for food. Usually seen singly or in pairs. Flight is fast and low over the ground. Occasionally perches in a tree, usually low to the ground, sometimes high. Has an upright stance and flicks its wings and tail when alarmed.
Where to see it A chance anywhere throughout the rainforest, but perhaps Goldsborough State Forest Park, Jourama Falls National Park, Mission Beach, Dunk Island and Murray Falls State Forest Park offer the best possibilities. Usually difficult to get a clear sighting.

FAMILY CLIMACTERIDAE

WHITE-THROATED TREECREEPER *Cormobates leucophaeus*
Status A common resident of upland rainforest and adjacent wet sclerophyll forest, usually above 500 m but sometimes down to 300 m, from Mt Amos to Paluma. The endemic race *minor* present in the Wet Tropics is smaller and darker than the White-throated Treecreeper of south-eastern Australia.
Habits Usually seen singly, sometimes in pairs working up tree trunks, probing cracks and crevices for insects and spiders. Once at the top of a tree it will swoop down to the base of a nearby tree to repeat the process. The call is a series of high-pitched piping notes.
Where to see it More easily located around the edges of rainforest and in fringing eucalypt forest. Fairly easily seen.

BROWN TREECREEPER *Climacteris picumnus*
Status Generally scarce in drier woodland on the western fringe of the Wet Tropics from Cooktown south to the ranges behind Townsville. Reaches the coast about Ingham where it is rare. The population in the Wet Tropics region belongs to the distinct smaller and darker race *melanota* which was once regarded as a distinct species — the Black Treecreeper.
Habits Usually singly or in pairs, sometimes small groups. It spends much of its time searching for food on tree trunks and limbs, sometimes on open ground. Flight consists of rapid stiff wing-beats and a glide. Utters a sharp staccato call which is often the first indication of its presence.
Where to see it In drier woodland, especially in Poplar Gum *Eucalyptus platyphylla* forest at Big Mitchell Creek, Kaban and Mt Fox.

FAMILY MALURIDAE

LOVELY FAIRY-WREN *Malurus amabilis*
Status Formerly regarded as a race of the Variegated Fairy-wren but now rightfully a distinct species. Uncommon, with the main population scattered throughout coastal areas. A small population about Mt Molloy and Julatten. A few records from the Atherton Tableland.
Habits Usually in family groups, sometimes pairs. It often feeds in undergrowth, sometimes in trees, foraging up to 10–15 m above the ground.
Where to see it A chance anywhere on the coastal strip. Rifle Creek Reserve is one of the better places.

RED-BACKED FAIRY-WREN *Malurus melanocephalus*
Status A common and widespread resident.
Habits Usually in family parties with one fully-plumaged male, sometimes more, feeding close to the ground. From time to time it will fly up to a vantage point above the grass.
Where to see it Throughout denser, grassy areas and open woodland. Easily located.

FAMILY PARDALOTIDAE

SPOTTED PARDALOTE *Pardalotus punctatus*
Status Generally locally common breeding species in wetter, open eucalypt forest, especially about areas of Flooded Gum *Eucalyptus grandis* and casuarina *Allocasuarina* spp. at higher altitudes. Some minor altitudinal movement in winter.
Habits A bird of upper foliage where it feeds on insects. Usually seen singly or in pairs. In the Wet Tropics, it breeds exclusively in knot holes in trees (J. Young pers.comm.).
Where to see it About stands of Flooded Gum and wet sclerophyll at higher altitudes, e.g. Atherton Tableland, Ravenshoe, Kirrama State Forest, Seaview Range, and west of Paluma.

RED-BROWED PARDALOTE *Pardalotus rubricatus*
Status Rare visitor, mostly restricted to the drier north-western section, south to Herberton. One record from Townsville (Lavery and Hopkins 1963).
Habits Similar to those of other pardalotes.
Where to see it A remote chance in dry, open forest about Mts Carbine and Molloy; Herberton. More easily seen in inland Australia.

STRIATED PARDALOTE *Pardalotus striatus*
Status A common and widespread breeding species at most altitudes in suitable habitat, but rare or absent from wetter coastal areas from Innisfail northward. The black-headed race *melanocephalus* inhabits the Wet Tropics.
Habits Similar to those of the Spotted Pardalote.
Where to see it Throughout open woodland and eucalypt forest, moreso in western and southern parts of the region.

FERNWREN *Oreoscopus gutturalis*
Status A common resident usually above 600 m; sometimes down to 300 m from Mt Amos to Paluma. Endemic to the Wet Tropics.
Habits Quiet and unobtrusive, it lives on the rainforest floor. Usually seen singly, sometimes in pairs, it feeds amongst ferns and undergrowth. Moves about, almost mouse-like, sometimes elevating its tail. It has a distinctive series of high-pitched, long, drawn-out whistling notes as well as a harsh churring like that of a scrubwren.
Where to see it Throughout upland rainforest. Nearly always difficult to locate.

YELLOW-THROATED SCRUBWREN *Sericornis citreogularis*
Status A widespread, common resident of upland rainforest from Mt Amos to Mt Elliot.
Habits Usually seen singly or in pairs. It is an active bird, feeding on the rainforest floor or in low undergrowth. Fairly tame, it will scold when an observer approaches its nest — a large, blackish, debris-like structure suspended from foliage some 2 m or more above the rainforest floor.
Where to see it Throughout upland rainforest. Easily located.

WHITE-BROWED SCRUBWREN *Sericornis frontalis*
Status An uncommon to common resident in denser eucalypt forest and rainforest edges at higher altitudes. Very common about Ravenshoe and south to Tully Gorge, but less common farther south. Appears to be absent north of the Atherton Tableland.
Habits Spends most of its time on the ground, actively hopping through undergrowth, over logs and other debris. It is a fairly unwary species and will come close if an observer makes a squeaking sound. Usually seen singly or in pairs.
Where to see it Best chance is in southern areas of the Atherton Tableland, about Ravenshoe, especially along creeks in open forest close to rainforest where the two habitats meet.

ATHERTON SCRUBWREN *Sericornis keri*
Status Generally a moderately common resident in upland rainforest above 700 m. Endemic to the Wet Tropics. The main population inhabits an area from Mt Windsor Tableland and Thornton Peak, to the southern Atherton Tableland. However, it has been recorded close to the summit of Mt Finnigan (J. McLean pers.comm.) and on the Seaview Range. Recorded breeding at Kirrama State Forest and Paluma (J. Young pers.comm.).
Habits Inhabits mostly the rainforest floor, feeding low to the ground or in leaf litter, searching over logs and in low shrubbery.
Where to see it Most rainforested areas on the Atherton Tableland, e.g. The Crater. Mt Lewis is one of the best areas.

LARGE-BILLED SCRUBWREN *Sericornis magnirostris*
Status A common and widespread rainforest resident, moreso at lower altitudes, but common at higher altitudes where the Atherton Scrubwren is generally absent, e.g. Mt Spec.
Habits Usually in small parties, sometimes pairs searching for insects on tree trunks, in foliage and occasionally in ferns close to the ground.
Where to see it Easily located in rainforest at lower altitudes.

TROPICAL SCRUBWREN *Sericornis beccarii*
Status Moderately common. Reaches the far northern part of the Wet Tropics in the vicinity of Cooktown and Helenvale.
Habits Usually seen singly, in pairs or small parties. Searches for food in the mid and lower strata of the forest. Its calls are almost identical to those of the Large-billed Scrubwren.
Where to see it About Keatings Gap, Mt Cook National Park, Quarantine Bay Road.

WEEBILL *Smicrornis brevirostris*
Status A generally common resident in drier woodland on the western fringe of the Wet Tropics. Uncommon in the southern part of the region, e.g. west of Ingham and Townsville.
Habits Seen in pairs or small parties. Usually quite vocal and utters a loud 're-hoo'. Feeds at all strata in the outer foliage of trees.
Where to see it In drier woodland about Mts Carbine and Fox; Walkamin, Granite Gorge, Kaban.

BROWN GERYGONE   *Gerygone mouki*
Status A common to abundant, widespread resident of mostly upland rainforest above 250 m from Mt Amos south to Mt Elliot.
Habits Its call, a repeated twittering 'what-is-it' can be heard commonly in the rainforest through the breeding season Oct.–Jan. Fairly silent during the remainder of the year. Searches for insects mostly in the mid and lower strata, actively hovering and fluttering as it goes. Usually seen singly or in pairs.
Where to see it Throughout upland rainforest. Easily located.

MANGROVE GERYGONE   *Gerygone levigaster*
Status A common breeding species in the southern part of the Wet Tropics about Townsville. Rare about Ingham. Absent north of about Cardwell. The few records from northern parts of the region are doubtful and are probably misidentified juvenile Large-billed Gerygones, the species which commonly occupies the mangrove habitat north of Cardwell.
Habits Usually seen singly or in pairs. It searches vigorously for insects in the foliage and outer branches of mangroves at all levels. Will occasionally hover to take insects. Song is rich and sweet.
Where to see it In mangroves about Townsville.

WESTERN GERYGONE   *Gerygone fusca*
Status A rare visitor to drier areas west of Ingham.
Habits Similar to those of other gerygones. It has a rich and beautiful 'falling' song which ends abruptly.
Where to see it A possibility in the Mt Fox area. Common in inland parts of Australia.

LARGE-BILLED GERYGONE   *Gerygone magnirostris*
Status Generally a common resident throughout the lowland areas. A small population on the Mitchell River system about Mareeba, Mts Molloy and Carbine and on the Barron River about Kuranda.
Habits Usually seen singly or in pairs. It is an unobtrusive species as it searches for insects in foliage, sometimes hovering as it goes. The call is a succession of rising and falling notes uttered continually through the breeding season, but not as rich and sweet as calls of some other gerygones, e.g. Mangrove, Western and White-throated.
Where to see it Best areas are along streams lined with dense forest, but it can be seen in many other places, such as mangroves. Easily located.

FAIRY GERYGONE   *Gerygone palpebrosa*
Status A moderately common resident, mostly at lower altitudes. Moderately common in the upper Mitchell River system about Mts Molloy and Carbine. Uncommon about Townsville and the Atherton Tableland. Two races occur in the Wet tropics — the dark-faced *personata* north of about Innisfail and the pale-faced *flavida* to the south.
Habits Usually singly, in pairs or small parties. It quietly forages for insects in the outer foliage of trees and shrubs. Has a soft twittering call which is often the first indication of its presence.
Where to see it Throughout coastal rainforests and vine scrubs. Unobtrusive, but usually a squeaking sound will bring one or two birds into view.

WHITE-THROATED GERYGONE   *Gerygone olivacea*
Status Uncommon to common. A bird of drier forest, moreso on the western fringe of the Wet Tropics. Occasional about Cooktown. Common and breeding about Mt Carbine and Mareeba. Locally common and breeding on parts of the Atherton Tableland. A regular visitor to Ingham. An uncommon breeding species about Townsville with a small influx through winter.
Habits Similar to those of other gerygones. During the breeding season its beautiful song is a feature of the drier forest.
Where to see it Moreso in the drier forest on the western part of the region, but also about Ingham and Townsville. Usually seen while one is looking for other species.

MOUNTAIN THORNBILL *Acanthiza katherina*

Status A common rainforest resident from Mt Finnigan to Paluma above about 600 m, sometimes lower. Endemic to the Wet Tropics.

Habits Usually singly or in pairs. It forages amongst the mid and upper strata of rainforest. Birds persistently twitter as they move about. Has a flitting, undulating flight.

Where to see it Throughout upland rainforest. Easily seen.

BUFF-RUMPED THORNBILL *Acanthiza reguloides*

Status An uncommon resident of the drier western fringe of the Wet Tropics from the vicinity of Atherton south to Hervey Range. Absent elsewhere.

Habits It is an active species feeding in foliage and on the trunks and limbs of trees; sometimes on or near the ground. Usually seen in pairs, sometimes small parties. A vocal species, its twittering call is often the first indication of its presence. Flight is rather slow and bouncy. Often associates with the Yellow Thornbill.

Where to see it In drier open forest, especially where there are casuarina *Allocasuarina* spp. thickets. About Herberton, Ravenshoe, Kaban and Mt Fox.

YELLOW THORNBILL *Acanthiza nana*

Status An uncommon resident of the drier western fringe of the Wet Tropics from the vicinity of Herberton to Mt Fox. A rare breeding species about Ingham.

Habits Usually singly or in pairs, sometimes small groups foraging unobtrusively in the mid and upper strata of the forest. Call is a sharp, rather harsh clipped note. A very active species always on the move. Often associates with the Buff-rumped Thornbill.

Where to see it In drier open forest often where casuarina *Allocasuarina* spp. thickets or a densely-foliaged fine-leaved melaleuca *Melaleuca minutifolia* is present. Also in open forest and woodland. Best areas are about Herberton, Kaban and Mt Fox.

FAMILY MELIPHAGIDAE

SPINY-CHEEKED HONEYEATER *Acanthagenys rufogularis*

Status Vagrant to the drier southern parts of the Wet Tropics. Recorded Mt Fox and Townsville. A common species of inland Australia.

STRIPED HONEYEATER *Plectorhyncha lanceolata*

Status Vagrant to the drier southern parts of the Wet Tropics. Recorded Mt Fox and Townsville. A common species of south-eastern Australia.

HELMETED FRIARBIRD *Philemon buceroides*

Status A common coastal species from Cooktown to Townsville, present throughout the year and breeding. Rare on the Atherton Tableland.

Habits Seen singly, in pairs or small flocks. Feeds mostly high in foliage on nectar and insects. It is an active, noisy and aggressive bird.

Where to see it Throughout the eucalypt forest, woodland, gallery forest and mangroves. Often in urban areas. Easily seen.

SILVER-CROWNED FRIARBIRD *Philemon argenticeps*

Status A tropical species confined to the northern parts of the Wet Tropics. Moderately common about Cooktown, Helenvale and Shiptons Flat. A few records from Bloomfield. Generally absent southward though J. Young (pers. comm.) has a breeding record from Mt Carbine. Records farther south, e.g. Lake Tinaroo and Hervey Range need confirmation.

Habits Similar to those of other friarbirds and often associates with them. Sometimes hawks for flying insects.

Where to see it The best place is about Cooktown.

NOISY FRIARBIRD *Philemon corniculatus*
Status Common and widespread breeding species in the drier forests of the western part of the Wet Tropics and about Townsville. Present most of the year but highly nomadic, following flowering trees. Breeds commonly in the region. Generally absent from the wetter coastal areas but influxes occur spasmodically when birds will breed.
Habits Similar to other friarbirds. Follows flowering trees (mostly eucalypts) when it gathers in noisy flocks. Often quite aggressive both when feeding and breeding.
Where to see it In the drier forests to the west, e.g. Mts Carbine and Fox; Kaban, Ravenshoe, and Townsville.

LITTLE FRIARBIRD *Philemon citreogularis*
Status A common and widespread nomadic species following blossom, and breeding in spring when conditions are suitable. Mostly in drier areas on the western edge of the Wet Tropics, but occasionally irrupting to the wetter coast. However, abundant about Ingham and breeding. Uncommon about Townsville.
Habits Similar to those of other friarbirds and often associates with them. Sometimes hawks for flying insects.
Where to see it Moreso in the drier forests to the west, e.g. Mts Carbine and Fox; Kaban; west of Ravenshoe; west of Ingham. Easily located and observed.

BLUE-FACED HONEYEATER *Entomyzon cyanotis*
Status Common in the drier areas on the western fringe of the Wet Tropics from Cooktown to Townsville and about Ingham. Present throughout the year and breeding. Absent from the wetter coastal lowlands.
Habits Feeds in foliage or on limbs and trunks of trees by probing under the bark. It is a somewhat noisy bird, vigorous and inquisitive. Flight is fast and undulating. Usually seen singly, in pairs or small family groups.
Where to see it Throughout the drier western areas, e.g. Mts Carbine and Molloy; Mareeba, Kaban. Also about Ingham and Townsville. Easily seen.

NOISY MINER *Manorina melanocephala*
Status Generally uncommon. Confined to drier western areas in scattered resident colonies, e.g. Herberton, Kaban, Ravenshoe, Townsville. A large population at Mt Fox. Absent from wetter coastal lowlands.
Habits It is a bold and inquisitive species giving a piping alarm call when danger approaches. Obtains most of its food from branches and foliage of eucalypts. Usually in loose family parties.
Where to see it In drier eucalypt forest to the west.

YELLOW-THROATED MINER *Manorina flavigula*
Status Reaches the Wet Tropics only in the southern areas. Rare about Townsville but more common west of Mt Fox. Resident.
Habits Similar to those of the Noisy Miner.
Where to see it In dry ironbark and box woodland *Eucalyptus* spp. west of Townsville and Mt Fox.

MACLEAY'S HONEYEATER *Xanthotis macleayana*
Status A common, widespread resident in and about rainforest at all altitudes from Cooktown to Paluma. Endemic to the Wet Tropics.
Habits A quiet and unobtrusive species, it is seen singly or in pairs mostly in the mid and upper strata of the forest. Takes insects, nectar and fruit. Often seen searching vines and dead leaves.
Where to see it About rainforest and its edges. Easily seen. At Ivy Cottage, Paluma, birds mill around tables competing for crumbs and feeding from one's hand.

LEWIN'S HONEYEATER *Meliphaga lewinii*
Status Common. Resident in upland rainforest from Big Tableland to Paluma. Some altitudinal movement in winter, reaching some lowland areas, e.g. Daintree village. Moderately common about Julatten, and Mt Molloy in winter.
Habits A bold, lively bird and rather aggressive. Usually seen singly or in pairs. It is an active feeder, taking insects, nectar and fruit. Flight is strong and direct.
Where to see it In upland rainforest. Conspicuous.

YELLOW-SPOTTED HONEYEATER *Meliphaga notata*
Status A widespread common resident mostly in lowland rainforest below about 600 m.
Habits Similar to those of Lewin's Honeyeater.
Where to see it Throughout lowland rainforest and its fringes. Easily seen.

GRACEFUL HONEYEATER *Meliphaga gracilis*
Status A widespread common resident mostly in lowland rainforest below about 400 m occasionally to 500 m. Rare south of Ingham.
Habits Similar to those of the Yellow-spotted Honeyeater but less bold and aggressive.
Where to see it Throughout the lowlands. Easily seen.

BRIDLED HONEYEATER *Lichenostomus frenatus*
Status A common widespread rainforest species from Mt Amos to Paluma, mostly above 600 m. Endemic to the Wet Tropics. Some altitudinal movement in winter, e.g. Mossman, Julatten, Atherton township, Tully Gorge State Forest Park, Jourama Falls National Park. There is a substantial wintering population in mangroves at the mouth of Noah Creek near Cape Tribulation. At Mt Molloy birds follow gallery forest well out into dry tropical woodland through winter, reaching the Mitchell River. Also reaches dry areas about Mt Garnet in winter (G. Holmes pers.comm.).
Habits It is usually seen singly, in pairs or small loose groups feeding in the canopy and mid strata of rainforest. Takes insects, fruit and nectar. Has clear, bubbling, descending notes.
Where to see it Throughout upland rainforest. Conspicuous and easily seen. In winter, from the Maardja Boardwalk at Noah Creek and about Silky Oaks Lodge. Feeds from the hand in some areas, e.g. The Crater.

YELLOW-FACED HONEYEATER *Lichenostomus chrysops*
Status Generally common in open forest on the ranges and about the Atherton Tableland north to Mt Finnigan. A winter influx to the Atherton Tableland (Bravery 1970). Present throughout the year and breeding.
Habits Usually seen singly or in pairs. Spends much of its time searching the foliage of eucalypts for food. Has a cheery call.
Where to see it In open wetter eucalypt forest moreso on the ranges; Julatten, Kuranda, Ravenshoe, Kirrama State Forest, Seaview and Paluma ranges.

SINGING HONEYEATER *Lichenostomus virescens*
Status Vagrant to the Wet Tropics. A few records from the drier country about Mt Fox. (A small population about Hurricane Station 50 km west of Mt Carbine.) Common in inland Australia.

VARIED HONEYEATER *Lichenostomus versicolor*
Status Generally common in the northern parts of the Wet Tropics south to Cardwell where it meets and interbreeds with the Mangrove Honeyeater. Rare north of the Daintree River where there is a substantial population at the river mouth, but moderately common about Cooktown.
Habits Usually singly, in pairs or small parties. Feeds on insects and nectar and also among the lower roots and trunks of mangroves. It has a clear rollicking song. Flight is fast and undulating, often low to the ground or water.

Where to see it Throughout mangroves and adjacent forest north from Cardwell. Easily seen about the Cairns Esplanade and Yule Point.

MANGROVE HONEYEATER *Lichenostomus fasciogularis*
Status Common in the southern section of the Wet Tropics south of about Cardwell where it meets and interbreeds with the Varied Honeyeater. A large population about Lucinda.
Habits Similar to Varied Honeyeater.
Where to see it Throughout the coastal mangroves and adjacent forest south from Lucinda. Easily seen about Townsville.

WHITE-GAPED HONEYEATER *Lichenostomus unicolor*
Status Absent from most of the Wet Tropics, but common in some coastal areas about Townsville and Forrest Beach. Uncommon about Helenvale and Ingham. A small population on the McLeod River, north of Mt Carbine.
Habits Usually in pairs or small groups. It is noisy and aggressive, chasing others of its kind through the forest. Feeds on fruit and insects, sometimes nectar. Flight is fast but erratic and jerky.
Where to see it Best places are about coastal suburbs of Townsville and Forrest Beach. Has a preference for patches of trees surrounding isolated farmhouses.

YELLOW HONEYEATER *Lichenostomus flavus*
Status A common and widespread resident but absent from higher altitudes.
Habits Usually seen in pairs, sometimes singly. Active and constantly on the move, it feeds on nectar, insects and small fruit. The call is loud and cheery and the flight strong and undulating.
Where to see it Throughout tropical woodland, especially about farmhouses, city parks and gardens. Easily located.

GREY-FRONTED HONEYEATER *Lichenostomus plumulus*
Status Accidental. One record of a single bird from Ingham (J. Young pers.comm.). A bird of inland Australia.

FUSCOUS HONEYEATER *Lichenostomus fuscus*
Status Common resident, but restricted to scattered colonies on the Atherton Tableland, about Ingham (numerous colonies about Broadwater State Forest Park) and Hervey Range.
Habits Living in colonies, it is an active and aggressive bird, chattering almost continuously.
Where to see it In eucalypt forest and woodland about Kaban, Broadwater State Forest Park, Hervey Range.

[YELLOW-TINTED HONEYEATER *Lichenostomus flavescens*
Fuscous and Yellow-tinted Honeyeaters were previously regarded as races of the same species. More recent work has resulted in two species being recognised. When seen in the field, it is difficult to understand how the two could be lumped together. The Yellow-tinted Honeyeater shows a greater affinity with the White-plumed Honeyeater *Lichenostomus penicillatus* which it seems to replace in northern Australia.
Records of the Yellow-tinted Honeyeater from the Wet Tropics have proved to be misidentifications of the northern yellow-faced population of the Fuscous Honeyeater (Parker 1971) (Lavery 1974). The Yellow-tinted is essentially a bird of the Gulf of Carpentaria drainage where it is common, following rivers up to the Great Dividing Range but not crossing it.
The Yellow-tinted is **distinctly yellow with a prominent black ear plume over an indistinct yellow plume**. Habits closely resemble those of the White-plumed Honeyeater rather than those of the Fuscous. It is not gregarious whereas the Fuscous is. The Fuscous is **greyish with yellowish face, flight feathers and tail** and black ear plume over an **obvious** yellow plume.]

WHITE-PLUMED HONEYEATER *Lichenostomus penicillatus*
Status A common bird of inland Australia with small numbers reaching the drier southern parts of the Wet Tropics about Hervey Range. Also about Mt Fox where it is a rare visitor. Five breeding pairs located Mt Fox 1977 (J. Young pers.comm.).
Habits Usually occurs singly, in pairs or small groups. Feeds mainly in foliage where it takes insects, small fruits and nectar. Flight is fast and slightly undulating.
Where to see it Worth watching for if visiting Mt Fox or Hervey Range. Easily observed in inland Australia.

BLACK-CHINNED HONEYEATER *Melithreptus gularis*
Status Uncommon to rare, well-scattered, mostly in the drier western fringe. Probably nomadic but in some areas present locally most of the year. Breeding June–Aug. The olive-backed race *gularis* normally occurs in the Wet Tropics, but a record of a golden-backed bird at Abattoir Swamp Mar. 1994 possible hybrid with bright golden back and bright blue skin above eye.
Habits Singly, in pairs and small parties. It is an active bird feeding on insects taken from foliage, limbs and trunks of trees usually high above the ground. Has an attractive, bubbly call.
Where to see it In tropical woodland, especially where there are tall Blue Gum (Forest Red Gum) *Eucalyptus tereticornis*. Recorded from Julatten, Atherton, Kaban; west of Ingham and base of Hervey Range.

WHITE-THROATED HONEYEATER *Melithreptus albogularis*
Status A common widespread resident mostly at lower altitudes, but also common on the Atherton Tableland and west of the Paluma Range about Hidden Valley.
Habits It is an active bird, searching the upper foliage for insects, often hanging upside down in its quest. Similar in habits to the White-naped Honeyeater.
Where to see it In most eucalypt forest and woodland in the lowlands and on the Atherton Tableland. Easily seen.

WHITE-NAPED HONEYEATER *Melithreptus lunatus*
Status A locally common species which replaces the White-throated Honeyeater in eucalypt forest at higher altitudes. Occurs from Mt Carbine Tableland to Paluma.
Habits Seen singly, in pairs or small groups feeding through upper eucalypt foliage. Searches strips of hanging bark high in treetops. An active bird, it rarely comes down to lower levels.
Where to see it About eucalypt forest on the higher ranges, especially stands of Flooded Gum *Eucalyptus grandis*. Can be seen fairly easily about Atherton, Ravenshoe, Davies Creek National Park, Wallaman Falls and west of Paluma.

BROWN HONEYEATER *Lichmera indistincta*
Status Locally abundant, especially about the Atherton Tableland, Ingham and Townsville. Rare in the wetter coastal lowlands north of Ingham and about Cooktown. In small numbers locally about Cairns, e.g. in mangroves. Breeding. Highly nomadic.
Habits Usually seen singly or in pairs and often first noticed by its beautiful and cheery song heard throughout the day. It follows blossom, showing a preference for shrubby flowering plants such as bottlebrush (*Callistemon* and *Melaleuca* spp.) and mistletoe.
Where to see it Easily located in areas where it is more common. One of its favourite haunts is the border of mangrove forest and paperbark swamp.

WHITE-STREAKED HONEYEATER *Trichodere cockerelli*
Status A population about Cooktown reaches south to Shiptons Flat. Moderately common.
Habits Usually seen singly or in pairs. Searches for insects and nectar in low foliage and from limbs of trees and shrubs. Flight is fast and undulating. Has a variety of calls including a pleasant warbling song.
Where to see it About Cooktown and Shiptons Flat.

PAINTED HONEYEATER *Grantiella picta*
Status A rare, irregular visitor to the Atherton Tableland and Ingham.
Habits Usually seen singly or in pairs. Feeds on insects, nectar and fruits. Flight is swift and erratic. Has a loud, rich, double-note call.
Where to see it Sightings are by chance.

WHITE-CHEEKED HONEYEATER *Phylidonyris nigra*
Status Common in its restricted habitat, from Mt Windsor Tableland to Paluma. Resident, but probably locally nomadic, e.g. sometimes recorded at Julatten when blossom is present.
Habits Usually seen singly or in pairs, sometimes loose groups. Feeds on nectar and insects for which it will sometimes hawk in the air. During the breeding season in winter/spring, males perform a conspicuous territorial song flight, flying steeply up, calling, then dropping back to cover.
Where to see it About margins of rainforest at higher altitudes, especially about flowering banksias. Visits the garden at Ivy Cottage, Paluma. Also can be seen fairly easily at Mt Lewis, Davies Creek, Hasties Swamp and about gardens at Atherton.

BROWN-BACKED HONEYEATER *Ramsayornis modestus*
Status A common, widespread breeding species Aug.–May to paperbark swamps and mangroves in coastal lowlands. Rare over much of the Atherton Tableland but moderately common in paperbark swamps about Julatten. Most of the population is absent from the Wet Tropics between May and Aug., wintering in New Guinea. A small number, probably immature birds, winters locally in mangroves along the coast. Present most months at Cooktown.
Habits Usually in pairs or small flocks. Feeds on insects taken from foliage and under bark. Catches flying insects in short sallies. Also feeds on nectar, associating with other honeyeaters. Breeds in large, loose colonies.
Where to see it In paperbark swamps and mangroves about the lowlands. Easily seen at such places as Abattoir Swamp, Centenary Lakes, Dunk Island and suburbs of Townsville.

BAR-BREASTED HONEYEATER *Ramsayornis fasciatus*
Status Rare, occurring south to the Townsville area where there is a small population at Serpentine Lagoon. Two breeding records from Ingham (J. Young pers.comm.). Shows preference for paperbark swamps.
Habits Usually seen singly or in pairs. It is an active but quiet, inconspicuous species as it feeds through flowering trees at all levels. Usually nomadic, wandering in search of flowering plants, mainly eucalypts, melaleucas and grevilleas.
Where to see it Has been recorded from Cooktown, Mt Carbine, Rifle Creek, Rocky Creek, Ingham, Toolakea and Serpentine Lagoon.

RUFOUS-BANDED HONEYEATER *Conopophila albogularis*
Status Vagrant. One record from Forrest Beach (J. Young pers.comm.). A bird of coastal northern Australia.

RUFOUS-THROATED HONEYEATER *Conopophila rufogularis*
Status A common breeding species about Ingham. Uncommon about Townsville. Rare on the Atherton Tableland. Absent elsewhere.
Habits Usually in small groups or larger loose flocks. Feeds on nectar, but also takes insects, sometimes on the wing. Aggressive to its own kind when feeding. Often hovers to catch insects or to drink.
Where to see it Best place is at the Ross River Bush Garden on the southern outskirts of Townsville. Can be seen about Ingham, especially to the south, about Frances and Cattle creeks, in paperbark swamps, though these areas are difficult to access.

EASTERN SPINEBILL *Acanthorhynchus tenuirostris*
Status Generally common at higher altitudes from Mt Amos to Paluma. Resident.
Habits Usually seen singly, in pairs or sometimes larger loose groups when blossom is present.
It is a very active bird, flitting about with a distinctive sound of its wings as it flies.
Where to see it About most upland rainforest, e.g. Mt Lewis, Atherton Tableland, Kirrama
State Forest, Wallaman Falls, and Paluma. Easily located.

BANDED HONEYEATER *Certhionyx pectoralis*
Status An irregular visitor to the drier areas from Cooktown south to Ingham. Rare about
Townsville. Influxes occur in some years when it sometimes becomes abundant. Follows
flowering paperbarks and eucalypts, often breeding when conditions are suitable. Highly
nomadic, appearing suddenly and vanishing just as quickly.
Habits Feeds mostly on nectar, but sometimes takes insects caught on the wing in short flights.
Active and conspicuous. Appears singly, in pairs or in large loose flocks. Flight is jerky and
undulating.
Where to see it Always a possibility in drier areas where eucalypts and paperbarks are
flowering, e.g. Cooktown, Mts Carbine and Molloy; Julatten, Mareeba, Kaban and Ingham.

DUSKY HONEYEATER *Myzomela obscura*
Status A common and widespread species present throughout the year and breeding.
Habits Usually occurs singly or in pairs, sometimes small groups about a food source. It
inhabits the foliage of trees, feeding on nectar. Catches insects by darting into the air. Can be
quite pugnacious and aggressive while feeding. Flits rapidly throughout the foliage as it feeds.
Where to see it Throughout rainforest and other dense habitats, e.g. mangroves and coastal
scrubs, often about the edges. Easily located.

RED-HEADED HONEYEATER *Myzomela erythrocephala*
Status Extends southward from Cape York to vicinity of Princess Charlotte Bay. A small
isolated population in mangroves in Hinchinbrook Channel known through 1970s (J. Young
pers.comm.). Some unconfirmed reports in mangroves between Cairns and Ingham in recent
years.
Habits Usually seen singly or in pairs. Feeds about flowers and foliage, sometimes associating
with other species. It has a fast, slightly undulating flight.
Where to see it Always worth checking any small red-headed honeyeater in mangroves. Note
that the Scarlet Honeyeater sometimes occurs in mangroves.

SCARLET HONEYEATER *Myzomela sanguinolenta*
Status Generally a common, widespread nomadic species in most areas. Rare about Cooktown.
Follows trees in flower, breeding when conditions favourable. Sometimes may be absent for months.
Habits Mostly seen in larger loose flocks, sometimes in small groups, rarely singly. Brownish
females and immature males predominate. Very active and vocal, its beautiful song sounds like
the tinkling of small bells. It is often aggressive towards its own kind, chasing others through
and about the treetops.
Where to see it About flowering eucalypts and paperbarks and the tops of flowering rainforest
trees at all altitudes. Easily located by its sweet song.

CRIMSON CHAT *Epthianura tricolor*
Status Vagrant. Recorded Mt Fox 1978 (J. Young pers.comm.). A common nomadic bird of
inland Australia.

ORANGE CHAT *Epthianura aurifrons*
Status Vagrant. A flock of 21 birds at Blakey's Crossing, June 1985 (Wieneke 1988). A
common nomadic bird of inland Australia.

FAMILY PETROICIDAE

JACKY WINTER   *Microeca fascinans*
Status   A common resident in parts of the drier western fringe of the Wet Tropics, e.g. Kaban, Mt Fox. Uncommon about Townsville and the Atherton Tableland. Rare north of Mareeba. Absent from coastal areas north of Townsville.
Habits   Usually seen singly or in pairs. Flies into the air to take insects. Sometimes hovers close to the ground. Perches on stumps, fence posts and dead trees. Has a beautiful call usually uttered from a prominent perch such as the top of a dead tree.
Where to see it   In open sparsely timbered areas about the western fringe of the Wet Tropics.

LEMON-BELLIED FLYCATCHER   *Microeca flavigaster*
Status   Generally a common, widespread resident. Uncommon south of Ingham.
Habits   Rather inconspicuous. Usually seen singly or in pairs. It darts out to catch insects from a horizontal branch or amongst foliage. Has a sweet clear song.
Where to see it   Throughout most woodland and drier eucalypt forest. Fairly easily seen.

[YELLOW-LEGGED FLYCATCHER   *Microeca griseoceps*
Status   It seems likely that the Yellow-legged Flycatcher existed on the Atherton Tableland and nearby areas up until at least the 1960s and probably until the mid-1980s. There are persistent reports in the literature by competent observers from that time. Earlier, two specimens were supposedly taken — one since destroyed, the other with some doubt placed on the collecting locality.
P.A. Bourke and A.F. Austin (Bourke and Austin 1947) apparently frequently encountered it during an 18 months' residence on the Atherton Tableland 1943–45. S.R. White (1946) recorded it from the 'lower Barron River' and from 'jungle' to the north of Cairns and at Mossman during a 20 months' residence in north-eastern Queensland. J.A. Bravery (1970) described it as a 'rare resident in rainforest and wet sclerophyll' during a 20-year residence near Atherton. In Jan. 1967, B.J. Wallace (Noske and Sticklin 1979) watched a pair for four hours, 6 km north of Malanda. In most cases these observers mention the distinctive feeding habits which distinguish it from other similar species in rainforest/wet sclerophyll habitat. Bourke and Austin's report is especially convincing.
More recently, P. Nagle (1987), while banding 5 km south-east of Ravenshoe (probably about 1986), netted a bird with 'distinctly bright yellow legs, grey head and white throat, with lower bill lighter in colour than its upper bill', features 'which were not consistent with Pale-yellow Robins' which he had been netting.
The Yellow-legged Flycatcher is largely **arboreal, feeding actively in the manner of a flycatcher, foraging through branches and foliage and often taking insects on the wing.** Grey upperparts (especially on the head); pale-lemon underparts; whitish-grey throat; **bright yellow legs; dark horn upper mandible and cream to yellow lower mandible.]**

RED-CAPPED ROBIN   *Petroica goodenovii*
Status   Scarce. A regular visitor in small numbers to the south-western parts of the Wet Tropics in the vicinity of Mt Fox. Sometimes reaches Hervey Range.
Habits   Usually seen singly or in pairs. Most food, such as insects and spiders, is taken from the ground. Occasionally flicks its wings and tail as it sits watching for prey.
Where to see it   Worth watching for if in the vicinity of Mt Fox and Hervey Range, especially in winter. Easily seen in inland Australia.

HOODED ROBIN   *Melanodryas cucullata*
Status   A rare breeding species in the south-western parts of the Wet Tropics in the vicinity of Mt Fox.
Habits   Usually seen singly or in pairs. Spends much time on the ground searching for insects or sits on low perches such as stumps, watching for prey. Flight undulating.
Where to see it   West of Mt Fox, often in areas of dead trees. More common farther inland.

PALE-YELLOW ROBIN   *Tregellasia capito*
Status   A common widespread resident in rainforest at all altitudes from Mt Amos to Paluma.
Habits   Similar to those of the Eastern Yellow Robin.
Where to see it   Throughout rainforest. Despite being unobtrusive, it can be fairly easily located.

EASTERN YELLOW ROBIN   *Eopsaltria australis*

Status An uncommon to common resident, moreso at higher altitudes. Rare or absent in coastal areas.

Habits Mostly seen singly or in pairs. Has a habit of clinging sideways to a tree trunk, watching the ground below for prey. A tame and trusting bird.

Where to see it In tropical woodland and denser eucalypt forest in the ranges, e.g. about Atherton Tableland, Kaban, Black Mountain Road, Paluma, and Hervey Range.

MANGROVE ROBIN   *Eopsaltria pulverulenta*

Status Generally a common resident in its restricted habitat, but rare or absent about Cooktown and rare about Townsville. A major population in Hinchinbrook Channel.

Habits Usually seen in pairs, sometimes singly, or family groups. It is a trusting species, quietly flitting from perch to perch in the mid to lower strata of mangroves. Often drops down to the mud, hopping over the surface to take prey. Has a mournful double-note whistle.

Where to see it Only in dense, tall mangroves and often difficult because of the inaccessibility of its habitat. Some of the better places are beside the boat ramp at the end of Thomson Road, the boat ramp at Meunga Creek, along the mangrove-lined channel at Centenary Lakes and along some of the lower reaches of the larger rivers, e.g. Daintree. Birds will often respond to a squeaking sound.

WHITE-BROWED ROBIN   *Poecilodryas superciliosa*

Status Locally common resident but absent from many areas. Uncommon about Cooktown. Common about Ingham. Small populations are scattered about some of the drier areas, e.g. Townsville, Mt Molloy and Mareeba.

Habits Usually singly or in pairs. A quiet species, but active as it moves through the mid and lower strata of the forest. Has a jerky and rapid manner when feeding, frequently cocking its tail. Often takes prey from the ground. Sometimes takes insects on the wing.

Where to see it In gallery forest, e.g. Big Mitchell Creek, Emerald Creek Falls State Forest Park, Jourama Falls National Park, along creeks about Mareeba, Frances and Cattle creeks south of Ingham.

GREY-HEADED ROBIN   *Heteromyias albispecularis*

Status A common, widespread rainforest resident, mostly at altitudes above 400 m. Occasionally close to sea level, e.g. a large resident population at Broadwater State Forest Park. Some minor altitudinal movement in winter, e.g. Julatten, Cape Tribulation.

Habits Usually found singly or in pairs. It inhabits the lower stratum of rainforest, often perching sideways on a tree trunk and pouncing on prey below, or hopping for a short distance over the rainforest floor. It has a distinctive, piping call as well as other whistling notes.

Where to see it Easily seen in most upland rainforest, e.g. Mt Lewis, Atherton Tableland, Kirrama State Forest, Wallaman Falls and Paluma. The Crater is one of the best places.

FAMILY ORTHONYCHIDAE

CHOWCHILLA   *Orthonyx spaldingii*

Status A common resident of upland rainforest from Big Tableland to Paluma, but also present in some lowland areas, e.g. Tully Gorge State Forest Park, The Boulders, Lacey Creek State Forest Park and Cooper Creek. Endemic to the Wet Tropics.

Habits An active, ground-dwelling bird, it scratches in leaf litter for insects. During early morning, from dawn, its resonant, rapid, rhythmic calls are a feature of most upland rainforest. Runs across the rainforest floor, seldom flies. Usually in pairs or family groups.

Where to see it Throughout rainforest at higher altitudes. One of the best places is Mt Spec National Park and around Paluma township.

FAMILY POMATOSTOMIDAE

GREY-CROWNED BABBLER *Pomatostomus temporalis*
Status Generally a common resident in drier woodland on the western edge of the Wet Tropics. Uncommon about Townsville. Absent elsewhere.
Habits A lively bird, usually in small communal groups of up to a dozen individuals. The group bounces energetically over the ground, overturning objects and searching through leaf litter for food. Sometimes searches through trees and shrubs. At the approach of an observer, the birds become noisy and agitated.
Where to see it In drier forests about Mts Carbine and Fox, and Mareeba.

FAMILY CINCLOSOMATIDAE

EASTERN WHIPBIRD *Psophodes olivaceus*
Status A common breeding resident from Mt Amos to Mt Elliot mostly at higher altitudes, but in some places at low altitudes close to the coast, e.g. Mission Beach.
Habits A bird of the lower strata of the forest, it is often seen feeding in leaf litter on the forest floor and sometimes in vines and tangled vegetation up to 10 m above the ground. It moves quickly when surprised, bouncing and hopping through the undergrowth. Its whip-crack call is one of the unique sounds of the Australian bush.
Where to see it Throughout rainforest or tall eucalypt forest with undergrowth at higher altitudes. Though frequently heard, it can be difficult to observe. One of the best places is at Chambers Wildlife Rainforest Apartments.

FAMILY NEOSITTIDAE

VARIED SITTELLA *Daphoenositta chrysoptera*
Status Scarce to common resident in the drier western fringe of the Wet Tropics from Cooktown to the ranges behind Townsville. Common about Mt Fox and parts of the Atherton Tableland. The race *striata* inhabits the Wet Tropics region. However, J. Young has a record of the race *leucoptera* (White-winged Sittella) nesting near Mareeba, while Bravery (1970) recorded birds which he took to be this race from Walkamin in 1956 and 1959.
Habits Usually in pairs or small parties. When feeding, it works along and down the branches of trees (mostly eucalypts) Often clings to the underside of branches.
Where to see it Mostly in drier eucalypt forest, but sometimes in wet sclerophyll. Mts Carbine and Fox; Mareeba, Kaban.

FAMILY PACHYCEPHALIDAE

CRESTED SHRIKE-TIT *Falcunculus frontatus*
Status A rare to uncommon resident in the western fringe of the Wet Tropics, but moderately common about Kaban and Herberton.
Habits Mostly seen singly or in pairs. It tears bark from branches in its search for insects in the upper stratum of the forest. Flight is strong and direct as it swoops from tree to tree.
Where to see it Best areas are in open forest about Kaban and Herberton. Has also been recorded Hasties Swamp, Wongabel and Kirrama state forests, west of Ingham and west of Paluma. Easily overlooked, but can be located by its mournful whistle. Will respond to an imitation of its call.

GOLDEN WHISTLER *Pachycepala pectoralis*

Status A common breeding resident in rainforest usually above 300 m. Sometimes coastal in winter, e.g. Innisfail and Broadwater State Forest Park where fully-plumaged males have been recorded at this time.

Habits Usually seen singly, sometimes in pairs. Searches through foliage for food, sometimes with feeding flocks of other small birds. Apart from males becoming vocal through the breeding season, it is mostly an unobtrusive species.

Where to see it Throughout rainforest at higher altitudes, e.g. Mt Lewis, Atherton Tableland, Wallaman Falls, and Paluma. During the breeding season, males are easily located by their constant song.

MANGROVE GOLDEN WHISTLER *Pachycephala melanura*

Status A small resident population in Hinchinbrook Channel appears to be the only one in the Wet Tropics. A single record of a female on Dunk Island (K. Uhlenhut pers.comm.). A similar record from Innisfail (J. Young pers.comm.).

Habits Generally similar to those of the Golden Whistler. Feeds in the mid and lower strata of mangrove forest, but sometimes takes prey from the mud or debris.

Where to see it In mangroves of Hinchinbrook Channel, but access without a boat is difficult.

GREY WHISTLER *Pachycephala simplex*

Status Generally a common and widespread resident throughout lowland rainforest. Uncommon or rare over much of the Atherton Tableland and Paluma Range.

Habits Usually seen singly or in pairs. Feeds mostly in the mid and upper strata of rainforest, usually in a quiet manner, sometimes fluttering in outer foliage to take insects in the fashion of a flycatcher. However, quite vocal through the breeding season.

Where to see it Throughout lowland rainforest. Unobtrusive and can be passed over easily if one is unfamiliar with its call.

RUFOUS WHISTLER *Pachycephala rufiventris*

Status Common and widespread over much of the Wet Tropics, present throughout the year and breeding. An irregular winter visitor to Cooktown. Numbers increase about Townsville in winter with immature birds predominating.

Habits Usually seen singly, sometimes in pairs, sometimes larger loose groups. Males are quite vocal through the spring breeding months when their beautiful notes can be heard throughout the day. Responds to loud noises, e.g. thunder, hand-clapping.

Where to see it Easily seen throughout open forest and woodland.

LITTLE SHRIKE-THRUSH *Colluricincla megarhyncha*

Status Common resident at most altitudes, but generally absent from wetter upland rainforest especially in the northern parts of the Wet Tropics.

Habits Usually seen singly or in pairs. Searches for food in vines and on tree trunks, often high in the canopy, sometimes on the ground. Has a repertoire of many sweet clear notes.

Where to see it In most rainforest and scrubby areas at lower altitudes. Often one of the first birds encountered in these habitats.

BOWER'S SHRIKE-THRUSH *Colluricincla boweri*

Status A common, widespread resident of the upland rainforest from Mt Amos to Paluma. Appears to be some minor altitudinal movement in winter, birds appearing at lower levels, e.g. Julatten. Endemic to the Wet Tropics.

Habits Singly or in pairs, it is rather quiet and unobtrusive as it feeds mostly in the mid and lower strata of rainforest. One of its calls is a loud 'chuck'. Song is a series of loud, rich and varied notes. Feeds in masses of vines in undergrowth, on tree trunks and sometimes just below the canopy, sometimes on the ground.

Where to see it Rainforest at higher altitudes, e.g. Mt Lewis, Atherton Tableland, Kirrama State Forest, Wallaman Falls.

GREY SHRIKE-THRUSH *Colluricincla harmonica*
Status Occurs at all altitudes. Common at higher altitudes in the western part of the Wet Tropics, but rare in lower altitudes to the east. Resident, but may be some minor movement into lower altitudes in winter.
Habits Usually seen singly or in pairs feeding through the branches of trees or sometimes hopping over the ground. Has a beautiful rich voice which is heard at its best through the breeding season in spring.
Where to see it In eucalypt and casuarina *Allocasuarina* spp. forests on the ranges, e.g. Atherton, Mt Fox and Paluma.

FAMILY DICRURIDAE

YELLOW-BREASTED BOATBILL *Machaerirhynchus flaviventer*
Status Common to very common at lower altitudes, uncommon to rare at higher altitudes but moderately common at Paluma. Resident.
Habits Usually in pairs. It is an active feeder, working its way through foliage in the mid and upper strata of the rainforest. Also hawks flying insects. Has a soft trilling call.
Where to see it Rainforest at all altitudes, often at the edge of rainforest.

BLACK-FACED MONARCH *Monarcha melanopsis*
Status A common breeding species in rainforest at higher altitudes from Sept.–Mar./Apr. A passage migrant at lower altitudes. Winters in New Guinea, vacating the Wet Tropics region almost entirely at this time. The few winter records are probably stragglers from south-eastern Australia.
Habits Usually seen singly or in pairs. Its rather attractive call is a feature of the rainforest during the breeding season. It feeds amongst foliage and will take insects in mid-air.
Where to see it Throughout the rainforest.

BLACK-WINGED MONARCH *Monarcha frater*
Status A breeding visitor to rainforest farther north on Cape York Peninsula. Widespread in New Guinea where the Cape York population winters. One record of a single bird from Edmonton Jan. 1982 (Magarry 1983). Three records of single birds: Cooktown, Mar. 1991, Apr. and Nov. 1992 (J. McLean pers.comm.) and one of a single bird at Julatten Apr. 1993.
Habits Similar to those of the Black-faced Monarch.
Where to see it Worth checking all grey monarchs. The Black-winged Monarch apparently 'overshoots' when migrating to and from northern Cape York Peninsula.

SPECTACLED MONARCH *Monarcha trivirgatus*
Status A common breeding species in lowland rainforest where it is present throughout the year. Generally scarce in upland rainforest though a moderately common breeding species at Paluma. It vacates some upland rainforest in winter, e.g. Paluma and Mt Lewis, but is present throughout the year on the Atherton Tableland. Probably some migration through the region from south-eastern Australia A winter visitor only, to Magnetic Island.
Habits Usually seen singly or in pairs. Very active when feeding about foliage, often tumbling, hovering and performing other antics. Feeds mostly in the mid stratum of rainforest.
Where to see it Best areas are lowland rainforest. Easily encountered.

WHITE-EARED MONARCH *Monarcha leucotis*
Status Scarce to moderately common in lowland rainforest throughout the year from Cairns to Ingham. Breeding about Innisfail and Mission Beach (J. Young pers.comm.). Rare from Cooktown to Cairns and on the Atherton Tableland. Winter visitor to Dunk and Magnetic islands and about Townsville. Uncommon at Paluma with most records in June and July (A. Griffin pers.comm.). Common in winter about Ingham, especially in mangroves.

Habits A very active bird, fluttering amongst the outer foliage of rainforest to disturb insects. Often resembles a fantail in action when feeding. Usually seen singly or in pairs.
Where to see it Can appear anywhere throughout the lowland rainforests. Most reliable areas are Lacey Creek State Forest Park; about Tully, and on Dunk and Magnetic islands in winter.

PIED MONARCH *Arses kaupi*
Status A moderately common resident of lowland rainforest. Less common in upland rainforest, e.g. uncommon on Mt Lewis and the Atherton Tableland, rare at Paluma. Endemic to the Wet Tropics.
Habits Usually seen in pairs, sometimes singly. It has a specialised feeding habit resembling that of a treecreeper. Feeds mostly on tree trunks and branches and will flit rapidly over them to flush insects. Often holds its wings open and jerks its tail repeatedly downwards as it moves. Fans its tail and raises its collar in a slight frill.
Where to see it Throughout rainforest at lower altitudes. Rather unobtrusive. Will often appear while one is searching for other species.

BROAD-BILLED FLYCATCHER *Myiagra ruficollis*
Status A small resident population in mangroves about Hinchinbrook Channel; another about Victoria Creek near Ingham. Unconfirmed reports from Mossman to Mission Beach in recent years. An old specimen from Cooktown (Boles 1984).
Habits Usually seen singly or in pairs. Habits similar to those of the Leaden Flycatcher.
Where to see it About Victoria Creek and Hinchinbrook Channel both of which can only be accessed by boat.

LEADEN FLYCATCHER *Myiagra rubecula*
Status A moderately common to abundant widespread breeding species, but less common north of the Atherton Tableland. Numbers increase about Townsville in winter, but decline on the Atherton Tableland at the same time. The population from south-eastern Australia winters in north-eastern Queensland north to southern New Guinea.
Habits Usually seen in pairs, sometimes singly. Keeps mostly to the upper stratum of the forest. Catches insects in the air or in foliage.
Where to see it Throughout eucalypt forest and woodland.

SATIN FLYCATCHER *Myiagra cyanoleuca*
Status A rare passage migrant in spring and autumn, wintering in New Guinea. It is a breeding species of south-eastern Australia with a few scattered breeding records as far north as central Queensland. However, J. Young (pers.comm.) found several pairs breeding in the tops of rainforest trees on the western side of Paluma Range, where it is usually a passage migrant, Dec. 1982 and in 1984. The few winter records from the Wet Tropics are probably stragglers from southern Australia.
Habits Similar to those of the Leaden Flycatcher.
Where to see it Sightings in the Wet Tropics are purely by chance, mainly during Aug.–Sept. and Mar.–Apr.

SHINING FLYCATCHER *Myiagra alecto*
Status Generally common. Resident.
Habits Usually seen singly or in pairs. Catches flying insects by sallying out from a perch or forages through the maze of mangrove roots close to the mud, also taking small shellfish and crabs. Has a frog-like croaking call as well as several whistling notes.
Where to see it Throughout mangroves, adjacent forests or along rivers. Fairly easily encountered.

RESTLESS FLYCATCHER *Myiagra inquieta*

Status A somewhat rare, irregular but widespread visitor. Breeding has been recorded at Ingham. More common in drier woodland farther west of the Wet Tropics.

Habits Usually seen singly or in pairs. It is an active and restless bird, sallying out to catch insects. Will hover in a near vertical position with tail down, often close to the ground, to take insects and spiders from leaves and branches. Sometimes hovers against walls of buildings to take spiders. Utters an unusual grinding or churring note while hovering — hence the old name 'Scissors Grinder'.

Where to see it Usually by chance. Turns up while one is looking for other species. More common in south-eastern Australia.

MAGPIE-LARK *Grallina cyanoleuca*

Status A common and widespread bird in most open habitats. Breeding adults are usually resident throughout the year. Non-breeding birds sometimes gather into large nomadic flocks in winter.

Habits Spends much of its time on the ground, searching for food often about damp areas. Has a buoyant flight, slow and direct.

Where to see it Throughout the open areas and about urban areas. One of the first birds seen.

RUFOUS FANTAIL *Rhipidura rufifrons*

Status A moderately common breeding species in rainforest at higher altitudes south from the Atherton Tableland. Uncommon about Mts Windsor and Carbine tablelands and Mt Lewis. Generally absent from upland areas during autumn and winter, but common at this time at lower altitudes from Cooktown to Townsville, though rare between the Daintree and Bloomfield rivers. Populations of south-eastern Australia winter from the Wet Tropics region into New Guinea.

Habits A bird of the lower stratum of rainforest, often seen on or close to the ground with tail fanned. Very active with a quick, jerky flight. Usually singly or in pairs.

Where to see it Throughout upland rainforest in summer and in denser vegetation in the lowlands in winter. An obvious species, it is unwary, allowing a close approach.

GREY FANTAIL *Rhipidura fuliginosa*

Status A common, dark-coloured endemic race *keasti* is resident in upland rainforest above about 500 m. A paler migratory race *alisteri* (and perhaps *albiscapa*) from southern Australia winters north to Cooktown. Common throughout the open forest and woodlands at most altitudes at this time.

Habits Usually seen singly or in pairs. It is an extremely active bird performing some incredible aerial manoeuvres when catching insects in flight. It droops its wings frequently and fans its tail constantly.

Where to see it In upland rainforest throughout the year and in open forest in the lowlands in autumn and winter.

NORTHERN FANTAIL *Rhipidura rufiventris*

Status An uncommon to common resident throughout the lowland areas. Common about Ingham, generally uncommon on the Atherton Tableland and about Townsville. Rare north of the Daintree River but moderately common about Cooktown.

Habits Usually seen singly or in pairs feeding in the upper stratum of the forest, sallying out for flying insects from an exposed branch. It does not perform the tail-twitching or aerial antics of other fantails. Has a short, sweet, melodious song.

Where to see it Throughout eucalypt forest and woodland at lower altitudes. Unobtrusive but fairly easily located and observed.

WILLIE WAGTAIL *Rhipidura leucophrys*

Status A common widespread breeding species present throughout the year with an increase in numbers about Townsville in winter.
Habits It is a confiding bird usually seen singly or in pairs. Sits on low branches, stumps, posts, often on the ground and sometimes on the backs of farm animals, darting out in a twisting flight to take insects. Seems to be constantly on the move.
Where to see it Throughout open areas. One of the more obvious birds.

SPANGLED DRONGO *Dicrurus bracteatus*

Status A common widespread breeding species mostly at lower altitudes with smaller numbers reaching some upland areas, e.g. Atherton Tableland, Seaview Range and Paluma. There is considerable spring and autumn migration through the Wet Tropics and a large wintering population in some areas, e.g. Cape Tribulation, Ingham, Townsville.
Habits Usually seen singly or in pairs, or in flocks on migration. Sits on an open perch such as a thin horizontal branch and dashes out to catch insects. Call is a variety of harsh metallic notes.
Where to see it Throughout much of the Wet Tropics. Easily seen.

FAMILY CAMPEPHAGIDAE

BLACK-FACED CUCKOO-SHRIKE *Coracina novaehollandiae*

Status Common and widespread. Present throughout the year. Limited breeding. Numbers increase on the Atherton Tableland Apr.–Aug. with many immature birds present. Present about Cooktown Apr.–early Nov. only.
Habits Usually inhabits the canopy of eucalypt forest and woodland, working its way through the branches searching for insects. Undulating flight consists of several fast wingbeats and a glide on closed wings. Occurs singly or in pairs, sometimes in small flocks.
Where to see it Throughout the open forest and woodland, often about urban areas.

BARRED CUCKOO-SHRIKE *Coracina lineata*

Status Fairly common in both upland and lowland rainforest. Some populations appear to be migratory, e.g. those about Daintree and Mt Lewis where the birds appear through Oct. and Nov., breed and depart about Mar. and Apr. It is present throughout the year about Helenvale and Shiptons Flat, and the Atherton Tableland. Most likely that birds from southern Queensland winter in the Wet Tropics.
Habits Usually seen singly or in pairs though a number of birds may congregate at a fruiting tree. It is active, moving quickly through the canopy and over the rainforest.
Where to see it Fairly easily seen about rainforest on the Atherton Tableland, Kuranda, Kirrama State Forest, Wallaman Falls, and Paluma. More easily seen from roadways and open areas beside rainforest.

WHITE-BELLIED CUCKOO-SHRIKE *Coracina papuensis*

Status A common, widespread species, present throughout the year and breeding.
Habits Similar to those of the Black-faced Cuckoo-shrike.
Where to see it Throughout open forest and woodland, often about urban areas.

CICADABIRD *Coracina tenuirostris*

Status Two distinct populations are present in the Wet Tropics. A coastal population south to Ingham inhabits denser forest such as rainforest and mangroves at low altitudes; the other, open forest and tropical woodland to the west. There appears to be no overlap of the two populations. Both are common and both appear to be migratory. Calls are considerably different and distinctive. Both calls are faithfully reproduced on David Stewart's tapes, see p. 316.
Habits Usually seen singly. A bird of the upper foliage where it feeds on insects. The female is quite unobtrusive. Movements are quick and flight rapid and direct. Does not refold its wings as other cuckoo-shrikes do. It is a shy species, usually difficult to approach.
Where to see it In most open forest and woodland and throughout the coastal plain. The peculiar buzzing calls of the male usually alerts an observer.

GROUND CUCKOO-SHRIKE *Coracina maxima*

Status A rare visitor to the south-western section of the Wet Tropics and to the western edge of the Atherton Tableland.

Habits Usually seen in pairs, sometimes in family parties. It is a rather shy species, moving off as an observer approaches. Feeds mostly on the ground, walking and running back and forth. Perches on fence posts and in dead trees.

Where to see it Most records are from Hervey Range and west of Mt Fox. More easily seen in inland Australia.

WHITE-WINGED TRILLER *Lalage sueurii*

Status Scarce to moderately common. Uncommon about Mt Carbine but common in drier areas of the Atherton Tableland; moderately common about Ingham; uncommon about Townsville. Rare in coastal areas north of Ingham. Inclined to be erratic in occurrence and movements. Breeds when conditions are favourable.

Habits Usually unobtrusive, but the male is quite conspicuous when breeding, flying from tree to tree and calling loudly in courtship display. Feeds amongst foliage and on or close to the ground. Usually seen singly or in pairs.

Where to see it In drier open forest and woodland, especially small isolated patches of eucalypts.

VARIED TRILLER *Lalage leucomela*

Status Common and widespread, moreso at lower altitudes. Present throughout the year and breeding.

Habits Usually seen singly or in pairs. Moves through foliage in a quiet and unobtrusive manner. Tends to feed in the outer foliage of trees, sometimes high up, taking insects and sometimes small fruit. Often first noticed by its distinctive rolling trill call.

Where to see it In denser forested areas and rainforest. Not difficult to locate and observe.

FAMILY ORIOLIDAE

YELLOW ORIOLE *Oriolus flavocinctus*

Status A common resident of lowland rainforest, gallery forest and mangroves from Cooktown to Ingham. Rare south of Ingham. Scarce visitor to the Atherton Tableland.

Habits Usually seen singly or in pairs, sometimes small loose flocks. Feeds on fruit taken in the upper stratum of the forest and seldom leaves the shelter of the canopy. It is rather unobtrusive but during the spring breeding season its bubbly call is a feature of denser forests in coastal lowlands.

Where to see it The best areas are in gallery forest along streams and in mangroves. Fairly easily located and observed.

OLIVE-BACKED ORIOLE *Oriolus sagittatus*

Status Generally common, widespread and breeding. Less common on the Atherton Tableland (Bravery 1970). A common winter visitor to Dunk Island (K. Uhlenhut pers.comm.).

Habits Mostly seen singly or in pairs, its rollicking call is heard frequently through the breeding season in spring and summer. It inhabits the upper stratum of eucalypt forest. Flight is strong and undulating.

Where to see it Easily seen through eucalypt forest and tropical woodland.

FIGBIRD *Sphecotheres viridis*

Status A common to abundant, widespread breeding species, especially in lowland areas but also common on the Atherton Tableland. Present throughout the year. Moves from area to area according to availability of food. Two races occur, meeting about Townsville. Males of the southern race have olive-green breasts while males of the northern race have yellow breasts. Females of both races are similar. Interbreeding occurs where the two races meet resulting in much variation in breast colour of males, being mostly an unattractive shade between the two colours.

Habits Usually in loose flocks which are quite vocal. Brown birds with striated underparts (females and juveniles) outnumber fully-plumaged males. Very active with a swift flight. Feeds on rainforest fruit.

Where to see it   Mostly at lower altitudes wherever trees are fruiting. Easily located, especially in some towns were it feeds in fruiting trees lining roadways.

FAMILY ARTAMIDAE

WHITE-BREASTED WOODSWALLOW *Artamus leucorynchus*

Status Abundant. Mostly coastal. Less common on the Atherton Tableland.

Habits Occurs mostly in pairs and small groups often close to fresh or brackish water. Feeds in the air, catching insects with an easy soaring circling flight. Like other woodswallows, a number will often perch together in a group.

Where to see it On powerlines throughout the Wet Tropics.

MASKED WOODSWALLOW *Artamus personatus*

Status Rare. Erratic passage visitor in flocks of varying size to western areas of the Atherton Tableland and about Ingham and Townsville. Sightings more frequent in drier years. Flocks are usually on the move but may remain from several days to several weeks.

Habits Migrating flocks fly high in the air, accompanied by much calling. Will sometimes stay aloft for hours. Flocks often consist of both Masked and White-browed Woodswallows. Much of its food is taken in the air.

Where to see it Chance sightings only, in the Wet Tropics. Common in arid inland Australia.

WHITE-BROWED WOODSWALLOW *Artamus superciliosus*

Status Similar to the Masked Woodswallow with which it often associates.

Habits Similar to those of the Masked Woodswallow.

Where to see it Chance sightings only, in the Wet Tropics. Common in arid inland Australia.

BLACK-FACED WOODSWALLOW *Artamus cinereus*

Status Scarce to uncommon in drier open areas about the western edge of the Atherton Tableland. Absent in some years. Common and breeding about Ingham, uncommon about Townsville.

Habits Occurs singly, in pairs or small loose flocks. It perches on tops of fence posts, shrubs and on telephone wires, sallying out from a vantage point to catch insects in a graceful manner. Often hovers.

Where to see it In open, lightly-timbered areas. Best places are about Ingham and south-west of Townsville. Sometimes about Lake Mitchell. Very common in inland Australia.

DUSKY WOODSWALLOW *Artamus cyanopterus*

Status Scarce. Small resident populations about Kaban, Yungaburra and south-west of Townsville. Few records elsewhere.

Habits Usually in pairs, sometimes small loose groups. Similar to other woodswallows in habits. A number of birds will cluster together to roost at night.

Where to see it In open woodland, especially in areas with dead trees. About Kaban or the Yungaburra Cemetery provides the most likely chances. Common in south-eastern Australia.

LITTLE WOODSWALLOW *Artamus minor*

Status Rare. Occurs in small numbers in south-western parts of the Wet Tropics, e.g. Mt Fox where it is a regular visitor, Hervey Range and Hidden Valley. Only a few records elsewhere. A flock at McLeod River, north of Mt Carbine in June 1993.

Habits Similar to those of the Dusky Woodswallow.

Where to see it A chance sighting only, in the Wet Tropics, but worth watching for if visiting Mt Fox or Hervey Range. Best areas are drier open grassy woodland with standing dead trees.

BLACK BUTCHERBIRD *Cracticus quoyi*

Status Uncommon to common widespread resident of denser vegetation throughout the Wet Tropics. More common at lower altitudes. Less common on Atherton Tableland and uncommon about Townsville.

Habits Usually seen singly or in pairs, sometimes small family groups. Its loud clonking call can be heard within its dense habitat, mostly during early morning and late afternoon.

Where to see it Throughout most denser vegetation at lower altitudes. Sometimes shy and difficult to approach.

GREY BUTCHERBIRD *Cracticus torquatus*

Status An uncommon resident in drier open forest on the Atherton Tableland, north to Mts Molloy and Fox, and inland from Townsville.

Habits Usually seen in pairs or family groups. Takes prey mostly from the ground. Flight is fast and direct.

Where to see it In drier open woodland, often in the same area as the Noisy Miner. Best areas are between Kaban and Ravenshoe and inland from Townsville.

PIED BUTCHERBIRD *Cracticus nigrogularis*

Status A common resident in open forest about Mt Carbine, Ingham and Townsville. Scarce about farmland on the Atherton Tableland. Absent from the wetter coastal strip north from about Cardwell.

Habits Usually in pairs or family parties. Takes some of its food from the ground, but will pursue and catch small birds. Flight is strong and undulating. A pair of birds will often perch high in a dead tree in an open area and perform a beautiful duet.

Where to see it Conspicuous about Mt Carbine, Ingham and Townsville.

AUSTRALIAN MAGPIE *Gymnorhina tibicen*

Status A common resident about Mt Carbine and open areas on the Atherton Tableland. Uncommon about Ingham, moderately common about Townsville. Absent from wetter coastal areas north of Ingham. Small numbers between Cooktown and Lakeland.

Habits Usually seen singly, in pairs or small family groups. Flight is fast and direct. It is a tame and approachable species but aggressive towards other groups of magpies and some other species, such as Magpie-lark and birds of prey.

Where to see it Conspicuous throughout its range.

PIED CURRAWONG *Strepera graculina*

Status Common on the Atherton Tableland throughout the year. Uncommon in forested hills west of Ingham and Townsville, but common on Magnetic Island. Rare about Bloomfield. Winter visitor to Innisfail and Tully. Nomadic flocks sometimes occur in winter throughout its range with some altitudinal movement. A common winter visitor to Cooktown occurring in flocks numbering up to 60 birds.

Habits Often a noisy species especially when in flocks, though some of its notes are lovely ringing sounds. Feeds in the foliage of trees, sometimes on the ground, often feeding its own young on nestlings of smaller birds during the breeding season.

Where to see it Easily seen throughout its range, especially in upland areas.

FAMILY PARADISAEIDAE

VICTORIA'S RIFLEBIRD *Ptiloris victoriae*
Status A common rainforest resident at all altitudes from Mt Amos to Paluma. A bird of paradise, endemic to the Wet Tropics.
Habits Feeds in the mid and upper strata of rainforest. Sometimes searches tree trunks in a manner resembling that of a treecreeper. Probes cavities in branches, rotting tree trunks and limbs as it searches for insects. Also eats fruit. Flight is swift and direct, the wings of the male sounding like the rustle of taffeta. Call is a single harsh rasping note.
Where to see it Throughout the rainforest, e.g. Mt Lewis, Lakes Barrine and Eacham, Mission Beach, Paluma. Usually difficult to locate, but at Ivy Cottage, Paluma, birds will take food from one's hand.

[TRUMPET MANUCODE *Manucodia keraudrenii*
Sometimes recorded from the Wet Tropics region, but undoubtedly misidentified Spangled Drongos in moult or with abraded tails (*see* Frith 1994). A resident rainforest species of northern Cape York Peninsula.]

FAMILY CORVIDAE

AUSTRALIAN RAVEN *Corvus coronoides*
Status An uncommon, well-scattered resident of the southern part of the Wet Tropics, reaching north to Ingham in coastal areas and extending up the Herbert River to the vicinity of Mt Garnet. Absent north of Ingham and Mt Garnet. A common species of south-eastern Australia.
Habits Usually seen singly or in pairs. Flight is strong and direct. Call is very distinctive, like a loud wail.
Where to see it In open forest and open areas about Ingham and Townsville.

TORRESIAN CROW *Corvus orru*
Status A common resident about Mt Carbine, Ingham and Townsville. Scarce about farmland on the Atherton Tableland. Rare in the wetter coastal strip north from Ingham and generally absent north of about Edmonton. A few sightings from Daintree.
Habits Usually seen singly or in pairs but sometimes in large nomadic flocks. It is a wary but cheeky bird and a pair will sometimes establish itself about a farmhouse. Feeds mostly on the ground.
Where to see it Easily seen throughout its range.

FAMILY CORCORACIDAE

WHITE-WINGED CHOUGH *Corcorax melanorhamphos*
Status Uncommon. Reaches the south-western corner of the Wet Tropics in small numbers about Hervey Range.
Habits Lives in family groups of about 5–10 birds. Feeds on insects, spiders and sometimes seed on the ground. Becomes quite noisy if alarmed. Flight is rather slow with flapping, interspersed with short glides.
Where to see it A few scattered groups about Hervey Range. Very common in south-eastern Australia.

APOSTLEBIRD *Struthidea cinerea*
Status A common to rare resident of parts of dry woodland on the north-western and south-western edges of the Wet Tropics. Common about Mt Carbine.
Habits Mostly occurs in groups of 6–12 birds and feeds on the ground. Has a slow flight, usually low and direct with several wing beats and a glide. When disturbed, it leaps from

branch to branch, uttering harsh notes. A family group will sometimes establish itself about a farmhouse.

Where to see it Easily seen about Mts Carbine and Fox; Granite Gorge, Walkamin, and south-west and west of Townsville.

FAMILY PTILONORHYNCHIDAE

SPOTTED CATBIRD *Ailuroedus melanotis*
Status A common resident throughout the rainforest from Mt Amos to Paluma.
Habits Usually inhabits the mid and upper strata of rainforest. Often wary and will sometimes hop higher and higher into the canopy at the approach of an observer. Movements are quick. Sometimes several will gather in a fruiting tree, but mostly seen singly or in pairs. Has a distinctive, cat-like call.
Where to see it Throughout the rainforest. Fairly easily located, especially in spring and summer when its calls are frequently heard.

TOOTH-BILLED BOWERBIRD *Scenopoeetes dentirostris*
Status A common resident of upland rainforest above 600 m, sometimes lower in winter, e.g. Julatten. Ranges from Mts Amos to Elliot. Endemic to the Wet Tropics.
Habits Usually seen singly. During the breeding season Oct.–Jan. each male maintains a display court — a small, cleared area about 1 m in diameter on the rainforest floor. This he adorns with a dozen or more large freshly-picked green leaves turned upside down. His extensive, varied and remarkable repertoire can be heard throughout the rainforest at this time.
Where to see it Throughout the upland rainforest, e.g. Mt Lewis, Lakes Barrine and Eacham, Kirrama State Forest, Seaview Range and Paluma. Easily located during the breeding season when males are at their display courts. Elusive for the rest of the year when it remains high in the canopy.

GOLDEN BOWERBIRD *Prionodura newtoniana*
Status A common resident of upland rainforest above 900 m, sometimes as low as 700 m, from Mt Windsor Tableland and Thornton Peak to Paluma. Endemic to the Wet Tropics.
Habits Usually seen singly, it is an unobtrusive species feeding on fruit and occasionally insects. The male builds a large bower usually consisting of twin towers of sticks constructed around two close saplings. He will sit for hours on a nearby branch, occasionally preening and calling.
Where to see it The best place to see a male is about a bower usually Oct.–Jan. but sometimes throughout the year. Females are sometimes seen about bowers, but are also encountered through the rainforest. Local birdwatchers usually know the location of bowers.

SATIN BOWERBIRD *Ptilonorhynchus violaceus*
Status Rare to common resident of upland rainforest and its margins from Mt Lewis to Paluma. Common on Mts Carbine and Windsor tablelands, parts of the Atherton Tableland, Seaview Range and at Paluma. Rare on Mt Lewis. Possibly some altitudinal movement in winter.
Habits Usually seen singly, sometimes in small groups made up of females and immatures. Sometimes seen hopping over short, grassy areas close to rainforest. Feeds on rainforest fruits taken at all levels. Fully-plumaged males are mostly solitary and remain close to their bowers for most of the year.
Where to see it About the edges of upland rainforest and adjacent areas. Not difficult to locate. Best areas are the Atherton Tableland and about Paluma.

SPOTTED BOWERBIRD *Chlamydera maculata*
Status Vagrant. A few records from the dry south-western parts of the Wet Tropics about Mt Fox. A single bird at Paluma June 1993. A species of dry open woodland of central eastern Australia replaced in northern Australia by the Great Bowerbird.

GREAT BOWERBIRD *Chlamydera nuchalis*

Status A common widespread resident of drier woodlands from Cooktown to Townsville. Absent from wetter coastal areas.

Habits Usually solitary, sometimes in pairs or loose groups at a fruiting tree. Active and inquisitive. Flight is undulating, strong and direct. The male builds a large bower (usually partly concealed by low foliage) on the ground, and decorates it with snail shells and other objects.

Where to see it Throughout drier tropical woodland. Fairly easily seen about Cooktown, Mt Molloy, Mareeba, Granite Gorge and Townsville.

FAMILY ALAUDIDAE

SINGING BUSHLARK *Mirafra javanica*

Status Scarce to common. Fairly widespread, present throughout the year and breeding. More common in drier grassland, e.g. about Townsville. Moderately common about sugar-cane fields at Mossman, scarce in pasture at Daintree. Bravery (1970) reported it as very common on Atherton Tableland in pasture and crops until *Glycine javanica* (a pasture plant) was introduced, from which time it became scarcer.

Habits Spends its time on the ground where it lives on seeds and insects. During the breeding season, the male performs an aerial song flight high in the air on quivering wings, circling and flying back and forth accompanied by beautiful song, before suddenly dropping down to cover.

Where to see it Best places are in open grassland and crops, e.g. Blakey's Crossing, Forrest Beach, Atherton Tableland.

FAMILY MOTACILLIDAE

RICHARD'S PIPIT *Anthus novaeseelandiae*

Status An abundant widespread resident.

Habits Usually seen singly or in pairs feeding in open grassy areas or perched on fence posts or rocks, or in small dead trees. During spring it performs an undulating courtship display high in the air, flying up with wings quivering and tail elevated, then dipping down only to repeat the display.

Where to see it On most areas of shorter grass.

YELLOW WAGTAIL *Motacilla flava*

Status A rare but regular non-breeding summer visitor from the Northern Hemisphere, usually Nov.–Feb. Small numbers appear about Mossman, Cairns and Innisfail. A few records from Ingham and Townsville Town Common.

Habits Mostly seen singly. Spends much time on the ground where it takes insects, sometimes dashing into the air for them. Perches in small trees, on posts or stumps.

Where to see it Best places are the turf farm at Edmonton and Innisfail aerodrome.

GREY WAGTAIL *Motacilla cinerea*

Status A rare, non-breeding summer visitor from the Northern Hemisphere appearing Nov.–Mar. and recorded from Mt Lewis, Lake Tinaroo, Kauri Creek, Innisfail and Paluma. Probably more regular than records indicate because of the inaccessibility of much of the habitat it prefers.

Habits Seen singly. Similar in habits to the Yellow Wagtail.

Where to see it A chance at higher altitudes, especially close to water.

FAMILY PASSERIDAE

HOUSE SPARROW *Passer domesticus*

Status Introduced. First recorded at Innisfail Sept. 1964, Atherton Oct. 1965 and Townsville 1965. Now abundant in most cities and towns.

ZEBRA FINCH *Taeniopygia guttata*

Status Occurs sporadically about Ingham, and Townsville where it is resident in some urban areas. Irrupted into the Mareeba, Dimbulah areas in 1985, remained and bred for several years and eventually disappeared (J. Squire pers.comm.). Absent from other areas.

Habits Usually in pairs or flocks. It feeds on the ground, eating fallen seed or takes seed from grass heads by pulling them down. Flight is fast and direct.

Where to see it Blakey's Crossing is one of the most reliable places. Very common in inland Australia.

DOUBLE-BARRED FINCH *Taeniopygia bichenovii*

Status Generally uncommon to common and breeding. Fairly common about Townsville. Moderately common about Mareeba and Mt Molloy. Uncommon elsewhere. Rare about Cooktown but a common winter visitor to Annan River gorge.

Habits Usually in pairs or flocks. It feeds on the ground, eating fallen seed, but sometimes pulls grass heads down to pluck the seed. When disturbed it will fly to a nearby bush to take cover where it will hop about uttering a mournful squeaking call.

Where to see it In grassy woodland about Mt Molloy, Mareeba, Granite Gorge, Townsville Town Common. Fairly easily seen.

BLACK-THROATED FINCH *Poephila cincta*

Status Generally uncommon in dry country about Mt Molloy, Mareeba, the drier parts of the Atherton Tableland and west of Townsville. Small numbers about Cooktown. Rare about Ingham. The black-rumped race *atropygialis* inhabits areas about Mts Carbine and Molloy; Mareeba and Kaban and has been recorded from Ingham. The white-rumped race *cincta* occurs from Townsville southward.

Habits Spends much time feeding on grass seed on the ground and will often pull grass heads down to pluck the seed. Similar in habits to other finches.

Where to see it Can be difficult to locate. Best places are in dry open forest about Mts Molloy and Carbine; Mareeba and west of Townsville.

MASKED FINCH *Poephila personata*

Status Vagrant or aviary escapee. A breeding pair (white-eared race *leucotis*) on Cardwell Range 1975 (J. Young pers.comm.). This race inhabits Cape York Peninsula as far south as about Princess Charlotte Bay and inland to about Georgetown.

CRIMSON FINCH *Neochmia phaeton*

Status A common resident of coastal lowlands from Cairns to Ingham. Less common about Townsville. Absent north of Cairns but one record of a flock on Laura River west of Cooktown, Sept. 1989 (J. McLean pers.comm.).

Habits Usually seen singly, in pairs or small groups. It is an active bird and aggressive to its own kind. Feeds on seeds of grasses and herbs by climbing amongst the grass stems or taking them from the ground.

Where to see it In swampy areas where pandanus and paperbarks occur. Also about sugar-cane fields. Easily seen south of Cairns, Thomson Road, Cairns Crocodile Farm and about Innisfail, Tully and Ingham.

STAR FINCH *Neochmia ruficauda*

Status The eastern race *ruficauda* is apparently extinct in the Wet Tropics region. Last recorded at Cardwell in 1926 when it was not uncommon (Storr 1984). A small population still exists to the north about Lakefield National Park.

PLUM-HEADED FINCH *Neochmia modesta*

Status Rare. A nomadic and irregular visitor, usually in small numbers, sometimes larger flocks. Birds suddenly appear, remain for some time, occasionally breed and then disappear. Has been recorded from Mareeba, Atherton, Kuranda, Ingham and more occasionally about Townsville.

Habits Similar to those of other finches. Gregarious. Its flight is fast and slightly undulating. Usually unwary, allowing a close approach.

Where to see it The chance of a sighting is remote, but drier, lightly timbered habitat provides the best opportunity.

RED-BROWED FINCH *Neochmia temporalis*

Status A common to abundant species at all altitudes, but more common in higher areas. Present throughout the year and breeding.

Habits Usually seen singly or in pairs, but often in small flocks feeding on the ground amongst grass where it searches for seed. Flight is fast, direct, slightly undulating and often accompanied by a thin, high-pitched call.

Where to see it Margins of rainforest and adjacent grassy areas throughout most of the Wet Tropics.

NUTMEG MANNIKIN *Lonchura punctulata*

Status Introduced. Generally moderately common to common throughout most open grassy areas. Well-established in Townsville by 1951 and then spreading rapidly north and south. First recorded Apr. 1956 at Innisfail where it was common by 1965. Reached Cairns 1960; Cooktown 1961. First recorded at Atherton June 1964, common by 1969.

CHESTNUT-BREASTED MANNIKIN *Lonchura castaneothorax*

Status A common to abundant breeding species in most areas east of the Great Dividing Range. Present throughout the year, but probably nomadic. Uncommon about Townsville where it is mostly a dry season visitor.

Habits Usually in small flocks feeding on the seeds of grasses. Sometimes feeds on the ground. Call is a soft rather attractive bell-like note. Flight is fast, flocks twisting and turning in unison.

Where to see it Throughout taller grassland and about sugar-cane fields. An easy species to locate.

BLUE-FACED PARROT-FINCH *Erythrura trichroa*

Status A rare breeding species of upland rainforest from Helenvale to Wallaman Falls. A single breeding record from Seaview Range (J. Young pers.comm.). Little is known of its movements. On Mt Lewis, small flocks appear in grassy clearings, usually mid-Jan.–Apr., but sometimes as early as Oct. From late Apr. the entire population vanishes, though in some years an occasional juvenile remains. Present throughout the year with some movement about Shiptons Flat and Upper Annan River.

Habits Usually seen singly or in small groups. Lives on seed taken from most strata of the rainforest and from grass by roads and clearings. Often feeds with Red-browed Finches. Has a thin, high-pitched call which is often the only indication of its presence. Seems to be able to move through rainforest foliage without being detected. Wary.

Where to see it Elusive and difficult to locate. The best chance is by grassy roadsides and edges of clearings in rainforest when grasses are seeding. It is worth scanning feeding flocks of Red-browed Finches. When flushed, the red-brows fly off low to the ground while the parrot-finches often fly steeply up to foliage. The most reliable and accessible areas are Mt Lewis, Butchers Creek and Topaz.

GOULDIAN FINCH *Erythrura gouldiae*

Status Populations of Gouldian Finch have declined rapidly in recent decades throughout northern Australia. Before 1900 it was regularly reported from north-eastern Queensland as far south as Homestead, approximately 80 km south-west of Charters Towers (Smedley 1904). Reported as abundant about Innisfail in 1947 (Garnett 1992). Formerly occurred about Dimbulah, Clohesy River, Biboohra, Mareeba and Walkamin (Holmes 1995). Now probably extinct in the Wet Tropics region. Small populations remain about Hurricane Station to the north and Chillagoe to the west of the region.

Habits Usually in small flocks never far from water, visiting pools to drink through the day. Feeds on grass seeds taken from seeding heads or sometimes from the ground. During the Dry, sometimes seen feeding over recently-burnt areas.

Where to see it Always worth watching for in dry eucalypt woodlands on the western edge of the Wet Tropics, e.g. north and west of Mt Carbine, about Dimbulah and west to Chillagoe.

FAMILY NECTARINIIDAE

YELLOW-BELLIED SUNBIRD *Nectarinia jugularis*

Status A common widespread resident in lowlands. Generally absent from high altitudes but moderately common on parts of the Atherton Tableland. Present on some offshore islands.

Habits Usually seen singly or in pairs flitting and hovering about foliage. Feeds on nectar, insects and spiders. Often seen about houses and buildings where it commonly builds its nest under eaves and on verandahs and patios. Flight is direct and swift.

Where to see it Throughout coastal areas. An obvious species.

FAMILY DICAEIDAE

MISTLETOEBIRD *Dicaeum hirundinaceum*

Status Abundant and widespread at all altitudes. Present throughout the year and breeding.

Habits Usually keeps to the upper foliage. Flight is swift and direct, though occasionally erratic. Sometimes it will fly a long distance high in the air. Usually seen singly, sometimes in pairs. Its staple diet consists of mistletoe fruits.

Where to see it Throughout the Wet Tropics.

FAMILY HIRUNDINIDAE

WHITE-BACKED SWALLOW *Cheramoeca leucosternus*

Status A rare but regular winter visitor in small numbers (mostly pairs) about Ingham and Mt Fox. One record near Mareeba July 1986 (J. Squire pers.comm.). Another from Watsonville 1994.

Habits Similar to those of other swallows.

Where to see it A slight chance about Ingham during winter. Easily seen in inland Australia.

BARN SWALLOW *Hirundo rustica*

Status A regular non-breeding summer visitor in small numbers from the Northern Hemisphere from about Nov.–Mar. Mainly occurs regularly at several localities along the coast, especially about Mossman and Innisfail.

Habits Similar to the Welcome Swallow with which it often associates. Appears singly or in small numbers. Mostly seen resting on overhead powerlines.

Where to see it One of the best places is Newell Beach, north of Mossman. At Garradunga, birds perch on powerlines near the hotel. Worth checking swallows anywhere along the coast at this time of year.

PACIFIC SWALLOW *Hirundo pacifica*

Status A small population of the New Guinea race *frontalis* recently discovered between Daintree and Port Douglas. Appears to be present throughout the year though no breeding recorded.

Habits Similar to those of the Welcome Swallow with which it associates.

Where to see it On powerlines between Daintree and Port Douglas, especially about Newell Beach, north of Mossman. Difficult to distinguish with certainty from the Welcome.

WELCOME SWALLOW *Hirundo neoxena*

Status Generally abundant, widespread and present throughout the year and breeding. Less common in open areas at high altitudes. Scarce in coastal areas north of Daintree River. A considerable increase in numbers in coastal lowlands from Townsville to Daintree during autumn and winter.

Habits Usually seen hawking over open areas or sitting on powerlines. Often hawks low to the ground with an easy and graceful flight. Usually in loose flocks, sometimes singly or in pairs. Associates with other swallows and martins. Forms large communal roosts, e.g. at Babinda.

Where to see it In most areas, especially about cities and towns. One of the most common birds in north-eastern Queensland.

RED-RUMPED SWALLOW *Hirundo daurica*

Status A scarce non-breeding summer visitor from the northern hemisphere. First Australian record near Daintree (Squire 1984). Recorded with increasing regularity in other areas since then, e.g. Mossman, Garradunga, and Edmonton. Probably previously overlooked.

Habits Similar to those of the Welcome Swallow with which it often associates.

Where to see it Always worth scanning flocks of swallows and martins resting on powerlines during late spring and summer. One of the best places is Newell Beach, north of Mossman.

TREE MARTIN *Hirundo nigricans*

Status Generally common and widespread but present throughout the year. Nomadic and irregular in non-breeding season when numbers increase. A winter visitor to northern areas of the region. Rare in coastal areas north of Daintree River. Possibly migrates through Atherton Tableland (Bravery 1970). Breeding in southern areas.

Habits Spends most of its time sweeping and fluttering about the heads of large trees (usually eucalypts) or hawking for insects over open areas. Gathers in loose flocks with Fairy Martins and swallows.

Where to see it Over most open areas, often on powerlines.

FAIRY MARTIN *Hirundo ariel*

Status Generally common, widespread and present throughout the year. Large flocks have been recorded on the Atherton Tableland Jan.–Sept. where there is a small spring breeding population. Rare in coastal areas north of the Daintree River.

Habits Usually seen sitting on powerlines, hawking for insects or milling about culverts where it breeds. Associates with Tree Martins and swallows.

Where to see it Over most open areas, often on powerlines.

FAMILY SYLVIIDAE

CLAMOROUS REED-WARBLER *Acrocephalus stentoreus*

Status Scarce to moderately common, more common in the southern parts of the Wet Tropics. A small summer breeding population and a large wintering population at least as far north as Ingham and the Atherton Tableland. Scarce at all times north of the Atherton Tableland.

Habits When breeding, utters a beautiful rich song, but remains silent and secretive in the non-breeding season. Singly or in pairs. Usually remains well-concealed within its habitat.

Where to see it Always a possibility in most freshwater reedbeds and along some of the larger rivers, e.g. Herbert. Sometimes in sugar-cane in the lowlands.

ORIENTAL REED-WARBLER *Acrocephalus orientalis*
Status Probably a regular but rare, non-breeding summer visitor to the Wet Tropics region. Two birds mist-netted at Townsville Jan. 1989. Two 6 km north of Mossman Mar. 1996 in 3 m tall sugar-cane with sedges, vines and rank herbage intermixed. Recent records from farther south (NSW). A non-breeding summer visitor to New Guinea and Indonesia from its breeding grounds in Asia.
Habits Similar to those of the Clamorous Reed-Warbler.
Where to see it Worth being aware of it when visiting reedy swamps or about sugar-cane.

TAWNY GRASSBIRD *Megalurus timoriensis*
Status A generally widespread breeding species. Very common on the Atherton Tableland where numbers increased about 1948 following the planting of Guinea Grass *Panicum* sp. (Bravery 1970). Numbers drop markedly from autumn when most of the population appears to vacate the region. A single bird sighted on Snapper Island Aug. 1984 (J. McLean pers.comm.).
Habits Usually singly or in pairs, it is a shy species which will drop to cover when approached but will also climb a grass stem to watch an observer. During the breeding season, males perform display flights.
Where to see it Wherever there is rank grass, pastures or crops. The Atherton Tableland and sugar-cane fields about Cairns, Innisfail and Ingham are some of the best places.

LITTLE GRASSBIRD *Megalurus gramineus*
Status Generally rare. Probably nomadic. A few scattered breeding records. Probably a small regular breeding population in wetlands about Townsville. Very rare in the northern part of the Wet Tropics.
Habits A timid species remaining hidden in cover and disappearing when approached. Feeds amongst tussocks, shrubbery and reeds in freshwater swamps. During the breeding season it has a thin, two or three-note whistle which is usually the first indication of its presence.
Where to see it The best chance is probably the more permanent reedbeds about Townsville Town Common and Blakey's Crossing. Sightings have also been made at Bromfield Swamp and parts of the Atherton Tableland. Also at Eubenangee Swamp.

RUFOUS SONGLARK *Cincloramphus mathewsi*
Status Scarce in southern parts, rare in northern areas. A few small isolated breeding populations occur on the drier south-western fringe of the Wet Tropics, with another breeding population at Abergowrie (J. Young pers.comm.). A male performing song flight at Julatten Aug. 1993. Recorded Millaa Millaa Dec. 1994. Usually a winter visitor elsewhere. A single bird at Annan River June 1992 (J. McLean pers.comm.).
Habits Rather conspicuous while breeding in spring, when the male flies over his territory, uttering a rich song. Unobtrusive during the non-breeding season. Males are polygamous. During the breeding season, it often perches on stumps, branches of trees and fence posts. Usually seen singly, in pairs or loose groups.
Where to see it In dry tropical woodland about Mt Fox and Abergowrie during the breeding season. A chance sighting only, in the non-breeding season. Common in southern Australia.

BROWN SONGLARK *Cinclorhamphus cruralis*
Status An uncommon winter visitor to the Ingham/Townsville area. Rare and erratic winter visitor elsewhere. A record of four birds at Cairns Esplanade and another of 20 which stayed for four months at Innisfail aerodrome. In each case, these are the only records by longstanding resident observers.
Habits Usually seen singly or in small loose groups. Usually shy, silent and unobtrusive during the non-breeding season.
Where to see it Only by chance in the Wet Tropics. Common in many inland areas of Australia.

ZITTING CISTICOLA *Cisticola juncidis*

Status Rare. Small scattered populations on the central Queensland coast north to Ingham.
Habits Occurs singly, in pairs or family groups. The male has a conspicuous song flight throughout the breeding season Nov.–Apr. He flutters up, usually to a height of about 30 m, and with undulating flight circles over his territory, uttering a peculiar 'tick'. During display, the tail is fanned, exposing cinnamon panels. After a minute or so he swoops down to the grass. Inconspicuous during the non-breeding season.
Where to see it Best possibility is in saline grassland, e.g. couch grass *Sporobolus* sp. close to mangroves or beach from Ingham south, e.g. Forrest Beach and Giru.

GOLDEN-HEADED CISTICOLA *Cisticola exilis*

Status Abundant, widespread, present throughout the year and breeding.
Habits Usually occurs singly or in pairs. During the breeding season the male is very obvious, calling from favoured vantage points such as fence posts, tops of thistles or grass stems. From there he flies into the air, sometimes quite high, fluttering about with a jerky flight over his territory and uttering a peculiar buzzing note before dropping back to cover.
Where to see it Throughout grassland and farmland.

FAMILY ZOSTEROPIDAE

[PALE WHITE-EYE *Zosterops citrinellus*

Status Unconfirmed reports of this species occur from time to time from Green Island. The Pale White-eye occurs on islands off the north-eastern coast of Cape York Peninsula. The most southerly confirmed record is from Rocky Islets, 75 km north-north-east of Cooktown (Holmes 1986). The resident birds on Green Island belong to the Great Barrier Reef form of the Silvereye which is brighter than its mainland relatives, with more yellow throat and pale-yellowish under tail-coverts. It is likely that these have been misidentified as Pale White-eyes. The Pale White-eye can be distinguished from the Silvereye by its **uniform,** plain greenish back, **bright** greenish-yellow throat (reasonably well-demarcated from **uniform** off-white underparts) and greenish-yellow under tail-coverts.]

YELLOW WHITE-EYE *Zosterops luteus*

Status Two records from Brook Islands, each of a single bird (J. Young pers.comm.). A moderately common breeding species in mangroves about the mouths of Barratta Creek and the Burdekin River to the south of the region.

SILVEREYE *Zosterops lateralis*

Status Common and widespread in most habitats and at all altitudes from Cooktown to Paluma. Uncommon about Townsville. Present throughout the year and breeding.
Habits Usually seen in small flocks searching through foliage for food. The call most commonly heard is a single, high-pitched note usually uttered while feeding.
Where to see it Throughout the Wet Tropics and easily located.

FAMILY MUSCICAPIDAE

BASSIAN THRUSH *Zoothera lunulata*
RUSSET-TAILED THRUSH *Zoothera heinei*

Status Until Ford (1983) demonstrated clearly that there were two distinct species of ground-thrush inhabiting eastern Australia, in places partly sharing habitat, only one species with several races was recognised.
Both species inhabit upland rainforest in the Wet Tropics. A distinct race of the Bassian *cuneata* is isolated in the Wet Tropics. However, being larger than southern populations, it is contrary to Bergmann's rule where birds become smaller nearer the tropics. While some taxonomists regard it as a large montane race, it will probably prove to be a distinct species.

Little is known of each bird in north-eastern Queensland. They do not inhabit adjacent altitudinal zones as in southern Queensland. Both coexist in the Seaview and Paluma ranges. Neither is common anywhere except possibly the Seaview Range where the Russet-tailed is moderately common.

The Bassian occurs in an area at least from Bakers Blue Mountain, across the Atherton Tableland south to Paluma Range, while the Russet-tailed appears to have a disjunct distribution, occurring mainly on the Seaview and Paluma ranges. Northwards, the only recent record is of a small population at the base of Mt Spurgeon at 1150 m. The only record from the intervening area seems to be of a specimen taken in 1910 and simply labelled *Barron River*.

Habits Both species have similar habits and are usually seen singly or in pairs on the ground searching for food in leaf litter. The call of the Russet-tailed is a sweet double-note 'pee-poo' usually uttered at dawn and dusk, while that of the Bassian is a distinctive, sweet warble like that of the introduced Common Blackbird *Turdus merula*, again uttered at dawn and dusk.

Where to see it Infrequently encountered. Both can be seen at Paluma; the Bassian on the Atherton Tableland, e.g. The Crater.

FAMILY STURNIDAE

METALLIC STARLING *Aplonis metallica*
Status A common to abundant breeding species Aug.–Apr. south to Ingham. Mostly a rare passage migrant about Townsville. Usually coastal but reaches higher altitudes, e.g. Atherton Tableland where it is locally moderately common, and almost to Paluma township. Migrates to New Guinea after breeding but small numbers overwinter in coastal lowlands, e.g. Cairns.

Habits A gregarious species which travels in small to large flocks. Noisy. Feeds on rainforest fruits. Breeds in colonies, building large-domed nests in the crowns of huge rainforest trees, sometimes in street trees. Flight is swift and direct.

Where to see it Throughout coastal lowlands and nearby areas. Very obvious.

COMMON STARLING *Sturnus vulgaris*
Status Introduced. Only a few records from the Wet Tropics region. Port Douglas 1944, Innisfail 1965, Ingham 1990 — a single bird in each instance.

COMMON MYNA *Acridotheres tristis*
Status Introduced to north-eastern Queensland late last century and now abundant throughout all settled areas from Mossman to Townsville where it has become a pest. Rare about Cooktown where it was last recorded in 1986 (J. McLean pers.comm.). First recorded Atherton Tableland 1931.

To the best of my knowledge, the information concerning facilities and permits for national parks and state forest parks was valid at the time of writing. Following proclamation of Queensland's Wet Tropics, the Wet Tropics Management Authority was formed to administer the World Heritage area. Much of it then was under the control of the Departments of Environment and Heritage and Forestry. This process is still under way. As a result place names have sometimes been changed. Therefore, to avoid confusion in some instances, I have referred to place names as they are popularly known locally. As an example, Wallaman Falls National Park has become the 'Wallaman Falls Section of Lumholtz National Park'. It seems much simpler to refer to it as 'Wallaman Falls', the name by which it will always be known!

Generally permits are not required for most public areas throughout the Wet Tropics. If in doubt a telephone call should be made to the relevant departmental office. Permits are usually issued on the spot free of charge for such activities as birdwatching, though in some instances one may have to quote driver licence number and vehicle registration.

Note the following changes to telephone and facsimile numbers, planned to take effect late 1997. (070) numbers will become (07) 40 followed by the current number; (077) numbers will become (07) 47 followed by the current number.

National Parks:
Department of Environment

COOKTOWN	(070) 695777
MOSSMAN	(070) 982188
ATHERTON	(070) 914262
CAIRNS	(070) 523092 or (070) 523096
TOWNSVILLE	(077) 225211
INNISFAIL	(070) 614291
CARDWELL	(077) 668115
INGHAM	(077) 761700

State Forests:
Department of Primary Industries (DPI) Forest Service

CAIRNS	(070) 523287
ATHERTON	(070) 911844
TOWNSVILLE	(077) 222688
INGHAM	(077) 762777
CARDWELL	(070) 668804

Great **Barrier Reef Wonderland** — information centre, aquarium, theatre, Museum of Tropical Queensland, ferry terminal. 2–68 Flinders Street East, Townsville. Telephone (077) 727122.

ALTITUDE (METRES)

Atherton 790	Mareeba 420
Bluewater SF 500	Millaa Millaa 850
Dimbulah 470	Mt Carbine 360
Henrietta Creek 370	Mt Fox 810 (surrounds average 600)
Herberton 880	Mt Lewis 1220 (surrounds average 1000)
Irvinebank 760	Mt Molloy 400
Julatten 420	Mt Whitfield 360
Kaban 960	Paluma 920
Kirrama SF 900 (at highest point)	Ravenshoe 940
Koombooloomba Dam 770	Shiptons Flat 240
Kuranda 350	The Crater 1000
Lake Tinaroo 670	Tully Gorge SFP 80
Malanda 740	Wallaman Falls 620

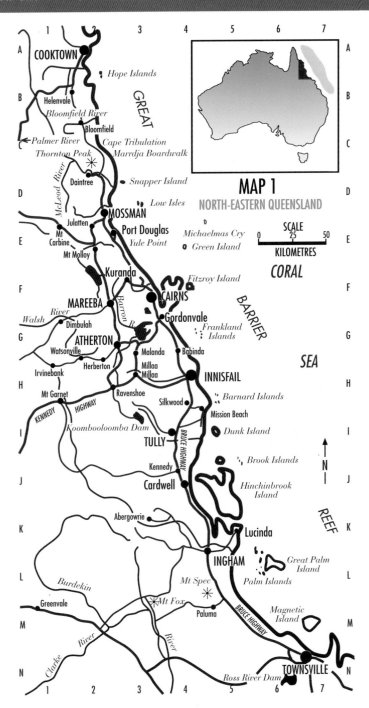

MAP 1
NORTH-EASTERN QUEENSLAND

SCALE
0   25   50
KILOMETRES

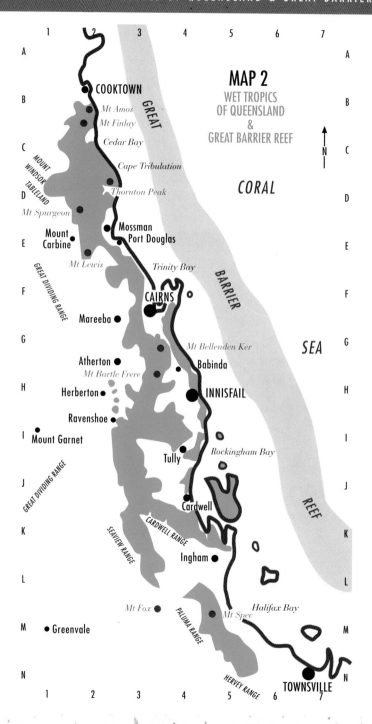

MAP 2

WET TROPICS
OF QUEENSLAND
&
GREAT BARRIER REEF

N

CORAL

BARRIER

SEA

REEF

COOKTOWN
Mt Amos
Mt Finlay
Cedar Bay
Cape Tribulation
Thornton Peak
Mt Spurgeon
Mossman
Port Douglas
Mount Carbine
Mt Lewis
Trinity Bay
CAIRNS
Mareeba
Mt Bellenden Ker
Atherton
Mt Bartle Frere
Babinda
Herberton
INNISFAIL
Ravenshoe
Mount Garnet
Tully
Rockingham Bay
Cardwell
CARDWELL RANGE
SEAVIEW RANGE
Ingham
Mt Fox
PALUMA RANGE
Halifax Bay
Mt Spec
Greenvale
HERVEY RANGE
TOWNSVILLE

MOUNT WINDSOR TABLELAND

GREAT DIVIDING RANGE

GREAT DIVIDING RANGE

GREAT

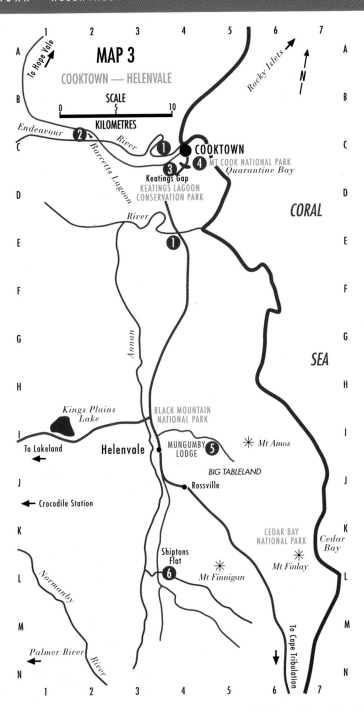

MAP 3

COOKTOWN — HELENVALE

SCALE

0   5   10

KILOMETRES

To Hope Vale

Endeavour   River

Barretts Lagoon

COOKTOWN

MT COOK NATIONAL PARK
Quarantine Bay

Keatings Gap

KEATINGS LAGOON
CONSERVATION PARK

Rocky Islets

N

A B C D E F G H I J K L M N

River

CORAL

Annan

SEA

Kings Plains
Lake

BLACK MOUNTAIN
NATIONAL PARK

To Lakeland

Helenvale   MUNGUMBY
LODGE

Mt Amos

BIG TABLELAND

Rossville

Crocodile Station

CEDAR BAY
NATIONAL PARK   Cedar
Bay

Shiptons
Flat

Mt Finlay

Normanby

Mt Finnigan

To Cape Tribulation

Palmer River   River

1   2   3   4   5   6   7

BEST AREAS

1 Endeavour and Annan Rivers The Endeavour is a moderate river which widens into an estuary just before reaching the sea. An extensive area of mangroves covers much of the lower reaches. Birding about the Endeavour can be rewarding either by boat or by taking the Hope Vale road which follows the river for 15 km or so. This traverses some interesting habitat including small areas of rainforest.

Birding along the Annan River by dingy (starting from the Annan River bridge boat ramp 8 km south of Cooktown) is also recommended for an array of species including the Great-billed Heron which is occasionally seen upstream.

Any heathland (particularly with flowering *Banksia dentata* Feb.–May or flowering *Melaleuca* spp.) is worth checking for the White-streaked Honeyeater.

Notable species Great-billed Heron, Striated Heron, Black Bittern, Osprey, Brahminy Kite, White-bellied Sea-Eagle, Marsh Sandpiper, Common Greenshank, Common Sandpiper, Beach Stone-curlew, Pacific Golden Plover, Grey Plover, Red-capped Plover, Greater Sand Plover, Pied Imperial-Pigeon, Fork-tailed Swift, Little Kingfisher, Large-billed Gerygone, Helmeted Friarbird, Varied Honeyeater, White-streaked Honeyeater, Dusky Honeyeater, Spectacled Monarch, Shining Flycatcher, Northern Fantail, Yellow Oriole, Black Butcherbird.

Facilities All facilities at Cooktown.

Access By road, take the airport road from Cooktown and follow on. Boat ramp in town, and also beside Annan River bridge, 8 km south. Good access to the Endeavour River can be gained at lower town, Cooktown Airport 12 km, Knight's Caravan Park 33 km and Hope Vale 46 km.

2 Barretts Lagoon is a small 'L' shaped lagoon or billabong. The dense southern section of vegetation is private property. Be aware that estuarine crocodiles can appear any time of year.

Notable species Orange-footed Scrubfowl, Wandering Whistling-Duck, Green Pygmy-goose, Black-necked Stork, Comb-crested Jacana, Emerald Dove, Superb Fruit-Dove, Wompoo Fruit-Dove, Pied Imperial-Pigeon, Red-winged Parrot, Large-billed Gerygone, Yellow Honeyeater, Brown-backed Honeyeater, Shining Flycatcher, Cicadabird, Black Butcherbird.

Facilities None.

Access Fifteen kilometres north of Cooktown on the Hope Vale road, on the left hand side.

3 Keatings Lagoon Conservation Park An interesting wetland which supports a large number of birds, the lagoon fills through the Wet and dries out through the late Dry. The surrounding forest usually supports a good variety of forest birds such as Silver-crowned Friarbird.

Notable species Magpie Goose, Wandering Whistling-Duck, Radjah Shelduck, Green Pygmy-goose, Black-necked Stork, Whistling Kite, Brahminy Kite, White-bellied Sea-Eagle, Brolga, Common Greenshank, Comb-crested Jacana, Black-winged Stilt, Black-fronted Dotterel, Red-kneed Dotterel, Red-winged Parrot, Red-backed Fairy-wren, Silver-crowned Friarbird, Yellow Honeyeater, Brown-backed Honeyeater, Lemon-bellied Flycatcher, Northern Fantail, Great Bowerbird, Golden-headed Cisticola.

Facilities There is a bird hide 250 m from the road on the southern side of the lagoon. An educational self-guiding walk, jointly created by the Gungarde aborigines and Department of Environment, focuses on aboriginal bush foods and medicines. Picnic area.

Access The main road from the south crosses the wetland at Keatings Lagoon about 6 km before Cooktown.

4 **Mt Cook National Park — Quarantine Bay** Both of these areas are in close proximity to Cooktown and provide some good birding opportunities. One of the avian attractions about Cooktown is the Tropical Scrubwren, usually to be found in patches of rainforest in these localities. One can sometimes find Silver-crowned Friarbirds in the open forest.

Notable species Nankeen Kestrel, Red-necked Crake, Bush Stone-curlew, Pied Imperial-Pigeon, Chestnut-breasted Cuckoo, Gould's Bronze-Cuckoo, Large-tailed Nightjar, Buff-breasted Paradise-Kingfisher, Blue-winged Kookaburra, Noisy Pitta, Lovely Fairy-wren, Tropical Scrubwren, Silver-crowned Friarbird, Macleay's Honeyeater, Dusky Honeyeater, Yellow-breasted Boatbill, White-bellied Cuckoo-shrike, Varied Triller, Yellow Oriole, Black-throated Finch, Yellow-bellied Sunbird.

Facilities None.

Access From Cooktown Hospital, follow Ada Street east about 1 km. Mt Cook National Park lies about 3 km south of Cooktown. Follow signs to the start of the Mt Cook walking track which leads to the summit. The track is rather steep. The road to Quarantine Bay leads off to the right, before Mt Cook NP, when approaching from the south. Further information may be obtained from The Ranger, telephone (070) 695777.

5 **Mungumby Lodge** Mungumby is situated below Big Tableland on the banks of Mungumby Creek near Helenvale about 35 km south of Cooktown. Within an hour by 4WD, there is a variety of habitat including upland and lowland rainforest, eucalypt forest and savannah woodland, wetland, coastal heathland and estuarine mangrove. The lodge operates day trips to all these areas or can provide a guide.

Notable species: Brown Goshawk, Grey Goshawk, Superb Fruit-Dove, Pied Imperial-Pigeon, Brush Cuckoo, Gould's Bronze-Cuckoo, Papuan Frogmouth, Large-tailed Nightjar, Azure Kingfisher, Buff-breasted Paradise-Kingfisher, Lovely Fairy-wren, Fairy Gerygone, Silver-crowned Friarbird, Yellow-spotted Honeyeater, Yellow-faced Honeyeater, Graceful Honeyeater, Bridled Honeyeater, Grey Whistler, Yellow-breasted Boatbill, Pied Monarch, Rufous Fantail, Cicadabird, Varied Triller, Yellow Oriole, Spotted Catbird, Great Bowerbird, Black-throated Finch, Yellow-bellied Sunbird.

Facilities Ten cabins each with ensuite for twenty guests, set in a beautiful garden with a swimming pool. Breakfast is included and packed lunches can be provided. There is also a barbecue and cool room for food storage. Alternatively, evening meals are available at The Lion's Den Hotel, Helenvale (15 minutes drive) or at several restaurants in Cooktown. Contact owners, Nick and Lizzie Marshall, telephone and facsimile (070) 603972.

Access From Cooktown, take the Cairns road then the Helenvale road. The road to Mungumby turns to the left a few kilometres from the junction. From Cairns, travel either via inland route — Mt Molloy and Lakeland or via coastal route — Mossman, Cape Tribulation and Helenvale (4WD only) — through some spectacular tropical scenery. Daily air service from Cairns to Cooktown.

6 **Shiptons Flat** Shiptons Flat has a mixture of lowland rainforest and tropical woodland. The road follows the upper section of the Annan River for a few kilometres. Most of the region is private property but one can find some interesting birds from the road. The Blue-faced Parrot-Finch occurs in the general area.

Notable species Orange-footed Scrubfowl, Grey Goshawk, Superb Fruit-Dove, Pied Imperial-Pigeon, Topknot Pigeon, Chestnut-breasted Cuckoo, Gould's Bronze-Cuckoo, Papuan Frogmouth, Blue-winged Kookaburra, Buff-breasted Paradise-Kingfisher, Lovely Fairy-wren, Red-backed Fairy-wren, Fairy Gerygone, Silver-crowned Friarbird, Macleay's Honeyeater, White-streaked Honeyeater, Grey Whistler, Yellow-breasted Boatbill, Spectacled Monarch, Pied Monarch, Cicadabird, Victoria's Riflebird, Spotted Catbird, Blue-faced Parrot-Finch, Yellow-bellied Sunbird.

Facilities None.

Access From Cooktown, take the Cairns road, then the Helenvale road near Black Mountain National Park. At about 7 km, the Shiptons Flat road turns to the right.

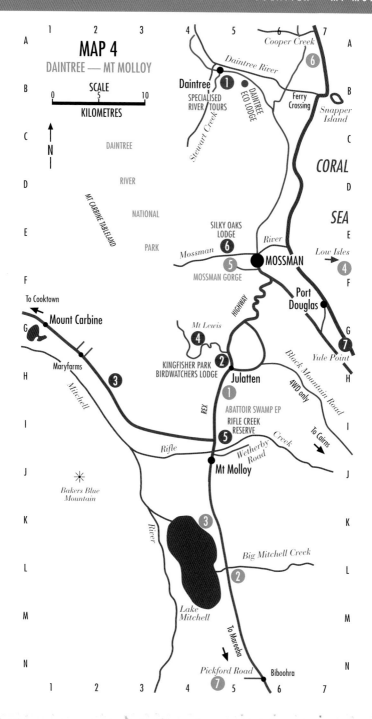

MAP 4
DAINTREE — MT MOLLOY

SCALE

KILOMETRES

N

DAINTREE

RIVER

NATIONAL

PARK

MT CARBINE TABLELAND

To Cooktown

Mount Carbine

Maryfarms

Mitchell

Bakers Blue
Mountain

River

Lake
Mitchell

To Mareeba

Pickford Road

Daintree River

Cooper Creek

Daintree

SPECIALISED
RIVER TOURS

DAINTREE
ECO LODGE

Ferry
Crossing

Snapper
Island

Stewart Creek

CORAL

SEA

SILKY OAKS
LODGE

River

MOSSMAN

Low Isles

Mossman

MOSSMAN GORGE

Port
Douglas

HIGHWAY

Mt Lewis

Yule Point

KINGFISHER PARK
BIRDWATCHERS LODGE

Julatten

Black Mountain Road

4WD only

To Cairns

ABATTOIR SWAMP EP

RIFLE CREEK
RESERVE

REX

Rifle

Creek

Wetherby
Road

Mt Molloy

Big Mitchell Creek

Biboohra

BEST AREAS

1 Daintree River An excellent area for some of the more elusive species such as Great-billed Heron and Little Kingfisher. A wide diversity of habitats in the general area produces a good variety of birds many of which are best seen from the river.

Chris Dahlberg and Denise Collins own and run Specialised River Tours which caters primarily for birdwatchers. By operating a small boat Chris is able to explore the more interesting reaches of the river which larger craft cannot access. Usually 50 or more species are seen on the two-hour dawn trip, which undoubtedly provides the best chance of seeing a Great-billed Heron in the Wet Tropics.

There are no walking tracks in the vicinity of Daintree village, but roads lead to Upper Daintree and along Stewart Creek, both of which offer worthwhile birding opportunities.

Notable species Great-billed Heron, Black Bittern, Black-necked Stork, Green Pygmy-goose, White-bellied Sea-Eagle, Comb-crested Jacana, Beach Stone-curlew, Wompoo Fruit-Dove, Pied Imperial-Pigeon, Double-eyed Fig-Parrot, Gould's Bronze-Cuckoo, Channel-billed Cuckoo, Barking Owl, Papuan Frogmouth, Little Kingfisher, Collared Kingfisher (lower reaches), Large-billed Gerygone, Helmeted Friarbird, Mangrove Robin (lower reaches), Shining Flycatcher, Barred Cuckoo-shrike, Yellow Oriole, Black Butcherbird.

Facilities For bed and breakfast at Red Mill House or bookings for Specialised River Tours, telephone (070) 986169. Various other bed and breakfast establishments. General store with licensed eating area, post office, camping and caravan park, public toilets. Daintree Eco Lodge provides first class amenities in an undisturbed rainforest setting, telephone (070) 986100.

Access From Mossman, take the Daintree road to Daintree village. Travel through the town and down to the jetty. Specialised River Tours depart from this jetty.

2 Kingfisher Park Birdwatchers' Lodge A well-known north Queensland birdwatching destination, Kingfisher Park nestles in an attractive rainforest setting. Here an impressive array of birds can be seen at close quarters. One of the more sought-after species for which the park is noted is the elusive Red-necked Crake. Buff-breasted Paradise-Kingfishers breed about the grounds through the summer months, while a pair of Lesser Sooty Owls rear young in most years. It is an excellent place to see platypuses. Local spotlighting excursions are occasionally conducted.

Notable species Orange-footed Scrubfowl, Pacific Baza, Red-necked Crake, Buff-banded Rail, Bush-hen, Bush Stone-curlew, Emerald Dove, Wompoo Fruit-Dove, Superb Fruit-Dove, Common Koel, Barking Owl, Lesser Sooty Owl, Papuan Frogmouth, Buff-breasted Paradise-Kingfisher, Large-billed Scrubwren, Macleay's Honeyeater, Dusky Honeyeater, Grey Whistler, Yellow-breasted Boatbill, Pied Monarch, Victoria's Riflebird, Spotted Catbird, Metallic Starling.

Facilities The park offers modern self-contained units, bunkhouse units, powered caravan sites, tent sites, community kitchen, showers, toilets, laundry, small food store. Telephone (070) 941263 or facsimile (070) 941466. Hotel, fuel, post office with arts and crafts, general store, baker, butcher and takeaway at Mt Molloy. Tavern at Julatten. Coffee shop near Julatten school.

Access Situated at Julatten on the Rex Highway 10 km from Mt Molloy or 23 km from Mossman.

3 Mts Carbine and Molloy There is a remarkable contrast in the few kilometres between these two areas and Mt Lewis which towers to the east and north. The rich wet upland rainforest of Mt Lewis gives way to very dry tropical woodland which allows some inland and arid habitat species to reach this region. Australian Bustard, Squatter Pigeon, Galah, Red-winged Parrot, Red-backed Kingfisher, Grey-crowned Babbler and Apostlebird can be seen within a few kilometres of Chowchilla, Fernwren, Tooth-billed Bowerbird, Golden Bowerbird. In the drier woodland, the Buff-breasted Button-quail sometimes occurs, while the Painted Button-quail is sometimes present in adjoining habitat.

Mt Molloy is situated amidst what is probably the richest birding area in Australia. Nearly 300 species have been recorded within a 15 km radius of the town, including all 13 Wet Tropics endemics.

A dam near the old Mt Carbine mine site is a well known spot for birdwatching, not only for a good variety of aquatic species but also Squatter Pigeon, Black-throated Finch and other dryland species. A vehicular track to the dam leads off to the left, less than 1 km north of Mt Carbine.

Notable species Square-tailed Kite, Spotted Harrier, Australian Bustard, Buff-breasted Button-quail, Common Bronzewing, Squatter Pigeon, Red-tailed Black-Cockatoo, Galah, Red-winged Parrot, Pale-headed Rosella, Little Bronze-Cuckoo, Red-backed Kingfisher, White-throated Gerygone, Blue-faced Honeyeater, Banded Honeyeater, Scarlet Honeyeater, White-winged Triller, Torresian Crow, Apostlebird, Great Bowerbird, Double-barred Finch, Black-throated Finch.

Facilities Mt Molloy: Hotel, fuel, post office with arts and crafts, general store, baker, butcher, takeaway, public camping ground at Rifle Creek has toilets only. **Mt Carbine:** General store, takeaway, hotel, limited accommodation.

Access Mts Molloy and Carbine are on the highway leading north to Cooktown from Mareeba.

4 Mt Lewis The area surrounding Mt Lewis averages over 1000 m and is covered with upland rainforest. Though usually lacking an abundance of bird numbers compared to some areas on Atherton Tableland and Mt Spec, Mt Lewis nevertheless has all the upland rainforest species. Here is one of the best places in north-eastern Queensland to see the Blue-faced Parrot-Finch during a rather short summer/autumn season. Cassowaries are sometimes seen, but in such a large area of rainforest sightings are infrequent and purely by chance.

The best place for birdwatching is about a grassy clearing (about 12 km off the Rex Highway) from which a few disused logging tracks run. The road travels on much further but one need only travel this far. It is here where Blue-faced Parrot-Finches are mostly seen.

Notable species Southern Cassowary, Grey Goshawk, White-headed Pigeon, Wompoo Fruit-Dove, Superb Fruit-Dove, Topknot Pigeon, Australian King-Parrot, Chestnut-breasted Cuckoo, Shining Bronze-Cuckoo, Southern Boobook, Lesser Sooty Owl, Papuan Frogmouth, White-throated Treecreeper, Fernwren, Atherton Scrubwren, Brown Gerygone, Mountain Thornbill, Bridled Honeyeater, White-cheeked Honeyeater, Eastern Spinebill, Grey-headed Robin, Chowchilla, Bower's Shrike-thrush, Barred Cuckoo-shrike, Victoria's Riflebird, Spotted Catbird, Tooth-billed Bowerbird, Golden Bowerbird, Blue-faced Parrot-Finch.

Facilities None. Camping is not permitted.

Access The road leads off the Rex Highway to the left, 2.5 km from Julatten when travelling towards Mossman. Most of the road is unsealed and usually has a good surface suitable for small cars, but should not be traversed after heavy rains. Parts of the Mt Lewis area are designated 'Restricted Access' and a permit is required from Department of Primary Industries (DPI) Forest Service, 83 Main Street, Atherton. However, all species and the best birding areas are located well before the Restricted Access sign.

5 Rifle Creek Reserve This 300 ha reserve on the flood plain of Rifle Creek at Mt Molloy comprises mixed tropical woodland with areas of rainforest interspersed with small dry hills. With its mix of forest types, this reserve supports an amazing variety of birdlife and 220 species have been recorded. It is one of the best areas for Grey Whistler, Northern Fantail and Lovely Fairy-wren. The local community has provided access tracks from the road which lead to various lagoons.

Notable species Orange-footed Scrubfowl, Black Bittern, Brahminy Kite, Collared Sparrowhawk, Buff-banded Rail, Bush-hen, Emerald Dove, Double-eyed Fig-Parrot, Little Bronze-Cuckoo, Common Koel, Channel-billed Cuckoo, Pheasant Coucal, Large-tailed Nightjar, Macleay's Honeyeater, Yellow-faced Honeyeater, Yellow Honeyeater, Brown-backed Honeyeater, Scarlet Honeyeater, Grey Whistler, Yellow-breasted Boatbill, Northern Fantail, Olive-backed Oriole, Double-barred Finch, Chestnut-breasted Mannikin, Yellow-bellied Sunbird.

Facilities None.

Access One kilometre north from Mt Molloy, turn right into Wetherby Road. About 1 km along Wetherby Road one enters the reserve. The road continues for 3 km through mixed tropical woodland to Wetherby Station which is private property.

6 **Silky Oaks Lodge** Surrounded by rainforest on three sides, Silky Oaks Lodge is attractively situated overlooking the Mossman River beside the Daintree River National Park. While the surrounding gardens of the lodge have a good variety of birds, a walking track leads from the lodge up into some excellent lowland rainforest which can produce Noisy Pitta, Buff-breasted Paradise-Kingfisher, Yellow-breasted Boatbill and other lowland species. Another track leads down to the Mossman River where the lovely bubbling notes of Yellow Oriole can be heard on a summer's day and Azure Kingfishers fly low over the water. Walking back along the road leading into the lodge can be quite rewarding, especially during early morning. The lodge conducts special weeks for birdwatching guests led by expert local guides.

Notable species Orange-footed Scrubfowl, Grey Goshawk, Wompoo Fruit-Dove, Superb Fruit-Dove, Double-eyed Fig-Parrot, Azure Kingfisher, Buff-breasted Paradise-Kingfisher, Noisy Pitta, Large-billed Scrubwren, Lovely Fairy-wren, Red-backed Fairy-wren, Helmeted Friarbird, Macleay's Honeyeater, White-throated Honeyeater, Grey Whistler, Yellow-breasted Boatbill, White-eared Monarch, Pied Monarch, Cicadabird, Yellow Oriole, Spotted Catbird, Yellow-bellied Sunbird, Metallic Starling.

Facilities Luxury wilderness lodge providing all amenities. Telephone (070) 981666 or facsimile (070) 981983.

Access From Mossman, travel north on the Daintree road. The first lodge sign is about 4 km from Mossman.

7 **Yule Point** The extensive sandflats provide an excellent area for shorebirds from Sept.–Mar. Though bird numbers are not as prolific as those at the Cairns Esplanade, some interesting species appear here including on occasions some of the oceanic terns. Yule Point was once a good spot for Beach Stone-curlew, but over more recent times has become unreliable, probably because of human disturbances.

Notable species Eastern Reef Egret, Striated Heron, Osprey, Black-tailed Godwit, Bar-tailed Godwit, Whimbrel, Eastern Curlew, Common Greenshank, Grey-tailed Tattler, Great Knot, Red Knot, Sanderling, Red-necked Stint, Sharp-tailed Sandpiper, Curlew Sandpiper, Pacific Golden Plover, Lesser Sand Plover, Greater Sand Plover, Pied Imperial-Pigeon, Varied Honeyeater.

Facilities None.

Access From the Port Douglas intersection on the Captain Cook Highway travel 8 km south. Just before rounding a rocky headland, there is ample parking on either side of the road. A rough walking track leads through the mangroves and across a tidal creek to the sandflats. Access should be made when tides are low, as the tidal creek can rise quickly.

OTHER AREAS

1 **Abattoir Swamp Environmental Park** Though this swamp is inclined to dry out towards the end of the year, it usually supports an interesting variety of both aquatic and open forest birds and is well worth a visit for a couple of hours.

The Wet Tropics Management Authority in conjunction with Mareeba Shire Council have constructed a boardwalk to a bird hide overlooking the water, whilst adjacent areas are gradually being revegetated. Abattoir Swamp is presently undergoing a vegetation management programme designed to ensure control of exotic aquatic plant species and maximise prime habitat for birds. Aquatic species recorded include Black Bittern, Black-necked Stork, Wandering Whistling-Duck, Green Pygmy-goose, Buff-banded Rail, White-browed Crake, Bush-hen, Comb-crested Jacana, Marsh Sandpiper.

Open forest birds include Brown Quail, Blue-winged Kookaburra, Lemon-bellied Flycatcher, Northern Fantail, Golden-headed Cisticola, Tawny Grassbird, Red-backed Fairy-wren, Yellow Honeyeater, Brown-backed Honeyeater, Chestnut-breasted Mannikin.

Access Four kilometres north of Mt Molloy off the Rex Highway.

2 Big Mitchell Creek Much of this area is private property. A good variety of open forest birds inhabits the open woodland on either side of the road and is well worth a stop when travelling the highway between Mareeba and Mt Molloy.

A small population of White-browed Robin inhabits the creek and birds can be found on both sides of the bridge. A Great Bowerbird has a bower in dense bushes on the western side just beyond the fence. Other interesting birds which may be seen are Northern Fantail, Fairy Gerygone and Lemon-bellied Flycatcher.

Access The creek is signposted and situated about 23 km north of Mareeba and 17 km south of Mt Molloy. There is an open area on the south-eastern side of the bridge where a vehicle can be parked.

3 Lake Mitchell Known locally as Southedge Lake or Quaid's Dam, Lake Mitchell can be seen to the west of the Mareeba – Mt Molloy road. Following the Wet, shallow water spreads to the road providing habitat for an interesting variety of aquatic species including some Asiatic shorebirds. Some interesting raptors such as White-bellied Sea-Eagle, Wedge-tailed Eagle, Spotted and Swamp Harriers, Australian Hobby and Brown Falcon are sometimes seen here. Presently Lake Mitchell is private property.

Access Approximately 12 km south of Mt Molloy and 25 km north of Mareeba.

4 Low Isles Sometimes Low Isles is promoted as a good area for birdlife, but apart from the large colony of breeding Pied Imperial-Pigeons, Low Isles does not provide much in the way of ornithological interest. Some shorebirds occur here but it does not compare with the Cairns Esplanade or Yule Point. For seabirds, a reef trip to Michaelmas Cay or the outer Great Barrier Reef is a much better proposition.

5 Mossman Gorge Part of Daintree National Park, Mossman Gorge is sometimes promoted as a good area for birds, but is quite disappointing, apart from a large colony of Metallic Starlings which establishes itself in a huge tree beside the car-park each spring. There are fewer birds present here than one would expect to see in lowland rainforest. The noise of the river flowing through the boulders obliterates most bird sound. Mossman Gorge, however, is one of the more scenically spectacular areas in north-eastern Queensland with a circuit walking track through some beautiful lowland rainforest. It is a popular spot for swimming and attracts large numbers of tourists each year. Further information may be obtained from Department of Environment, Mossman.

Access Approaching Mossman from Cairns, the road to Mossman Gorge turns to the left on the outskirts of town. It is well-signposted.

6 North of the Daintree River Some visitors to tropical Queensland have a preconceived notion that rainforest becomes richer in birdlife the further north one travels. However, this is not generally so. Though the spectacular rainforest north of the Daintree River (known locally as the Daintree Rainforest) is one of the oldest and richest (in plant species) in the world, it is strangely poor in birdlife. However, there are some isolated areas, mostly closer to the foothills of the nearby ranges, which hold a reasonable variety of species. Further information may be obtained from the Department of Environment, Mossman.

Access Take the Cape Tribulation road north from Mossman.

7 Pickford Road (Biboohra) Once renowned for its abundance of birdlife due to rice growing activities, the farms about Pickford Road now grow sugar-cane which is one of the most sterile crops for birdlife. Sugar-cane fields, however, do attract species of native rats and hence some species of owls, but intense poisoning of the rats is presumed to be the cause of the rapid decline in owl populations.

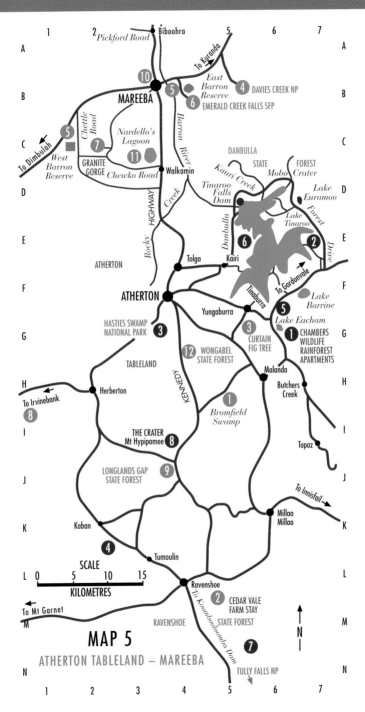

MAP 5

ATHERTON TABLELAND — MAREEBA

BEST AREAS

❶ Chambers Wildlife Rainforest Apartments An excellent variety of birds can be seen in the surrounding rainforest. One of the best places to see Wompoo Fruit-Doves and Eastern Whipbirds. Grey-headed Robins feed on the lawns. In late spring and summer, Tooth-billed Bowerbirds build their courts beside the forest pathways and Victoria's Riflebirds display in the rainforest clearing. Spotted Catbirds and Lewin's Honeyeaters visit the verandahs. The leafy entrance road and rainforest clearing provide worthwhile birding, especially early morning. Wary Red-legged Pademelons graze in open areas from dusk and Sugar Gliders glide in to your patio after dark.

Chambers is centrally situated at Lake Eacham and provides a delightful base for those wanting to spend a few days on the Atherton Tableland. John Chambers is most helpful and will provide visitors with current wildlife spotting information and detailed maps to other places of interest on the tablelands.

Notable species White-headed Pigeon, Wompoo Fruit-Dove, Superb Fruit-Dove, Rose-crowned Fruit-Dove, Topknot Pigeon, Australian King-Parrot, Crimson Rosella, Southern Boobook, Lesser Sooty Owl, White-throated Treecreeper, Grey-headed Robin, Eastern Whipbird, Golden Whistler, Yellow-breasted Boatbill, Rufous Fantail, Barred Cuckoo-shrike, Cicadabird, Victoria's Riflebird, Spotted Catbird, Tooth-billed Bowerbird.

Facilities Comfortable self-contained holiday apartments. Walking trails through rainforest.

Access From Yungaburra, travel via the Gordonvale road. Turn right at the Lake Eacham signpost and follow the road past the lake. Turn left into Eacham Close, 500 m past the lake. Telephone and facsimile (070) 953754.

❷ Danbulla Forest Drive Entering Danbulla Forest Drive from the Gordonvale road, one travels initially through farmland and then through some 8 km of excellent upland rainforest which provides good birding, especially during early morning. There are some worthwhile stops on the way, such as the Cathedral Fig. Mobo Crater, with its 600 m circuit walking track, is an example of tropical upland rainforest and creek scenery at its best.

The road passes into regrowth and pine plantations and then into dry sclerophyll with access at a few points to Lake Tinaroo. The walking track along Kauri Creek is worthwhile if time permits.

Notable species: White-headed Pigeon, Brown Cuckoo-Dove, Superb Fruit-Dove, Rose-crowned Fruit-Dove, Topknot Pigeon, White-rumped Swiftlet, White-throated Needletail, Lovely Fairy-wren, Lewin's Honeyeater, Bridled Honeyeater, Yellow Honeyeater, Eastern Spinebill, Chowchilla, Golden Whistler, Bower's Shrike-thrush, Northern Fantail, Victoria's Riflebird, Spotted Catbird, Tooth-billed Bowerbird, Chestnut-breasted Mannikin, Tawny Grassbird.

Facilities Camping grounds and various picnic areas around Lake Tinaroo, kiosk at Tinaroo Falls.

Access From Yungaburra, travel the Gordonvale road. Turn into Boar Pocket Road 3.8 km after the Lake Barrine road. This is the commencement of Danbulla Forest Drive. It can also be approached via the road past the Tinaroo Falls Dam spillway, travelling the route in the opposite direction.

❸ Hasties Swamp National Park A temporary swamp which fills during the Wet. By the late Dry it has dried out completely. As it dries, large areas of muddy edges and shallow water are available to aquatic species and shorebirds. It is one of those interesting areas where one never knows what may turn up. Often large numbers of Sarus Cranes roost at Hasties from late afternoon and large numbers of Magpie Geese are often present which is a spectacle in itself. Often some interesting raptors can be seen over adjacent farmland.

Notable species Magpie Goose, Plumed Whistling-Duck, Wandering Whistling-Duck, Pink-eared Duck, White-necked Heron, Glossy Ibis, Royal Spoonbill, Spotted Harrier, Swamp Harrier, Sarus Crane, Buff-banded Rail, Purple Swamphen, Latham's Snipe, Marsh Sandpiper, Sharp-tailed Sandpiper, Comb-crested Jacana, Black-fronted Dotterel, Red-kneed Dotterel, Sacred Kingfisher, Singing Bushlark, Tawny Grassbird, Golden-headed Cisticola.

Facilities None.

Access From Atherton, take the Herberton road. Watch for Hasties Road on the left, a few kilometres from Atherton. Access to the swamp is gained from this road.

4 Kaban The district of Kaban lies on the western edge of the Atherton Tableland. Here, dry sclerophyll forest offers the opportunity to view some species of the dry interior of the continent. A breeding population of Sacred Kingfisher and others such as Eastern Yellow Robin, Jacky Winter, Grey Shrike-thrush and Dusky Woodswallow can be seen. Colonies of the northern yellowish-headed form of the Fuscous Honeyeater can be located where denser forest still stands. Checking the various roads about Kaban usually provides good opportunities for an unusual sighting and a chance for a few species not seen elsewhere about the Wet Tropics.
Notable species Common Bronzewing, Crested Pigeon, Galah, Red-winged Parrot, Pale-headed Rosella, Tawny Frogmouth, Red-backed Kingfisher, Sacred Kingfisher, Brown Treecreeper, Red-browed Pardalote, White-throated Gerygone, Buff-rumped Thornbill, Yellow Thornbill, Noisy Miner, Fuscous Honeyeater, Black-chinned Honeyeater, Jacky Winter, Eastern Yellow Robin, Varied Sittella, Crested Shrike-tit, Grey Shrike-thrush, White-winged Triller, Dusky Woodswallow, Grey Butcherbird, Black-throated Finch.
Facilities None.
Access Turn right from the Atherton–Ravenshoe road into Tumoulin road 29 km from Atherton. A road, signposted 'Airport' which turns to the left 7 km along the Tumoulin road, leads back towards Herberton and follows the railway line. The first few kilometres of this road usually provides excellent birding. Alternatively from Herberton, take the Ravenshoe road. Turn right about 5 km from Herberton and follow through to Tumoulin.

5 Lakes Barrine and Eacham These lakes are extinct volcanic craters now filled with water and surrounded by rainforest. Each lake has a circuit walking track winding through the rain-forest and a good variety of birds can be seen, though a few of the high altitude species are absent. Lake Barrine, with a reedy fringe, is the better for such aquatic species as Wandering Whistling-Duck, Cormorants and sometimes Great Crested Grebe, as well as Hardhead and Dusky Moorhen. Both lakes are situated on the busy tourist circuit, so early morning birding is recommended.
Notable species Wandering Whistling-Duck (Barrine), Great Crested Grebe, White-headed Pigeon, Wompoo Fruit-Dove, Topknot Pigeon, Australian King-Parrot, Crimson Rosella, Southern Boobook, Lesser Sooty Owl, White-throated Treecreeper, Lewin's Honeyeater, Bridled Honeyeater, Grey-headed Robin, Golden Whistler, Bower's Shrike-thrush, Yellow-breasted Boatbill, Barred Cuckoo-shrike, Victoria's Riflebird, Spotted Catbird, Tooth-billed Bowerbird.
Facilities Picnic grounds and toilets at both lakes. Kiosk at Lake Barrine, telephone (070) 953474.
Access From Yungaburra, take the Gordonvale road. The Lake Eacham signpost is 3 km past Yungaburra. Lake Barrine is a further 6 km towards Gordonvale.

6 Lake Tinaroo — Tinaroo Falls Dam Lake Tinaroo is a man-made dam with an irregular shoreline, supporting large numbers of waterfowl. In the Dry, and as other waterways recede, many birds such as Pygmy-geese take refuge on the lake. Numbers of Asiatic shorebirds inhabit the muddy shores of the lake through the summer season. It is worthwhile spending some time about the lake, perhaps visiting in conjunction with Danbulla Forest Drive which circles the backwaters, providing access points on the way. Tinaburra, a few kilometres from Yungaburra, is one of the better spots.
Lake Tinaroo is a popular area for water-sports, picnickers and campers, and can often become overcrowded at peak holiday periods and weekends.
Notable species Plumed Whistling-Duck, Wandering Whistling-Duck, Black Swan, Australian Wood Duck, Cotton Pygmy-goose, Hardhead, Great Crested Grebe, Glossy Ibis, Black-necked Stork, White-bellied Sea-Eagle, Swamp Harrier, Sarus Crane, Brolga, Dusky Moorhen, Little Curlew, Marsh Sandpiper, Common Greenshank, Red-necked Stint, Sharp-tailed Sandpiper, Comb-crested Jacana, Pacific Golden Plover, Red-kneed Dotterel, Caspian Tern, Whiskered Tern.
Facilities Several camping areas about the shores of Lake Tinaroo, caravan park, picnic area, kiosk at Tinaroo Falls. The towns of Atherton and Yungaburra are nearby. Motel and caravan park at Tinaburra. Further information may be obtained from Atherton Tableland Promotion Bureau, telephone (070) 914222.
Access From Atherton or Tolga, travel via Kairi to Tinaroo Falls Dam, then via Danbulla Forest Drive from which there are various access points. From Yungaburra, taken the Tinaburra road.

7 **Ravenshoe State Forest** The road travels through more than 13 km of tropical rainforest and then 15 km of mostly wet sclerophyll before reaching Koombooloomba Dam. Both habitats are excellent for birds. Though bird numbers are sometimes not over-plentiful, these two habitats can provide an interesting list of species. Most of the area is in excess of 1000 m. All of the high altitude species are present.

Ravenshoe State Forest has the added benefit of generally being off the tourist track. No permit is required as access through the forest is via a public road. Koombooloomba Dam itself is generally poor for aquatic species.

Notable species Grey Goshawk, Red-tailed Black-Cockatoo, Crimson Rosella, Brush Cuckoo, Pheasant Coucal, White-throated Nightjar, Australian Owlet-nightjar, White-throated Treecreeper, Spotted Pardalote, Fernwren, Brown Gerygone, Mountain Thornbill, Bridled Honeyeater, Yellow-faced Honeyeater, White-naped Honeyeater, Eastern Spinebill, Grey-headed Robin, Chowchilla, Eastern Whipbird, Bower's Shrike-thrush, Victoria's Riflebird, Tooth-billed Bowerbird, Golden Bowerbird.

Facilities Picnic areas at Koombooloomba Dam and Tully Falls National Park. A short walking track to the top of Tully Falls overlooks some spectacular gorge scenery.

Access Take Tully Falls road from Ravenshoe. There is 24 km of sealed road and a further 15 km of good unsealed road to the dam.

Note: Tully Falls National Park which is approached from Ravenshoe should not be confused with Tully Gorge State Forest Park which is approached from Tully.

8 **The Crater (Mt Hypipamee National Park)** This popular tourist spot is probably the best of the rainforest habitat on the Atherton Tableland, being higher in altitude than most other areas. Good birding can be had during early morning about the picnic ground and parking area, and along the entrance road which is often a good spot for Fernwren, Atherton Scrubwren and Victoria's Riflebird. The Fernwren can sometimes be found close to the edge of the rainforest surrounding the picnic area, or across the bridge to the left, at the start of the walking tracks. Bridled Honeyeaters, Grey-headed Robins and Spotted Catbirds come to the picnic tables. Birding is usually not as good along the walking tracks which in places follow the Barron River — the noise of the river drowns out calls.

The Crater is famous for viewing nocturnal animals, but unfortunately too much zealous spotlighting by some tour operators appears to have forced the animals to retreat into the rainforest. As a consequence, authorities now apply strict controls on spotlighting activities.

Notable species White-headed Pigeon, Wompoo Fruit-Dove, Superb Fruit-Dove, Topknot Pigeon, Australian King-Parrot, Crimson Rosella, Lesser Sooty Owl, White-throated Treecreeper, Fernwren, Atherton Scrubwren, Lewin's Honeyeater, Bridled Honeyeater, Grey-headed Robin, Eastern Whipbird, Golden Whistler, Rufous Fantail, Barred Cuckoo-shrike, Victoria's Riflebird, Spotted Catbird, Tooth-billed Bowerbird, Golden Bowerbird.

Facilities Picnic grounds, toilets.

Access From Atherton, take the Ravenshoe road. The road to The Crater turns off at 25 km.

OTHER AREAS

1 **Bromfield Swamp** This extinct volcanic crater is now an extensive swamp. Many waterbirds inhabit the area, the great attraction being the roosting of Sarus Cranes and Brolgas which are present from June–Dec. when hundreds of birds occur. The swamp is privately-owned and permission to walk around the swamp is required from the owner at the nearby farmhouse. An observation platform has been erected beside the road, but it is so far from the swamp that one needs a telescope to identify the birds. This area is only worth a visit if one has missed the Sarus Crane elsewhere. However, hundreds of Sarus Cranes and Brolgas coming to roost at dusk is a spectacle worth experiencing. The area about the platform is a good spot for Tawny Grassbirds during the summer months.

Access From Malanda, travel via the Atherton road. Two kilometres out turn left at Upper Barron Road where there is a sign to Bromfield Swamp. The observation platform is 5.5 km along this road.

2 Cedar Vale Farm Stay Situated a short distance from the dry forest about Kaban and close to Ravenshoe State Forest, Cedar Vale is within easy access to some of the better birding spots on the southern edge of the Atherton Tableland. There is a considerable area of upland rainforest on the property which adjoins World Heritage rainforest. Some of the upland species such as Chowchilla may be seen along a series of marked walking tracks. Identification tags have been attached to several hundred trees, shrubs and ferns for those also interested in botany. Platypuses and tree-kangaroos may also be seen. Owned and operated by Les and Ros Buglar, Cedar Vale provides accommodation in the homestead with shared facilities or in a self-contained cabin. Telephone and facsimile (070) 976782.
Access From Ravenshoe, take the Atherton road. At 3 km turn right into the Millaa Millaa road. Turn right into Harris Road. Cedar Vale Farm Stay is 1 km along Harris Road.

3 Curtain Fig A small area of rainforest typical of the little which still remains on the Atherton Tableland. Variety of birds is similar to that of most rainforest on the Tableland though some of the high altitude species are absent. The forest beside the sealed road beyond the Curtain Fig is often good for a variety of birds including Yellow-breasted Boatbill and Pied Monarch. The Curtain Fig Tree is well worth a visit for those interested in botany.
Access Approaching Yungaburra from Atherton, watch for the Curtain Fig signs on the right on the outskirts of the town. The Curtain Fig is about 1.5 km along this road.

4 Davies Creek National Park Davies Creek consists mostly of dry sclerophyll with denser forest along the creek. A good variety of open forest birds is present, though most can be seen elsewhere. However, King Quail and Painted and Buff-breasted Button-quail have all been sighted in this park. A circuit track follows the creek for a short distance. There are facilities for self-registered camping.
Access Approximately 23 km from Kuranda or 15 km from Mareeba off the Kuranda–Mareeba road. Take the Davies Creek National Park road and travel 6 km to the park.

5 East and West Barron Reserves These two locations are water storage systems for the Tinaroo irrigation scheme. A large variety of waterbirds usually inhabits these reservoirs during the latter half of the year. Permission to access these reserves should be obtained from DPI Water Resources, Mareeba, telephone (070) 922555.
Access West Barron: From Mareeba, take the Dimbulah road. Turn off at approximately 12 km into Chettle Road. The reservoir is 1.5 km on the right. **East Barron:** From Mareeba, take the Cairns road, then at 5 km the Emerald Creek Falls road. One will see the earthen wall of the reservoir approximately 3 km further, on the left.

6 Emerald Creek Falls State Forest Park A dry sclerophyll area with denser forest along Emerald Creek, this is a good spot for White-browed Robin. A general list of common open forest species can be seen in the vicinity.
Access From Mareeba, take the Cairns road. The Emerald Creek turnoff is 5 km from Mareeba on the right. Emerald Creek Falls picnic area and walking tracks are 12 km down this road. No camping is permitted.

7 Granite Gorge Some of the dryland species such as Red-backed Kingfisher and Red-browed Pardalote occur about Granite Gorge. A fine example of a Great Bowerbird's bower is situated a few hundred metres from the entrance. A highlight are the tame rock wallabies which inhabit the gorge. Granite Gorge is privately-owned and camping facilities are available for a modest fee. Telephone (070) 932259.
Access Travelling from Atherton to Mareeba, turn left at Chewko Road and follow signs for about 16 km to the Gorge.

8 Irvinebank   An interesting historical town, Irvinebank is situated in dry sclerophyll forest. There is a lagoon on the Petford road at the western edge of the town where a few pairs of Cotton Pygmy-geese as well as other waterbirds can sometimes be seen.
Access   Irvinebank is 23 km west of Herberton via a reasonable unsealed road.

9 Longlands Gap State Forest   This is excellent rainforest with good birds, but unfortunately access is limited, although it is worth wandering about here if The Crater is overcrowded with sightseers. The Golden Bowerbird frequents this rainforest, as well as Fernwren, Atherton Scrubwren, Victoria's Riflebird, Tooth-billed Bowerbird and other rainforest species.
Access   Longlands Gap State Forest is 2.5 km past The Crater (Mt Hypipamee National Park) on the Atherton–Herberton road, or about 27.5 km from Atherton.

10 Mareeba Rotary Park   This attractive park in an open setting consists of two lagoons built into Granite Creek. Some interesting aquatic birds appear through the Dry. It is often the best place on the tablelands to see Pygmy-geese. Clamorous Reed-Warblers inhabit the bulrushes fringing the lower lake. Unfortunately, the main detraction is the number of domestic ducks and geese which have been allowed to proliferate.
Access   Mareeba Rotary Park is situated at the northern end of the town before crossing Granite Creek. Watch for the signs on the left. Turn left before the park into Railway Parade. The paved pathway encircles the two lakes.

11 Nardello's Lagoon   Another storage dam for the Tinaroo irrigation system, usually with a reasonable variety of aquatic species. Often Cotton and Green Pygmy-geese are present. A pair of White-bellied Sea-Eagles breed each year. Unfortunately close access is difficult and birds are a long way off making a telescope essential equipment. The best approach is from Chewko Road, though viewing from this position is useless during the afternoon because of the western sun.
Access   From Mareeba, take the Atherton road. Chewko Road is 16 km from Mareeba or 14 km from Atherton.

12 Wongabel State Forest   This State Forest contains a good variety of rainforest species and some open forest species though all can be easily seen elsewhere. There is a population of White-cheeked Honeyeaters about the perimeter. The Queensland Forest Service has constructed an interesting botanical walk where many tree species display their botanical and common names.
Access   From Atherton, take the Ravenshoe road. Wongabel State Forest is on the left 9.5 km from Atherton.

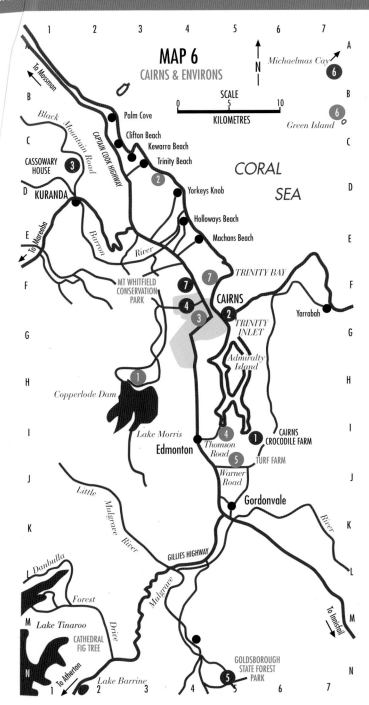

MAP 6
CAIRNS & ENVIRONS

N

SCALE
0   5   10
KILOMETRES

Michaelmas Cay   6

Green Island   6

Palm Cove

Clifton Beach

Kewarra Beach

Trinity Beach   2

CASSOWARY
HOUSE   3

KURANDA

Black
Mountain Road

CAPTAIN COOK HIGHWAY

To Mossman

To Mareeba

Barron

River

Yorkeys Knob

Holloways Beach

Machans Beach

CORAL

SEA

TRINITY BAY

MT WHITFIELD
CONSERVATION
PARK   7   7

4   CAIRNS   2

3   TRINITY
INLET

Yarrabah

Admiralty
Island

1

Copperlode Dam

Lake Morris

Edmonton

Thomson
Road   1   CAIRNS
CROCODILE FARM

4

5   TURF FARM

Warner
Road

Gordonvale

River

Little

Mulgrave

River

GILLIES HIGHWAY

Danbulla

Forest

Lake Tinaroo

CATHEDRAL
FIG TREE

Mulgrave

Drive

To Atherton

Lake Barrine

GOLDSBOROUGH
STATE FOREST
PARK   5

To Innisfail

BEST AREAS

1 **Cairns Crocodile Farm** With the construction of large freshwater ponds for crocodile farming, the subsequent reed growth has attracted many elusive birds such as rails and crakes. It is undoubtedly the best place to see White-browed Crake and Buff-banded Rail. Baillon's and Australian Spotted Crakes, Lewin's Rail and Painted Snipe have all been recorded in recent times. Other aquatic species take advantage of the more open ponds. It is becoming one of the popular birdwatching spots in the Wet Tropics and one can easily spend a few hours there.
Notable species Australasian Grebe, Little Egret, Royal Spoonbill, Brahminy Kite, Buff-banded Rail, Baillon's Crake, White-browed Crake, Marsh Sandpiper, Common Greenshank, Wood Sandpiper, Red-necked Stint, Sharp-tailed Sandpiper, Black-winged Stilt, Pacific Golden Plover, Red-capped Plover, Black-fronted Dotterel, Whiskered Tern, Little Kingfisher, Yellow Honeyeater, Crimson Finch, Chestnut-breasted Mannikin.
Facilities Open seven days from 8.30 a.m. to 4.30 p.m. Modern kiosk. Toilets.
Access From Cairns City, travel south through Edmonton. About 4 km south of Edmonton turn left into Warner Road, 6 km north of Gordonvale. Follow Warner Road for about 2 km and turn left at the sign for the crocodile farm. Follow the road for about 6 km to the end. The crocodile farm is on the right. An admission fee applies. The farm may be reached by other means other than self-drive. Telephone (070) 563095 for further information.

2 **Cairns Esplanade** One of the most interesting birdwatching spots in north-eastern Queensland where well over 200 species of birds have been recorded. It is one of the best spots for Asiatic shorebirds on the eastern coast of Australia and is recognised worldwide for its importance as shorebird habitat, with large numbers of birdwatchers visiting each year.
Regrettably, it is continually under threat from development. A number of very rare and vagrant species has appeared over the years — species such as Common Redshank, Asian Dowitcher, Pectoral Sandpiper, Long-toed Stint and Dunlin to name a few.
Usually the most productive section is about the grassy areas on the mudflats close to where Florence Street meets the Esplanade, but it is often worth walking the full 2.5 km. The best time is about two hours before high tide or from about an hour or so after high tide. John Crowhurst works on the Cairns Esplanade (for Cairns City Council). Part of his duties include assisting birding visitors with information, identification, recent sightings and places to visit. John will make himself known to birdwatchers, if he is in the vicinity.
Notable species Australian Pelican, Striated Heron, Nankeen Night Heron, Black-tailed Godwit, Terek Sandpiper, Grey-tailed Tattler, Great Knot, Red Knot, Sanderling, Red-necked Stint, Sharp-tailed Sandpiper, Curlew Sandpiper, Broad-billed Sandpiper, Beach Stone-curlew, Pacific Golden Plover, Grey Plover, Lesser Sand Plover, Greater Sand Plover, Gull-billed Tern, Little Tern, Pied Imperial-Pigeon, Helmeted Friarbird, Varied Honeyeater, Yellow Honeyeater.
Facilities Easy access to all facilities. Public toilets on the Esplanade.
Access Within walking distance of the centre of Cairns.

3 **Cassowary House** Owned and managed by John and Rita Squire, Cassowary House is a small, homely guest house situated in rainforest near Kuranda. Most middle altitude birds can be seen about the house, as well as the more difficult seasonal species. Red-necked Crakes and Musky Rat-kangaroos inhabit the garden. During a week's stay, John can take you to all habitats within a 100 km radius where about 200 species of birds may be seen.
Notable species Southern Cassowary, Red-necked Crake, Wompoo Fruit-Dove, Superb Fruit-Dove, Double-eyed Fig-Parrot, Azure Kingfisher, Buff-breasted Paradise-Kingfisher, Noisy Pitta, Lovely Fairy-wren, Macleay's Honeyeater, Chowchilla, Yellow-breasted Boatbill, White-eared Monarch, Pied Monarch, Northern Fantail, Barred Cuckoo-shrike, Black Butcherbird, Victoria's Riflebird, Spotted Catbird.
Facilities Well-known for comfortable accommodation, good food and excellent guiding, Cassowary House mainly offers all-inclusive birdwatching stays for up to a week, although sometimes accommodation and meals only, or a self-contained unit are available. Telephone and facsimile (070) 937318.
Access Situated about 2.5 km along Black Mountain Road, which turns to the left 3 km from Kuranda, just across the Barron River bridge off the road to Cairns.

4 **Centenary Lakes and Flecker Botanical Gardens** Like the Esplanade, this excellent area is usually quite rewarding and should be a mandatory stop of a few hours for all dedicated birdwatchers. There is always a chance for some of the more elusive species such as Black Bittern, White-browed Crake and Little Kingfisher, as well as Pygmy-geese. A boardwalk has been constructed through a palm swamp between the gardens and the lakes. This swamp is dry in the latter part of the year. The boardwalk leads to a footbridge over a tidal mangrove channel where Common Sandpiper, Mangrove Robin and Large-billed Gerygone are often seen.
Notable species Orange-footed Scrubfowl, Magpie Goose, Green Pygmy-goose, Black Bittern, Brahminy Kite, Bush-hen, Common Sandpiper, Whiskered Tern, White-winged Black Tern, Double-eyed Fig-Parrot, Gould's Bronze-Cuckoo, Azure Kingfisher, Little Kingfisher, Large-billed Gerygone, Helmeted Friarbird, Yellow Honeyeater, Brown-backed Honeyeater, Mangrove Robin, Shining Flycatcher, Varied Triller, Black Butcherbird, Yellow-bellied Sunbird.
Facilities Pleasant licensed kiosk. Toilets.
Access From Cairns City, travel 3.5 km north on the Captain Cook Highway. Turn left into Collins Avenue. Flecker Botanical Gardens are on the right, 1 km from the highway. The boardwalk commences opposite the entrance to the Gardens. Alternatively, turn left into Arthur Street about 3 km from Cairns City to go directly to Centenary Lakes. There is a regular bus service to the Gardens from Cairns City.

5 **Goldsborough State Forest Park** Also called Goldsborough Valley State Forest, this is a gem for lowland species in late spring and early summer when many trees are in fruit. From mid-Nov.–Mar. Buff-breasted Paradise-Kingfishers can be easily seen about the camping ground, while the Noisy Pitta inhabits the floor of the surrounding rainforest. At night, Lesser Sooty Owls sometimes call about the camping ground. A walking track just under 1 km in length leads to Kearney's Falls. Not far from the entrance are two good examples of Orange-footed Scrubfowl mounds. However, the best birding is about the camping and picnic grounds situated beside the beautiful Mulgrave River and back along the road leading to the camping ground. The road continues past the camping ground to the Goldfields track through open forest and grassland where additional species can be found.
Notable species Orange-footed Scrubfowl, Grey Goshawk, Red-necked Crake, Wompoo Fruit-Dove, Superb Fruit-Dove, Rose-crowned Fruit-Dove, Double-eyed Fig-Parrot, Australian King-Parrot, Gould's Bronze-Cuckoo, Azure Kingfisher, Buff-breasted Paradise-Kingfisher, Lesser Sooty Owl, Papuan Frogmouth, Large-tailed Nightjar, White-rumped Swiftlet, Noisy Pitta, Fairy Gerygone, Grey Whistler, Yellow-breasted Boatbill, Pied Monarch, Barred Cuckoo-shrike, Varied Triller, Black Butcherbird, Victoria's Riflebird, Spotted Catbird, Tawny Grassbird, Metallic Starling.
Facilities Well-maintained camping ground, fireplaces, water to all campsites, toilets, picnic area, no showers. Self-registration with a modest camping fee. Hotel 18 km, Gordonvale 23 km.
Access From the Bruce Highway at Gordonvale travel via the Gillies Highway for 6.5 km. Turn left at the Goldsborough State Forest sign and travel about 15 km to the camping ground.

6 **Michaelmas Cay** Michaelmas Cay is famous for its spectacularly large number of nesting seabirds, mostly terns and noddies. In recent years the breeding of these birds has become a tourist attraction. Consequently, the Department of Environment has been forced to restrict visitor access to a small area of the cay. A number of tours operate from Cairns to Michaelmas Cay, but the most profitable from a birdwatching point of view is one which also visits the outer Great Barrier Reef via Michaelmas Cay for there is always the chance of rarities further out on the Reef. An hour or two on the cay itself is usually ample time.
Notable species Wedge-tailed Shearwater, Masked Booby, Brown Booby, Red-tailed Tropicbird, Great Frigatebird, Lesser Frigatebird, Lesser Crested Tern, Crested Tern, Roseate Tern, Black-naped Tern, Bridled Tern, Sooty Tern, Common Noddy, Black Noddy.
Facilities All tours provide amenities.
Access Most boats leave from the vicinity of The Pier Marketplace or adjacent jetties at the southern end of the Esplanade in Cairns City. Travel east via Spence Street, across the Esplanade and follow the road into the car-park.

7 Mt Whitfield Conservation Park A walk up Mt Whitfield on the northern edge of Cairns will introduce newly-arrived visitors to some of the rainforest birds for which north-eastern Queensland is noted.

The Noisy Pitta is sometimes seen by the walking tracks, while from mid-Nov.–Mar. there is a good possibility of sighting a Buff-breasted Paradise-Kingfisher. Other birds such as Fairy Gerygone, Lovely Fairy-wren and Yellow Oriole are usually easily seen.

A walking track leads up into the rainforest, consisting of a shorter circuit of 1.3 km named the Red Arrow. A longer 7.5 km circuit named the Blue Arrow leads off the Red Arrow circuit.

Notable species Orange-footed Scrubfowl, Emerald Dove, Wompoo Fruit-Dove, Superb Fruit-Dove, Buff-breasted Paradise-Kingfisher, White-rumped Swiftlet, Noisy Pitta, Lovely Fairy-wren, Fairy Gerygone, Yellow-spotted Honeyeater, Graceful Honeyeater, Pale-yellow Robin, Grey Whistler, Yellow-breasted Boatbill, Pied Monarch, Varied Triller, Yellow Oriole, Spotted Catbird, Metallic Starling.

Facilities None in the park. Toilets and kiosk in nearby Flecker Botanical Gardens.

Access From Cairns City, travel north 3.5 km on the Captain Cook Highway and turn left into Collins Avenue. Watch for the Mt Whitfield Conservation Park sign about 1 km along Collins Avenue just before the Flecker Botanical Gardens. There is a regular bus service from the city centre to the Gardens.

OTHER AREAS

1 Copperlode Dam Also known as Lake Morris, Copperlode Dam is a pleasant drive from Cairns to an interesting area and usually a good spot for birds, although all species can be seen elsewhere. Kiosk.

Access From Cairns City, travel north along Sheridan Street for 2 km. Turn left into James Street, which runs into Anderson Street. About 1.5 km along Anderson Street, turn right into Reservoir Road. Travel 2.5 km and turn left into Lake Morris Road. Continue to Copperlode Dam.

2 Northern Beaches: Machans Beach, Holloways Beach, Yorkeys Knob, Trinity Beach, Kewarra Beach, Clifton Beach, Palm Cove These beachside suburbs of Cairns still retain some original tropical woodland and are ideal places to stay when visiting Cairns. Many of the more common open forest and woodland species can be seen and occasionally Beach Stone-curlew appear on the beaches. Double-eyed Fig-Parrots are usually fairly common.

Access From Cairns City or the airport, take the Captain Cook Highway and travel northwards. Once across the Barron River, one will see signposts for each locality as one progresses north.

3 Pioneer Cemetery Also known as Little Street Cemetery, Pioneer Cemetery is one of the best places in the Wet Tropics to see Bush Stone-curlews at close range. Birds rest by day amongst the headstones or under the few trees scattered throughout the old section. Other species are few. Pioneer Cemetery can be easily visited on the way to or from Centenary Lakes and Flecker Botanical Gardens.

Access From Cairns City, travel north along Sheridan Street on the Captain Cook Highway for 2 km. Turn left into James Street, then right into Little Street which runs past the cemetery.

4 Thomson Road Thomson Road runs through sugar-cane fields where Crimson Finches and Chestnut-breasted Mannikins are easily seen. It leads to a boat ramp and mangrove channel where Little Kingfisher and Mangrove Robin are occasionally seen, though it is not always a reliable spot. Other birds such as Collared Kingfisher and Shining Flycatcher sometimes occur in the vicinity. A rough walking track, 150 m before the boat ramp and running beside the Edmonton Fishing Club building, leads into a larger mangrove channel where most sightings have been made. Insect repellent is essential.

Access From Cairns City, travel south towards Edmonton. The Thomson Road signpost is on the left at the town centre.

5 Turf Farm at Edmonton Some interesting migratory birds appear on the short grass of this turf farm Oct.–Mar. It is one of the best places in the Wet Tropics to see Little Curlew and Yellow Wagtail, both regular summer visitors. Others which occasionally appear are Pacific Golden Plover, Oriental Plover, Sharp-tailed Sandpiper, and Oriental and Australian Pratincoles. Crimson Finches and Chestnut-breasted Mannikins can often be seen about the nearby sugar-cane fields. The turf farm is private property but one can see everything from the road sides. A telescope is not entirely necessary but a distinct advantage.
Access From Cairns City, travel south through Edmonton. About 4 km south of Edmonton, turn left into Warner Road which is 6 km north of Gordonvale. The turf farm is about 1 km along this road. Parking space beside the road is narrow.

6 Green Island National and Marine Park From a birdwatching perspective, Green Island is only worth a visit for the island form of the Silvereye and perhaps the chance of a Rose-crowned Fruit-Dove. Apart from these, Michaelmas Cay is much more rewarding. Green Island Resort offers all amenities, telephone (070) 313300.
Access A number of cruises depart The Pier Marketplace at the southern end of Cairns Esplanade.

7 Mangrove Boardwalk near Cairns Airport Two boardwalks each about 600–700 m in length have been constructed in mangroves close to the airport. The mangrove forest is impressive, but bird species are usually quite poor even though the Little Kingfisher and Mangrove Robin have occasionally been recorded. It is usually worth a visit only if one has time to spare whilst awaiting aircraft departure.
Access From the airport, travel towards Cairns City for 1.5 km. The car-park and entrance are on the left.

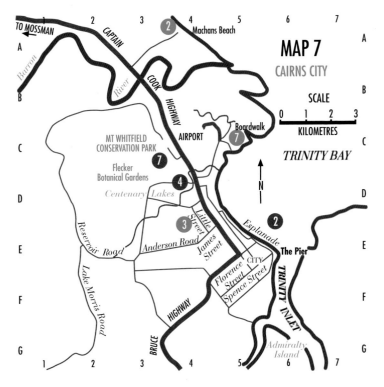

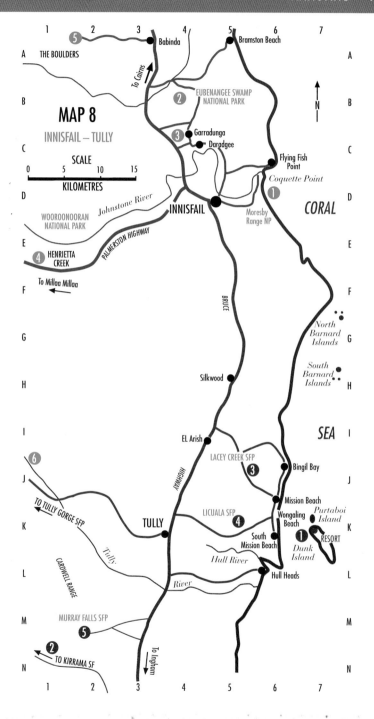

THE BOULDERS

Babinda

Bramston Beach

EUBENANGEE SWAMP
NATIONAL PARK

To Cairns

N

MAP 8

INNISFAIL — TULLY

Garradunga

Daradgee

SCALE

Flying Fish
Point

Coquette Point

CORAL

0   5   10   15

KILOMETRES

Johnstone River

INNISFAIL

Moresby
Range NP

WOOROONOORAN
NATIONAL PARK

PALMERSTON HIGHWAY

HENRIETTA
CREEK

To Millaa Millaa

BRUCE

North
Barnard
Islands

South
Barnard
Islands

Silkwood

SEA

EL Arish

TO TULLY GORGE SFP

LACEY CREEK SFP

Bingil Bay

Mission Beach

Purtaboi
Island

HIGHWAY

LICUALA SFP

Wongaling
Beach

TULLY

South
Mission Beach

RESORT

Dunk
Island

Tully

Hull River

CARDWELL RANGE

River

Hull Heads

MURRAY FALLS SFP

TO KIRRAMA SF

To Ingham

BEST AREAS

1 **Dunk Island** An attractive island with a small section occupied by a resort. Some varied forest habitats together with oceanic habitat provide good birding opportunities and an impressive variety of bird species may be seen.

Various terns, e.g. Black-naped and Lesser Crested, and sometimes the Roseate occasionally rest at the Spit. Other species such as Noisy Pitta often can be seen on the walking tracks ascending the mountain and about E. J. Banfield's grave site. The White-eared Monarch, a winter visitor only, is fairly easy to observe around the forest edge and about the farm. The Little Kingfisher inhabits the mangroves past the airstrip while Beach Stone-curlews inhabit the area between the end of the airstrip and the mangroves. It is interesting to note that the Yellow-spotted Honeyeater is common on the island while the Graceful Honeyeater is absent.

Notable species Orange-footed Scrubfowl, Osprey, Brahminy Kite, White-bellied Sea-Eagle, Grey Goshawk, Beach Stone-curlew, Lesser Crested Tern, Roseate Tern, Black-naped Tern, Bridled Tern, Wompoo Fruit-Dove, Rose-crowned Fruit-Dove, Pied Imperial-Pigeon, White-rumped Swiftlet, Little Kingfisher, Noisy Pitta, Yellow-spotted Honeyeater, Varied Honeyeater, Brown-backed Honeyeater, Spectacled Monarch, White-eared Monarch, Rufous Fantail, Tawny Grassbird, Metallic Starling.

Facilities Resort offers all amenities and caters for day trippers. Camping ground, walking tracks. Visitors may obtain a permit to camp from the Resort, telephone (070) 688199 or contact Department of Environment, Cardwell.

Access By water taxi from South Mission Beach or from Wongaling Beach in the Mission Beach area. A ferry service is available from the jetty at North Mission Beach. The island can be reached by air from Townsville.

2 **Kirrama State Forest** With access to four habitat types, Kirrama State Forest provides an excellent opportunity for a long list in a day's outing.

Kirrama Range is another of the high altitude rainforest areas where some endemic species such as Golden and Tooth-billed Bowerbirds can be found. The road passes through lowland rainforest as it begins to ascend, giving a good opportunity for some lowland species such as Pied and Spectacled Monarchs. At the top of this range past the upland rainforest, the road passes through some excellent wet sclerophyll with White-throated Treecreeper, White-naped and Yellow-faced Honeyeaters and Eastern Spinebill. Dry sclerophyll forest then appears, which Eastern Yellow Robin, Grey Shrike-thrush and Rufous Whistler inhabit. An old, disused logging track in the rainforest leads off beside a bridge displaying a faint '10' roughly painted on it. Birding along this track is usually quite good. The track is 21.7 km from the highway.

Notable species Grey Goshawk, Brown Cuckoo-Dove, Emerald Dove, Superb Fruit-Dove, Topknot Pigeon, Red-tailed Black-Cockatoo, Shining Bronze-Cuckoo, Gould's Bronze-Cuckoo, Lesser Sooty Owl, Buff-breasted Paradise-Kingfisher, White-throated Treecreeper, Lovely Fairy-wren, Brown Gerygone, White-naped Honeyeater, Scarlet Honeyeater, Lemon-bellied Flycatcher, Eastern Yellow Robin, Grey-headed Robin, Bower's Shrike-thrush, Grey Shrike-thrush, Yellow-breasted Boatbill, Pied Monarch, Victoria's Riflebird, Tooth-billed Bowerbird, Golden Bowerbird.

Facilities None. Camping is not permitted.

Access From the township of Kennedy on the Bruce Highway north of Cardwell, turn left and follow the road to Kirrama State Forest. It is 34 km over Kirrama Range to a field station set in dry sclerophyll forest and run by James Cook University.

3 **Lacey Creek State Forest Park** Lacey Creek and Licuala state forest parks are two of the most reliable areas in the Wet Tropics for cassowary sightings. Lacey Creek State Forest Park is one of the best areas for White-eared Monarch and excellent for fruit-doves during the winter. A 1.2 km walking track leads initially to a clearing which is often a reliable spot for the monarch. The track then follows a creek leading back to the picnic ground. Cassowaries are likely to be seen anywhere along this track or about the clearing. This lowland rainforest is typical of the huge tract of forest which once existed on the coastal plain.

Notable species Southern Cassowary, Orange-footed Scrubfowl, Red-necked Crake, Double-eyed Fig-Parrot, Wompoo Fruit-Dove, Superb Fruit-Dove, Rose-crowned Fruit-Dove, Azure Kingfisher,

Buff-breasted Paradise-Kingfisher, Macleay's Honeyeater, Grey Whistler, Yellow-breasted Boatbill, Spectacled Monarch, White-eared Monarch, Pied Monarch, Barred Cuckoo-shrike, Varied Triller, Victoria's Riflebird, Spotted Catbird, Yellow-bellied Sunbird, Metallic Starling.
Facilities Picnic areas, barbecues.
Access Take Mission Beach road from El Arish on the Bruce Highway. Lacey Creek State Forest Park is on the left, 10 km along this road. **Note:** The walking track across the highway to join Licuala State Forest Park does not exist as shown on some maps and information boards, but starts 2 km further along the road towards Mission Beach.

4 Licuala State Forest Park This park is almost entirely a Fan Palm *Licuala ramsayi* forest and though initially seemingly poor for birds, results can be reasonably good. Being a more open forest, birds are consequently more easily seen. A boardwalk has been erected through the forest. Like Lacey Creek State Forest Park, Licuala is one of the best places in the Wet Tropics for the Southern Cassowary. Among the more open undergrowth, Noisy Pittas may be seen. The open foliage of the forest usually provides a good opportunity for Victoria's Riflebird. A 4.6 km walking track terminates at the El Arish–Mission Beach road and can give some worthwhile birding as well as another chance for a cassowary. The longer 7 km walk to Lacey Creek is no longer in use.
Notable species Southern Cassowary, Orange-footed Scrubfowl, Double-eyed Fig-Parrot, Noisy Pitta, Grey Whistler, Yellow-breasted Boatbill, Spectacled Monarch, Barred Cuckoo-shrike, Varied Triller, Victoria's Riflebird, Spotted Catbird, Metallic Starling.
Facilities None.
Access Take the Tully–Mission Beach road at the turnoff 2 km north of Tully. At 16.5 km a gravel road leads to the left. This is well-signposted. Licuala car-park is 1 km along this road.

5 Murray Falls State Forest Park Another excellent birding spot with a mix of tropical woodland and lowland rainforest. This is a very pleasant area with a trail through the rainforest leading to an observation platform and spectacular waterfall.
During the summer, Buff-breasted Paradise-Kingfishers are fairly easily seen in the rainforest. The floor of the rainforest is quite open making it excellent for sighting the Noisy Pitta which is reasonably common. Lovely and Red-backed Fairy-wrens and Northern Fantails inhabit the open forest leading to the park. This is another worthwhile place to try for White-eared Monarch. It is also a fairly reliable spot for Red-tailed Black-Cockatoo. During late afternoon these birds often fly back and forth overhead. One small drawback is the sound of the waterfall which tends to stifle bird calls around the camping ground.
Notable species Orange-footed Scrubfowl, Emerald Dove, Superb Fruit-Dove, Red-tailed Black-Cockatoo, Double-eyed Fig-Parrot, Large-tailed Nightjar, Australian Owlet-nightjar, Buff-breasted Paradise-Kingfisher, Noisy Pitta, Lovely Fairy-wren, Red-backed Fairy-wren, Fairy Gerygone, Macleay's Honeyeater, Dusky Honeyeater, Scarlet Honeyeater, Lemon-bellied Flycatcher, Grey Whistler, Yellow-breasted Boatbill, Pied Monarch, Northern Fantail, Cicadabird, Black Butcherbird, Spotted Catbird, Metallic Starling.
Facilities Camping ground with self-registration (modest camping fee), cold showers, picnic area, tables, barbecues, toilets, swimming.
Access From the Bruce Highway 21 km north of Cardwell or 18 km south of Tully, turn at the Murray Falls State Forest Park sign. The partly-sealed road leads 20 km to the park.

OTHER AREAS

1 Coquette Point Sometimes promoted as a good birding spot but often bird numbers are poor. The road terminates at the Johnstone River amongst a small stand of mangroves. One can make one's way at low tide through the mangroves to the beach.
Access Coquette Point is confusing to find. Cross the Johnstone River in Innisfail over the old bridge near the Police Station and watch for the small signs on the way. Turn left and travel 4.5 km generally following the river but taking some lefts and rights through South Innisfail to the rainforest and national park. It is 6 km from the bridge near the Police Station to the end of the road on the Johnstone River. Further information may be obtained from the Department of Environment, Innisfail.

2 Eubenangee Swamp National Park Eubenangee Swamp is an important wetland covering 1520 hectares where large numbers of aquatic species gather after the Wet. An impressive list of aquatic, lowland rainforest, forest and grassland birds has been recorded from this area. A walking track, half a kilometre in length, follows the Alice River and then ascends a grassy hill top which overlooks part of the wetlands. During early morning some interesting rainforest birds can be seen along the river walk, e.g. Double-eyed Fig-Parrot, Noisy Pitta, Grey Whistler, Pied Monarch, Victoria's Riflebird, sometimes White-eared Monarch and others. Unfortunately, one is restricted to observing the wetlands from the crest of the hill where a telescope is necessary. It is the great pity that one cannot gain closer access. Nevertheless, this wetland is a very interesting spot and also worth a visit for the rainforest birds. Further information may be obtained from the Department of Environment, Innisfail or The Ranger, telephone (070) 676304.

Access About 24 km north of Innisfail travelling towards Cairns, turn right into Bramston Beach road. Turn right into Cartwright Road. The Alice River and entrance to the walking track are 1.5 km down this road.

3 Garradunga and Daradgee Garradunga's attraction is the small number of visiting Barn Swallows sometimes present Dec.–Jan. There is little else of interest in the surrounding sugar-cane fields. The Barn Swallows are usually seen on powerlines about the hotel and sometimes in nearby Daradgee. Garradunga is only a short distance from the highway and worth a detour at that time of year.

Access Turn right 10 km north of Innisfail at the Garradunga signpost. The hotel is about 2 km along this road.

4 Henrietta Creek (**Wooroonooran** *formerly* **Palmerston National Park**) Situated below the Atherton Tableland in the Johnstone River valley, Henrietta Creek consists of very attractive, mostly lowland tropical rainforest. However, with most of it lying between 300 m and 600 m in altitude, some of the upland endemic birds are missing. Though some other rainforest areas have a greater variety of birds, Chowchillas can be seen feeding by the tracks about the picnic grounds, while Australian King-Parrots, Double-eyed Fig-Parrots, Macleay's Honeyeaters, Yellow-breasted Boatbills and others can be seen in the rainforest. Southern Boobook and Lesser Sooty Owl as well as the weird calls of the Orange-footed Scrubfowl can be heard through the night.

Access Take the Palmerston Highway – Atherton Tableland turnoff just north of Innisfail. Henrietta Creek camping ground is 33 km along the highway from Innisfail.

5 The Boulders Very popular with tourists and day trippers, The Boulders is a beautiful spot with short walking tracks through some spectacular lowland rainforest and riverine scenery, with a good variety of the more common lowland rainforest birds. A better area for birds than nearby Josephine Falls.

Access Turn off the highway at Babinda and travel west through the town. Follow this road for 7 km to The Boulders.

6 Tully Gorge State Forest Park Situated in a very attractive setting by the Tully River, this park usually offers a good variety of the more common lowland rainforest birds. In addition, some interesting species can be seen through the farming and grazing land leading to the park. The scenery in the gorge is spectacular with tropical rainforest sweeping steeply down to the river. It is worth a trip from this aspect alone.

Further information may be obtained from DPI Forest Service, Ingham.

Access From Tully, take the Cardstone road. The park is about 40 km from Tully.

Note: Tully Gorge State Forest Park should not be confused with Tully Falls National Park which, though at a much higher altitude only a few kilometres away, can only be approached from Ravenshoe on the Atherton Tableland.

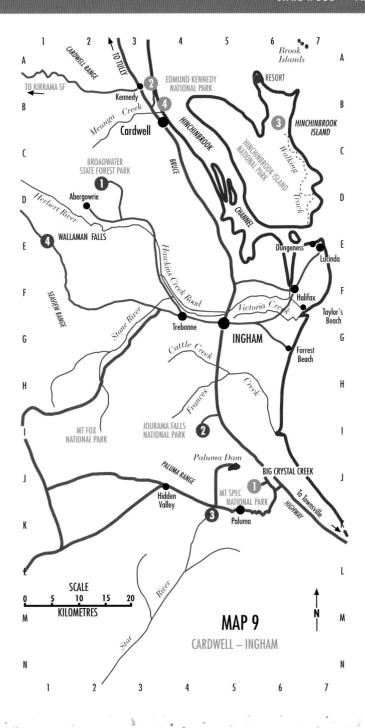

CARDWELL RANGE

TO TULLY

TO KIRRAMA SF

Brook Islands

RESORT

EDMUND KENNEDY NATIONAL PARK

Kennedy

Meunga Creek

Cardwell

HINCHINBROOK

BRUCE

HINCHINBROOK ISLAND

Walking Track

HINCHINBROOK ISLAND NATIONAL PARK

CHANNEL

BROADWATER STATE FOREST PARK

Abergowrie

Herbert River

WALLAMAN FALLS

Dungeness

Lucinda

SEAVIEW RANGE

Hawkins Creek Road

Stone River

Trebonne

Victoria Creek

Halifax

Taylor's Beach

INGHAM

Cattle Creek

Forrest Beach

Frances

Creek

MT FOX NATIONAL PARK

JOURAMA FALLS NATIONAL PARK

Paluma Dam

BIG CRYSTAL CREEK

PALUMA RANGE

Hidden Valley

MT SPEC NATIONAL PARK

Paluma

To Townsville

HIGHWAY

River

SCALE
0 5 10 15 20
KILOMETRES

Star

N

MAP 9
CARDWELL – INGHAM

BEST AREAS

1 **Broadwater State Forest Park** Set in open forest beside an extensive tract of rainforest, Broadwater State Forest Park is one of the more pleasant places to do some good birding. A 1.6 km walking track leads through the rainforest which contains the only lowland population of Grey-headed Robins in north-eastern Queensland. A longer track follows up Broadwater Creek through open forest and gallery forest where Pacific Baza, Northern Fantail and Lovely Fairy-wren are often seen.

Notable species Pacific Baza, Red-necked Crake, Wompoo Fruit-Dove, Superb Fruit-Dove, Red-tailed Black-Cockatoo, Double-eyed Fig-Parrot, Lesser Sooty Owl, Large-tailed Nightjar, Australian Owlet-nightjar, Azure Kingfisher, Noisy Pitta, Lovely Fairy-wren, Fairy Gerygone, Brown-backed Honeyeater, Eastern Yellow Robin, Grey-headed Robin, Eastern Whipbird, Crested Shrike-tit, Spectacled Monarch, White-eared Monarch, Pied Monarch, Northern Fantail, Barred Cuckoo-shrike, White-bellied Cuckoo-shrike, Spotted Catbird.

Facilities Basic camping with self-registration (modest camping fee), picnic area, barbecues, toilets.

Access From Ingham, take the road to Trebonne. Broadwater State Forest Park is 47 km from Ingham over a good, mostly sealed road, well-signposted. An alternate route is via Hawkings Creek Road about 10 km north of Ingham.

2 **Jourama Falls National Park** Another excellent birding area, set in dry sclerophyll with rainforest along the creek. A walking track leads up to a fairly spectacular waterfall and gorge. Best birding is about the picnic area and camping ground set beside the creek. This is one of the best places in north-eastern Queensland to see White-browed Robins. Also excellent for Noisy Pitta as well as Pied Monarch and Yellow-breasted Boatbill. Large-tailed Nightjars call about the camping ground at night and are not difficult to see from dusk. The Australian Owlet-nightjar can also be heard about the camping ground at night.

Notable species Brown Cuckoo-Dove, Emerald Dove, Rose-crowned Fruit-Dove, Red-tailed Black-Cockatoo, Brush Cuckoo, Gould's Bronze-Cuckoo, Large-tailed Nightjar, Australian Owlet-nightjar, Azure Kingfisher, Noisy Pitta, Lovely Fairy-wren, Yellow Honeyeater, Brown-backed Honeyeater, Dusky Honeyeater, Scarlet Honeyeater, Lemon-bellied Flycatcher, White-browed Robin, Grey Whistler, Yellow-breasted Boatbill, Spectacled Monarch, Pied Monarch, Northern Fantail, Great Bowerbird, Yellow-bellied Sunbird, Metallic Starling.

Facilities Basic camping with self-registration (modest camping fee), picnic ground, barbecues, toilets. Further information may be obtained from The Ranger, telephone (077) 773112.

Access Turn off the Bruce Highway 22 km south of Ingham or 88 km north of Townsville at the Jourama Falls National Park sign. The road leads 6 km to the park.

3 **Paluma, Mt Spec National Park, Hidden Valley** The area about Paluma provides some of the best upland rainforest birding in the Wet Tropics region. The Chowchilla is more easily seen about Mt Spec National Park and Paluma township than elsewhere in north Queensland.

Best birding is towards Paluma Dam. About 4 km past Paluma towards Hidden Valley, the road to the dam turns to the right. Approximately 11 km further there is a small parking area and a track to Birthday Creek Falls. There are recent records of Grey Wagtail appearing near these falls. Birding along the road for a few kilometres on either side of the car-park (especially about the creek crossing and the old hut a couple of kilometres before the car-park) is usually excellent. The road continues to Paluma Dam which is usually poor for aquatic birds. In fact, the rainforest about the dam never seems to be as productive as that further back towards Paluma. However, about the camping area, there are some bowers of the Satin Bowerbird.

The Golden Bowerbird is fairly common in this rainforest but bowers are difficult to locate without the assistance of local observers.

A highlight at Paluma is Ivy Cottage Tea Rooms where birds such as Macleay's Honeyeater and Victoria's Riflebird come to take crumbs from dining tables. A walk through the garden usually provides a good list of birds.

The road to Hidden Valley passes initially through some wet sclerophyll where one will find Eastern Yellow Robin, Grey Shrike-thrush, White-browed Scrubwren and White-naped Honeyeater, before entering dry sclerophyll with such species as Squatter Pigeon and Red-tailed Black-Cockatoo.

Notable species Southern Cassowary (irregular), Red-necked Crake, White-headed Pigeon, Squatter Pigeon, Wompoo Fruit-Dove, Superb Fruit-Dove, Topknot Pigeon, Red-tailed Black-Cockatoo, Crimson Rosella, Lesser Sooty Owl, Noisy Pitta, Spotted Pardalote, Fernwren, Mountain Thornbill, Macleay's Honeyeater, Lewin's Honeyeater, Bridled Honeyeater, White-cheeked Honeyeater, Eastern Yellow Robin, Grey-headed Robin, Chowchilla, Eastern Whipbird, Bower's Shrike-thrush, Grey Shrike-thrush, Yellow-breasted Boatbill, Black-faced Monarch, Barred Cuckoo-shrike, Victoria's Riflebird, Tooth-billed Bowerbird, Golden Bowerbird, Satin Bowerbird, Bassian Thrush, Russet-tailed Thrush.

Facilities Some holiday units and houses are occasionally available. Contact Paluma Accommodation and Information Service (077) 708520. There is no food store as such in the township, but light refreshments and basic food items may be purchased at Ivy Cottage, telephone (077) 708533. Basic camping at Paluma Dam. Picnic ground at Mt Spec National Park entrance. Contact Department of Environment, Ingham, or Paluma (077) 708526. Rustic cabins at Hidden Valley with meals available and some supplies, telephone (077) 708088.

Access The Paluma turnoff from the Bruce Highway is 42 km south of Ingham or 66 km north of Townsville. Paluma township is a further 18 km up a rather narrow sealed road. Conditions on the partly-sealed road to Hidden Valley (26 km past Paluma) should be checked during the Wet.

④ Wallaman Falls A worthwhile birding area with some spectacular waterfall and gorge scenery. The road travels for some kilometres through rich upland rainforest. Cassowaries have been seen fairly regularly about the picnic and camping ground and through the rainforest. Walking tracks are few and birding is done along the roads. There is an impressive stand of wet sclerophyll in the vicinity of the camping ground and towards the Falls.

Notable species Southern Cassowary, Square-tailed Kite, Superb Fruit-Dove, Southern Boobook, Lesser Sooty Owl, Noisy Pitta, White-throated Treecreeper, Fernwren, Bridled Honeyeater, Yellow-faced Honeyeater, White-naped Honeyeater, Grey-headed Robin, Chowchilla, Eastern Whipbird, Victoria's Riflebird, Spotted Catbird, Tooth-billed Bowerbird, Satin Bowerbird, Bassian Thrush, Russet-tailed Thrush.

Facilities Basic camping with self-registration (modest camping fee), picnic ground, toilets and barbecues, swimming.

Access From Ingham, travel to Trebonne, turn left and follow the national park signs. Much of the 51 km from Ingham to the camping ground is unsealed. Further information may be obtained from The Ranger, telephone (077) 775125.

OTHER AREAS

① Big Crystal Creek Big Crystal Creek is part of the Mt Spec National Park and situated in open eucalypt woodland at the base of the Paluma Range. Gallery forest lines the creek. It has a reasonable variety of more common species, most notable of which is a population of White-browed Robin, but it lacks the large variety seen at Jourama Falls National Park.

Access Take the Paluma – Mt Spec National Park road from the Bruce Highway, 42 km south of Ingham or 66 km north of Townsville. Follow the signs to Big Crystal Creek before the ascent to Paluma township.

2 Edmund Kennedy National Park This park consists mostly of coastal or dune scrub and mangroves. It is rather disappointing as far as birds are concerned, especially the mangrove species. However, the Orange-footed Scrubfowl is common and some good examples of large mounds can be seen. The pale-faced race of the Fairy Gerygone is also common. Most other species can be more easily seen elsewhere. The best area is about the old beach camp and car-park and back along the road for 1.5 km to the exit of a walking track circuit. A boardwalk has been erected through the mangrove forest.
Access Turn right off the Bruce Highway 4 km north from Cardwell. Drive 1 km to the park entrance and a further 4 km to the beach.

3 Hinchinbrook Island National Park Spectacular and rugged, Hinchinbrook Island has many diverse habitats from rainforest on Mt Bowen at 1142 m to mangroves about the coastline. Most of Hinchinbrook Island is inaccessible though there is a 32 km walking track down the east coast, mostly through open forest. A list of about 150 birds, all of which can be seen reasonably easily elsewhere, has been recorded from the island.
The extensive mangrove forest of Hinchinbrook Channel is of most interest for it is here where the Great-billed Heron is sometimes sighted and the only known population of Mangrove Golden Whistler in the Wet Tropics region occurs. The Broad-billed Flycatcher has been recorded from this forest. However, the mangrove forest is accessible only by boat.
Access By charter boat from Cardwell or Lucinda, or private boat from ramps at Lucinda and Cardwell (high water) and Dungeness.

4 Meunga Creek Boat Ramp Usually a good spot to see Mangrove Robin though generally little else. To the left of the ramp is the remains of a small timber jetty built through the mangroves where the Mangrove Robin is sometimes seen.
Access Travel north through Cardwell, turn right 1.6 km from the town centre into Toohey Street. Turn left into Winter Street and right into White Street. Travel via Coral Sea Drive over a gravel road to the boat ramp which is 3 km from the highway.

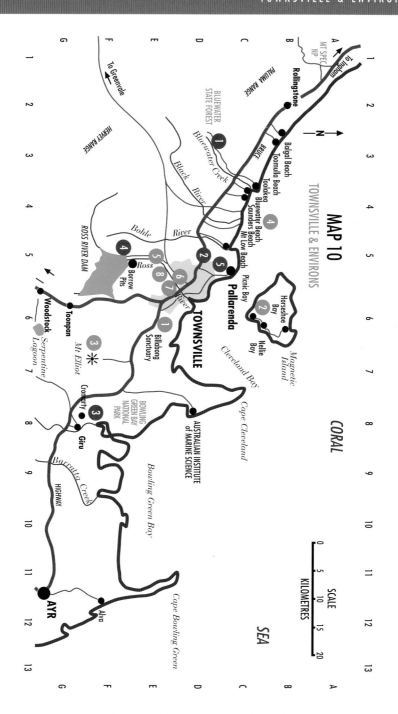

MAP 10

TOWNSVILLE & ENVIRONS

CORAL

SEA

SCALE

0
5
10
15
20

KILOMETRES

311

BEST AREAS

1 Bluewater State Forest Situated on the southern part of the Paluma Range, this is the nearest large area of rainforest to Townsville. In places, areas of open forest with casuarinas adjoin the rainforest. Looking drier than lush tropical rainforest further north, it nevertheless supports a good number of bird species. However, being a mid-altitude rainforest, some of the endemics from higher altitudes are absent.

Notable species: Grey Goshawk, Emerald Dove, Wompoo Fruit-Dove, Superb Fruit-Dove, White-rumped Swiftlet, Noisy Pitta, Mountain Thornbill, Macleay's Honeyeater, Yellow-faced Honeyeater, White-cheeked Honeyeater, Scarlet Honeyeater, Chowchilla, Eastern Whipbird, Yellow-breasted Boatbill, Pied Monarch, Victoria's Riflebird, Spotted Catbird, Silvereye.

Access Travel 30 km north of Townsville and after crossing Bluewater Creek, turn left into Forestry Road. This road ascends the range for 20 km becoming rather rough as one progresses. Best birding is along this road.

2 Blakey's Crossing Fed by Louisa Creek and flowing through the Town Common into the Bohle River, this is one of the more important wetlands about Townsville. It is one of the last to dry out after the Wet with water present well into the Dry and quite spectacular at the end of the Wet with huge numbers of waterfowl. A mixture of swamp and grassland gives a good variety of birds and quite a number of interesting and rare species have turned up over the years. The Mt St John sewage ponds are adjacent the wetlands.

Notable species Brown Quail, Plumed Whistling-Duck, Wandering Whistling-Duck, Pink-eared Duck, Black-necked Stork, Swamp Harrier, Australian Bustard, Red-backed Button-quail, Red-chested Button-quail, Latham's Snipe, Wood Sandpiper, Sharp-tailed Sandpiper, Red-kneed Dotterel, Australian Pratincole, Whiskered Tern, White-winged Black Tern, Singing Bushlark, Zebra Finch, Clamorous Reed-Warbler, Tawny Grassbird, Little Grassbird.

Access Take Ingham road from Townsville and travel north. One kilometre past the RAAF (Air Force) base, there is a depression on either side of the road. Turn right immediately past this depression (near the caravan park) into a short, unsealed road. The track leads to the sewage ponds, but after climbing through a gate, walk to the right and down through grass to the wetlands.

3 Cromarty Part of a large coastal wetland which surrounds Townsville, this area is seen at its best following the Wet. Much of the area is privately-owned, but a public road traverses the wetlands. One can watch birds from this road. It is one of the best areas in north Queensland to see huge numbers of Brolgas and Magpie Geese, both of which breed there. Patches of forest along the road (including dry rainforest) contain some interesting tropical forest species. This is the best area for finches around Townsville, including the Crimson.

Notable species Magpie Goose, Black-necked Stork, Brolga, Latham's Snipe, Bush Stone-curlew, Black-winged Stilt, Red-kneed Dotterel, Whiskered Tern, White-winged Black Tern, Pallid Cuckoo, Red-backed Fairy-wren, White-gaped Honeyeater, Black-faced Woodswallow, Great Bowerbird, Crimson Finch, Chestnut-breasted Mannikin, Singing Bushlark.

Access Take the Bruce Highway south from Townsville. Watch for the Australian Institute of Marine Science (AIMS) turnoff on the left. Nine kilometres south of the AIMS road, turn left into Cromarty Siding Road. Once through the 'Cromarty' gate, travel left into unsealed Reed Beds Road and follow to a T-junction. Turning right will take you back to the highway. If you miss the Crimson Finch, turn left at the T-junction and check along the sugar-cane fields.

4 Ross River Dam This large dam, 25 km west of Townsville, supplies the city with most of its water. Though it is one of the better areas for waterfowl, access is restricted to a viewing area above the spillway. However, with a telescope, one can usually see a large number of birds. The borrow pits below the dam wall, which can be seen from the same aspect, are also excellent for aquatic species. Good birds can be found around the car-park and below the spillway. By following the road along the dam wall to the right of the parking area, one will often see raptors soaring off the uplift from the wall. It is also good for Brown Falcon and Red-backed Kingfisher in winter. At the end of the road (6 km from dam) is a locked gate. Climb over the gate and follow the track over the dam wall. From the top of the wall you will see an area of swamp to your right and Ross River to your left. This is the best area in Townsville for Black-throated

Finch. The river is one of the better places for both species of Pygmy-geese. Access to this area is permitted for birdwatching.

Notable species Plumed Whistling-Duck, Wandering Whistling-Duck, Black Swan (large numbers), Cotton Pygmy-goose, Green Pygmy-goose, Pink-eared Duck, Hardhead, Great Crested Grebe, all four species of Cormorant, Australian Pelican, Little Egret, Great Egret, Intermediate Egret, Glossy Ibis, White-bellied Sea-Eagle, Swamp Harrier, Brown Falcon (winter), Dusky Moorhen, Eurasian Coot, Latham's Snipe (borrow pits), Comb-crested Jacana, Black-winged Stilt, Whiskered Tern, Cockatiel, Red-backed Kingfisher (winter), Black-throated Finch.

Facilities Picnic area and toilets.

Access Take Upper Ross River Road from the city and follow it to the parking area at the dam wall.

5 Town Common Conservation Park *(formerly* **Townsville Town Common Environmental Park)** Known locally as 'The Common', this is an extremely interesting area and usually one of the best about Townsville, especially after a good Wet. However, bird numbers can be down considerably following a poor Wet. There are many different habitats within this 3245 ha park including tropical woodland, eucalypt forest, grassland, saltmarsh or saline grassland, mangroves and wetlands. A gravel road runs into the park for a distance of 3 km, and a number of walking tracks radiate from this road. There are four bird hides in the area. Further information may be obtained from the Ranger Station at the entrance. Entrance gates operate from 6.30 a.m. to 6.30 p.m. The Townsville Bird Observers Club of Australia (Townsville BOCA) conducts a bird walk on the first Sunday of each month. Meet at the entrance gate at 6.30 a.m.

Notable species Magpie Goose, Wandering Whistling-Duck, Cotton Pygmy-goose, Green Pygmy-goose, Hardhead, all four species of Cormorant, Royal Spoonbill, Yellow-billed Spoonbill, Black-shouldered Kite, Brahminy Kite, Swamp Harrier, Wedge-tailed Eagle, Brolga, White-browed Crake, Latham's Snipe, Oriental Pratincole, Whiskered Tern, Pied Imperial-Pigeon, Red-backed Fairy-wren, Helmeted Friarbird, Yellow-spotted Honeyeater, White-gaped Honeyeater, Yellow Honeyeater, Varied Triller, Great Bowerbird, Singing Bushlark, Zebra Finch, Clamorous Reed-Warbler, Tawny Grassbird.

Facilities Ranger Station, telephone (077) 741382.

Access Take the Cape Pallarenda Road to Rowes Bay Country Club which is 5 km from the city centre. Turn left at the Town Common Conservation Park sign and follow to the park entrance.

OTHER AREAS

1 Billabong Sanctuary Built about an area of wetlands with some pleasant surrounding forest, Billabong Sanctuary can produce some interesting birds. Whistling-Ducks and sometimes Pygmy-geese are often present on the lily-covered lagoons.

In conjunction with the Australian Species Management Programme, the sanctuary conducts a captive breeding programme designed to increase numbers of the endangered Southern Cassowary and release them into the wild. Open daily 8.30 a.m. to 5 p.m. Telephone (077) 788344.

Access Seventeen kilometres south of Townsville via the Bruce Highway.

2 Magnetic Island This 'mainland' island lies 10 km offshore from the heart of Townsville. Half of the island has been reserved as national park while the rest is still relatively under-developed with a few scattered holiday villages. There are 22 km of walking tracks in the national park which wind through a variety of habitats. Some seabirds such as Brown Booby and Lesser Crested and Crested Terns can sometimes be seen along the island's coastline. One of the attractions is the White-eared Monarch which regularly and commonly winters in forest about the island Apr.–Sept. The best place to see it is reputedly Gustav Creek, where the walking track meets the creek.

Access Passenger ferries leave the terminal at Great Barrier Reef Wonderland, 2-86 Flinders Street East, Townsville and the ferry terminal on Sir Leslie Thiess Drive, seven days a week. A vehicular ferry departs from near the Motor Boat Club in Plume Street. Bicycles, motorcycles and cars may be hired on the island.

3 Mt Elliot (Bowling Green Bay National Park) Situated south of Townsville, this outlier represents the southern-most extension of tropical rainforest in north-eastern Queensland. Mt Elliot rises to over 1300 m, with rainforest being confined to the higher altitudes above 600 m. However, most of the high altitude endemic birds are absent. Drier eucalypt woodland, denser along the creeks, is found on the southern side. The Plum-headed Finch has been recorded from grassland in the lower areas, as well as Red-backed Kingfisher, Weebill and a variety of honeyeaters. On the northern side, walking tracks lead into the forest and a reasonable variety of general forest species can be seen. Further information may be obtained from The Ranger, telephone (077) 788203.

Access **To camping ground:** travelling south along the Bruce Highway, turn right 28 km from Townsville. The camping ground is a further 6 km along this road. **To the drier western side:** take the Flinders Highway (which travels to Charters Towers) and turn left at Woodstock, then proceed towards Giru. There is no access to the park, but good birding along this road. After turning left at Woodstock watch for **Serpentine Lagoon.** This is good habitat for wetland and forest birds and one of the few sites around Townsville where Bar-breasted Honeyeater can be seen. This is private property and access requires permission. Contact Townsville BOCA (077) 891306.

4 The Northern Beaches
Mt Low Beach (Bushland Beach — mouth of Bohle River — turn 17 km from city centre into Mt Low Parkway)
Saunders Beach (turn 21 km from city centre)
Toolakea Beach (mouth of Bluewater Creek — turn 31 km from city centre)
Toomulla Beach (turn 44 km from city centre)
Balgal Beach (turn 51 km from city centre just before Rollingstone)
Mouth of Crystal Creek (turn 69 km from city centre — travel via Barrilgie Road just north of bridge over Crystal Creek).
These areas to the north of Townsville, though not supporting a large variety of birds, can be good for shorebirds especially Sept.–Oct. and Mar.–Apr. during migration. Ruddy Turnstone, Great and Red Knots, Pacific Golden Plover, Lesser and Greater Sand Plovers are some of the species which can be seen here in numbers, as well as other more common shorebirds. Some of the forest areas contain Fairy Gerygone, Varied Triller and fairy-wrens, while the mangroves contain Mangrove Gerygone, Mangrove Honeyeater and sometimes Great-billed Heron and Little Kingfisher. Often Osprey, Brahminy Kite and White-bellied Sea-Eagle can be seen, as well as more common birds of prey. Mangrove Robin can be called in at the mangroves at the southern end of Bushland Beach. In some areas short-term camping is permitted, usually free of charge. Some areas have well-established beach communities.

5 Ross River This river winds its way through tropical woodland across the coastal plain, eventually reaching Cleveland Bay. Most of the area below Ross River Dam has now given way to urban development. Ross River Road follows the river for some distance and some good general birdwatching can be done from the riverbank. Quite a few common species are present, including aquatic species and a variety of honeyeaters and other woodland birds in paperbarks and eucalypts along the riverbank.
Access From the city, travel via Ross River Road and Upper Ross River Road.

6 Ross River Bush Garden A reliable spot for Rufous-throated Honeyeater.
Access Via Thompson Street, Mundingburra.

7 South Bank of Ross River A wide variety of birds including shorebirds, seabirds, mangrove and bush birds may be seen here.
Access Via Racecourse Road, Cluden. Exercise care on the rough gravel section.

8 Palmetum This is a good birding spot close to the city, as well as displaying the largest palm collection in the Southern Hemisphere.
Access From the city, travel via Ross River Road and Nathan Street. The Palmetum is on the left just past the bridge over Ross River.

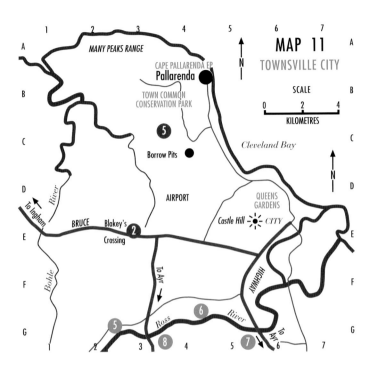

MAP 11
TOWNSVILLE CITY

MANY PEAKS RANGE

CAPE PALLARENDA EP
Pallarenda

TOWN COMMON
CONSERVATION PARK

Borrow Pits

Cleveland Bay

SCALE

0   2   4
KILOMETRES

N

River

To Ingham

AIRPORT

QUEENS
GARDENS

Castle Hill   CITY

BRUCE   Blakey's
       Crossing

Bohle

To Ayr

HIGHWAY

Ross   River

To Ayr

BIRDWATCHING ORGANIZATIONS

Royal Australasian Ornithologists Union (RAOU), 415 Riversdale Road, Hawthorn East, Vic. 3123. Telephone (03) 98822622 or facsimile (03) 98822677.

Bird Observers Club of Australia (BOCA):
183 Springvale Road, (Post Office Box 185) Nunawading, Vic. 3131. Telephone (03) 98775342 or facsimile (03) 98944048.
Cairns Branch: Post Office Box 2910, Cairns, Qld. 4870.
Townsville Branch: Post Office Box 756, Townsville, Qld. 4910.

Queensland Ornithological Society Inc.: Post Office Box 97, St Lucia, Qld. 4067.

ORNITHOLOGICAL GUIDING SERVICES

Australasian Birding Services Andy Anderson specialises in personal guiding (half or full day) from Cairns. He is also available for guiding groups locally and as far afield as Papua New Guinea and New Zealand. Write to Post Office Box 7999, Cairns, Qld. 4870. Within Australia: telephone and facsimile (070) 323387. Outside Australia: +61-70-323387. E-mail: birdo@internetnorth.com.au
Fine Feather Tours Del Richards operates a daily six-hour birdwatching tour to some of the better birding habitats about Mossman to Mount Molloy. A hot brunch is provided. He is available to guide groups as well as locate target species. Write to Post Office Box 853, Mossman, Qld. 4873. Within Australia: telephone and facsimile (070) 983103. Outside Australia: +61-70-983103.
Glenn Holmes Locally, Glenn's specialities are birds of the Atherton Tableland, seabirds and shorebirds. His other specialties include birds of the Gulf of Carpentaria (known as the Gulf) Wetlands, as well as Gouldian and Star Finches and Blue-faced Parrot-Finch. Glenn will also plan itineraries locally or Australia-wide. Write to 33 Twelfth Avenue, Atherton, Qld. 4993. Within Australia: telephone and facsimile (070) 914364. Outside Australia: +61-70-914364.
Kirrama Wildlife Tours Klaus Uhlenhut conducts birdwatching tours for small groups, mainly covering southern parts of the Wet Tropics. Fully-accommodated extended tours are undertaken to localities farther afield, e.g. Iron Range, the Gulf, Kakadu and the Kimberley. Klaus is also available for local charter of half-day duration or longer. Write to Post Office Box 133, Silkwood, Qld. 4856. Within Australia: telephone (070) 655181 or facsimile (070) 655197. Outside Australia: telephone +61-70-655181 or facsimile +61-70-655197.

BIRD CALL TAPES : WILDLIFE VIDEOS

Australian Bird Sounds: Queensland's Wet Tropics and Great Barrier Reef: Non-Passerines and Passerines.
Produced by David Stewart (NATURE SOUND) in two cassettes of high-quality sound recordings totalling 124 species. Recommended as companion tapes to this field guide. They feature all endemics and many of the more exciting and rare birds of the region. Available from RAOU, BOCA, or David Stewart, Post Office Box 256, Mullumbimby, NSW, 2482 and selected retail outlets.

Two videos from JOHN YOUNG WILDLIFE, distributed by Ray Smith Productions, Post Office Box 339, Maleny, Qld. 4552, telephone and facsimile (074) 999455.
The Greater Daintree and the Wildlife Within Produced in the heart of the Wet Tropics, this latest release shows seldom-seen tropical birds such as Great-billed Heron at its nest, Rufous and Lesser Sooty Owls at their breeding hollows, Little Kingfisher at a rainforest pool and Tooth-billed and Golden Bowerbirds tending their bowers, plus many more. (60 min.)
Birds of Tropical North Queensland features the intriguing display of Victoria's Riflebird, just one of 55 species filmed. (65 min.)

LIST OF REFERENCES

Blakers, M., Davies, S.J.J.F. and Reilly, P.N. 1984, 'The Atlas of Australian Birds', Melbourne University Press, Melbourne.
Boles, W.E. 1984, 'Southern specimen records of the Broad-billed Flycatcher', *Sunbird* **14**, 80.
Bourke, P.A. and Austin, A.F. 1947, 'The Atherton Tablelands and its Avifauna', *Emu* **47**, 87.
Bravery, J.A. 1970, 'The Birds of Atherton Shire, Queensland', *Emu* **70**, 49.
Burton, A.M., Chavez-Chavez, L.G., Cade, T.J. and Cade, R. 1991, 'A Red-footed Booby from Abergowrie State Forest, North Queensland', *Sunbird* **21**, 62.

Cameron, S.M. 1980, 'Grey Wagtail in North Queensland', *Sunbird* **11**, 44.

Cheshire, N.G. 1989, 'A Bulwer's Petrel *Bulweria bulwerii* off North-eastern Australia', *The Australian Bird Watcher* **13**, 61.

Christidis, L. and Boles, W.E. 1994, 'The Taxonomy and Species of Birds of Australia and Its Territories', *Royal Australasian Ornithologists Union Monograph* 2, RAOU, Melbourne.

Corben, C., Roberts, G. and Ingram, G. 1974, 'Sightings of Huttons Shearwater in Queensland', *Sunbird* **5**, 55.

Fisher, K. and Fisher, L. 1989, 'Laughing Gull *Larus atricilla*: A New Record for Australia', *The Australian Bird Watcher* **13**, 34.

Ford, J. 1981, 'Hybridisation and migration in Australian populations of the Little and Rufous-breasted Bronze-Cuckoos', *Emu* **81**, 209.

Ford, J. 1983, 'Speciation in the ground-thrush complex *Zoothera dauma* in Australia', *Emu* **83**, 141.

Frith, C.B. 1984, 'The Status and Distribution of the Trumpet Manucode *Manucodia keraudrenii* (Paradisaeidae) in Australia', *The Australian Bird Watcher* **15**, 218.

Garnett, S. (Ed.) 1992, 'Threatened and Extinct Birds of Australia', *Royal Australasian Ornithologists Union Report 82*, RAOU, Melbourne.

Gill, H.B. 1970, 'Birds of Innisfail and hinterland', *Emu* **70**, 105.

Griffin, A.C.M. 1976, 'A White Noddy in North Queensland', *Sunbird* 7, 49.

Griffin, A.C.M. 1995, 'An Annotated List of Birds of the Paluma Range, North Queensland', *Sunbird* **25**, 73.

Holmes, G. 1986, 'Notes on the Pale White-eye *Zosterops citrinella*', *The Australian Bird Watcher* **11**, 208.

Holmes, G. 1995, 'Survey of Gouldian Finch in Queensland during Dry Season of 1995: with Review of Distribution and Status', *Report to Conservation Commission of the Northern Territory*, Conservation Commission of the Northern Territory, Darwin.

King, B.R. 1993, 'The Status of Queensland Seabirds', *Corella* **17**, 65.

Lavery, H.J. 1974, 'Additional records of Yellow-tinted Honeyeater and Fuscous Honeyeater in North Queensland', *Sunbird* 5, 66.

Lavery, H.J. and Grimes, R.J. 1974, 'The Yellow Silvereye in north-east Queensland', *Sunbird* **5**, 42.

Lavery, H.J. and Hopkins, N. 1963, 'Birds of the Townsville District of North Queensland', *Emu* **63**, 242.

Longmore, N.W. 1985, 'Two new records of the Short-tailed Shearwater from North Queensland', *Sunbird* **15**, 84.

Mackay, R. 1991, ' Papuan Harrier in North Queensland', *The Australian Bird Watcher* **14**, 146.

Magarry, D. 1983, 'Black-winged Monarch near Cairns, North Queensland', *Sunbird* **13**, 36.

McKean, J.L. 1983, 'Some notes on the occurrence of the Great Reed Warbler *Acrocephalus arundinaceus* in the Northern Territory', *Northern Territory Naturalist* **6**, 3.

McLean, J.A. 1994, 'The Charadriiformes of the lower Endeavour and Annan rivers, North Queensland', *Sunbird* **24**, 49.

McLean, J.A. 1994, 'Recovery of a banded Southern Giant-Petrel in North Queensland', *Sunbird* **24**, 70.

McLean, J.A. 1995, 'The Family Meliphagidae of the Cooktown area, North Queensland', *Sunbird* **25**, 63.

Nagle, P. 1987, 'Yellow-breasted Flycatcher reported from the Atherton Region of North Queensland', *Sunbird* **17**, 31.

Nielsen, L. 1992, 'Spotless Crake at Paluma, North Queensland', *Sunbird* **22**, 85.

Noske, R.A. and Sticklen, R. 1979, 'Nest and Eggs of the Yellow-legged Flycatcher', *Emu* **79**, 148.

Parker, S.A. 1971, 'Distribution of *Meliphaga flavescens* and *M. fusca* in northern Queensland', *Sunbird* **2**, 41.

Smedley, J.H. 1904, 'Finches in northern Queensland', *Emu* **4**, 68.

Squire, J.E. 1990, 'Some Southern Records and Other Observations of the Buff-breasted Button-quail *Turnix olivei*', *The Australian Bird Watcher* **13**, 149.

Stokes, T. and Corben C. 1985, 'A survey of pelagic birds in the Western Coral Sea and Great Barrier Reef', *Corella* **9**, 25.

Storr, G.M. 1953, 'Birds of Cooktown and Laura districts, North Queensland', *Emu* **53**, 225.

Storr, G.M. 1984, 'Revised List of Queensland Birds', Western Australian Museum, Perth.

White, S.R. 1946, 'Notes on the Bird Life of Australia's Heaviest Rainfall Region', *Emu* **46**, 81.

Wieneke, J. 1988, 'The Birds of Magnetic Island, North Queensland', *Sunbird* **18**, 1.

Wieneke, J. (Ed.) 1989, 'Birds of Townsville and where to find them', Wildlife Preservation Society of Queensland, Townsville Branch, Townsville.

Wodzicki, K. and Stein, P. 1958, 'Migration and dispersal of New Zealand Gannets', *Emu* **58**, 289.

INDEX OF SCIENTIFIC NAMES

Erythrogonys cinctus 76, 78, 83, 169, **232**
Erythrotriorchis radiatus 179, **219**
Erythrura
  gouldiae **276**
  trichroa 32, 40, 92, 152, **275**
Esacus neglectus 96, 98, 106, 109, **230**
Eudynamys scolopacea 26, 54, 62, 107, 121, 130, **243**
Eurostopodus
  argus 148, 195, **245**
  mystacalis 151, 195, **245**
Eurystomus orientalis 26, 34, 84, 109, **249**

F

Falco
  berigora 134, 150, 179, **220**
  cenchroides 134, 180, **220**
  hypoleucos 180, **220**
  longipennis 180, **220**
  peregrinus 180, **220**
  severus 181
  subniger 29, 180, **220**
FALCONIDAE **220**
FALCONIFORMES **216**
Falcunculus frontatus 36, 73, 88, 91, **262**
Fregata
  ariel 24, 123, 156, 161, **213**
  minor 23, 123, 156, 161, **213**
FREGATIDAE **213**
Fregetta tropica 163
Fulica atra 25, 95, 165, **223**

G

GALLIFORMES **205**
Gallinago
  hardwickii 167, 175, 186, **224**
  megala 170, **225**
Gallinula
  tenebrosa 25, 83, 118, 165, **223**
  ventralis 25, 175, **223**
Gallirallus philippensis 61, 83, 117, 153, 174, **221**
Geopelia
  cuneata 41, 54, 103, 120, **237**
  humeralis 58, 147, **237**
  striata 41, 58, 59, 91, 104, 120, **237**
Geophaps scripta 90, 103, 147, **237**
Gerygone
  fusca 41, 49, 135, **252**
  levigaster 41, 49, 101, 135, **252**
  magnirostris 41, 49, 135, **252**
  mouki 41, 49, 100, 135, **252**
  olivacea 72, 77, 135, **252**
  palpebrosa 72, 76, 94, 135, **252**
Glareola maldivarum 75, 111, 126, 157, **232**
GLAREOLIDAE **232**
Glossopsitta pusilla 39, 92, **239**
Grallina cyanoleuca 23, 95, 105, **266**
Grantiella picta 20, 84, **258**

GRUIDAE **221**
GRUIFORMES **221**
Grus
  antigone 47, 99, 167, **221**
  rubicunda 47, 99, 167, **221**
Gygis alba 193, **235**
Gymnorhina tibicen 24, **270**

H

HAEMATOPODIDAE **230**
Haematopus
  fuliginosus 29, 86, 99, 103, **230**
  longirostris 24, 86, 99, 103, **230**
HALCYONIDAE **247**
Haliaeetus leucogaster 30, 48, 177, **218**
Haliastur
  indus 80, 177, **218**
  sphenurus 150, 157, 177, **218**
Hamirostra melanosternon 176, **217**
Henicopernis longicauda 181
Heteromyias albispecularis 110, 134, 140, **261**
Heteroscelus
  brevipes 137, 185, **227**
  incanus 137, 185, **227**
Hieraaetus morphnoides 150, 179, **219**
Himantopus himantopus 22, 169, **230**
Hirundapus caudacutus 20, 154, **246**
HIRUNDINIDAE **276**
Hirundo
  ariel 112, 156, **277**
  daurica 69, 114, 155, **277**
  neoxena 75, 155, **277**
  nigricans 22, 112, 155, **277**
  pacifica 75, 155, **277**
  rustica 75, 79, 155, **276**
HYDROBATIDAE **210**

I

Irediparra gallinacea 129, **229**
Ixobrychus
  flavicollis 28, 71, 173, **215**
  minutus 173, **215**

J

JACANIDAE **229**

L

Lalage
  leucomela 22, 60, 65, 101, **268**
  sueurii 21, 146, **268**
LARIDAE **233**
Larus
  atricilla 189, **233**
  crassirostris 190
  dominicanus 189, **233**
  novaehollandiae 161, 189, **233**
  pipixcan 190, **233**
  ridibundus 190
  sabini 190